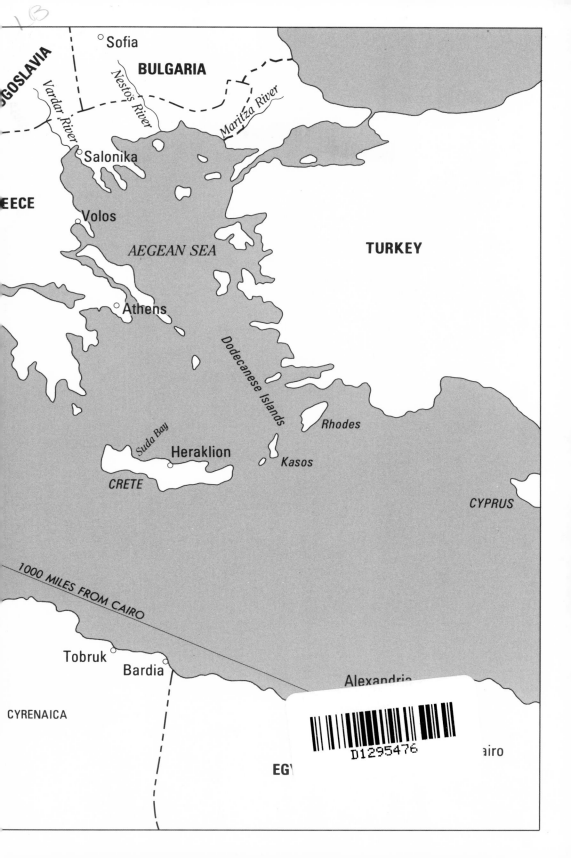

ATLANTIC

OCEAN

Moscow ○

London ○    Berlin ○

Belgrade ○    Ploesti ○

Rome ○    Istanbul ○

Ankara ○

Gibraltar ○    Athens ○

ALGERIA    Malta ○    *MEDITERRANEAN SEA*

Tripoli ○    Benghazi ○

MOROCCO    Cairo ○    RED

SEA

SUDAN

Dakar ○    Khartoum ○

AIR  REINFORCEMENT  ROUTE

Lagos ○    EAST AFRICA

Takoradi ○

├─────── 1000 MILE RADIUS FROM LONDON AND CAIRO ───────┤

Diary of a Disaster

# Diary of a Disaster

## *British Aid to Greece 1940-1941*

ROBIN HIGHAM

THE UNIVERSITY PRESS OF KENTUCKY

FOR BARBARA
for thirty-six years of love and friendship

The University Press of Kentucky:
scholarly publisher for the Commonwealth,
serving Bellarmine College, Berea College, Centre
College of Kentucky, Eastern Kentucky University,
The Filson Club, Georgetown College, Kentucky
Historical Society, Kentucky State University,
Morehead State University, Murray State University,
Northern Kentucky University, Transylvania University,
University of Kentucky, University of Louisville,
and Western Kentucky University.

*Editorial and Sales Offices:* Lexington, Kentucky 40506-0024

**Library of Congress Cataloging-in-Publication Data**

Higham, Robin D. S.
    Diary of a disaster.

    Bibliography: p.
    Includes index.
    1. World War, 1939-1945—Campaigns—Greece.
2. World War, 1939-1945—Diplomatic history.   3. Great
Britain—Foreign relations—Greece.   4. Greece—Foreign
relations—Great Britain.   I. Title.
D766.3.H53   1986        940.53'22'4109495        86-9177
ISBN 0-8131-1564-7

# Contents

Preface & Acknowledgments    vii

Introduction    ix

I  Prologue    1

II  The Metaxas Phase    11
28 October 1940 to 29 January 1941

III  The Garden of Eden    76
29 January 1941 to 4 March 1941

IV  Denouement and Disaster    154
5 March 1941 to 26 April 1941

V  Conclusion    234

Notes    238

Bibliographical Comment    260

Index    265

*Illustrations follow page 118*

Other books by Robin Higham:

*Armed Forces in Peacetime; Britain, 1918-1940* (1963)
*The Military Intellectuals in Britain, 1918-1939* (1966)
*Air Power: A Concise History* (1973, 1985)
Edited by Robin Higham:
*Official Histories* (1970)
*A Guide to the Sources of British Military History* (1971)
*Civil Wars in the Twentieth Century* (1972)
*Intervention or Abstention* (1975)
*A Guide to the Sources of U.S. Military History* (1975)
 and with Donald J. Mrozek Supplements I (1981) and
 II (1986)
*Soviet Aviation and Air Power* with Jacob W. Kipp (1977)
*The Garland Bibliographies in Military History* with Jacob W.
 Kipp (1984- )

# Preface & Acknowledgments

In approaching this story of a modern Greek tragedy I have taken the view that what is important is *what the British knew and could have known at the time*. The tale is told from the British point of view, but I have searched both British and American archives and memoirs, and visited Greece as well.

One considerable difficulty for anyone working in the area of Greek history is that no one can seem to agree on the spelling of place names. Modern maps, for instance, have as many variants of spellings as there are mapmakers. Another difficulty is that during the Greek civil war from 1944 to 1949 a number of villages were removed and no longer appear on the maps. And when the official historians came to make maps they either used such a scale that a number of names do not appear on their charts, or made gross errors—for example in locating railway lines—such as to make the maps suspect. I have usually chosen to use spellings that were standard in the documents of the time, particularly as they appeared in the military or diplomatic signals and other communications. I have taken the liberty of editing the signals themselves, when quoting them, to make them more readable.

My thanks are due to the Controller of Her Majesty's Stationery Office for permission to quote from numerous documents in the Public Record Office, and to the Keeper of the Department of Photographs at the Imperial War Museum and the Greek Army Directorate of History for permission to use their copyrighted photographs.

I am grateful for the support of the Bureau of General Research at Kansas State University many years ago when the project started, and to many individuals who have assisted me. Since 1972, when the British government opened the World War II archives, I have had the invaluable help of Commander Edward May, former associate director of the National Maritime Museum at Greenwich, who has followed up references and ferreted out sources at the Public Record Office in London and sent photocopies of the documents cited in these pages. As these materials and others from the National Archives in Washington have accumulated, I have experienced the excitement of seeing the truth unfold, often in contradiction to statements in memoirs and official histories.

In Greece, Lieutenant-General Ioannis Metaxakis, Head of the Greek Army History Directorate, was particularly helpful, as were Major-General Konstantinos Kanakaris and other Greek officers. General Kanakaris not only took me on tours in 1979 and 1980 from Athens to Florina, Thessalonika, the Monastir Gap, and Kalamata, so that I could view the ground, but also in 1981 translated the newly released Greek documents so that I could cross-check the British and Greek versions of key meetings. He also checked the manuscript of the book for errors. Dr. Michael Llewellyn Smith was kind enough to show me the old British legation building in Athens in 1980.

I must also add my thanks to two participants in the events of 1940-1941, the late Major-General Sir Guy Salisbury-Jones and General Sir James Marshall-Cornwall, who together with my colleagues on this side of the Atlantic, Alan Wilt of Iowa State University, Edward M. Coffman of the University of Wisconsin at Madison, and R.H. Roy of the University of Victoria, read and commented upon the manuscript. To them all I am most grateful. Errors remaining, of course, are my own.

# Introduction

Wars are not won solely by the powers of personality and diplomacy, however attractive these may be to publishers and readers. Ultimately wars have to be fought and won by adherence to the principles of war, which in the modern day include not only the concentration of forces upon defined objectives but also an understanding of the needs and limits of available technology.

At the heart of this story is the study of the interplay between heroic and popular personalities of the likes of Churchill and Eden, who had only a vague comprehension of the realities of war in a distant theater in 1940-1941, and the military generals Wavell and Metaxas, who were making decisions in the threatened area. The real issues were not the great themes of Western Civilization, as personified by all that "Greece" stood for from Pericles to Byron, but what was a sensible grand strategy, what should be the priorities for action, what were the means to accomplish the goals, and when would they be available? Inevitably these questions required technical and technological answers; they also demanded intelligence operations and skillful deception. Wavell met the challenges in a surprising way.

The events chronicled here took place almost entirely before ULTRA, the decoded German signals, became available. In the early years of the Second World War the British high command had yet to learn how to run a modern war efficiently; it was a task that required hard work, patience, and accurate information as well as theoretical knowledge. Perception and interpretation played a part: there was a certain disbelief in ULTRA until June 1941, because it was said to be from a Secret Intelligence Service agent; since the SIS had been wrong before, ULTRA was discounted by some. What the British needed to know, however, was reaching them through normal diplomatic or intelligence channels; even without ULTRA the British knew of German intentions from a variety of sources. If they made the wrong decisions, it was because they failed to read the messages correctly, their minds being set to see things only from their own perspective.

The involvement in Greece was never more than a limited campaign in an unlimited war, as far as the British were concerned, but they were never quite sure that Greece was not their last foothold in Europe. They had wonderful dreams of holding on to this last bastion of civilization and of protecting it with a diplomatic and military alliance, a Balkan bloc. These dreams bore little relation to military and economic realities, and so the stage was set for tragedy.

---

"The margin is narrow and the risk is considerable."
> Eden and Dill to Churchill
> from Athens, 5 March 1941

"This very unfortunate adventure. . . ."
> Lieutenant-General Thomas A. Blamey,
> Commanding General, Australian Forces,
> Middle East, 7 August 1941

"I need not give you a long account of the campaign in Greece: it was a series of misfortunes."
> General Sir Archibald P. Wavell,
> Commander-in-Chief, Middle East,
> 1939-1941, to the Indian Legislature,
> 1 August 1941.

"One frequently hears the expression 'lesson of Greece' used in conjunction with another one, even more widely used, 'lack of air support.' We did not lose Greece solely because we were weak in the air. We lost it because we did not have ready and thoroughly organized in Greece a *Balanced Force* of all arms, including ground and air of equal strength to the German invaders, with secure communications having sufficient capacity to maintain that force."
> Air Chief Marshal Sir Arthur Longmore,
> former Air Officer Commanding-in-Chief, Middle East,
> to the Royal Empire Society, May 1942.

# I

# Prologue

Moving through the receiving line at a postwar reception, the taciturn Field Marshal Earl Wavell came to Major-General Sir Frederick de Guingand. He stopped, poked him in the chest, and said, "Freddie, there was more to Greece than you'll ever understand."[1]

In the months between the Italian invasion of Greece on 28 October 1940 and the British evacuation at the end of April 1941, General Sir Archibald Wavell was the British commander-in-chief, Middle East, and de Guingand was a major on his planning staff. The British decision to aid Greece changed both their careers. It led Wavell to the thankless task of viceroy of India, while de Guingand rose to become Field Marshal Viscount Montgomery of Alamein's chief of staff in the victorious campaigns of 1942 to 1945.

In 1940 Wavell, the best-known and -loved general in the army, had a greater grasp of the political side of war than most of his contemporaries. He was once again to prove true a claim of General James Wolfe, often quoted by Wavell himself, that "war is an option of difficulties."[2] He commanded a vast theater which stretched from Malta in the west to Aden in the east, and from Macedonia in the north to Kenya in the south. When the Italians closed the Mediterranean, his Middle East command had to be supplied largely by a twelve-thousand-mile sea route from the United Kingdom and the United States around the Cape of Good Hope. Wavell had instantaneous communications with London, but a pedestrian supply system; there was a large gap between words and goods.

What makes this tale of a disaster so frightening is that it could easily happen again.

In order for grand strategy to be viable it must be based upon solid facts and realistic appraisals. In 1940 London regarded the Middle East as a colonial area whose center was the Suez Canal. Farther to the east lay a second important focus in the oil wells of Iran and Iraq. The first area was vital because the "lifeline of the Empire" flowed through the Canal and across the Mediterranean, connecting the British Isles to India and Australia; the second, because oil was the lifeblood of the war economy. But after Italy severed the lifeline, there was no sound British reappraisal and no consistent policy that assigned grand-strategic priorities to the various factors in the area; there was only a vague idea that the Italians should be cleared from eastern Africa and from the Dodecanese Islands, where their airfields were a threat to the Suez Canal. No plans were laid for Crete, though that 160-mile-long island could obviously be an important bastion if properly developed.

To the north of Crete lay an area in which it was believed by Englishmen that Lord Byron (the Thomas Phillips portrait still hangs in the Residence in Athens) had heroically liberated the Greeks from Ottoman rule; somewhere to the north of that lay the Balkans and the noble Serbs. In that mountainous countryside were the Bashi-Bazouks and the Bulgars, and from a place called Salonika the British had eventually launched a successful campaign at the end of the First World War. To the east of Macedonia lay Gallipoli, a peninsula upon which a brilliantly conceived Churchillian campaign had foundered because of military incompetence in 1915. It now lay in the land of the Turks, a swarthy, taciturn, tough race. London was not quite sure whether Greece and Turkey were part of the Balkans or of the Levant; it really did not matter too much, for they would do what the British told them to do.

Unfortunately, that naive picture was badly flawed in relation to the realities of geopolitics. Most of the commerce of Greece, the Balkans, and Turkey was with Germany, along the natural water and rail routes of the Danube valley. If many of the smaller powers in the area were not ruled by pro-German factions, they were linked to Berlin economically, and they were susceptible to the immediate physical threat of German power. Vital to German interests were the Rumanian oilfields, which by the winter of 1940 Hitler was already arranging to occupy in force. Against such naked military power the British had virtually nothing to offer. The United Kingdom had barely survived the Battle of Britain in the summer of 1940, and through the winter was still afraid of a German invasion. Her forces in the Middle East were pitifully small, as anyone like the neutral Turks could see by simply going visiting.

Notwithstanding the realities, the British and the French had insisted on guaranteeing Greek and Turkish neutrality by treaty in April and May 1939, and the British had then incautiously renewed these assurances after France fell. Seeing which way the power seemed to be shifting, and anxious to protect his own interests in the Balkans, Mussolini of Italy had seized Albania in early 1939 and decided that he should also have Greece. Aware of this ambition the Greek prime minister, the doughty little soldier General Ioannis Metaxas, was most anxious to maintain a strict neutrality; in spite of the pleas of his French-trained chief of staff, General Alexander Papagos, he refused to go to full mobilization in October 1940, unwilling to give the Italians an excuse for invasion. But he had in August sought British help.

The Greek army was small and tough, based largely upon reserves. It suffered from a number of basic weaknesses that need to be kept in mind. It was largely equipped with obsolete French, Polish, and Czech arms, for which there was now no other source than captured Italian matériel. There was only a single small-arms factory in Greece, and it depended upon imported raw materials. That the army was short of motor transport was not so vital as that Greece lacked all-weather roads, had but a single railway line north from Athens to Salonika and Florina, and had no all-weather airfields. Geographically the country was in most places very suitable for defense, provided that the troops had time to dig in and were equipped with adequate artillery and signals networks. As most roads were donkey tracks, and as the wireless sets of the day would not work in the mountains, most communication had to be by telephone or runner. Both were very slow, and once an active campaign started the country began to run short of donkeys, then of man- and woman-power.

Even if the British had been in top political, diplomatic, military, and economic form in 1940, Greece was not an area for which they were mentally or physically fitted. And there was another weakness. The link between diplomatic and military action in wartime has to be through intelligence services. In London the Foreign Office handled secret intelligence and was mainly interested only in Germany; there was little vital coordination at the top until 1942. Like most other organizations, too, intelligence at all levels was suffering from rapid expansion and territorial imperatives. Though a Middle East Intelligence Centre was opened at Cairo in 1939, the Balkans were excluded from its purview, while the Foreign Office denied it political and diplomatic information. (Nevertheless, its staff of enthusiastic young amateurs was soon putting out appreciations on twenty countries, including those in the Balkans; this so infuriated the War Office that only Wavell's intervention saved MEIC from abolition in May 1940.)

After Italy entered the war the Cairo branch of the Bletchley Code and Cypher School, which Wavell had managed to establish, began to receive signals intelligence ("sigint") directly over the teletype from London, giving Wavell access to filtered ULTRA from the Luftwaffe in Sicily and Rumania. But it was not until May 1941 that this unit was allowed to reveal the real sources of its information, and even then many chose not to believe it.[3]

The British were weak on photo-reconnaissance (PRU) also. One flight of Glenn Martin Marylands operated from Malta in the autumn of 1940, and a second was built up in the Middle East in early 1941. But there were too few aircraft to cover the necessary targets on anything but a spasmodic basis.[4] Middle East Command had only three Blenheim IVs in

Egypt which could reach Benghazi, in northern Libya, and they did not have the right spark plugs for long-range work.[5] It was not until March 1941 that London finally agreed that British estimates of German air strength had been too high and that more RAF aircraft could be released from the home command and sent to the Middle East; alas, that was too late to help Greece or this tale.[6]

Moreover, if intelligence was not yet cranked up to wartime efficiencies, the same was also true of the British services. The army and the RAF, particularly, suffered not merely from the usual post-peacetime shortages of tested men and equipment, but also from the fact that their officers were simply not trained for war. And just as the highest governmental levels had no grand strategy for the Mediterranean–Middle Eastern theater, so also the services had not developed their doctrines. For instance, though it had spent the First World War as a tactical air force, the RAF between the wars had become enamored of grand-strategic bombing independently of the army, and was opposed to undertaking tactical work; in fact, "army cooperation" was almost a dirty word. This would affect the Greek tragedy, because it placed the air officer commanding-in-chief, Middle East, Air Chief Marshal Sir Arthur Longmore, in conflict with his superiors at home. The trim, handsome Longmore, 5 feet, 8 inches tall, 150 pounds, was a former senior Royal Naval Air Service officer, a veteran of Jutland, who had risen in spite of his Mediterranean naval background in a service dominated by former Royal Flying Corps airmen who had served on the Western Front in the Great War. Longmore was also that rare senior British officer who still flew himself. Because of RAF theory Longmore's subordinate after November 1940, Air Vice Marshal John D'Albiac, became embroiled in tactical arguments in Athens, which were largely irrelevant since his bombers often could not get over the mountains to strategic targets.

Wavell's problems as commander-in-chief included not only the vast size of his theater but the diplomatic and economic necessities with which he was also saddled. These ranged from a hostile Vichy French force in Syria to the continentalism of the Boers in Cape Town, six thousand miles away. Not until 1942 was a Cabinet minister based in Cairo to take the civilian side off the C-in-C's shoulders, and a Middle East supply center established to handle the complexities of the regional economy. When in November 1940 Greece came within Wavell's purview, he had to deal with the fact that the coal for its railways came from England, and essential wheat supplements from India. Vitally affecting his planning was the miscalculation by the War Cabinet Office in London of ships available from September 1940 to the end of August 1941. (The error was due to failing to realize that the Norwegian and Greek fleets were already included in the British totals, and therefore could not be added in again, as they were under hire.[7]) The absence of a national inventory system in

Britain, together with the fear of invasion, had a doubly inhibiting effect on London's willingness to dispatch supplies to the Middle East.

On the eve of the Italian attack on Greece of 28 October 1940 Wavell, in Cairo, had roughly 500,000 men under his command, but of these the South Africans could only be used in East Africa, and the Australians and New Zealanders could not be employed without the consent of their home governments. (Those from "down under" well remembered Gallipoli and Chanak, in both of which Churchill had had a hand.) Wavell was desperately short of modern equipment for anything but an 1898-style "Fuzzy-Wuzzy" colonial war, which is what London basically thought he would be waging. Indicative of this is the fact that in July 1939, in spite of the size of his command, Wavell had a staff of only five officers, of whom one was part-time.

Air Chief Marshal Longmore's air force was equally pitiful, composed of biplanes and early modern monoplanes with a handful of more modern machines. He had on hand 40 Gladiators with 40 in storage, 70 Blenheims with 70 in storage, 24 Bombays and Valentines, 24 Lysanders with 24 in reserve, and 10 Sunderlands. There was no radar in Egypt. The attitude in the Air Ministry, conscious or not, was that matériel that was of no use in Europe could be sent to the Middle East. As a result, Longmore (with Wavell's backing) was constantly making himself unpopular for calling his very real needs to the attention of those at home. London also appeared to have forgotten that in 1938 it had added to Middle East Command Malta, Palestine and Transjordan, Iraq, and Aden.

The naval commander, that irascible, red-faced seadog, the popular Admiral Sir Andrew Browne Cunningham, was based at Alexandria rather than at Cairo. He was often incommunicado when the Fleet was at sea, and he was desperately short of destroyers for all tasks. There was no joint headquarters in Cairo, and not until 15 February 1940, when Wavell was appointed, was there a clearly nominated C-in-C ME. And each C-in-C still reported to his own service chief in Whitehall.

To complicate matters, in October 1940 the secretary of state for war, the debonair Anthony Eden (known as the "film star at the War Office," or "Robert Taylor"), was visiting the Middle East. One of the principal *dramatis personae* of this play, Eden seems as secretary of state for war to have deferred to senior military officers, for he had been but a captain in the First World War. When he returned for another visit in 1941, as Foreign Secretary and the Prime Minister's legate, he operated in an entirely different manner: then, he thought he had full authority to make any decision.

The C-in-C's had not remained mentally closeted in Cairo in the first three-quarters of 1940.[8] Starting on 10 May Longmore had sent home the first of his many requests for reinforcements to bring his command up to establishment. By August he had noted that, with the Italians in the war (from 10 June), he was twenty-two and a half squadrons short of requirements and that, even if his losses rose no higher than those suffered on restricted operations, he needed 35 to 50 Blenheims and 24 Hurricanes a month as replacements, rather than the 12 of each the Air Ministry had promised on 6 July.

On 27 May Wavell had proposed to London that the British should support Greece, since it was regarded as part of the Levant rather than of the Balkans, and that they should attempt to deny Rumanian oil to Germany. But he was told early in June by the Chiefs of Staff (the COS) that it would be unwise to repeat the mistakes of 1914-1918 war by backing weak countries liable to be overrun, so he was to take no action.

On 16 July Churchill handed one of his general directives to the Chiefs of Staff, who after making changes passed it to Wavell, noting that, as the ministerial committee had pointed out to the Prime Minister, the Middle East had neither the modern equipment nor the air support needed to face the impending Italian invasion of Egypt. Strangely, in as small a land as England, and with their interests and reputations, Churchill and Wavell had never met. The Prime Minister (also minister of Defence) now asked the C-in-C ME to fly home so he could meet him.

Wavell, therefore, took the risk of the long flight via Malta and Gibraltar and arrived in London on 8 August, just as the Battle of Britain started in earnest. He met at once with the Chiefs of Staff, to whom he gave a verbal appreciation of the situation: the Egyptian frontier was holding, but he was short of vehicle parts and tanks. What he feared, and there were already rumors of this, was not the Italians, but the arrival of Germans. He had no intelligence network behind the Italian lines, and thus two German armored divisions might reach Benghazi before being detected by photo-reconnaissance. The Italians had 280,000 troops in North Africa, and in an advance this force would have air support from some 300-400 bombers, 300 fighters and 200 transports. On his own side, the 7th Armoured Division had only 65 tanks (against an establishment of 220) and was seriously short of spares; the 4th Indian Division lacked a brigade and most of its artillery; and the Anzacs (Australians and New Zealanders) could only be used as yet for internal security duties because of their lack of equipment. Internal security itself was complicated by the fact that, since Egypt and Italy were not at war, some fifty thousand Italians were free to move around in Egypt, and Wavell was hampered by rules that forbade him to gather secret intelligence or prepare for subversive activities.

The GOC-in-C ME also had an artillery problem: units in his command were equipped with 18-pounders and 4.5-inch howitzers, but ammunition for these guns was in short supply, since production had been stopped when the new 25-pounder gun-howitzer was introduced in England. The same was true for the 37-mm antitank guns, for which he had only 21,000 rounds on hand. This meant that sooner rather than later all his units had to be re-equipped.

Wavell also met with Anthony Eden, and after their conversation Eden noted in his diary that "his deficiencies are shocking."[9] The reasons for the shortages were, of course, the vast loss at Dunkirk of equipment originally given to the British Expeditionary Force in France, and the need to re-equip the forces in the United Kingdom to be able to resist invasion. Shipping to the Middle East was slow, now that the Mediterranean was closed (the route around the Cape of Good Hope quadrupled the distance), and the arrival of convoys at Middle East ports congested the limited dock facilities and delayed unloading.

On 12 August Wavell met with the Defence Committee, chaired by the action-minded Churchill, from ten in the evening until two the next morning. Wavell was annoyed at the Prime Minister's wanting to know where every battalion was and why it was not someplace else. Eden says he commiserated with him, for he was used to it, but at nine o'clock on the morning of Tuesday, 13 August, Wavell offered his resignation. No sooner had Eden smoothed this over than a letter arrived from the Prime Minister refusing to meet again with Wavell. In his epistle the voluble Churchill asserted that Wavell lacked mental vigor and the resolve to overcome obstacles, and accepted too tamely the difficulties in the various theaters in which he was conducting operations so that he failed to concentrate on the decisive point. (Yet it would be exactly this dispersion of effort that Churchill himself was most guilty of instituting in the Greek case.)

Eden sent back a note to the Prime Minister saying that weapons, not men, were the problem in modern war, and urged him to support Wavell. He might have added that war had changed a good deal since young Churchill had charged the Fuzzy-Wuzzies on the way to Khartoum with Kitchener in 1898, but it really would not have helped. Churchill did not know or respect Wavell, though the British army did. According to Eden, Churchill regarded Wavell as a "good average colonel"; he constantly referred to him that way and said he would make a good chairman of a Tory association, thus damning him with faint praise. Eden tried to point out that Wavell had always been against appeasement and that he was a noted scholar at Winchester and—he might have added—a distinguished author of books on the successful campaigns of the First World War in the Middle East, in which he had participated. Unfortunately, Churchill at sixty-six still had his boyhood prejudices: as a Harrovian, he disliked Wykhamists. The secretary of state for war felt that the truth was that Churchill never understood Wavell, and that the general—quiet, poetic, and withdrawn as he was—never encouraged the Prime Minister to get to know him in the few days he was in England.

Meanwhile the Battle of Britain swirled overhead. On Thursday, 15 August, the Germans sent over some two thousand sorties, against which the RAF sent up 974 fighters.[10] That was also the day on which Churchill asked Eden who could replace Wavell and got the reply that General Sir Claude Auchinleck, GOC, Southern Command, could, but that there was not sufficient evidence to warrant such a move. On Friday Wavell left England, to return again but once until 1947, after he had fought fourteen campaigns and served as viceroy of India.

By the end of August it was becoming evident that the Greeks were concerned about their neutrality, and that the Chiefs of Staff were taking the view that no forces could be spared for Greece, Turkey, or Crete until Egypt was secure. Eden, who had wanted to aid the Balkans in 1936,[11] claims that on the twenty-first he told Churchill that, as the British might have to become involved in Greece, the Middle East would have to be reinforced.[12] The next day the Greeks asked what help they could expect under the guarantee treaty. After London discussed the political consequences for Anglo-Greek relations and the military realities of the supply line around the Cape of Good Hope, the British ambassador in Athens, the Etonian Sir Michael Palairet, was instructed to tell General Metaxas that little could be done except to try to prevent the Italian occupation of Crete, which lay on the line from Italy to the Italian Dodecanese Islands. Unfortunately Palairet was emotionally involved in Greece and did not follow instructions. Instead he called for British forces to be sent to Greece and told London that Britain was letting down a country to whom she had given a guarantee. On 26 August the War Cabinet reconsidered and informed Palairet that, in addition to promises of British support at the postwar peace table, some financial aid might be available. Churchill also sent Metaxas a personal message, saying that Britain expected shortly to be stronger in the Mediterranean.[13] On 5 September Lord Halifax, the Foreign Secretary, reaffirmed the 1939 Anglo-French guarantee, in spite of the fact that France had fallen.

As Wavell was leaving London in mid-August, British Somaliland, an unimportant colony consisting mostly of barren land, was evacuated by its small garrison. Churchill angrily sent Wavell a disapproving signal. Later, when the chief of the Imperial General Staff (the CIGS), Sir John Dill, was in Cairo in February 1941, he told Wavell that the Prime Minister had never forgiven the C-in-C ME for his response: "Heavy butcher's bill not necessarily indication of good tactics."[14] At a long Cabinet meeting on 4 October Churchill spent some time attacking Wavell, of whom he was increasingly uncertain. But on that same Friday Hitler and Mussolini met in the Brenner Pass, and the next day the British intelligence service presented the Prime Minister an account of their conversations, including proposals to send German troops to Libya and mount a drive on the Suez Canal from Syria. Churchill's immediate reaction was that, as the countries of eastern Europe could not stop the Germans, the Middle East army had better be built up as quickly as possible. On Sunday, 6 October, faced with increasing evidence that the enemy objectives were Greece and Yugoslavia and not an invasion of Britain, Churchill reluctantly ordered reinforcement of the Middle East.[15]

On 7 October Longmore signaled congratulations to Sir Charles Portal on his appointment as chief of the Air Staff (CAS), but pointed out that the Middle East was still terribly weak and would remain so for some time to come, in spite of attempts to reinforce it by sending aircraft out via Malta and via Takoradi in West Africa, both at a wastage of about 10 percent.[16]

On and off there had been mention of garrisoning Crete. It was discussed while Wavell was in London, but he had no troops to spare. With the arrival of three more Italian divisions in Albania in the autumn, the matter was raised again in Athens but, as the British attachés could make no promises, no headway was made. In any case, Metaxas wanted no foreign troops on his soil until war broke out. So the Joint Planning Staff in London took the view that a small force should be earmarked to move to Crete as soon as Greece was attacked, but that that action should be the limit of a British commitment to Greece. This was accepted in London, and Cairo was ordered to hold such a force in readiness.

In fact, though Suda Bay, on Crete, was a desirable naval refueling base, it would have to be protected by A/A guns and fighters from nearby airfields, and there was no grand-strategic reason why, in an air age, Crete should be held. Wavell knew what he had to do—clean the Italians out of East Africa while holding on to Egypt—but there was still no British grand-strategic plan for the Middle East. Part of the reason for this may have been personality conflicts and misunderstandings.

The principals on the British side may be divided into two groups, the civilians and the military. In the former group were Winston Churchill and Anthony Eden and their lesser associates, principally Palairet in Athens. In the latter were Wavell and Longmore in Cairo, Dill in London, and their subordinates, particularly Air Vice Marshal John D'Albiac in Athens. Making a third group were four important Greek leaders—King George II, Metaxas (who was prime minister and president of the Council), Papagos, and Metaxas' successor as prime minister, Alexander Koryzis.

All of these players had various bonds of sympathy which drew them to others on the stage at one time or another. Churchill, Eden, and Metaxas had been soldiers, but were now politicians. Wavell, Longmore, Dill, Metaxas, and Papagos had a common understanding of military realities, which King George II in his British-style uniforms also shared. But the Greeks, except perhaps for Metaxas, always felt themselves to be in an inferior position, while Eden, at least, tended to feel that as an Englishman he was superior.

Another thread woven through this tale is that of the personal relationship between Churchill and Eden, who were at moments like father and son. Indeed, Eden later wrote that the Prime Minister told his young secretary of state for war that after the conflict he was to succeed him as prime minister.[17]

Even in the matter of language there were interesting contrasts. The Greeks all spoke at least one language besides their own. Some of the British spoke a second language, but this was not always useful in Greece: Wavell was fluent in Russian, and Eden's ability to quote Persian poetry was at best misleading. So most discussions took place in English or with interpreters, with minutes kept in English and Greek and protocols in French.

The final moves made before the Italians struck against Greece on 28 October were the Cabinet decision on the ninth that Eden should pay a visit to the Middle East, an unusual step, and the agreement on the twelfth that, owing to the needs of Home defense, no more RAF squadrons should be sent to the Middle East. On 14 October Eden teletyped that he had arrived safely in Cairo; two days later he reported that Wavell was planning a January offensive in the Western Desert, if the equipment arrived, and in the Sudan, unless the Italians attacked first. On the seventeenth Palairet telegraphed Eden that Metaxas, an internationally respected strategist, predicted an Axis attack on Greece and Turkey and advised that the British could protect their left flank if they would pay attention to Greece and listen less to Turkey. Metaxas felt sure that the Greeks could hold the Italians on the Albanian front if they had some air support and antiaircraft and antitank weapons.[18] The ambassador's signal had been repeated to London, and Longmore was asked by the Chiefs of Staff what he could do, to which he replied, "Nothing." (Wavell supported this opinion.)[19] The next evening Dill told the War Cabinet that there was no truth to the rumors that Mussolini intended to attack Greece.[20]

On Saturday, 16 October, the new chief of the Air Staff, Portal, dropped a handwritten note to his deputy chief: "You mentioned this evening that we now had lots of fighters in store and were just becoming well off for pilots. Are you satisfied that we have done all we should for AOC-in-C ME (I don't mean necessarily that he should use them to help Greece)?"

On the twenty-seventh the first decrypt from BONIFACE (later called ULTRA) hinted that the German invasion of Britain was off.[21]

The stage was now set for the British decision to aid Greece. The record is a diary of a disaster.

# II

# The Metaxas Phase
## 28 October 1940 - 29 January 1941

*The rattle of gunfire had begun to involve western European troops in the drama that became the Second World War as early as Mussolini's invasion of Ethiopia in 1935. Hitler had honed his weapons in Spain, and in the spring of 1940 he swept through Denmark, Norway, Holland, Belgium, and France, until brought up short by the English Channel. In the last few days of the German blitzkrieg the Italians had joined in, and all of a sudden the Allied planners' worst possible case had gone out the window and been replaced by an undreamed-of nightmare: a hostile Continental coast from the North Cape to Spain without a single ally in power on the mainland of Europe, the Mediterranean closed to British shipping, and Italian troops threatening Egypt from two sides.*

*Grim as the summer of 1940 was, with a weaponless army back from Dunkirk, as the year waned into fall General Wavell began to make slow headway in his vast Middle East Command. Without informing Winston Churchill, the belligerent new prime minister who had taken over in May, Wavell was even planning an offensive strategy and setting up his own intelligence organization.*

*In the Balkans the Germans were beginning a military penetration that flowed down the normal lines of their economic well-being and might reach the Persian Gulf. Far to the west in the United States Franklin D. Roosevelt campaigned for, and on 2 November won, a third term.*

## 28 October 1940

The Greek prime minister, General Ioannis Metaxas, was a pudgy little man with a pasty face, who had not the slightest physical resemblance to either a general or a dictator, according to C. L. Sulzberger of the *New York Times*.[1] He was spending the weekend at his country villa at Kifisia, then ten miles outside Athens on the road to Marathon. At three o'clock on Monday morning, 28 October, he was roused by the Italian ambassador, Count Emmanuel Grazzi, who handed him an ultimatum, properly couched in diplomatic French, which demanded the right of the Italians to occupy certain strategic positions within Greece. Metaxas refused to dignify the ultimatum with a written reply. Rubbing the sleep from his eyes, and realizing that he was faced with a declaration of war, he said simply, "*Ochi!*" (no).

Though the timing may have been unexpected—the Italian service staffs were throwing a party—the note was not. The Greeks had anticipated an Italian attack on the Epirus front since 3 October and had been partially mobilized.[2] Metaxas dismissed the ambassador, called the king, got into his car, and drove straight to the British legation, where at 3:30 he handed the Italian note to the minister, Sir Michael Palairet. Palairet later wrote of the ultimatum, "It would be difficult to find a better specimen of lying effrontery even among the numerous similar productions of the Axis Powers." He added that Metaxas' first step had been to ask for British help; Metaxas' diary gives a slightly different version.[3]

Metaxas then went to army headquarters to consult General Alexander Papagos, the chief of staff. They agreed that the British might not be able to do much in support of the guarantee of April 1939, but that they would press for what they could get; they judged that Turkey would probably remain neutral, since she had failed to act when Italy had brought the war to the Mediterranean in June.[4] They then spoke with King George II.

Palairet at once dispatched a copy of the ultimatum to London by diplomatic pouch, where it arrived on 14 November, and fired off a telegram to the Foreign Office, repeated to Cairo, giving the news and asking for help. The chain effects of this were immediately evident: the Foreign Office telephoned the War Office at 5:25 a.m., and nineteen minutes later the Admiralty dispatched a war signal to all flag officers at home and abroad. The Mediterranean Station had already warned all submarines at 0715 Cairo time, a message received in London at 0650Z (Greenwich, the base time). In midmorning the military attaché in Angora (as Ankara was then often called) telegraphed to say that he would pass on information from the Turkish general staff on the situation in Greece unless told otherwise; Turkish action, however, would be confined to the neutralization of Bulgaria.

The military attaché in Belgrade reported that the Yugoslav chief of the general staff "was evidently surprised by the turn of events and was in a depressed and nervous state. . . . He repeated several times, What can we do? We are completely surrounded. I received the impression that it was unlikely that Yugoslavia would come to the aid of Greece." Nevertheless, some Yugoslav divisions were brought to a war footing.

As soon as the news of the Italian attack on Greece reached London, a signal was sent to Wavell in Cairo, stressing that Crete was vitally important as a Fleet base and authorizing the dispatch of up to one infantry brigade with field and A/A guns, despite the risks that would have to be run in Egypt and Malta.[5] At 5:45 in the afternoon Churchill sent off a characteristic word of encouragement to General Metaxas: "We will give you all the help in our power. We fight a common foe and we will share a united victory."[6] Churchill wished to bomb Rome but was promptly overruled.[7]

That night Sir Alexander Cadogan, the under-secretary of state for foreign affairs, noted in his diary, "The dirty ice-creamers attacked Greece at 6 am. Luckily I wasn't woken."[8]

Early on what proved to be a beautiful sunny Monday there were Italian air attacks on various places in Greece, including an ineffective one on the Tatoi Palace about fifteen miles north of Athens. The Greek general staff began to move into the imposing Hotel Grand Bretagne, on the northeast corner of Sýntgama Square just across from Parliament House and a short walk from the Italian embassy.

When the news reached Cairo, Eden, Wavell, and Longmore were in Khartoum. Their deputies had, therefore, to act for them until late morning when they flew back into town.[9] At 1:45 Wavell sent a personal signal to Dill, the CIGS, in which he reported that he and the senior Air Staff officer, Air Vice-Marshal Drummond, had met with Admiral Cunningham at Alexandria. The navy intended to use Suda Bay at once as a temporary base, and the assistance which the army and the RAF could render had been discussed. Several officers would be dispatched the next day by flying boat to make a reconnaissance. The Malta battalion of the Yorks and Lancashire Regiment was being held in readiness to move by cruiser to Crete, with another battalion on short notice, but no further action would be taken without London's authority except in an emergency. One commando troop of a hundred men was being placed at the disposal of the C-in-C Med' for use if urgently required. Wavell further asked that the burden of sending a battalion to Malta be transferred to the Home command. The movement of A/A guns to Crete was being examined, while air matters were covered in a signal to the chief of the Air Staff.

Secretary of War Eden sent his own assessment to London, to the effect that the security of Egypt came before everything else and that, while the army was almost up to strength, the RAF was way behind. Moreover, any land forces sent from the Middle East to Greece could not possibly be strong enough to have a decisive influence on the fighting there, and by dividing resources the British would risk failure in both places. Even more important, such action might jeopardize the plans Wavell was preparing in great secrecy, plans of which Eden would tell Churchill when he got home.[10] Eden sent this message in his own personal code and it was decoded in London and passed to the Prime Minister in an uncopied handwritten note.

Drummond, in the absence of Longmore, had already that morning signaled to Portal, the chief of the Air Staff, that he had agreed to send a Sunderland with a party to Suda Bay on the twenty-ninth, including an

RAF officer charged with looking over the area to see if a full-sized airfield could be built near Suda Bay. Drummond was also arranging for three Sunderlands to be refueled there while undertaking naval reconnaissances. At the same time another signal requested that the Greeks be informed that Sunderlands, Blenheims, and Glenn Martins would be flying over Greek territory.[11]

At this time someone in Cairo ran through a personnel index and came up with the name of a Lieutenant Hunt, who could speak Greek. He was called in, promoted to captain, told a British force was being sent to Greece, made intelligence officer, and put in command of a cipher section. And so began OPERATION BARBARITY.[12]

In London the Cabinet met at five o'clock that afternoon and listened to Eden's cable declaring, "We are not in a position to give effective help by land or air, and another guaranteed nation looks like falling to the Axis." The Cabinet also heard that Metaxas had asked for air and naval aid to protect Corfu and Athens. Such requests had been made for some time, and only guarded replies had been given. It was now suggested that Rome be bombed, avoiding of course the Vatican, but that the Fleet be kept away from Corfu. The line, however, to be taken with the Press was that all possible aid was being given to Greece.[13] Bombing Rome was in accord with a thought from Sir Miles Lampson, the British ambassador in Cairo, who added Taranto, the Italian naval base, using Wellingtons based in Egypt. The Cabinet also heard that Admiral Cunningham, C-in-C Med', was most anxious about the state of his destroyers, as it was their condition which would limit his operations to the west of Greece. Convoys to Greece would further extend his limited resources, though use of Suda Bay would help.[14]

The War Office was aware that Hitler might send aid to the Italians in North Africa.[15] This was confirmed the next day when Sir Samual Hoare, formerly secretary of state for air and now British ambassador in Madrid, cabled the contents of the discussions that Mussolini and Hitler had held in Florence on the afternoon of the twenty-eighth. At that time Hitler had offered Mussolini his parachute troops—but to occupy Crete, a strategic stepping-stone bastion for both sides.

The War Cabinet concluded that there was not much that could be done at that moment, though—as the official historian, Sir Llewellyn Woodward, would comment later—"During the next few days there was a considerable change of policy."[16]

Part of that change was reflected in an Air Ministry memorandum prepared in response to the Prime Minister's direction on the twenty-eighth to move four heavy bomber squadrons (Wellingtons then fell into that category) to the Middle East to work from advanced bases in Greece. The four-page study concluded that for security reasons only four aircraft a night could be dispatched to Cairo via Malta and that the four squadrons would need a minimum of 500 personnel, 50 specialist vehicles, and 500 tons of shipping stores. The aircraft would have to have tropical filters and other modifications fitted. It would take five weeks for stores to arrive. Personnel could only be rushed out through the Mediterranean, and that would take a major naval operation during a moonless period. The only alternative, and it was unacceptable to the planners, was to rob personnel from the Middle East in order to get aid to Greece at once. Some 3,800 personnel were already scheduled to sail from the United Kingdom in November to bring the RAF in the Middle East up to strength just for its existing units. So the conclusion was "that timely air support for Greece cannot be provided from RAF resources except at the expense of Middle East Command. Flying out additional aircraft would not affect this unless the appropriate personnel and equipment could also be got out." Not to be ignored was Eden's signal of 16 October, "Reinforcement of the RAF is the pressing need of the hour here and will, I am convinced, prove to be the decisive factor," a statement that was reinforced on the twenty-sixth by another saying that he was frankly disappointed in the air reinforcements and stressing their need even for defense.

In Greece itself, the planners pointed out, there was a problem of the location of suitable airfields. There were some on the plain around Larissa, which did have a railway and was connected to the small but usable port of Volos. There were only two good airfields near Athens (both of which were bombed on the morning of the twenty-eighth), which did have the adequate port of the Piraeus. There was one field on Crete, but it was too small for modern bombers and was within easy reach of the Italian airfields in the Dodecanese. Larissa was within range of Albanian airfields, and Athens could be reached from both Rhodes and Albania. Greek air defenses were negligible, so airfield defense would have to come from the Middle East Command, which was already woefully short. "The risks of relying on A/A. defences, dispersal, and quick refuelling would have to be accepted."

To set up a refueling base would require roughly 110 personnel, 100 tons of shipping stores, 25 vehicles, and 65 tons of bombs and 6 tons of small-arms ammunition weekly. "The impracticability of providing adequate defences in Greece compels us to use Egypt as the main base for the operation," a plan that involved 1,400 miles of unproductive flying to and from the refueling point per sortie. This, coupled with the limited scale of operations from improvised bases and likely higher wastage, would limit operations to eight to ten sorties per day, so the best scheme was thought to be for squadrons to move up to the advanced refueling base for three or four days at a time and then return to Egypt for major maintenance. The planners disliked this arrangement, however, because it involved large numbers of maintenance personnel at both ends and many aircraft on the ground in daylight. Overall, the report concluded that the only means of

affording quick air aid to Greece was to send it from the Middle East, yet
"We have abundant evidence that the Middle East is already dangerously
weak in its air defence."[17]

## 29 October 1940

The Defence Committee of the Cabinet met that evening, and the next day
(the twenty-ninth) Churchill asked Eden to stay on in the Middle East.
The advanced British reconnaissance party reached Crete and at once
found that the only airfield was at Heraklion, seventy miles from Suda
Bay, and that it was only suitable for Gladiators. Approval was received to
move a brigade to Crete at once.

From Athens the naval attaché reported to Admiral Cunningham that
Metaxas had said that he "will chase the Italians out of Albania in a month
if you can cut their maritime communications for that period." The naval
attaché reported that he had said that that was impossible, two or three
days at a time being more likely, though submarines might be able to
operate in the Adriatic for longer. Metaxas was delighted that the flagship
had already used Suda Bay and said that all Greek bases were entirely at
the British navy's disposal. In response the Admiralty signaled about
mining Greek waters to deter the Italians, but added that the C-in-C Med'
was "free to act as circumstances dictate in the event of Greece being
overrun."[18] Meanwhile the Air Ministry had been offered places for fifty
men and twenty-five tons of stores on a naval vessel sailing from Glasgow
the next day and had ordered Bomber Command to have the men aboard.

And from Belgrade the British minister, Ronald Ian Compbell, telegraphed that Prince Paul ("our friend") was under increasing German
pressure and more and more felt the isolation of Yugoslavia. This telegram made its slow rounds of the Foreign Office, where on 12 November
Philip Nichols, head of the Southern Department, noted that it was far the
most encouraging message from Belgrade because, as Pierson Dixon
(recently back from Rome) had commented, thinking about war was a
mental effort Prince Paul had hitherto refused to make.[19] In fact the
Foreign Office underrated the man.

## 30 October 1940

On Wednesday a long telegram at the expensive day rate arrived in
London from Palairet reporting on the war situation: according to the
Yugoslavs the Italians now had fifteen divisions in Albania with twelve
on the Greek front. Palairet appealed for help and especially requested
the bombing of Italian concentrations in Albania, using Greek airfields for
refueling as required. Otherwise, he said, he would not signal in daytime
unless it was urgent.[20]

And from Ankara Sir Hughe Montgomery Knatchbull-Hugessen, His Britannic Majesty's Ambassador, signaled that the best course was to keep Turkey out of the war until the spring, as general assurances were all that Turkey had to give until she was well supplied and equipped, an opinion with which Wavell's chief of staff, General Arthur Smith, concurred, and so did R.J. Bowker, deputy head of the Southern Department in the Foreign Office.[21] Ankara also sent word that the Turkish ambassador in Berlin had advised that the German Foreign Office had "expressed complete surprise and dismay" when shown a copy of the Italian ultimatum to Greece.[22]

Also on Wednesday the CAS, Portal, signaled Longmore that he thought it made better sense to operate the Wellingtons from Malta against the Italian lines of communications to Greece, while Longmore's aircraft should concentrate on direct aid to Greek forces. "You will appreciate the advantages of Crete vs the mainland as an advanced base, but we leave the final decision to you."[23]

A further long telegram from Knatchbull-Hugessen, who was unaware that his valet Cicero was a German spy, said that it was agreed that the Turks would not enter the war for some time unless compelled to do so. They regarded the German line that Greece had been refueling the Royal Navy as economically absurd and considered the Italian attack "a dishonourable, dirty business" that would recoil on Germany. What the Turks would do was to ship to the Greeks the antitank ammunition with which the British had supplied them.[24]

## 31 October 1940

The tempo of a changing policy can begin to be detected on Thursday, 31 October. That morning a Sunderland flying boat landed in Phaleron Bay with British officers aboard. They disembarked and motored up to Athens to talk with the Greek authorities. In the close community that was Athens in 1940, the American naval attaché soon knew what was afoot and cabled home a diplomatic appreciation, which took the view that, if the Germans attacked, they would widen the war unacceptably; and so they were likely to seize only strategic targets and leave the older part of Greece alone. He had the impression that what shocked the Germans was not the Italian attack but the Greek resistance.[25] The American ambassador, Lincoln MacVeagh, added that one of the British officers had said that "it took some courage to risk another Norway."[26]

In Cairo, No. 30 Squadron, a mixture of fighter and bomber Blenheim I's, was ordered to Greece. Each airman was issued two blankets, and S/Ldr. U.Y. Shannon was told, "Plans are to be prepared for the evacuation of personnel and material should such action become necessary. These plans to include arrangements for demolition of such material as cannot be evacuated. . . . Items saturated with petrol should be ignited by firing a Very pistol into the dump from an upwind position." His fifteen aircraft ("Too few" Metaxas told his diary) were to leave in two groups, the first on 3 November and the second on 5 November, accompanied by four Bombay transports, which would refuel at Heraklion on Crete and then proceed to Eleusis.[27]

After tea Wavell signaled that he was sending Major-General M.D. Gambier-Parry to join the military mission in Athens at the first opportunity; he was assuming that the military attaché there could provide an interpreter. He added that he would like to have Gambier-Parry, a useful field commander, relieved in Athens by Major-General T.G.G. Heywood, as he did "not want Heywood as a commander in the Middle East."[28] (Heywood, who had served on "Tim" Harrington's staff in Constantinople after World War I, was a Balkan specialist, a linguist who when military attaché in Paris had failed to report on the poor state of the French army before 1940. *Persona non grata* to fighting soldiers in the Middle East, Heywood was killed in an air crash in May 1941.)[29]

A row between the C-in-C's ME and the Chiefs of Staff in London over the slowness in breaking Italian ciphered messages was finally resolved with the agreement on 31 October that a deciphering unit composed of staff from the Bletchley Code and Cypher School should be set up at RAF Heliopolis, Cairo, to be administered by the army with specialists from all three services attached.[30] This became known as the Combined Bureau, Middle East. At the same time on the intelligence front London was beginning to get strong evidence that the Germans were going to undertake a major campaign in the Balkans. Up to this time information had flowed in from normal diplomatic and Secret Intelligence Service channels. Now it was supplemented by ULTRA as German Air Force units began to move into the Balkans and transmit over the airwaves. But because of other priorities and the learning process, it would be February 1941 before some of this Enigma traffic was deciphered and the information made available.

In Athens, the fact that the Germans were not at war with the Greeks enabled them to keep their embassy open all during this period.

Churchill told the War Cabinet that afternoon that Britain had shown that she could stay in the war, although she could not yet launch an offensive; meanwhile invasion had to be safeguarded against, while Germany was master of Europe.[31] Alexander Cadogan at the Foreign Office confided to his diary that he had tried to tell Halifax and Churchill what a great opportunity the Greek conflict was for an attack on Italy, but they had a "Narvik/Dakar complex"; he therefore had to tone down a very discouraging telegram from the Prime Minister to Palairet.[32]

It had been agreed in London that an interservice military mission should be formed in Athens which would be headed by Rear-Admiral

Charles Turle, sometime head of the British naval mission to Greece, 1927-1929; he had been brought out of retirement in 1939 because he spoke Greek, and sent as naval attaché to Sofia and Athens. A signal was sent to Middle East headquarters announcing this decision, with a request that they supply the rest of the personnel.

With signals coming in from Athens urging air attack on the Italian lines of communication, the Air Ministry became concerned, and the chief of the Air Staff minuted his deputy: "We cannot allow the AOC-in-C to maintain an altogether non-posthumous [*sic*] attitude failing the discovery of a landing ground in Crete where bomber aircraft of his command could be refuelled. He should at once consider sending a token force to Athens or some other aerodrome on the Greek mainland where refuelling facilities can be made available. A demonstration bomber flight near the Albanian frontier would do much to hearten Greek troops and need not necessarily commit the AOC-in-C to the permanent detachment of bombers from his force."

But before anyone could act, Longmore, back in Cairo from his visit to Khartoum, had seen Palairet's signal and taken it upon his own shoulders to respond, signaling Portal, "It seems that it has become politically absolutely essential to send a token force to Greece even at the expense of my force here. I have therefore arranged to despatch to Athens without delay one Blenheim Mark I Squadron of which half the aircraft are equipped as fighters and half as bombers. This makes no provision for Fighter Defence of the Fleet Base Crete for which no aerodrome in the locality is available. It also reduces by small proportion the fighter defence of Alexandria."[33]

That signal, sent at 1127 from Cairo, was received in the Air Ministry at 1405. The reply, originated at 1503 and dispatched at 1700, shows the speed with which action could sometimes be taken. Portal fully approved of Longmore's action; he reiterated the instructions to find a good landing ground in Crete or, if that proved impossible, to establish a more permanent base in Greece.[34]

In the meantime the cruiser *Berwick* had left the United Kingdom with the RAF contingent and 12 Bofors guns for the defense of Crete.

## 1 November 1940

Lecturing at the United States National War College in Washington after the war, Wavell said that "because they took away some of my very limited air support to aid Greece, I had to tell Eden that I was planning to attack the Italians in the Desert; otherwise I wished to keep it a secret."[35] As a man of deception long at home in a wartime Cairo in two world wars, Wavell was only too well aware of the likelihood of leaks.

It was against this background that Eden sent from Cairo a long report of his initial conversations with the C-in-C's; he dealt with the strengthening of the defense of Crete and came to the conclusion that the first line was the Fleet. But he then went on to point out that the RAF was so weak that it could not afford a high proportion of losses on the ground. It was essential that, as Graeco-Italian hostilities escalated, British minds should be clear as to the main issues. "The following are my conclusions," said Eden:

> We cannot from Middle East resources send sufficient air or land reinforcements to have any decisive influence upon the course of fighting in Greece. To send such forces from here or to divert reinforcements now on their way or approved would imperil our whole position in the Middle East and jeopardize plans for offensive operations now being laid in more than one theatre.
>
> After much painful effort and at the cost of grave risks we have, so far as our land forces are concerned, now built up a reasonably defensive force here. We should presently be in a position to undertake certain offensive operations which, if successful, may have far-reaching effect on the course of the war as a whole. It would surely be bad strategy to allow ourselves to be diverted from this task and unwise to employ our forces in fragments in a theatre of war where they cannot be decisive.

This opinion reflected that of the C-in-C's ME and of their Joint Planning Staff in Cairo, who felt that a whole brigade might be necessary for Crete's defense because it was such a crucial island.[36] What no one said was that Crete was far larger than Malta and much farther removed from the main Axis coast. It was potentially of great value, and yet everyone had more hesitation about defending it and the aircraft on it than they had about defending Malta. But at least something was done about Crete this day. One battalion arrived there to join the 130 officers and men with medical stores who had been landed at Suda Bay when the cruiser HMS *Liverpool*, severely damaged by a torpedo on 14 October, was docked for repairs.[37]

In Athens the Germans told Metaxas that they would not regard the RAF in Greece as a *casus belli* unless the RAF were given airfields in the north.

Major-General Gambier-Parry, an amiable Etonian, now an armored corps general officer, arrived in Athens as the Chiefs of Staff's personal representative at the new military mission on 1 November and met immediately with Palairet and Col. Jasper Blunt, the military attaché. Both thought that Gambier-Parry had been sent in response to an appeal from General Papagos and were unaware of the limitations in his instructions from both the Chiefs of Staff and the Foreign Office. Unfortunately it seemed that Papagos had been informed that Gambier-Parry was the answer to his prayers. Blunt took the general along to see the Greek commander-in-chief at seven in the evening and was much impressed with Papagos' reasonable attitude when it was explained to him that Gambier-Parry was not in a position to make any decision upon a general plan of campaign or upon British cooperation.

Gambier-Parry reported home that he could not see, since GHQ was in Athens, how a British military mission could do a better job than the military attaché. He was not wanted further forward, as communications were so bad in Greece that it took two days to get to the front, and the field communications system was heavily overloaded; it scarcely needed foreigners trying to get priorities on it.[38]

On this Friday in London the War Cabinet was told of Eden's report and discussed the aid that could be given to Greece. Those present agreed that if the Greeks put up a good resistance the British would have to help at once. On the other hand Turkey might be more important to the United Kingdom in the long run. The Chiefs of Staff then expressed their concern that the Germans would advance into Turkey and Syria once they had taken Greece.[39]

## 2 November 1940

The next morning, at the request of the Greek king and Metaxas, Gambier-Parry saw each of them for about fifteen minutes. Both urged the need for maximum British air action in Albania to protect the Greek field army until mobilization was completed; given ten days, they expected to be able to go onto the offensive. Metaxas suggested that fully armed RAF bombers should fly to Greece to be refueled and briefed, and then attack the enemy. Further, the Royal Navy should occupy Suda Bay and operate from there to prevent an Italian landing behind the Greek lines in the west. Both impressed upon Gambier-Parry the need for the British to make a maximum cooperative effort: actions would speak louder than words.

That night Gambier-Parry sat down and drafted a sketch of the three principal Greek leaders for the benefit of London and Cairo. He started with Papagos, a commander, he felt, who knew his stuff and thought before he made his points. Tall and aristocratic in appearance, he was very likable, although possibly too austere to command affection or popularity. But the English general liked his quiet, confident manner, which could not fail to communicate itself to his staff and subordinates. Though Papagos was obviously tired and suffering from lack of sleep, he took the greatest pains to explain the situation. Gambier-Parry was much taken by the Greek commander's patience and knowledge of detail, but he also got the impression that Papagos thought he was empowered to discuss a plan of campaign with him. Unfortunately the rest of Gambier-Parry's description of Papagos was lost to a garbled transmission in which a large number of groups were undecipherable.

Turning then to the king, Gambier-Parry was obviously fooled, for he believed that George II had a completely English outlook and was very easy to talk to. Though a little shy, he had great charm of manner, a grand sense of humor, and a witty way of putting things. He struck Gambier-Parry as having the utmost confidence in Metaxas and Papagos and in being wisely determined not to interfere. Nevertheless, the king was thoroughly well informed and had a detailed knowledge of the military situation and of the requirements of the services.

But "General Metaxas is the big noise in Greece at present and I should describe him as a really outstanding personality even by international standards." Although he spoke almost no English, he understood a good deal, and Gambier-Parry naturally found that his distinguished military record (he had been chief of staff in World War I) facilitated discussions. A very shrewd man, Metaxas went straight to essentials, but appeared thoroughly to understand the difficulties of immediate cooperation with the British when they were explained to him.

At Greek GHQ itself there was a general quiet confidence which bespoke the efficiency of a well-trained team. The effects were evident even in the lower ranks: it was notable that although the Greeks had allowed five days for the call-up, 80 percent of the reservists had reported on the first day.

But if the leadership and the spirit of the Greeks were excellent, their equipment was something else altogether. The four tanks in the Greek army consisted of 2 obsolete Vickers and 2 ancient Carden-Lloyds used at the training schools. As for antitank weapons, they had 22 .55-inch antitank rifles plus 19 sent by the British from the Middle East; they hoped for 22 more, with 60,000 rounds of ammunition from the British and 5,000 rounds from the Turks. Seventeen hundred antitank rifles and 120 guns had been on order from France for more than a year but, like other prewar purchases, had not been delivered. What the Greeks wanted were 60 two-gun antitank pack sections and 25 four-gun sections for mountain use, as they feared an Italian sweep through southern Yugoslavia down into Greece through the Monastir Gap.[40]

Also on 2 November a plane carrying British officers flew low over Athens, to the cheers of the crowds. These new arrivals necessitated a hunt for space for a headquarters for the RAF. The Near East Foundation's building was, therefore, requisitioned, presaging greater things to come.

As early as 2 November, however, discussions with the Bulgarian minister in Athens made MacVeagh and others suspicious that the Bulgarians would provide passage for the Germans to attack Greece. To the American ambassador and the Greek Foreign Office the future seemed like a chess game in which Moscow was the red queen and Greece, as usual, but a pawn of the great powers.[41]

Eden was hot in Cairo and anxious to get back to London and tell the fidgety Prime Minister of Wavell's plans, but on the second Churchill signaled, "The Greek situation must be held to dominate others now. We are well aware of our slender resources." And added that Eden should stay on another week. In frustration Eden scribbled across the message sheet, "Egypt more important than Greece."[42] And in his diary he noted, quite correctly, that the idea that Greece should dominate was strategic folly; the C-in-C's, the British ambassador at Cairo, and he all agreed that the key was Egypt.[43]

In London the vice chief of the Naval Staff, Vice-Admiral Sir Tom Phillips, said, "For God's sake don't lets go fighting in Macedonia. We must not commit ourselves to fighting on land at present—and so we mustn't go into Greece."[44] Ivone Kirkpatrick, the Foreign Office representative on the Committee on Foes, later recalled that the committee at this time came to the conclusion that if they were Hitler they would lay off Spain, maintain the threat of invasion of the United Kingdom, send substantial reinforcements to North Africa, and attack in the Balkans. At the same time, he noted, Churchill said that the trouble with the Chiefs of Staff Committee was that it always presented the sum total of its fears.[45] The Prime Minister saw it that way because it spent half its time shooting down his more ill-conceived schemes.

The big issue of the day was really the Greek shopping list, part of which was cabled by the military attaché in Athens, while a full copy was sent to London by air from Cairo. Basically what the Greeks needed was artillery—pack, mechanized, and A/A. They needed 100,000 boots, helmets, 150,000 rifles of 7.92 caliber, 70,000 pistols, 1,000 motorcycles with sidecars, and a like number of ambulances, tires and tubes, binoculars, 60 fighter aircraft, 24 Blenheims, spares for the Fairey Battles already delivered, parachutes, petrol and lubricants, and medical supplies and beds for a 5,000-bed hospital. The navy needed mainly ammunition in a variety of calibers.[46]

The War Cabinet agreed to the Greek requests for guns, aircraft and supplies that could come from the United States, but at the same time the Prime Minister insisted that Greece be given more British help by land and air. So two more Blenheim squadrons and two Gladiator squadrons were ordered to be sent, even though this left the Middle East dangerously weak. Churchill said that Britain could back out by explaining that the 1939 guarantee had been Anglo-*French*, and that all the plans had been in General Weygand's hands, but that public opinion would not be satisfied by this sort of subterfuge; in addition Britain would lose the Turkish alliance if her help to Greece was on a smaller scale than had been proposed. And he claimed that Britain had just as great a strategic interest in keeping the Italians out of Athens as out of Khartoum. It was a political argument.[47]

While it can be argued that the duty of leaders is to lead, it can also be held that they must be responsible and measure ends against means. A frequent failing of administrators and politicians is that they want to take a shortcut and pull off one great coup. Churchill was always desperate to do that, and in this case he was jumping the gun because he disliked and distrusted Wavell and Longmore. They were both rational, systematic officers, insistent on remedying the deficiencies in their commands for which he was partly responsible. Having to operate at the disadvantage of using signals rather than holding face-to-face meetings, neither Wavell nor Longmore could handle Churchill in the emotional way that was, in his case, most effective. Nor would either of them have been capable of doing so.

As Sir John Dill left Chequers after spending the evening with Churchill, Winston said to him, "Don't forget, the maximum possible for Greece!" Churchill's maxim for decades had been "Neglect no means," but now, as Martin Gilbert commented in his 1983 biography, the means were too few.[48] Dill went back to the Chiefs of Staff conference and was no help to Wavell there either. He opposed sending an expeditionary force to Greece, arguing instead for securing Crete as a naval and air base. An appreciation was sought from the joint planners, but this was not available until Monday the fourth.

But 2 November was still one of the turning-point days when the policy of nonintervention other than at Suda Bay was being changed into all aid short of troops. That evening the Air Ministry asked the British air attaché in Athens to supply information immediately on what airfields would be available for four to five RAF squadrons, and what facilities they would have.

## 3 November 1940

Eden reminded London that extensive discussions that morning in Cairo had reaffirmed the principles laid down in numerous Foreign Office telegrams to Athens, especially in No. 651 of 22 September that "any assistance that we may be able to give to Greece cannot be given until the German-Italian threat to Egypt is finally liquidated, the security of Egypt being vital to our strategy and incidentally to the future of Greece." And he went on later in the same message, "The security of Egypt is the most urgent commitment, and must take precedence of attempts to prevent Greece being overrun. It is also essential if we are to retain the support of Turkey." And in view of the fact that all that had been sent was one battalion to Crete and one squadron to Greece, would London please stop the BBC and Reuters from giving the misleading impression that more was being done, so as "not to raise hopes which cannot be realized."[49]

Later the same day Eden sent another signal summing up some items about aid to Greece not contained in his first telegram. These included the well-taken points that the things the Greeks were most likely to need were exactly those things the British themselves were so short of at this time—A/A guns, antitank guns, and rifles. Moreover, the British had but one spare trained brigade, and to send it would deprive the Western Desert Force of its only reserve, while the brigade could not reach the front in Greece for three weeks. Convoys due from Britain would contain only two regiments of artillery immediately available for the field, and the A/A regiments which had arrived were lacking equipment. So the British should adhere to their position and strengthen the units in Egypt rather than help the Greeks.

Sunday the third was not a happy day at the top. Eden in Cairo was irked that Churchill, having opposed sending reinforcements to the Middle East, was now insisting that Greece was more important than Khartoum and Kenya. "The weakness of our policy is that we never adhere to the plans we make," Eden grumbled to his diary. If Britain had thought to aid Greece, plans should have been made long ago, but the deliberate decision had been taken not to send aid, "so high sounding phrases only make matters worse."[50] The trouble that day lay in the fact that the ever-bellicose Churchill failed to understand that Eden and Wavell were for assuming the offensive, but, since Wavell was going to have to use deception, he wanted to be extremely secretive and he did not wish to send signals about his plans in case they were intercepted in the ether or in Cairo. Eden had all the information necessary to convince Churchill, but the Prime Minister would not let him fly home to deliver it. And so Churchill assumed that Wavell was yet "another cautious general."[51]

In London, the Chiefs of Staff agreed to send three RAF squadrons and A/A artillery from the Middle East, which would be replaced with 34 Hurricanes and 32 Wellingtons from home, in a policy of "all aid to Greece."

The RAF was finally able to move to Greece on this rainy Sunday because of the arrival of a British tanker in the Piraeus with aviation fuel. Eight Blenheim fighters of No. 30 Squadron and 4 Bombay transports of No. 216 Squadron left Egypt in the morning; 6 Blenheim bombers followed on the fifth. They landed at Eleusis airfield to the west of Athens, not far from the famous ancient naval battlefield of Salamis. Wing-Commander Willetts, who went with them, soon reported that the Greek air force was badly in need of direction and would welcome RAF advice, especially since those Royal Hellenic Air Force officers who had trained abroad had done so in England. He also reported that the 11 new Blenheim IV's in the RHAF were grounded because of a lack of spares. So

Longmore signaled London later in the day that he proposed to send Air Commodore John D'Albiac to be temporary air officer commanding (AOC) and adviser to the Greek general staff, if the secreatary of state for air approved.[52]

In London Col. Raymond E. Lee, the American military attaché, met the permanent secretary of the War Office, Sir James Grigg, at Lady Astor's house, Clivenden, and told him that Britain had a great opportunity to seize a string of bases in the Mediterranean and that he hoped that they would hold Crete strongly.[53] In the Foreign Office someone wrote on a minute on taking over Crete that it was a pity the British had not gotten in before Italy attacked, "but the Greek government learned nothing from the fate of Norway, Belgium and Holland, and were not ready to grant us the necessary facilities."[54]

Churchill's biographer wrote that at Chequers that Sunday Churchill lay in his four-poster bed with the flowered chintz hangings, chewing his cigar and dictating to his faithful typist, Kathleen Hill. He rapped out the precise phrases of a telegram to Eden, while sipping iced soda water and wiggling his toes under the covers.[55]

## 4 November 1940

On Monday the Foreign Office told Palairet to start marking his military attaché's telegrams "Immediate," as they had been delayed by lack of any priority. Palairet told the Foreign Office that the Italian minister had finally left with 190 Italians and 65 Germans including secret-service agents.[56] The service attachés in Athens reported that the Greek concentration would be complete in about ten days, but that even so the Greeks would be inferior to the Italians; they continued to press for air attacks on Italian communications: the sooner more aircraft could reach Greece, the greater would be their impact. In Cairo, however, Wavell was alarmed that Metaxas wished to withdraw the garrison in Crete, now that the British were there; he reluctantly concurred, even though it once more stretched his resources.

In London the Joint Planning Staff reported to the COS that it would be a mistake to move forces to Greece, as it would hazard the position in the Middle East, but that Crete should be secured. This position the COS Committee endorsed the next day. As D. M. Davin, the New Zealand official historian, notes, "The point is an important one. For if this line of action had been adhered to in the circumstances later to develop, the focus of British attention would have been Crete, and the troops sent to Greece might have been sent instead to Crete with consequences that can now only be the subject of conjecture."[57]

The War Cabinet approved the recommendations of the Chiefs of Staff only to have the Prime Minister skew their plan: Churchill declared that "the loss of Athens would be as serious a blow to us as the loss of Khartoum, and a more irreparable one." He then went on to aver that the British public was most anxious for intervention in Greece, as it felt that Britain could not welch on another guarantee. The War Cabinet responded to this sentiment, and to Lord Halifax's report of the Greek ambassador's request for arms and the use of the British Purchasing Commission in Washington, by steadily increasing the British commitment.[58]

After the War Cabinet meeting on the fourth, the Chiefs of Staff signaled the C-in-C's in Cairo their plan, beginning, "It has been decided that it is necessary to give Greece the greatest possible material and moral support at the earliest possible moment. Impossible for anything from the United Kingdom to arrive in time. Consequently only course is to draw upon resources in Egypt and to replace them from the United Kingdom as quickly as possible."

The COS then went on to spell out what should be sent to Greece, noting that 34 Hurricanes were being sent on the aircraft carrier HMS *Furious* to Takoradi, to be flown across Africa to Egypt, while their ground crews would be sent on a fast convoy through the Mediterranean, due to arrive about 2 December. In addition 34 Wellingtons were being flown out via Malta, with their ground crews also to be in the same convoy. The COS concluded, "It is fully appreciated that this plan will leave Egypt very thin for a period. Every endeavour is being made to make this period as short as possible."[59] Eden responded unenthusiastically to this telegram the next day that "these risks must be faced in view of the political commitments to aid Greece."[60]

Longmore was ordered to send to Greece as soon as possible, once defended airfields were available, BARBARITY FORCE, five RAF squadrons. This was in addition to No. 30 Blenheim squadron, which had just arrived in Greece. These actions, the Cabinet hoped, would encourage Turkey to offer help.[61] How naive the Cabinet was to think that one squadron was going to make realists like the Turks risk their national independence in such a confused situation! But in London Cadogan, at least, wrote "Thank Heavens we *are* doing all we can in the air for Greece."[62] "All" was not much. The CIGS said 22 antitank rifles had been sent from Egypt and he might be able to find 50 more.[63]

And, at last released, the secretary of state for war reported that after flying to Malta and Gibraltar he would arrive at Plymouth at 0900 on the eighth.[64]

The one piece of good news that London sent out was a signal to Longmore saying that the appointment of D'Albiac was approved and "Sending you earliest possible opportunity Air Officer to act as second in command to yourself."[65]

## Guy Fawkes Day, 5 November 1940

Among a number of signals from Athens was one reporting that the minister of war was delighted with the antitank rifles that had been flown in from the Middle East on the second; on the Epirus front they had been used on 4 November to destroy nine Italian tanks. Now the Greeks could use at least another hundred on that front alone. Gambier-Parry added that he had seen Metaxas and Papagos late the day before to establish a close working relationship well beyond what the military attaché could achieve: they would discuss future intentions and reactions to current events. He also noted that Metaxas had reserved "the right to assume the supreme direction of operations."[66]

In another signal Jasper Blunt, the military attaché, reported that General Papagos was "not a popular figure, but commanded respect owing to his quiet confident manner and sound common sense. Greek staff impress with their complete absence of excitement. . . . Majority of public transport commandeered. Complete black-out and curfew imposed for foreigners. All Italians arrested and some fifth column Germans but latter mostly free owing to undefined German position. . . . All are convinced that we are sending aircraft and arms, and, from aspect of morale, swing of public opinion . . . if we are found not to have done so will be [violent?]."

Blunt added that the BBC's assertion of British air superiority everywhere in the wake of the Battle of Britain did not help matters. British aid in Crete was considered by the Greeks to be "ineffective self-help" and the last bombing of the Dodecanese a waste of effort better employed against troop concentrations in Albania.[67]

Later in the afternoon the Admiralty said that the C-in-C's of the Mediterranean and East Indies could decide between them if the 36 magnetic mines at Aden could be used. Further supplies were being shipped.[68] In the meantime a slow convoy filled with fuel, coal, and RAF stores had left for the Piraeus, and the next day a fast one had come up the Suez Canal and left for Suda Bay and Malta carrying guns, troops and fuel.

In Cairo this Guy Fawkes Day D'Albiac received his orders from Drummond, the senior Air Staff officer, to proceed to Athens and relieve Wing-Commander Willetts as AOC, British Air Forces in Greece:

> You will have the status of an independent Air Force Commander but although not under the control of the Greek general staff, the conduct of air operations by the R.A.F. should, as far, as practicable . . . conform as closely as possible to the Greek plan for the defence of the country. . . .
>
> The fighters are being provided for the defence of your aerodromes and vulnerable . . . rear area. The attack of . . . enemy

lines of communication and . . . rear areas appear to be suitable tasks for the Blenheim bombers. You are not to allow the bombers to be used as artillery or to participate in the actual land operations unless the military situation becomes so critical as to justify the temporary diversion of our bombers from strategic bombing to support the Greek land forces. . . . Appropriate objectives for the Wellington bombers are points of disembarkation and concentration areas on the Albanian coast. . . .

Bombing is to be confined to military objectives and must be subjected to the following general principles: (a) Intentional bombardment of civil populatin as such is illegal. (b) It must be possible to identify the objective. (c) The attack must be maade with reasonable care to avoid undue loss of civil life in the vicinity of the target. (d) The Provisions of the Red Cross Convention are to be observed.

And after sundry instructions about not attacking Rome and coordinating operations with the AOC-in-C ME, "You are empowered to refuse to undertake any operation which, in your opinion, would jeopardize the security of the air forces under your command. In such an event you are to report the circumstances direct to this Headquarters."

He was also to inform the AOC-in-C of important discussions with the Greek general staff and to keep the British military mission in Athens informed, for "the possibility of a sudden and complete collapse of Greece must not be lost sight of when making your decisions on the location of the squadrons." If time did not allow for consultation with the AOC-in-C, he was to use his discretion as to the appropriate moment to evacuate the RAF from Greece.[69]

Meanwhile the AOC-in-C had reported to London that he was sending D'Albiac (with his wife) to Athens and requested that the Air Ministry "deal entirely with this HQ in all that concerns RAF matters in Athens otherwise grave danger of three-cornered interchange of signals resulting in complete confusion." As a staff was being improvised from Middle East Command personnel that Longmore expected Portal to replace, the AOC-in-C understandably later complained that one thing that was wrong with the RAF at this time was its lack of trained staff officers for just such emergencies. Further, despite explanations by the chief of the Air Staff about serviceability, spares, hours flown, type of operations, and the like, London still tended to make grandiose schemes based upon paper figures which included all training and communications aircraft in the whole command.[70] Longmore, who had been commandant of the Imperial Defence College in 1939, was well aware of the political and other aspects of the problem, but, nevertheless, he had every right as the AOC-in-C to object when his fighter force was reduced by 30 percent and his bomber force by 50 percent at a time when aircraft deliveries were well behind schedule. Yet just before Eden left for England, Wavell, Longmore, and Eden had agreed that more aircraft would have to go to Greece for political reasons.[71]

Back in London the Chiefs of Staff completed their study of the possibilities of German intervention in Greece, seeing the Italian attack as a diversion to draw the British away from Egypt and agreeing that the Greeks might hold up against an Italian attack, but not against a German one. Nor would any forces which Britain could send delay the Germans; and the Turks were not likely to help. Furthermore, it would be a mistake to divert forces from Egypt and tie them up in Greece, so help should remain restricted to sea, air, and technical aid.[72]

Others in London were fretting over the list of supplies the Greeks wanted and trying to see if the British Purchasing Commission in Washington could obtain most of them. But these requests raised the whole problem of Allied needs, and so a reduced Foreign Requirements Committee was established to handle them. And it had a not uncommon problem of its own: "As for the possibility of Greece getting war material in the U.S.A., it is not clear from the minutes of yesterday's War Cabinet meeting exactly what our policy is to be. The North American Supplies Committee are finding out from the Minister without Portfolio (Mr. Greenwood) what was decided." It was intended that the small committee should be chaired by the Third Sea Lord, but, as it "never materialized," a new committee was established under the ubiquitous Lord Hankey, longtime secretry of the Committee of Imperial Defence, and it met at last on the eighth.[73]

On that Tuesday evening of Guy Fawkes Day Churchill told the House of Commons that so carefully had Britain respected Greece's neutrality that the United Kingdom did not even know Greek dispositions or intentions. And it might be added that no one in British service seemed to know much about modern Greece at all.


## 6 November 1940

On arrival in Athens D'Albiac reported that it was expected to take three weeks to mobilize the Greek army and get it into position to make the country generally safe from the Italians. During this period, since the Greek road and rail network was so limited and many reservists had still to come from the islands, the Italian air force should have been able to play havoc, if properly handled, which it was not. The Greek air force had done well with limited numbers. Its pilots were keen, but with mostly French and Polish aircraft and limited spares, they suffered from an abnormally high rate of unserviceability. In addition the general staff used the air force solely for a tactical role, never to achieve air superiority, with the result that they soon suffered heavy casualties. D'Albiac had at once had a conference with the Greek prime minister and the commander-in-chief which resulted in a long-drawn-out argument over the proper employment of air forces, ending with agreement that the RAF bomber force should be employed against ports of disembarkation and centers of concentration behind the Italian lines. The big problem was still that Greece had no all-weather airfields, and there were few areas on the mainland in which fields large enough for modern aircraft could be constructed.[74]

In Cairo orders were issued for one flight of No. 84 Squadron of Blenheims to join No. 30 at Eleusis. Evidently Cairo had now learned that Greece was not as balmy as Egypt, for the airmen were kitted up to six blankets apiece and blue uniforms. In addition every airman was to carry a rifle with ammunition, and every officer a pistol.[75]

On his way home on 6 November Eden telegraphed from Malta that the more he thought about it, the more dangerous it was to withdraw one of the three fighter squadrons in the Western Desert, as "a third of our fighter forces is a very drastic cut, and, unless we can improve upon present plans, cannot be replaced for some weeks." And he added that Wellingtons were no use for daylight work and so were not half as good to the theater as were Blenheims, more of which were urgently needed along with four-gun Martin fighters, then known to be in the United Kingdom and which could be flown out.[76]

On the sixth little else happened. Wavell proposed to use New Zealanders on Crete. This was seconded by Freyberg but dropped when the government in Auckland opposed it on the grounds that one brigade of the New Zealand Division was still in the United Kingdom.[77] S/Ldr. T.H. Wisdom arrived in Athens by Sunderland flying boat, checked in at the King George hotel next to the Grande Bretagne on Sýntgama Square, and then sought out RAF headquarters. When he got back to his room his baggage had been gone through most carefully, as had that of all the others in his party. He also noted that soldiers leaving for the front were so ill equipped that people in the crowds along the streets were taking off their socks and shoes and giving them to the troops.[78]

In London the War Office was telling the Foreign Office that it had at last been able to look at the list the Greeks had sent and was shipping out 50 antitank rifles and 5,000 rounds of ammunition by air, together with some telephone cable. The Greek minister told Cadogan that the Yugoslavs were concentrating tanks near Monastir apparently with the intention of making it clear to the Italians that any drive for Salonika, which contained a Yugoslav free port, would be opposed. And the Air Ministry signaled Longmore that it was pleased that he was going to use Wellingtons from Greece, but hoped that they would be available again for Libyan targets if needed. The Air Ministry also noted that it was passing control of the Wellingtons based in Malta over to the Middle East. Bombers in Greece, the Air Staff said, should be used against targets agreed on with the Greek general staff; as for the fighters in Crete, Heraklion was too far from Suda Bay for effective defense, so the fighters were better employed in Greece. Since he could not spare another squadron for Crete, Longmore should leave it unguarded but press on with the development of airfields and facilities to allow operations there if required.[79]

Other British officials were meeting in the War Cabinet offices in Richmond Terrace, across Whitehall from Downing Street, to decide whether or not the Greeks should be allowed to have the £5 million credit that Britain had given them in dollars so that they could buy some sixty aircraft in the United States. The Foreign Office view was that the Greeks would not be able to use the aircraft if they could get them, so it would be better to see that the RAF got them (though, in fact, at the time the RAF was shorter of trained pilots than the Greeks were). The matter was finally resolved on the eighth by the Greek Requirements Committee, which decided that Greece had plenty of dollars and that "there was no need whatever for the time being to consider granting her a dollar credit."[80]

In the meantime a much more volcanic row had been building in the Prime Minister's own realm. He was demanding to know how the army, naval, and air intelligence services were organized and who was in charge. The basic problem was that the Joint Intelligence Committee (the JIC) was loaded with many administrative as well as interpretive responsibilities, and with the sifting of materials which properly should have been handled by the service departments.[81] This meant, because of the abrupt way in which war in the twentieth century expanded across the face of the earth, that senior people were apt to ask embarrassing questions about little-known places which suddenly came into prominence. A 6 November minute from Churchill illustrates the dilemma: "It was a disappointment to me to learn yesterday that the Air Ministry knew nothing about airfields in Crete. It seems that there should be a close investigation of our Air Force dispositions in the whole of the Middle East, for it is probable that inquiry will disclose a similar lack of information in other directions."

A week later Churchill exploded that he was receiving too many intelligence summaries, most of which contained no more than he had already read in Foreign Office and individual service directorates summaries and telegrams. It appeared that more than a year after Britain declared war the Higher Direction was still trying to get geared up. (It was not running smoothly until 1943.) Unfortunately, in democracies at least, it seems that by the time the apparatus is working well the war is running down. In many ways the Greek campaign of 1940-1941 came at the wrong end of the war.

## 7 - 12 November 1940

On the seventh, Thursday, a large supply convoy reached Greece with RAF ground crews and equipment; Squadron Leader Wisdom felt that German and Vichy French spies were a real nuisance; Cable & Wireless reported that all lines east of Athens in the Balkans were out; and in London Major-General Heywood was appointed head of No. 27 Military Mission in Athens and was told, "You will not commit His Majesty's Government even by implication to the provision of any such requirements as may be referred to you by the Greek Government. Nor will you encourage any expectation of specific support without prior sanction in order that false hopes may not be raised."[82] The policy, he was told, was to sustain Greek resistance without committing forces to Greece which were vital elsewhere. The BARBARITY force was to be made expandable to take two divisions, but on no account were the Greeks to be told this.

From Athens Gambier-Parry told Wavell that the king and Metaxas stressed the urgency of getting the six Greek battalions out of Crete and up to the Epirus front. Vice-Admiral H.D. Pridham-Wippell, second in command of the Mediterranean Fleet, was in Athens with HMS *Orion*, and he agreed with the others that the danger to Crete was not as great as the danger to Greece, and that if Greece went, Crete was useless. Gambier-Parry added that if the reinforcements for the Epirus were late, naturally the British would get the blame. The War Office at the same time was telling Wavell that "it is considered indispensible that further reinforcements be sent to Crete." To enable him to form a Cretan force, as suggested by the military mission, 20,000 rifles were being sent out. And the War Office told the military mission to inform Papagos that they fully understood his difficulties; they could not possibly object to his taking the six battalions, but would he please leave the twelve guns behind until the British could find replacements for them.[83]

The COS representative in Athens signaled Wavell that, in answer to a question on how Greece might employ a British military force if one were sent, the Greek prime minister replied that it was too early to tell. Metaxas was not as cheerful as he had been, because Italian air activity had increased; he stressed again the need for air support.[84]

However good his intentions, Gambier-Parry's signal sent palpitations of fear through certain quarters on the British side, and he was forced to send a long explanatory telegram about the hypothetical question that he had asked. Metaxas, he noted, was "a man with whom the utmost frankness is not only possible but desirable and will in no way be abused." Relations with all three Greek leaders were most cordial and lacking in suspicion. As Gambier-Parry saw it, the straws in the wind seemed to indicate that the wind was blowing in the direction of the dispatch of a British force to Greece. If this was so, then the commander-designate and the staff should be sent to Athens at the earliest possible moment. The terrain on and beyond the Albanian frontier was difficult, and the climate severe, and a British force would encounter both tactical and administrative problems. The country closely resembled the Northwest Frontier of India; he recommended that any force dispatched should have a high proportion of Indian and British forces "thoroughly experienced in mountain warfare." Moreover weather conditions were such in winter that the question of acclimatization needed to be seriously considered.

But London was not to be placated and on 9 November the War Office sent a sharply worded signal: "You are entirely wrong in supposing that wind is blowing in the direction of possible despatch of British Military Force to Greek Mainland and you are expressly forbidden by any word or suggestion of yours to imply that such a course is contemplated."

And so on the eleventh a contrite Gambier-Parry replied, "Much regret both my misinterpretation of the direction of the wind and my importunity resulting therefrom. Your expressed instructions are thoroughly understood and appreciated and I can only assure you that no harm has been done."[85]

But that apology crossed another signal from the War Office wanting to know if it was true that the head of the military mission had revealed to the press that the British squadrons in Greece would soon be followed by troops. Had he given an interview to the press? He was to leave that to the press attaché. He was in future neither to grant interviews nor to say anything at all regarding contemplated British action, hypothetical or otherwise.[86]

Poor Gambier-Parry was generally unlucky. After a spell in command of Crete, he returned to the Western Desert only to be captured by Rommel in the April 1941 retreat. He spent the rest of the war in an Italian prisoner-of-war castle.

Crete was another sensitive issue. The broad lines of policy had been laid down in discussions in early November, and it was eventually agreed that Suda Bay should become "a second Scapa Flow," which meant sending a mobile naval base team, consisting of 8,800 men with 72 antiaircraft guns and 10 to 15 coastal defense guns.[87] (Whether or not this organization actually was to be sent was still under discussion in April 1941, when Greece and then Crete fell.)

Again raised was the question of employing Australian and New Zealand troops. This had been discussed in September 1940, and leaders of the two Dominions had stipulated that the troops were to be used if properly equipped, and provided that such activity did not prevent their serving in their own divisions commanded by a Dominions officer.[88]

The South Africans were not to be employed outside of Africa at this time. When consulted on the matter of aid to Greece, Prime Minister Smuts had in early November indicated that northwest Greece would after mid-November be an impassible swamp, but that the Cretans were the best fighters in the Greek army. Queried as to the source of this strange—to London—opinion, Smuts (who had been a member of Lloyd George's War Cabinet in 1917 and was instrumental in creating the RAF) replied that it came from Professor Arthur Wellesley Falconer, formerly the assistant consulting physician to the British Salonika forces (1916-1918) and then principal and vice-chancellor of Cape Town University.[89]

In London there was another wide-ranging discussion of sending more air support to Greece, in which questions like the following were asked: Why did not the Greeks spend their dollars for aircraft? How many aircraft could they get for eight million dollars? Why not take over the air defense of Greece (and get blamed for the failures)? As this was a matter of supply, should not the Ministry of Aircraft Production be consulted? And would it really make much difference, because the Greeks did not have the trained personnel and so the wastage would be so high as not to be worth it?[90]

At the War Cabinet meeting on 7 November concern was expressed that Germans were still running around loose in Crete, since Greece was not at war with Germany. The Prime Minister suggested that they be disposed of by an accident, to which the very proper Foreign Secretary, Lord Halifax, replied that thirty-five "accidents" would hardly look accidental![91]

At this time the Greek government was asked by Lord Halifax to send a representative to the meeting of Dominion and Allied governments in London. But as the Greeks were the only ally fighting on their own soil under their own government still in their own capital city, they declined to do more than ask their minister in London, Simopoulos, to be present as an observer.[92]

To Metaxas' relief, at last it began to rain on 8 November, and Athens was hidden under clouds until the twelfth. Bombing was thus less likely.[93]

Middle East Command signaled the Air Ministry that it would start forwarding at noon daily an operational summary from Greece which would show the situation up to six o'clock the previous evening; the first of these reports gave the situation to eight o'clock on the morning of 8 November. This showed 15 Blenheims at Eleusis, 6 Wellingtons on the way in daylight for night operations, one flight of Blenheims warned to proceed from Egypt to Athens, and two squadrons withdrawn from the Desert to prepare to move.[94]

Eden himself got back to London on Friday, went to the War Office and saw Dill in his room overlooking Whitehall with the red London buses trundling by, and then went across to the War Rooms underneath the Foreign Office and saw Churchill. Winston gave him an affectionate greeting and was soon purring like a kitten as Eden at last could unfold the details of Wavell's bold plan for an offensive against the Italians early in December. After having spent the previous day approving all sorts of complicated plans to deny anything useful in the Middle East to the Germans and Italians (including ranging as far afield as Vichy-French Syria and the destruction of the oilfields in Iraq) as well as help for Greece, all Churchill could say when Eden laid out Wavell's plans was that he had wished that he had known earlier. Though Churchill later wrote that no harm had been done, nevertheless, as Parkinson notes, it had. There was in fact a very serious danger that Middle East Command had been saddled with more than it could handle with increasingly thin resources. In line with Wavell's desire for extreme secrecy for his forthcoming COMPASS offensive, only a very few people heard Eden's exposition of the plan; not even the War Cabinet knew about it until the troops actually attacked.[95]

It was hard for London to comprehend that although Greece was a European country and a founder of Western Civilization, it was in 1940 a relatively underdeveloped nation. For instance, the communications system was divided between the Hellenic Telephone Company, which owned the system in the towns, and the government TTT ministry, which controlled the landlines between them. While there was plenty of skilled manpower, there was a great shortage of equipment and wire, and all the exchanges were still manual. There were only fourteen teleprinters in the country, of which four were in Macedonia. There was a government point-to-point wireless system, but the Germans had a large part in it and most of the engineers in the telephone system were Germans. The Greeks were willing to help, and the telephones so far needed by the British had been installed; but at this time the RAF was manning only the airfields at Eleusis and Tatoi (a field later called Menidi, taking the name of a nearby village rather than that of the sylvan royal palace in the hills), and so the connections to Athens had not been difficult. As the RAF's signals operation was so efficient, it was recommended that the army signals units be placed under the chief RAF signals officer.[96]

Saturday the ninth started with what would be the routine signal summarizing operations in Greece. While more aircraft had arrived, two of the six Wellingtons dispatched to bomb Valona had not returned from that raid. Better news came to the Foreign Office from that old Etonion Sir Ronald Ian Campbell in Belgrade, who reported most confidentially that he had had a talk with Dr. M. Tupanjarin, the Serbian Peasant Party leader in British pay, who had talked on the fifth with Prince Paul. The situation appeared to be that Yugoslavia would join Greece if either Bulgaria herself or Germany via Bulgaria attacked Greece, or if there were a serious threat to Salonika, and that Yugoslavia would refuse passage to German troops going to Greece. Whether or not the Yugoslavs would fight rather depended upon the amount of help Britain gave Greece, and "in this respect the strategical and psychological presence of Salonika is very great. The whole Serb nation," Campbell continued, "remembered Salonika as the base from which Serbia was reconquered. The Bulgarians equally remembered it as the base from which they were defeated. Thus while the landing of a large force may now be out of the question, even the presence of a few officers and men would have an incalculable effect on Yugoslavia and Bulgaria. Naval support is vague and removed to the Serbs who are a nation of soldiers."[97]

Early on 10 November Prime Minister Metaxas apparently suffered a heart attack which was complicated by diabetes, for which insulin was flown in from abroad.[98] The next day the Air Ministry suggested to Longmore that it was up to him how much he told the king about supporting operations from Malta.[99] What was not said was how to tell the king that the air force which had only just won the Battle of Britain was so powerless. That night Longmore must especially have rejoiced when a dozen Swordfish biplane torpedo bombers struck the Italian fleet a severe blow at Taranto, a station Longmore had commanded at the end of the First World War.

On 12 November Professor F.A. Lindemann, Churchill's one-man research department, informed the Prime Minister that the United Kingdom could supply only 1 percent of the supplies Greece needed, "if indeed, we are ready to send anything." He then listed what might be made available. Churchill had this memo typed up, signed it, and sent it to the Chiefs of Staff, who then found some material including 20 Hurricanes at Malta for Greece. The Prime Minister vetoed the Hurricanes and ordered them to Egypt.[100]

## 13 - 23 November 1940

During these weeks Wavell's plans for Africa were explained to the Cabinet by Eden, the one politician with whom the taciturn Wavell could talk, and the air situation was constantly discussed. Churchill authorized sending Hurricanes to the Middle East to free Gladiators for Greece, an action to which Lord Beaverbrook vigorously objected. (Beaverbrook was overruled.)[101] But Churchill did not help matters by cabling Longmore on the thirteenth that he was astonished at how few fit modern machines he had operational from the vast numbers in his command, and demanding he report on steps being taken to remedy this and on the daily arrival of new aircraft. (A glance at what had happened to the Royal Hellenic Air Force in combat would have indicated the difficulties, as the RAF was to learn the next April: on 2 November the RHAF had 8 Blenheims and 8

Battles, and five squadrons of fighters of 6 to 8 serviceable aircraft each. By 15 November these had been reduced to 6 serviceable fighters.)[102] London tended to overestimate Longmore's strength by counting training aircraft in his command as operational aircraft.

A serious problem, both in the United Kingdom and abroad, was the lack of a repair organization in the RAF. This had almost led to disaster in the Battle of Britain. Damaged aircraft had accumulated until Lord Beaverbrook created a repair organization and forced the service to abandon peacetime acceptance standards: by October 1940 the number of aircraft being returned to service had begun to rise. But a similar organization was not created in the Middle East until mid-1941. Moreover, recovery of damaged aircraft was a much more serious problem than in Britain.

In Greece D'Albiac made a tour of potential airfield sites and urged that all-weather runways be constructed at Araxos and Agrinion. (Because of limited resources and shortage of labor, Araxos had not been completed in April 1941 when British engineers were forced to blow it up to prevent its use by the Germans.)

On 14 November the interservice mission, more correctly known as No. 27 Military Mission, was formally established under Rear-Admiral C.E. Turle.[103] He was told, among other things,

> Our policy in supporting Greece is based upon the hope that Greece will continue to resist the Italian attack, and upon the assumption that the Germans will not intervene against Greece in the near future. In present conditions it is not possible to issue instructions covering the eventuality of a German attack which would radically alter the military situation in Greece. . . .
>
> The object is to secure a firm foothold in Greece, when adequate forces have arrived in the Middle East in order to extend and intensify our offensive action against Italy, and possibly eventually to take effective action against the Roumanian oilfields and communications with Germany.

Turle's instructions went on to deal with the possibility of Greek withdrawals and demolitions and suggested holding, if possible, the line Naupaktos/Lamia, and if that fell to hold the lower mainland, the islands, and Crete. British forces in Greece were to conform in their movements to those of the Greeks, but if the latter collapsed, they were to be withdrawn to the Middle East. And, "In the event of German or Bulgarian attack, you will receive further instructions."

D'Albiac's position in Athens was one of some embarrassment and some power. In mid-November he was forced to have a showdown with Sir Michael Palairet and point out to him that his constant appeals to London for air power were awkward for all concerned. Sir Michael was persuaded that in the future all such messages should be sent through the

AOC, British Air Forces Greece. In addition D'Albiac pointed out that it was not much good asking for more support until there were airfields from which the aircraft could operate.[104]

In an attempt to resolve some of the tensions developing between the Air Ministry in London and the AOC-in-C ME and his staff in Cairo, Portal suggested that Air Chief Marshal Sir Edgar Ludlow-Hewitt, the Inspector- General, make a six- to eight-weeks' tour of the Middle East starting in January. In December Longmore sensibly declined this offer, and Portal accepted his claim that, given his small staff and operations on four different fronts, it was not the time for interrogations or spit and polish, no matter how well meant.[105]

Three more RAF squadrons were dispatched to Greece in four cruisers and four merchantmen on the 15 November, some 4,247 men and supporting equipment hastily gathered from RAF and army sources. But Metaxas told his diary they still came in "drop by drop."

Further to the north the Yugoslavs were partially mobilized, but professed to believe that they would not be attacked. From London King George VI responded to a melancholy letter from the Anglophile regent, Prince Paul, urging the prince to open negotiations with Greece and Turkey and hinting that Britain would in the not too distant future be able to supply armies other than her own with arms.[106] In Athens Metaxas continued to press Palairet for more help, suggesting on the sixteenth that, as nothing was happening in Egypt, surely Hurricanes could be sent over. Air Ministry intelligence pointed out that the rumors of Luftwaffe aid to Italy were contrary to the facts.[107] London learned that D'Albiac planned to deploy two Blenheim squadrons at Menidi with the Wellingtons based in Egypt rotating through for operations, one Blenheim and one Gladiator squadron at Eleusis, three bomber or fighter squadrons at Sedes, three at Larissa, one at Drama, and more squadrons further north, as more airfields there were inspected and became available.

Meanwhile early November had seen the genesis of OPERATION MANDIBLES, the plan to seize the Italian Dodecanese Islands located off the southwest coast of Turkey. These were a double threat to the British position, for they provided advanced air bases for attacks on the British center in the Middle East and they allowed the interdiction of the supply routes to Greece. Unfortunately, too often the subsequent operations failed for sending a boy to do a man's job, impelled by the Prime Minister's demand for action and a lack of a grand-strategic plan with objective priorities. As a result the Dodecanese were still in Axis hands when the war ended in 1945.

On 17 November Wavell sent in a "remarkably accurate" (in the official historian Playfair's words) appreciation that the Germans were massing in southeastern Europe to aid Italy and might attack Bulgaria and Yugoslavia. Metaxas told the American ambassador, MacVeagh, that if the Italians provoked Yugoslavia, the Germans would come in and Greece would be lost.[108]

In Washington the question of fighters for Greece was making its slow round of desktops and by mid-November had reached the stage where one hundred machines were available for export to Greece.[109] But, in fact, Washington never could get organized, in part because of British intrigues over aircraft to Greece, and so no machines were shipped before Greece was overrun in April 1941.[110]

In the meantime London had decided that a second squadron of Gladiators might be sent to Greece for close support of Greek troops, and that twelve additional aircraft should be turned over to the RHAF if suitable forward airfields were available.[111] In summing up this decision the next day to the War Cabinet, Churchill added that he did not think that the practical difficulties of moving aircraft from one country to another were quite realized by the lay mind, and evidently they were not realized in Greece. "It should be the business of our Air Attaché in Athens to acquaint our Minister there with them and thus prevent impossible and unreasonable requests being put forward."[112] (In the same message Churchill observed—interestingly enough, in the light of later decisions—that "the assistance which we now proposed to give to Greece would mean that our Air Force in Egypt would be greatly depleted and might be barely sufficient to cover requirements there should the enemy decide to stage an air offensive on that front.")

People in Athens were cheered on the twentieth by the news that one flight of No. 80 Squadron Gladiators had been in action the day before, flying from the grass field at Trikkala west of Larissa near the ancient monasteries of Meteora; but they were shocked also to learn of King Boris of Bulgaria's visit to Berlin. The Foreign Office in Athens took the view that Hitler would probably bypass the tough Yugoslavs in favor of an approach through Greece's old enemy Bulgaria.[113] In London Churchill was excited about Wavell's plans and had an argument with Eden in a Cabinet meeting because the latter tried to stop him from peppering the C-in-C with telegrams—which not only contained irritating gratuitous advice but also might breach security. At this time Churchill wrote President Roosevelt the fateful letter which stimulated the idea of Lend-Lease, a concept whose passage at times affected the course of this Greek tragedy.

On 22 November Longmore flew over to Athens to inspect and to consult with Metaxas. At the same time Papagos told Gambier-Parry that his 1912 field guns were wearing out and that, while he would welcome fully equipped British troops, what he really wanted was equipment so that he could raise his own divisions.[114]

On Longmore's plane to Athens was Stanley Casson, an old Greek hand who had already seen the Greeks fight four wars and only lose the one in Anatolia in 1921-1922. In his later memoirs Casson noted that the British knew little about the Greeks, overlooked their spiritual core and their history, and admired them in 1940 because they had done so much better at resisting than the British, who had had five years' warning that war was coming. The Greeks, he wrote, had absorbed all the lessons of the victims of Axis attacks. Casson, the chief intelligence officer, was the first member of No. 27 Military Mission to reach Athens. When he arrived the Greeks had just taken Koritza in Albania, and the crowds in the streets of Athens reminded him of those in 1912-1913 when the Greeks took Janina from the Turks. But he felt, as did the Greek general staff, that the Greek victories would bring in the Germans to save Italy (a decision Hitler had in fact made on the eighteenth). The deadly enemy, to anyone like Casson familiar with the Balkans, was Bulgaria, which saw the Greek advance into Albania drawing the troops further and further away from Macedonia and Thrace. According to Casson, the Greeks were still hoping that the Germans would referee a Graeco-Italian peace; for this reason they wanted British aid limited. The military mission, therefore, was only a token army. Casson concluded that though the Greeks were living in a fool's paradise, most really knew what would happen.[115]

Casson thought that the Greeks had a very modern mountain army, and that the average Greek was a very quick student who could learn how to use a new weapon in half the time it took the average Englishman. He told Gambier-Parry this at the time, and the latter told Wavell and the War Office that he was alarmed at what Casson was reporting to him. It appeared that the Greeks felt that after only twenty-five days of war they had scored the only Allied victory. Sending officers to instruct them in mountain warfare and modern weapons would be a very delicate matter. "I am convinced that the slightest signs of patronage or anything savouring of interference now or at any time would be bitterly resented and might have the most deplorable result." Gambier-Parry went on to suggest that the whole matter should be thoroughly discussed with his successor, Heywood. He added that Palairet agreed and had asked him to point out that the presence of a large military mission without troops would not be understood by the Greeks. "They would, he feels sure, particularly resent our sending people whom they know to be Archeologists and not soldiers."[116]

Coincidentally, arriving at the same time was David Hunt, the archeologist and Oxford don who had been plucked out of the card files to be the intelligence officer for BARBARITY. His observations on arrival were that the Greek army had mostly World War I equipment captured from the Austrians, and regimental transport consisting of carts captured from the Bulgars in 1912. The strength of the Greek forces was the infantry, which could fight on a loaf of bread and a handful of olives a day. Hunt, of course, had a lot of do with Stanley Casson, an old friend now, like Hunt, in intelligence. Casson had a bright collection of Greek-speaking young officers, some of whom would be left behind as liaison officers during the German occupation of 1941-1944. Hunt himself was the only army officer assigned to the RAF staff and, because he was the only Greek-speaking member of that team, the only one with ready access to the Greek GHQ and operations room in the Hotel Grande Bretagne. In Hunt's view Papagos had done wonders, but his army could only advance at a foot-pace.[117]

British Air Forces Greece headquarters was originally on the second floor of the Hotel Grande Bretagne, a wonderful late-nineteenth-century edifice which still graces (although with a 1950s facade) one corner of Sýntgama Square with its glass-roofed lobby and multistory interior court. Col. Guy Salisbury-Jones used to look out of his fourth-floor room in the morning to see what the weather was and would see General Papagos' balding head two floors below doing the same thing. The RAF staff liked being housed and fed in the Grande Bretagne and eating at Zonar's, but on 24 November D'Albiac moved them out to cheaper quarters in the Marasleon School on Aristomenous Street, on the northeast slope of Mount Lycabettus, above Evangelismos Hospital. The new quarters were about an eight-minute walk from the Grande Bretagne.

Meanwhile the army signals people had discovered that they had assigned call signs for BARBARITY which were already in use by the RAF, so these had to be changed from XBL and XBA to THE and THB. Other problems were the use of "bastard addresses" due to the scarcity of cipher staff, and the need to cut down on traffic and hours because of a shortage of RAF signals staff. This meant limiting the traffic to Greece to 5,000 groups daily, and traffic from Greece to 3,000. It also turned out that Cairo was not ready to receive messages until 2 December; even then its signalers had trouble keeping up with the RAF senders in Athens: "Operators this end are inexperienced." On top of that Cairo pointed out to Athens that its set faded off from 2359 to 0600 hours each night on 10,000 kcs, and suggested a switch for those hours to the 80-meter band. Signals continued to be a problem into January, when it was suggested that all messages be sent on the W/T links and not by commercial cables, which were liable to interruption, expensive, and being used to capacity. Complaints about operators also persisted. On the No. 5 net, the army's operators in Cairo were known to be guilty of acknowledging "X" code messages in plain language, so the RAF refused to use it.[118]

On 22 November Churchill told Wavell that he was disappointed in the ambiguity of Wavell's response about the date of COMPASS, and that he hoped that Wavell would realize his position. Sir Stafford Cripps, the British ambassador in Moscow, reported that the Germans were likely to attack Greece through Bulgaria, in which case, according to the Prime Minister, the Turks would either come in and need a lot of supplies, or they would stay out and Greece would fall. If Yugoslavia could be brought in, then the importance of getting that country and Turkey aligned against Germany would far outweigh any Libyan operation, and Wavell would be relegated to the very minimum defensive role in Egypt. If, however, Wavell could accomplish COMPASS within the first two weeks of December, that would create a changed situation. It was up to the C-in-C ME to judge whether or not he had the air forces he needed. "We may," the Prime Minister continued, "be forced to abandon Compass altogether, or there may be time to work it in before other things develop. I must, however, know what you are going to do, and when it would happen."[119]

Although in the end the Germans did not attack Greece until spring, in November there was plenty of evidence flowing into Athens and London from diverse sources that the Germans intended to intervene.[120] In London on Friday evening the twenty-second, the War Cabinet discussed Bulgaria. (The effort was largely vitiated by the news the next day that the Bulgarians had joined Hitler.) All that the War Cabinet did that night was to agree to send a signal to Campbell in Budapest and Knatchbull-Hugessen in Ankara urging them to get Turkey into the war. To this the British ambassador in Ankara quickly replied that Turkish participation at this time would be more of a liability than an asset.[121]

On 23 November Greek troops occupied Koritza, and there was great excitement in Athens. On the same day No. 211 Blenheim Squadron demonstrated what could be done when the pressure was on: it packed up its fifteen aircraft and left the Desert in three hours, arrived at Menidi just after its ground party, and was fueled, bombed-up, and ready for operations that night.[122]

## 24 November 1940

Longmore returned to Cairo late on the twenty-fourth, after visiting RAF units in Greece, and reported to London that he had met with the king, Papagos, and Metaxas. They were "proud of their success, the first allies to carry the offensive to enemy territory." Metaxas hoped that the Greek victory at Koritza would affect Turkey, Yugoslavia, and possibly even Bulgaria, and went on to speak of chasing the Italians out of Albania and of being the future Allied bridgehead in the Balkans from which the Allied armies might advance to right the final battle against the Germans. Where else, Metaxas asked, could it be fought? Static war had set in in North Africa. He wanted to know what was proposed by the British in the event of a German advance through Bulgaria toward Salonika. Longmore reported that he had assured the Greeks that planning staffs were considering these points, and had warned the Greek leaders that the Italians were likely to counterattack in Albania with heavy air support.

The king, Papagos, and Metaxas all expressed appreciation for the

work of the Royal Navy in the eastern Mediterranean and for the excellent
work of the RAF in Greece. They stressed the need for more aircraft, but,
said the AOC-in-C ME, completely ignored in their pleas for more aircraft
was the capacity of their indifferent airfields for large numbers of machines. (Moreover, most of the fields were on the wrong side of the
Pindus Mountains, where the weather either kept the aircraft grounded
or prevented them getting through to the battlefields. Longmore himself
had encountered such weather while trying to fly to the forward airfields.) After the meeting with the Greeks, he had then laid down to
Palairet the difficulties of getting aircraft reinforcements from Britain to
the Middle East in the next two critical months. He was disturbed by the
fact that no one seemed to have a very clear idea why the British military
mission, which had officially arrived that day, was in Athens. He doubted
if the Greeks needed or would tolerate advice on their kind of mountain
warfare. And the danger still remained that the roughly 3,000 army troops
which were servicing the RAF and providing its antiaircraft defenses were
assumed by some to be an advance guard of a larger force (a difficulty
which the BBC's evening broadcast of 23 November to Athens had reinforced).[123]

## 25 - 28 November 1940

On 25 November Major-General Heywood arrived in Athens to take over
officially as head of the No. 27 Military Mission. (Later, when Admiral
Turle was sent out to fill this position, Heywood became head of the army
section of the mission.) General Sir James Marshall-Cornwall, who shared
a house with Heywood and his wife in Constantinople after the First
World War, has since described Gordon Heywood as about five feet, nine
inches tall, rather bulky in figure. He spoke French perfectly, a legacy
from a French mother, but his judgment was not always to be trusted: as
military attaché in Paris he had misled the War Office about the quality of
the French army.

The mission's job were liaison, transmission of Greek requests, instruction, and "to prepare for the destruction of oil stocks in Greece in
case of necessity." It was established in the Hotel Grande Bretagne with a
Greek liaison team composed of a Major Kanakis and Capt. H.R.H.
Prince Peter of Greece as second-in-command (he took over in January
1941).[124] In fact the main function of 27 MM was to work with the
Deuxième Bureau of the Greek general staff and establish intelligence
links, which were used to obtain information on enemy forces in Albania
and later in Bulgaria. It also acted as liaison between the Greek intelligence service and the intelligence branch in Cairo. The operations
section kept in close touch with the Troisième Bureau of Greek GHQ to
keep track of Greek actions, making frequent visits to the front, and with

British liaison officers at army HQ at Janina and at corps HQ at Koritza, through direct W/T links to Athens. The "Q" side of 27 MM had a particularly heavy workload, since it was made the channel through which all Greek requests for aid had to be sent to the War Office, the Ministry of Supply, the Foreign Office, and the British Purchasing Commission in the United States. "Q" also had to work with the Greek Powder and Cartridge Factory and check and distribute all incoming supplies.[125]

The RAF Athens status report for 25 November showed what effect Longmore's gallant gesture, Churchill's prodding, and Palairet's pleadings had had. No. 30 Blenheim Squadron was at Eleusis; No. 70 Wellington was using Athens airfield as an advanced base; No. 84 Blenheim had one flight at Eleusis and the others at Menidi; No. 211 Blenheim had thirteen aircraft at Menidi; No. 80 Gladiator had one flight at Eleusis and the other at Trikkala; while No. 112 in Egypt would leave for Greece as soon as some Gladiators for it were available.

But as the AOC-in-C signaled later in the day, in elaborating on these dispositions, there were problems developing with winter coming on. Eleusis, for one, went unserviceable for periods after heavy rain; Menidi was more weatherproof than most; Trikkala was small and unserviceable after very heavy rain, but was not too far from Larissa, which was a large, reasonably weatherproof field. Araxos had been reported upon favorably by a survey party as being possible if runways were built; it could be used to refuel Blenheims currently when dry. Agrinion, situated north of the Gulf of Patras, was suitable only for Gladiators—though it was being extended—and had a bad approach.

An hour later London received word from Longmore that D'Albiac had so many administrative problems that he wished to avoid further commitments, so Longmore was arranging to have 12 Gladiators ferried over to the Greeks, while No. 112 Gladiator Squadron would fly over skeleton maintenance crews only with its B Section. Including his army support forces, D'Albiac now had over 5,000 officers and men, and Longmore therefore strongly recommended that he be given the rank of acting air vice-marshal, thus placing him on a more equal footing with the rear admiral and major-general of the British military mission, who had no executive responsibilities. London acted that night![126] Longmore also recommended that his senior air staff officer, Wing Commander Willetts, be upgraded to acting group captain.

The British Air Forces, Greece, now consisted of about 60 aircraft equally divided between bombers and fighters, of which a number were unserviceable. The RAF Wellingtons had been withdrawn to Egypt, as it was not advisable to operate them in a non-moon period until a west-coast airfield was available that was clear of mountains in its immediate vicinity. Longmore concluded, "My general impression as a result of this visit is very favourable. Air Force has settled down remarkably quickly and has carried out most successful operations contributing very largely to the Greek success."[127]

The Air Ministry responded to Wavell at lunchtime that construction work in Thrace and Anatolia should move as quickly as possible to prepare airfields for use by heavy bombers in the spring at the latest, with one runway 1,500 yards by 50 yards and three, 1,200 by 50 yards (dimensions adopted recently in the Canal Zone).[128] Also a top secret signal was sent to air force headquarters in Greece from the chief of the Air Staff: "You should on no account mention to anyone that dispatch of Hurricanes is being considered since the chance of its being sanctioned is remote and it is important not to risk disappointing the Greeks."[129]

In London on 25 November an element of tragedy was surfacing. Dill, whose wife was slowly dying of a paralytic stroke, was caught in a crossfire between Churchill and Wavell, and did not know what to do. Brigadier Dudley Clark, who was his military assistant at this time, has described Dill as upright, with thin fair hair, slightly greying, stern but with an Irish twinkle and a soft tuneful voice verging on a brogue. He spoke with the hesitation of a schoolboy trying to keep up with his thoughts. He had for years wanted to be chief of the Imperial General Staff and had taken infinite pains to prepare himself for the job in the total war he had foreseen coming; he knew Hitler personally and most Continental armies intimately. He had been recalled from Palestine in 1936 thinking he was going to be CIGS, but in the Hore-Belisha reforms Sir Cyril Devereux and then Viscount Gort, VC, had been given the job. Dill thought he had been assured of the British Expeditionary Force when war broke out, only to be disappointed again. Meanwhile Lady Dill was stricken and Sir John was sent, when the crisis came, as deputy to Gort in France. At last, in 1940, he had been made CIGS in place of Lord Ironside, VC, just when the army was in its deepest trouble and when he felt he could do little about it other than wait and encourage all efforts. That the unemotional Dill should clash with Churchill was probably inevitable; many service officers did, over working hours alone.

Dill liked to arrive at the War Office at 8:30 and be briefed by his staff for the next hour, which left him thirty minutes to read urgent mail before the Chiefs of Staff Committee met; then followed a Cabinet meeting at 11:30 and lunch. In the afternoon he conducted the domestic business of the army, because he was in all but name also commander-in-chief, that old position which both Wellington and the Duke of Cambridge had held in the nineteenth century. He was punctilious about this role. Then at 6:30 there was often another meeting of the Chiefs of Staff followed by dinner. By then the Prime Minister would have arisen late, read the papers, tended to some business during the middle of the day, had a nap and dinner, and would now be ready to roar along until the wee hours of the morning. To try to lighten the load on himself, Dill quickly brought in a vice chief and three assistant CIGS's; but, as he had trouble delegating, it did not help much.[130]

Dill was not treated very graciously by Churchill, as indeed the Prime Minister did not honor others who served the country well in arduous posts, notably Dowding and Wavell. When Dill reached the age of sixty on Christmas Day 1941, he was not retired but sent to work in Washington. (He died there and is buried in Arlington National Cemetery.) In part from the very first Dill was a victim of Churchill's old prejudices imbibed in his Hussar and World War I days. Though Dill may have seemed to be a bumbling brass-hat, he was not, and Winston badly underestimated his abilities. Unfortunately, the fact that Dill supported Wavell, that "ordinary colonel" in Egypt, did not endear him to the Prime Minister.

But further complicating the problem on the evening of 25 November was another shadow from the past and a very good example of Churchill's perversity. General Jan Christian Smuts played a decisive, even a sinister, role in British history on a number of occasions, and Churchill's fondness for him is an illustration of the old saying about an expert being a man five hundred miles from home. Smuts had been one of the Boer leaders in the war which humiliated the British army, in that colonial conflict in which young Churchill as a war correspondent had made a considerable name for himself. Then in the First World War the goateed Smuts had shown up in London as a lieutenant-general, victor of a bloody East African campaign against the Germans. He had been made a member of Lloyd George's inner War Cabinet and had been very largely responsible for the creation of the Royal Air Force. In 1939 he had been elected prime minister of South Africa, the culmination of a long and distinguished political career in his homeland.

Nor was Smuts going to be the only Dominion prime minister to have a direct hand in the British decision to aid Greece. On this November day, in Canberra, Australia, Robert Gordon Menzies had already told his Cabinet that he had decided to go to London to see Churchill and discuss Singapore, whose weakness had just been revealed.[131] Both Menzies and Smuts, who would be raised to the rank of field marshal by Churchill early in 1941, would pass through Cairo, and their visits would be influential.

After the Defence Committee broke up that night, Eden stayed behind and discussed with Churchill the future after COMPASS succeeded. Halifax, the Foreign Secretary, had reported that Germany had not made up her mind over the Balkans, though Churchill, correctly as it turned out, guessed that she would strike through Bulgaria at Salonika. The next day Halifax said that both Budapest and Sofia reported that no German activity was likely in the Balkans.

And Wavell cabled that he thought that the allocation of antiaircraft guns in his command was something that should be his responsibility; he advise that no more should go to Crete for the time being, and that when allocations were made they should be done by his own Interservices Committee in view of his shortages, and on the general understanding that as much as possible would be sent from the United Kingdom.[132]

On 26 November Major-General Sir John Kennedy, the director of military operations at the War Office, told the American Colonel Lee that because of a shortage of shipping, 16,000 troops for the Middle East were still standing by in the United Kingdom, and that the delay was affecting the rapidity with which the British could help the Greeks.[133] On Wednesday the twenty-seventh the planners tried to talk Churchill out of OPERATION WORKSHOP (which Admiral Cunningham called "a wildcat scheme . . . the height of unwisdom") to take the island of Pantelleria.[134] That evening the secretary of state for air was asked to report on the suitability of airfields in Greece as bases for possible action against the Rumanian oilfields, about which the British actually knew a good deal, and on the necessary preporatory measures. A few days later his report could not be found in the Cabinet office—it was not in the "Op. Box," nor in "Greece," nor in "Air," nor in "Gen. Wavell." Someone suggested that they had better contact the CAS,who had actually sent it over, to make sure that no action was necessary.[135] It seems that even the highest offices are not immune to gremlins!

### 29 November 1940

On Friday Longmore teletyped from Cairo to Portal in London that from signals received by Wavell and himself they had the feeling that London was thinking of air operations in the Middle East on a grand scale in 1941 without regard to supply routes: "It seems to me that there is the greatest danger of large scale operations being planned and timed to take place long before the necessary Air Forces to undertake or support them could possibly be expected to be ready to take part. Even our existing commitments are right out of step with our air strength even with what is immediately in sight yet we are already being asked what immediate assistance can be given Turkey in the event of her becoming involved."[136]

Longmore might have added that the Air Staff was guilty of bad staff work and quoted Portal himself, who as AOC-in-C of Bomber Command in 1940 had suggested to the Air Ministry that the means should govern the ends rather than vice versa.

Rear-Admiral Turle, having arrived in London from Greece, was present at 10:15 am at the Chiefs of Staff meeting for Item 10, Assistance to Greece. He outlined the situation at the time he left Athens on the eighteenth, reporting that the Greek government was in good fettle and confident that, provided the British continued to assist them, they could drive the Italians out of Albania. Metaxas had been sure on 16 November that they could hold Koritza and the mountains against the Italians during the winter. "There was no doubt that our assistance had turned the scale and the Greeks were aware of this. Nevertheless, it would be idle to imagine that the Greeks could hold out without considerable further consignments of materials and of increased air forces." Even so, Turle said, "The Greeks had expressed no desire for the despatch of British land forces." And, furthermore, he understood the disinclination of the authorities in the Middle East to release forces for Greece which could ill be spared; the scale of equipment which it was now intended to send Greece would be adequate.[137]

Actually Metaxas' diary on 16 and 17 November indicates that he thought he had briefed Turle that the first objective was to get the British to shift their primary effort to Greece, and to supply aircraft, weapons, trucks, and tanks to counter a German attack in the spring. He was gloomy: if the British could not supply aircraft to counter the Italians, how could the Greeks afford to provoke the Germans?

For the next few days bad weather in Greece canceled air operations. The Greeks rolled up successes during the following weeks, but these mountain operations were taking their toll, especially of the ubiquitous pack animals, mostly donkeys, which the Greeks used so much in mountain areas. The motor vehicles that had been requisitioned were already heavily worn in civilian life; the drivers were not trained, maintenance was ragged, and the roads were unpaved and treacherous, especially in the mountains. The British supplied some Canadian-made lorries and Italian booty captured in the Desert, and Casson claimed that this was having a direct effect on the front line by February.[138] Yet the report of 27 Military Mission shows that for the whole period of its existence the mission only handed over and obtained receipts for 62 ambulances, 13 Austin 3-tonners, 200 8-h.p. cars, 150 Bedford 3-tonners, 182 Chevrolet 3-tonners, 78 Ford 30-cwt and 44 Ford 15-cwt vans and 122 Fordson lorries, 86 Italian Spa and 60 Lancia lorries plus two other odd ones, 491 Norton motorcycles, and 104 horses. Some sources say that lorries arrived from the United Kingdom on Christmas Day but that their tires did not follow for another ninety days.[139] The only military material delivered to the Greeks before the arrival of the British Military Mission in Athens in late November were 100 Boys antitank rifles.[140] Almost all supplies for Greece came in the end from the Middle East. Four shiploads were sent direct from England in the first "Bullet Consignment," but only three arrived; and another large ship (the Clan Fraser) that came around the Cape became a total loss in the Piraeus harbor. No American orders arrived until the Greek government had moved to Crete in late April.

On 30 November 1940 Churchill was 66.

## 30 November 1940 - 8 January 1941

During nearly six weeks at the end of the year, as the snows fell in the mountains and the fighting on the Albanian front became a race between Italian morale and Greek supplies, action generally slowed down. Much that took place was preparatory.

Perhaps the most important development during the period was the growth of a misconception, later denied, that Britain would field a twenty-three-squadron air force in Greece in the spring. The rumor appears to have started while Rear-Admiral Turle was in London being briefed to become the head of the military mission. On 5 December the Air Ministry ordered Longmore—in a day of picks and shovels and steamrollers—to have ready by spring airfields in the Balkans for ten fighter squadrons, ten medium bomber squadrons, and three heavy bomber squadrons. At the same time Portal signaled that he was planning to fly out six fighter and six medium bomber squadrons during the December fine-weather period in the Mediterranean so that they could be put in storage until their ground and aircrews could arrive by sea in February or March. And in that signal he reinforced the idea that Longmore would have twenty-three squadrons in the Balkans in the spring. Somehow these figures were transmitted to the Australian commander, Blamey, but they were denied by Portal in November 1941 when a formal inquiry was made upon an Australian complaint of having been misled into the Greek adventure.[141] On 5 January Portal had to withdraw the idea of sending six of the bomber squadrons to the Middle East because he was short of aircrews and Churchill was demanding that Bomber Command be built up.[142]

On 5 December 12 replacement Gladiator biplane fighters were delivered to the Greek air force, the only aircraft the British or the Americans managed to give them before Greece was overrun four months later. That the Greeks were not better served was due in part—as Turle found in talking to the Prime Minister—to the fact that no one appreciated that time was not on the British side. Yet Turle believed that he had been assured by Portal that there would be fifteen squadrons in Greece in a few weeks and twenty-two by spring; he recorded this in his diary and reported it in Athens when he arrived there on the twenty-fourth.[143] In fact, there were four half-strength RAF squadrons in Greece.[144]

No one appears really to have grasped what Longmore was up against. When Wavell began his successful COMPASS reconnaissance in force, which turned into a rout of the Italians, the AOC-in-C had three fighter squadrons and four bomber squadrons with which to face approximately 250 Italian fighters and a like number of bombers.[145] But on 9 December, the day that COMPASS opened, an early model B-17 arrived in Cairo from London carrying a quiet, pipe-smoking deputy for Longmore, who had long requested such a person. Air Vice Marshal Arthur Tedder arrived with verbal orders to write back personally to Portal and his vice chief about Longmore.[146] By May 1941 this arrangement led to Longmore's recall for consultations and his replacement by Tedder as AOC-in-C.

In Greece D'Albiac's attempts to do something about more airfields was frustrated by the shortage of labor and supplies and by Metaxas' refusal to let British officers proceed north of Larissa to explore sites for airfields. The Greek prime minister, who had recently been overlooked at a tea with the British because, as he noted in his diary, he was too short, was convinced that the Germans would invade Greece in the spring and that the Greeks would have to lay down their arms as they would have nothing left with which to fight. He did not want the British pursuing schemes to build airfields from which it might be thought they could bomb Ploesti, the source of Germany's Rumanian oil, and thereby provoking the Germans into earlier or more destructive action.[147]

In London as Christmas approached Churchill continued to be buoyed up by the Desert victories; he promised more Hurricanes and urged his victorious general to rip the Italians out of Africa. Only when Wavell could go no further should he switch his offensive to the Dodecanese, which the C-in-C's in the Middle East had suggested should be taken in OPERATION MANDIBLES, (which might in the end have better been called NIBBLES).[148] On 23 December Eden became Foreign Secretary, and the secretary of war became a cipher under the minister of defence, Churchill. In Athens Metaxas had morbid dreams of Eden's elevation, which he overcame with prayers.

At the end of December Churchill ordered Portal to proceed with plans for nine new airfields in Greece south of the line Arta-Olympus, even though they would demand a large increase in military support staff and would strain the limited port and transportation facilities in that country.[149] At the same time the deputy quartermaster-general ME made a detailed report on Crete and Greece which backed up the report from Heywood on Papagos' need for lorries.[150] On the vital question of an artillery supply, General James Marshall-Cornwall, head of the military mission to Turkey and himself a gunner, sent Wavell a handwritten note on Christmas Day suggesting that the British ship out to the Greeks their four hundred new 1918 75-mm guns, obtained in the summer of 1940 from the United States.[151] But nothing was done. There were also proposals to re-equip the RHAF with Gladiators and older Blenheims and to replace these in the RAF with Curtiss P-36 Mohawks and P-40 Tomahawks, but these plans, too, were not carried out. And the year ended with yet a further exchange of signals all round about bases near Salonika and suitable aircraft for operations in Greece.[152] Longmore concluded that D'Albiac needed Group Captain John Grigson as a deputy in Athens and that the AOC himself should fly down to Cairo for a general consultation, while also taking over the post of air attaché. Portal agreed.[153]

On 1 January 1941 Metaxas reluctantly agreed in principle to the establishment of British bomber bases about Salonika. But no attacks to provoke Germany were to be made until Italy was defeated. He wanted to limit RAF activity to surveys.

In London early in January Churchill was testy and irritable, tired, angry, and strained. Eden was jumpy.[154] The War Cabinet kept changing its priorities from North Africa to the Balkans to Home defense. From ULTRA they had the impression that the Germans would attack Greece on 20 January, but it was still possible that England might be invaded, and now half the best tanks and much of the artillery was on its way to the Middle East. All the units in the United Kingdom were actually up to strength, but the British did not at this time sit down and systematically calculate what it would take for the Germans to land an army on a hostile coast, and they were more scared than they needed to be. As Churchill himself noted later in *The Grand Alliance,* in September 1940 the RAF still had fifty-one fighter squadrons and twenty-seven bomber squadrons, and the numbers were increasing. At the same time the army grew from twenty-six active divisions and a Home Guard of one million in September 1940 to thirty-four active divisions and five armored divisions plus one and a half million men a year later. Nevertheless, it is clear in Basil Collier's *The Defence of the United Kingdom,* and in contemporary documents, that almost everyone in London was fearful about invasion.[155]

At about this time the American military attaché in London, Colonel Lee, told his Russian colleague that in British opinion the new German armored divisions were being prepared for an attack on the USSR.[156] In Athens Metaxas was pleading for more lorries: his badly exposed and exhausted troops on the Epirus front needed to take Valona to stem the Italian effort, since the RAF was failing to do that. Palairet was questioning the role and duties of the military mission in Athens: in response London decided that it should be called a Liaison Delegation (but it never adopted the name), and should communicate only through the C-in-C in Cairo.[157] Longmore signaled that although reinforcements were en route, "they are not actually here. Risks we have run against Italians in denuding back areas defence cannot be repeated with impunity continuously and certainly not against Germans."[158]

On 4 January 1941, alerted by his military attaché in Berlin, Metaxas had his ambassador in London tell Eden that the Germans were concentrating twelve divisions against Yugoslavia in order to obtain free passage to Salonika, and that Greece would fight if attacked. Almost immediately Athens received telegrams from Berlin, Bucharest, and Belgrade saying that the German destination was Bulgaria. This was true, but the price of the ticket was to be Salonika for Bulgaria.[159]

On 6 January Churchill gave his merry-eyed chief of the Cabinet staff, General Sir Hastings Ismay, an appreciation for the Chiefs of Staff in which he made the destruction of the Italian army in North Africa the primary objective in the opening months of 1941. Once that had been accomplished by a force of 40,000 to 45,000 men (about four divisions), then the Army of the Nile would be free to go on to other things. He hoped that the East African campaign would also be over by April, thus freeing the 5th Indian Division. With these victories in hand, there would be a force of twelve divisions in the eastern Mediterranean and, with Egypt secure, the invasion of Sicily could then be given priority. But, he concluded, since nothing would suit the British better than that the Germans would delay attacking in the Balkans until spring, it had to be concluded that they would do so earlier. Thus as soon as Wavell had taken Benghazi, all forces must be switched to Greece so that Valona could be taken. It was clear to Churchill that unless this was done the Greeks would become dispirited and make a separate peace with the Italians. But above all, Hitler could not afford to have Britain with her airpower stabbing him from the west and so he would seek to destroy her: Britain had absolutely to be protected first.[160] And the next day he sent Wavell another reminder that waste in rear areas could not be afforded—he had far too few fighting men for his 350,000-ration strength. Wavell responded that he would carefully re-examine the situation, "but the more I see of war, especially present-day war, the more I am impressed by the part that administration plays."[161] How right he was.

Eden at this time sent Churchill a note that everything pointed to a German attack on Greece no later than the beginning of March.[162] Already the Germans had twelve modern divisions in Rumania, while all the Greeks had to defend the Bulgarian frontier with were three under-strength reserve divisions.[163] In Belgrade the Yugoslav Foreign Minister told the British ambassador that it was too late to repel a German invasion and to please pass that view along to his government. Sir Ronald Campbell did not take him seriously, but the Greek ambassador did and relayed the point to Athens.[164]

The seventh of January also saw two visitors arrive in Cairo. First came Col. "Wild Bill" Donovan, President Roosevelt's emissary, who, after talking to British officers, went on to Athens on the fifteenth to see what the Greeks needed, as if Washington had not been told. And later in the day D'Albiac flew in from Greece in the single-engined Percival Q6 piloted and owned by Wing-Commander Lord Forbes, his chief intelligence officer.

The next day in London the newly knighted Sir Alexander Cadogan was immensely cheered by the fact that Eden had told him to inform Palairet that His Majesty's government was prepared to send Wavell to Greece at once.[165] Churchill then told the Defence Committee that British help might not arrive in time to save Greece, but Eden added that it was vital to act to win over the Turks "furthermore, the Greeks are a temperamental race and we must do something to maintain their morale." Therefore it was decided that plans should be drawn up and that everything possible should be done within twenty four hours.[166] Wavell should halt his advance as soon as Tobruk was taken and switch all his forces to the Balkans. Prime Minister Smuts of South Africa and the Chiefs of Staff wondered if, in fact, perhaps Hitler was not making a feint to draw off strength from the United Kingdom prior to an invasion attempt.[167] The trouble was that no one on the British side was paying much attention to the German economic, diplomatic, and military grip on the Balkans, and no one would stand up to Churchill and say that the Greek armed forces were inadequately equipped, that the British could not re-equip them, and that Wavell did not have the forces to do the job envisioned.

As Churchill had only so recently noted and as Wavell's planners, including de Guingand, agreed, Wavell would not have any spare troops until mid-April, and these would then need rest and re-equipping. Thus Wavell's staff regarded the switch to Greece as unsound.[168] What they did see as just feasible was continuing the advance to seize Tripoli by a *coup de main* and joining up with the French in Tunisia, a much more desirable political objective which would open up the Mediterranean. The man who should have stood up for Wavell in the arguments in London was Dill, but he was mentally tired; by early 1941 the strain of his wife's slow death was causing him to sit ineffectively at COS meetings and ask irrelevant questions.[169]

In the meantime the RAF in Greece was having second thoughts about its doctrine, as Longmore admitted in his memoirs. Though the textbooks and staff college courses laid down that an air offensive should be an attack on rear lines of communications rather than an intimate participation in the ground battle, there was much to be said for close-range support visible to troops about to make an attack. Certainly it was a stimulant on the Greek front in Albania.[170] On 8 January Ambassador Lincoln MacVeagh was reporting exactly these views to Washington, pointing out that the RAF had not enough airfields and was limited in range in attacking the Adriatic ports, even when refueled at Larissa on the way from Athens; it was considering more bombing closer to the front lines because it often could not reach Durazzo. Moreover, while RAF officers, the ambassador reported, openly sympathized with Greek caution, privately they said that Greece would have to become a base for a war on Germany, and they had been laying their plans accordingly. As cabled by MacVeagh, the Greek under-secretary of state for foreign affairs said that the presence of the British made the chances of German mediation very unlikely, and Metaxas himself might have been behind the idea circulating in Berlin and in Athens that expulsion of Italy from the Balkans would be to Germany's advantage: some of the Greek leaders believed Germany not unsympathetic to Greece. Both the Greek prime minister and the Turkish ambassador in Athens thought that, if the Germans attacked Greece through Bulgaria, the Turks would attack the Germans.[171] (On the other hand, the Turkish Foreign Minister in Ankara told the Greek minister there just the opposite.)[172]

Between 7 and 9 January 1941 happy delusions, as Hinsley has called them, that the Germans were in Rumania only to protect the oilfields were swept away by Enigma messages that made it plain that Greece was the objective. Already on 27 December London had picked up mentions of OPERATION MARITA, and this confirmed diplomatic and other intelligence, including a note from Sofia that 1,800 trains were scheduled, enough for twenty divisions. In view of all this information, the Defence Committee, with a wonderful ignorance of winter conditions in the Bulgarian mountains (despite the sojourn of the Salonika Force not far from there in 1916-1918), decided that the Germans would attack Greece on 20 January. On the tenth they ordered Wavell to visit Athens.[173] What he could have done if the Germans had actually attacked on that schedule is entirely unexplained and does not seem to have crossed London's collective mind in any rational way related to movement timetables. Because of scarce shipping resources in the Middle East, for instance, when the decision was later made to send a force of only three and a half divisions, twelve weeks were required to transport it to Greece, let alone get it firmly in place to resist a professional blitzkrieg attack.

A further difficulty at this time was that general staff intelligence in Middle East Headquarters had not been informed of the Engima intercepts and was getting very little of this ultra-secret (ULTRA) information even secondhand. By 15 January London had begun to have second thoughts about an attack on the twentieth, a point the realists in Athens would have already reached.[174]

## 9 January 1941

Ambassador MacVeagh reported from Athens that the Rumanian premier had told the Yugoslav minister in Athens that he was 100 percent sure that the Turks would attack Bulgaria in relation to the build-up of German troops in Rumania, and 50 percent sure that Russia would act to prevent the Germans from gaining control of the Dardanelles. On the other hand, he thought that Germany's ultimate aim was certainly the conquest of the Ukraine and that she might attempt this directly without imperiling the very real economic advantages she was already enjoying from the Balkans.[175]

Longmore signaled Metaxas that on D'Albiac's advice he was sending two more squadrons to Greece, but neither would be at full strength until more aircraft were available.[176]

From London Portal told Longmore that he was reluctant to interrupt his successful chase of the Italians in Libya, but that political reasons necessitated a shift to major support for Greece: the Germans appeared likely to be going to move into Bulgaria and then strike rapidly at Salonika, supported by divebombers and Me109's "which would blast straight through the Greek defences unless we helped. Absence of British help might put Greece out of the war, keep Turkey out, and cause most serious political consequences both here and in America. I therefore regret that the reinforcements you propose must be considered quite inadequate. Most doubtful if two squadrons of Gladiators would do any good and think you should consider two or three squadrons Hurricanes and one or two Squadrons Blenheim IV."

He then went on to urge that these fighters be based on all-weather airfields about Salonika, from which they could cover both the Rupel Pass and the Albanian front. The withdrawals to Greece were to be considered immediate and urgent, and plans for the move were to be made at once. Portal ended by telling Longmore that this was a warning; a full order from the COS to the C-in-C ME would follow shortly. This order was dispatched the next day, and it warned of a possible German attack down the Struma valley on 20 January by three divisions, supported by 200 divebombers and employing air landings to disorganize the resistance. Support for the Greeks would have to come from the Middle East and the C-in-C ME was authorized to send up to one squadron of infantry tanks, one regiment of cruiser tanks, two field artillery regiments, two antitank regiments, two heavy and two light A/A regiments and two medium artillery regiments, as well as three Hurricane and two Blenheim squadrons and whatever was needed to maintain them. Speed was essential, and plans to move the force were to be made before Metaxas was consulted.[177]

Longmore replied with a detailed signal in which he pointed out that he had already warned that Hurricanes could not operate from Greek airfields then within range of the Italians, and could only sit around Salonika awaiting a German or Italian attack—which was considered unlikely in the winter. To send his Blenheims and Hurricanes from Libya would allow the Italian air force there to recover its balance. He reminded London of his slim resources and concluded by asking if the German threat might not be a feint to pull the British away from the Libyan front. Wavell cabled the CIGS that Portal's signal to the Longmore "fills us with dismay." He went on to say that nothing the British could do would stop a serious German advance; to attempt to do so would only disperse Britain's forces and lower Greek morale. "I am desperately anxious lest we play the enemy's game and expose ourselves to defeat in detail." Churchill responded stiffly that they were not; Wavell was to proceed at once to Athens.[178]

It was an unhappy Thursday in London. At noon, when Wavell's response to the signal ordering him to switch priorities to Greece was received at the War Office, Kennedy, the director of military operations, who had not seen the original signal before it was sent, immediately got hold of Dill. Kennedy told Dill forcefully that it was imperative that the British secure Libya so that they could pass convoys through the Mediterranean with fighter cover from North Africa. Further, he went on, to hold Salonika would require at least twenty divisions and an air force. The Germans could take Greece whenever they wanted and then menace British shipping in the Mediterranean, unless the British held the North African shore. In other words, the British stood to gain far more by clearing North Africa than by trying to hold Greece.[179] Dill was too dispirited to make a response.

Elsewhere in Whitehall on that day, the Hankey Committee on Supplies for Greece reported that some munitions had been found, including 70 percent of the Greek needs in 105-mm shells, from General de Gaulle, but not much else except shell steel. Anything ordered from the United States would not be ready until the end of 1941.[180]

## 10 - 13 January 1941

Over the next few days London and Cairo said many of the same things to each other and to their friends. In London Roosevelt's emaciated, chain-smoking emissary, Harry Hopkins, deplored Churchill's working habits, especially on weekends, while listening to him prepare the British for withdrawal in Greece.[181] Heywood flew over to Cairo from Athens and told Wavell that the reinforcements authorized by London were not what the Greeks needed—they wanted transport, A/A guns, aircraft, and clothing. Wavell agreed, but these were just the things that he was desperately short of himself.[182]

On 11 January Churchill told Wavell that London's information, which we now know was ULTRA, was reliable. They had to conform to the "larger interests at stake. . . . We expect and require prompt and active compliance with our decisions, for which we bear full responsibility." And he ordered Wavell and Longmore to make a joint visit to Athens.[183] It was a somewhat propitious moment, since three 10,000-ton ships escorted through the Mediterranean by the aircraft carrier *Illustrious* and several cruisers had at last delivered 200 Bedford 1½ ton trucks, some motorcycles, a few antitank guns and a snowplow.[184] (Metaxas grumbled to his diary that the British still refused to grant credits.) With these supplies No. 27 Military Mission officers could at last begin training the Greeks, to whom they shortly became advisers as the units pulled out for the front. Metaxas let it be known that he wanted two days of talks in Athens and three days to show his visitors the front.

Wavell got back from the Desert on the evening of the twelfth and left for Athens the next morning, followed by Longmore on the fifteenth. Before leaving Wavell indicated to London that he could not supply much: one squadron of light tanks, one regiment of cruisers, but no infantry tanks at all; artillery would be very thin, and the widely dispersed locations in Greece would create problems for medical and administrative units; additionally there was an acute shortage of signals. And he concluded that as Admiral Cunningham was still at sea he had not been able to discuss shipping, but it would be a serious matter, especially with the appearance of the German air force in the Mediterranean. On the thirteenth Longmore had to send London the unpleasant news that Heraklion airfield in Crete had been strafed by German aircraft from the Dodecanese.[185]

It was very cold that Monday morning when Wavell stepped out of the Sunderland flying boat in Phaleron Bay just east of the Piraeus. He went by launch to the Piraeus Yacht Club for lunch before meeting with Metaxas and Papagos.[186]

## 14 - 16 January 1941

Conferences were held at the Ministry of Foreign Affairs offices on both the fourteenth and the fifteenth. Present on the British side were Wavell and his staff, Palairet, Longmore (on the second day), Turle, Heywood, and D'Albiac; for the Greeks there were Metaxas, Papagos, Under-secretary of Foreign Affairs Mavroudis, and representatives of the Greek services. The minutes were kept in English by General Heywood and in Greek by Col. Stylianos Kitrilakis, the director of operations.

Wavell and Papagos each gave a summary in English of the operations in their respective commands. Metaxas noted that night in his diary that it was amazing that the British had survived and won in Africa, as they did not have anything. They obviously could not help against the Germans. Metaxas, in French, then reviewed the political situation in the Balkans and observed that in the event of Germany's (or Germany's and Bulgaria's) invasion of Greece, Yugoslavia would remain neutral, but that she would fight to protect her neutrality. Moreover, Prince Paul's government would not be pleased to see British troops at Salonika, as that would provoke the Germans and hasten the spread of the war to the Balkans. (This was information which the Greek minister had obtained that morning from the president of the Council in Belgrade.)[187] Metaxas, making his points by drawing maps on paper, also held that Turkey would remain neutral even if Bulgaria as well as Germany came in. From the information on hand the Greek prime minister did not foresee either Yugoslavia or

Turkey abandoning their reserved positions; Greece would resist the Germans or the Bulgarians by all possible means.

Papagos told the meeting all he knew about the German dispositions up to that time, including the fact that German air force officers in mufti were in Bulgaria setting up advanced observation posts, improving and building airfields, and restoring roads; the bridge across the Danube was being widened, and it appeared certain that the Germans would move through a partially mobilized Bulgaria first into eastern Macedonia and then into western Thrace. He then pointed out the Greek dispositions— twelve infantry divisions and three brigades plus one cavalry division on the Albanian front, and four infantry divisions on the Bulgarian front in addition to those in the fortifications; another division was shortly to be moved to the Albanian front to face more arriving Italians. In order to establish a good defensive position on the Bulgarian front he needed nine divisions, and he looked to the British to supply these. If the Germans were to be countered, the British had to land speedily and in security, and then concentrate rapidly, for the Greek staff estimated that the Germans could concentrate on the Greek border in eleven days. If the British landing could not take place before German troops entered Bulgaria, it should at least take place before they took up offensive positions along the Bulgarian frontier with Greece. For this it would be necessary to carry out rapidly, and in absolute secrecy, the following preparatory measures: (1) safeguard A/A defenses for ports in eastern Macedonia and western Thrace (which Papagos suggested the Greeks man during the Italian phase of the campaign); (2) make a start on air bases for the RAF, with the British providing the material and funds and the Greeks the work; (3) land supplies for the British Expeditionary Force and Greek forces, to be stored under Greek guard; (4) concentrate the BEF and its RAF wing in Egypt as soon as possible, ready for embarkation, but with rumors spread that they were going to take Tripolitania; (5) collect the shipping needed for the operation in the eastern Mediterranean as soon as possible.

On the assumption that this could be done without hastening the German descent, and taking into account the capacities of the ports of Salonika, Amphipolis, and Cavalla, it would be possible for the British to land in Greece and to take up positions along the Axios-Evros line, from the Vardar (sometimes called Axios) valley to the Maritza, on the Turkish border. From the political point of view such a successful operation might encourage Yugoslavia and Turkey to join the Allies.

Wavell replied that he had not sufficient forces in the Middle East; he had beaten Graziani with only very small forces and had none to spare. Britain could dispose of only two or three divisions and a few aircraft to aid Greece, and some of these would be Imperial troops used in the Cyrenaican campaign. Time had to be allowed to concentrate and transport them. The only forces immediately available were one regiment of artillery and a unit of about 65 armored cars; Wavell suggested that these be sent immediately. Metaxas replied that two to three divisions were inadequate, and the dispatch of armored cars and artillery would do nothing more than provoke the Germans. Wavell, as Metaxas put it, in the words of a commander-in-chief thrice insisted that his government wished the Greeks to accept the antitank regiment and the armored cars, which were all he could offer. Metaxas, therefore, refused them. He said that Greece could not fight for victory, only for honor, preferring to destroy herself. At that, Palairet shook his hand and Wavell, in a rare emotional moment, also congratulated him. Metaxas wondered that night in his diary if they would ever again consider him pro-German! And so the session broke up.[188]

At noon they adjourned for lunch at Sir Michael Palairet's.

On the afternoon of the fifteenth Wavell sent a long telegram to the CIGS in London. He reported that they had discussed in detail the problems of supplies for the Greeks and that he had promised to send a ship just arrived from the United Kingdom straight through with 200 vehicles. He noted that he had already sent from his own stocks 180,000 pairs of boots and 350,000 pairs of socks, as well as blankets and clothing, but that he was short of most other items the Greeks urgently needed, especially pack animals. There had been a long discussion of the Salonika problem in which Metaxas had argued that the appearance of any British troops would alarm the Yugoslavs and provoke the Germans. Metaxas' idea was that the British should provide material and that the Greeks would build defenses about Salonika which should only be occupied when the British could send a force that was capable of offensive as well as defensive action. "The President concluded that we must not interpret his attitude as a refusal to accept assistance at Salonika, but as a request for postponement." Metaxas was seeing the Salonika front as a new one after the Greeks had cleaned the Italians out of Albania, so Wavell recommended that the British should "make every possible arrangement as regards preparation of bases, which will in any case be necessary preliminary to despatch of troops, and we will examine defensive possibilities on this front."[189]

Longmore and "Wild Bill" Donovan arrived in time for lunch on the fifteenth, and in the afternoon Longmore discussed the future with the Greeks. He said that nothing could be done about greater RAF operations or about training the Greek air force until airfields for fourteen squadrons had been prepared with training fields around Salonika. At an evening conference Metaxas agreed to let the Greek air force re-form in the Salonika area, where their airfields could be used as advanced landing or refueling grounds in the event of a German attack. He would now allow RAF officers to visit Greek air force establishments in the area and reconnoiter landing grounds on Lemnos and Mytilene. Longmore asked for facilities for fourteen squadrons in the area south and west of Mount Olympus, which D'Albiac enumerated, and impressed upon the Greek prime minister that until these were available, with the capacity to meet British requirements, the RAF could not operate, no matter how many aircraft were sent: this would be the deciding factor in sending squadrons from Egypt. Mention was also made of the fact that 30 Wellingtons and Blenheims had been waiting for a week at Menidi for the weather to clear sufficiently for them to raid Albanian targets, while Eleusis was still unserviceable. Taking all these factors into account, Longmore was satisfied that no more than Nos. 112, 11, and 33 squadrons on standby to move to Greece could be handled there.[190]

That there was confusion as to the size of the British air force in Greece may be assumed from a report sent home by the American air attaché in Athens that he had been told in secret conversations with Metaxas and D'Albiac that after 15 January the RAF in Greece would consist of six heavy and six medium bomber squadrons and five fighter squadrons in two composite wings, totaling altogether seventeen squadrons, and that the Greek air force was to be expanded also. And in the course of the British discussions in Athens there was a specific mention of a force of nine British divisions supported by three weak Greek ones.[191]

Certainly no British landing in Greece made sense unless it was strong enough not to be overrun or thrown out. Prince Paul of Yugoslavia had made it plain that any British force at Salonika would be a provocation to Yugoslavia, which would then let the Germans in. And as Metaxas noted in his diary on 15 January, the British were too weak to influence the Balkans and everybody knew that.[192] To put a force in place as a rock upon which the Germans could stumble made sense, and parts of northern Greece lend themselves to that sort of positional warfare, provided that the forces placed there have enough men and support forces to invest and hold the ground. But the last thing the British could afford in 1941 was another fiasco such as Norway, where they had been overrun by German airborne troops, infantry, and air support, or another Dakar, where they had badly misjudged the military and political circumstances.

Just before Wavell flew back to Egypt, he and Heywood talked again with the Greek commander, Papagos, to try and persuade him at London's insistence to accept the two regiments (one of artillery and one of armoured cars) which had been proffered earlier. Papagos responded that it was mainly a political question (as Wavell had surmised at the end of his message to London on the fifteenth), and that it was not, therefore, up to him to reply. Wavell agreed and asked him to take it up with his government. Wavell then left for Egypt, and the Greeks went into conference. Papagos later wrote that they quickly concluded that the British did not have the means to send Greece adequate and timely help. The Germans already held the initiative with superior means and priority in preparation, and as soon as the weakness of the British was known to the Yugoslavs and the Turks it would only confirm them in their neutrality. Papagos suggested to the prime minister that an attempt be made to persuade the British that not only would the aid offered be politically disastrous to the Balkans, but also it would be contrary to sound strategic principles as far as operations in the Mediterranean theater were concerned. The two or three divisions that Wavell could send would be far more useful in Africa. The best course was not to halt the attack in Libya, but to defeat the Italian Marshal Graziani and seize Tripolitania (before any Germans got there). *Then* the British could undertake much more extensive operations in the Balkans. The abandonment, Papagos said— no doubt with Metaxas' full agreement—of a likely success in favor of operations in another theater already doomed to certain failure "would be to commit a strategic error in contradiction with the principles of a sound conduct of war."

The Greek discussions then entered the tricky ground of trying to outguess world opinion. If they refused outright the British offer, they might be accused of not being resolved to fight. Papagos countered this by arguing that militarily the British knew that their proposed intervention was undesirable. The other side of the argument was the unfortunate guarantee treaty of April 1939, which was likely to cause an outcry against Britain even within the island kingdom if Greece fell without a single British soldier on her soil. It would also adversely affect public opinion in America. (Both these arguments were in a sense specious, as the RAF was already on Greek soil, while it could be argued that the 1939 treaty became null and void at the fall of France.)

Fortunately, Metaxas still retained his clear head. He maintained his decision to refuse the British offer outright, so as neither to provoke the Germans nor to unsettle the Yugoslavs. But he would ask the British to land as soon as the Germans crossed the Danube or the Rumanian border into Bulgaria, as then their intentions would be unmasked. This decision was finally communicated to the British government on 18 January.[193]

As for Wavell, he was much relieved, for, as he told a postwar audience, "If Metaxas had accepted my offer of guns in January 1941 I should have had to stop my advance at Tobruk as that would have deprived me of the very considerable part of my technical arm . . . . I could not have gone any further.[194] (Wavell had become in many ways a Greek hero, like Metaxas. He caught the imagination—so very British, so very firm, so decided, so clearly impossible to ruffle or alarm; he was to the Greeks a legendary character. When he left on 17 January the Greeks felt lonely.)

As Casson pointed out, while the diplomats got excited about the German threat early in January, the soldiers could discuss it calmly since they knew the Germans simply could not get through the Bulgarian passes in the winter. But the real Greek tragedy began then, because the Greeks knew that a German attack was now inevitable.[195]

One of the interesting things about war and the mind of man is that something that is true of one side is never assumed to be true of the other. Thus on the one hand the British in London were suggesting in early January that the Germans could attack Greece on the twentieth, while D'Albiac was reporting on the fourteenth that weather had closed all but two of his airfields. At Larissa a squadron of Gladiators had been grounded by fog for fourteen days waiting for good enough weather to be able to fly across the mountains to Janina to support the Greeks. Eleusis was waterlogged.[196] The Germans were not credited with similar difficulties.

There were many reasons why the matter should have been left where it had fallen then. It was, as Casson suggested, a tragedy plodding towards its inevitable conclusion when the Greeks would run out of supplies and momentum just as the snows melted, the flowers bloomed, and the Germans attacked in April. But London was filled with noble thoughts and unnecessary miscalculations, which would lead to further tragedies and prolong the war. A better course would have been to secure North Africa before the Germans could cross over from Italy or establish the Luftwaffe. By mid-January Wavell was already concerned that the Luftwaffe was moving into the central Mediterranean to reinforce the Italians for an attack on Malta. This meant that Egypt's western flankguard had become Benghazi rather than Tobruk.

On another level, on 14 January the bureaucratic mind was at work in Cairo, dutifully reporting to London that the first estimate for services rendered to the Greeks for three months of campaigning amounted to the following sums, not large by the standards of the day:

> Hospital and other costs . . . . . . . . . . . . . . . . . . . £2000
> 12 old Gladiators . . . . . . . . . . . . . . . . . . . . . . . . . £1800 the lot
> Supplies & road transport. . . . . . . . . . . . . . . . . £4000
> _____
> £7,800

The Greeks paid Shell Oil Company directly for fuel, while airfields, billets, and the like were supplied free. So the *cost* of aid to Greece was hardly a consideration.[197]

In London Metaxas' refusal of the proffered help was accepted, but in order to cover his position Churchill insisted on 17 January that Wavell and Longmore tell the Greek prime minister that if the special force the British had proposed was not sent before the German advance began, it would certainly be too late, and no offensive British force would go to Salonika at any time; therefore nothing needed to be done to prepare ports in northern Greece.[198]

In mid-January Cunningham was planning a series of pin-prick sea-borne raids on the Dodecanese, but the Admiralty ordered him not to stir up a hornet's nest until their capture could be settled upon. Churchill told the Chiefs of Staff on the thirteenth that the arrival of the German air force in the central Mediterranean was evil, and promptly revived the idea of WORKSHOP, the taking of Pantellaria; the Defence Committee replied that the proper solution was the seizure of Sicily, but to this Churchill strenuously objected, declaring that the failure to take Pantellaria would be one of the classic mistakes of the war. So it was agreed to reconsider it in a week.[199]

Long a frustration for Metaxas and Papagos had been the failure to develop a Balkan alliance system or mutual security pact. At the heart of the problem lay the jealousies and suspicions of the various states—Yugoslavia, Albania, Bulgaria, Rumania, and Greece, as well as Turkey. There were religious differences as well as linguistic and racial ones. Yugoslavia itself was made up of Serbs, Croatians, and Slovenes. On top of this there were the enmities inherited from the three wars of 1912, 1913, and 1914-1918, as well as the Graeco-Turkish affair of 1922. Nor did geography help. Belgrade, the capital of Yugoslavia, was right on the Danube in the east central part of the country, while the principal seaport in the area was Salonika in Greece, long coveted by Bulgaria. Numerous conferences and exchanges had failed to solve these problems, though the Greeks kept trying. From 6 through 17 January 1941 there was an exchange between Metaxas and the Yugoslav regent, Prince Paul, which concluded with a still-secret conversation between the Yugoslav ambassador and the Greek prime minister. Evidently Prince Paul stressed his country's geographic disadvantages, bringing the whole discussion to an unsatisfactory conclusion as far as Metaxas was concerned.[200]

## 17 - 18 January

On 17 January the Luftwaffe bombed the Suez Canal, which had to be closed for twenty-four hours.[201]

The British minister in Sofia, George Rendel, reported in a telegram that the story in Bulgaria was that the Germans in Rumania were there mainly as a precaution against a British attempt to establish a Balkan front and were no menace to Bulgaria itself. Rendel was not so sure. Certainly the Foreign Office in London viewed the story as German propaganda.[202]

Late on the seventeenth Papagos sent for Heywood and passed along the word which the Hungarian regent, Admiral Horthy, had given to the Greek minister at Budapest: the Germans had 280,000 troops in Rumania with material for double that number. The Greek (or British?) military attaché in Bucharest put the number at 180,000.

On the evening of the eighteenth Heywood reported that Metaxas' policy was to gain time so that he could clean up Albania and shift troops to Macedonia while the British built up a strategical reserve in Egypt, "if His Majesty's Government concurs in his plan." Heywood then went on that Metaxas was "very anxious that it should be understood that his attitude is not one of refusal but is dictated by the latest date that the arrival of such assistance as we can give should be prepared and timed to effect surprise without provocation."[203]

Longmore signaled the Air Ministry from Athens that he recalled that he was to get 220 Mohawks (Curtiss P-36's) sometime, of which the Greeks were to get 30 early. A recent signal had indicated he was to get 500 Tomahawks (Curtis P-40's), but he did not know whether these were to be helpful or not, as he had heard that the Tomahawks were not yet satisfactory and might not meet RAF requirements. He needed to know at once as it affected the decisions he had to make on the re-equipment of both the RAF and the Greek squadrons.

From Cairo Wavell told the CIGS that on the sixteenth he had visited British units in and near Athens and had then spent a quarter of an hour in the evening each with the king, Metaxas, and Papagos. The Greek chief of staff had explained that they could not accept British troops for the Albanian front owing to administrative difficulties. Just as he was leaving Athens on the morning of the seventeenth, Wavell had received the COS signal relaying Churchill's warning, which he had immediately communicated to the king, emphasizing that London thought an attack on Salonika much more imminent than did Athens and stressing the point that British help could not arrive rapidly if an emergency arose. The king then asked Wavell what units he could supply, to which Wavell replied that he could send four or five regiments of artillery and one regiment of cruiser tanks. "He asked whether any infantry formations could be sent, and I said that I had no authority to send any." Late that night Wavell sent another telegram to the War Office giving his views of the Salonika situation:

1. Present proposal is a dangerous half measure. I do not believe that troops it is proposed to send are sufficient to enable the equivalent of three Greek divisions to hold Salonika if the Germans are really determined to advance on it. We shall almost inevitably be compelled to send further troops in haste or shall become involved in retreat or defeat. Meanwhile advance into Libya will be halted and Italians given time to recover.

2. Factor which may cause Germany to hesitate from move into Bulgaria is that, by doing away with Bulgarian neutrality, she at once exposes Rumanian oilfields to bombing attack. I have seen no reference to this fact in spite of many Foreign Office telegrams on Balkan situation, but surely it is most important one and Germany's fears in this respect may deter her moves.

Wavell then went on to point out that tying up technical troops in Salonika was poor investment if no attack came, and that with the poor communications in Greece they could do little to help on the Albanian front. He then further stressed the terrible weakness of his command in A/A and fighter aircraft. Moreover, while he had been assured that his forces were to be expanded and that troops sent to Salonika would be replaced, he was now finding convoys being cut of drafts and units essential even to keeping his present force up to strength. "If this represents a change of policy and we must be prepared to live on our own leanness for some time, may I please be informed; it would, of course, greatly increase dangers of sending forces to Salonika. . . . My conclusion is that we should accept Greek refusal, but shall make all necessary reconnaissances and preparations of Salonika front without giving any promise to send troops at future date."[204]

The Air Ministry told Longmore that he would get 300 Tomahawks from the United States over the next five months, though they would have American guns and be unusable until ammunition arrived. The 200 Mohawks, which he was to share with the South African air force, did need to have their engines modified before their next flight, so there would be a delay of a month while the fix was made; engines would be shipped out for the aircraft he already had. Longmore was naturally unhappy with this and complained that he needed then as many Hurricanes as possible until the supply of American aircraft was assured. Obviously, he continued, this affected the allocation of equipment and he hoped that it would be borne in mind when new commitments were made, especially now that the Luftwaffe had appeared in the Mediterranean. He, therefore, proposed to retain No. 33 Hurricane Squadron as insurance and only send No. 112 Gladiator and No. 11 Blenheim squadrons to Greece in order to assure cover for the newly reinstated advance on Benghazi.

A garbled signal from the COS had reached Athens earlier on Saturday, but it was not until five o'clock that Heywood could send on to Longmore the corrected version, which said that he was given both the option of retaining No. 33 Squadron in Egypt and permission to return to Egypt.[205]

Metaxas now began a more complicated game. He asked formally that British troops be landed as soon as the German army entered Bulgaria. This was to be the basis of staff talks from which large-scale planning was to come. The Greek prime minister also sent a copy of this note to Belgrade, knowing it would immediately be passed along to Berlin. The Greek dilemma was that if Yugoslavia joined the Allies, Salonika was needed as the port through which she would have to be supplied, and the Metaxas Line, those well-designed fortifications on the Bulgarian border, would be needed to cover Salonika. If Yugoslavia stayed neutral, then it was better to hold the shorter line along the Vermion Ridge through Edessa to Mount Olympus. But if Yugoslavia let the Germans pass through, then the Vermion Line could be turned and it was better to fall back on to the Aliakmon Line, which blocked the exits from the Monastir Gap. These three lines would keep cropping up in discussions over the coming weeks.[206] Unlike the Metaxas Line, the other two existed only on maps. In the note that Metaxas gave Palairet for London he pointed out that the Yugoslavs had withdrawn their pledge not to let the Germans pass through their country; and while on the one hand Metaxas had talked of a strategic reserve for which the shipping would be gathered, on the other he now observed that the British forces in the Middle East were inadequate to solve the problems of southeast Europe.[207]

## 19 - 28 January

Wavell's visit to Athens was intended to be secret, but Reuters in Istanbul published that it was for discussions with the Greek general staff on plans to counter a German thrust across Bulgaria into Greece, so Eden telegraphed Metaxas that they had given to the press and the BBC the story that Wavell had been over to consult about British aid to the Greeks against the Italians.[208]

Like an omen, at noon on 19 January a long-range German "Heinkel" photo aircraft (probably a Ju-86P at 33,000 feet) made a successful reconnaissance, lasting over two hours, of the Athens-Piraeus area, where twenty-one ships had arrived on the seventeenth carrying all sorts of vital war supplies, including parts for the Blenheims. Just after noon the next day 9 Italian SM-79's attacked the Piraeus from 1,500 feet and hit one empty 7,000-ton ship. The Italians lost one bomber and the British one fighter.[209]

"Will Bill" Donovan had since the fifteenth been staying with the Palairets at the British embassy, where he learned that the embassy in Moscow reported that the Russians felt that any German moves in the Balkans were no threat to them. Donovan also understood that the British were having no luck in Ankara either: the Turkish view was that the British should finish off the Italians in Libya so that they could shift their forces to meet the threat in the Balkans, and that it was inadvisable to provoke Germany as long as her concentration in Rumania was defensive.[210] By the twentieth Donovan had reached Sofia on his tour of the Balkans.[211]

Meanwhile in London on the night of 19 January the Chiefs of Staff had met to sort out the muddle left by the Greek refusal of inadequate aid. Admiral Sir Dudley Pound, the First Sea Lord, believed that the eastern Mediterranean should be consolidated so that later on forces could be sent to Greece and Turkey. To do this Cyrenaica should be cleared, Benghazi secured, and the Dodecanese occupied, especially now that the Germans were using the air bases there for attacks on the Suez Canal. He ruled out attempts to seize Sardinia and Sicily for lack of air support. Naturally, Churchill, still suffering from a week-old cold, reacted bitterly to this lack of offensive-mindedness, demanding instead that "the great forces in the Middle East" be used to open the lines of communication with Turkey, then blocked by the Vichy occupation of Syria. The victorious Army of the Nile, as Winston had recently renamed the Western Desert force, was to be a mobile reserve to be dispatched to Greece, or to Turkey if the Germans swung around through the Ukraine and down through the Caucasus. Orders were sent to the Middle East accordingly. But Longmore was allowed to retain No. 33 Gladiator squadron.[212]

Unlike the commanders at home, who had modern railway networks to save their motor transport, and vast civilian factories and repair organizations handy, as well as limited distances to travel, the commanders in the Middle East had to operate over distances commonly the length of the United Kingdom or more, almost always with motor transport fueled out of leaky four-gallon cans. But this was only one of the disadvantages faced by the AOC-in-C ME. For the Battle of Britain, Air Chief Marshal Dowding had twenty nine Hurricane and nineteen Spitfire squadrons, giving him about 760 first-class single-seat fighters, of which he could launch 570 at any one time because they were serviceable. In contrast, in January 1941 Longmore had yet to have in the theater 100 Hurricanes, of which he could normally not expect more than 70 to be serviceable, and these could not operate from all his airfields. Of the 26 Hurricanes and 15 replacements which landed in Greece for the campaign between mid-February and mid-April, 33 were lost and only 8 flew out to Crete. Forty-two of 47 Blenheim bombers and all 16 Gladiators sent were destroyed.[213] It was small wonder that Longmore's wastage in his fast-moving campaigns in remote areas was high. The Prime Minister should not have been surprised, but, as Eden said in November 1940, Churchill did not understand modern maintenance problems of motor transport, tanks, and aircraft operating in a country of desert spaces and devoid of industrial capacity.[214]

In the latter part of January, intelligence of various sorts was flowing into the Foreign Office from its consuls in the Balkans, all indicating the likelihood of German action and of Yugoslav inaction.[215] On the twenty-first the Chiefs of Staff ordered Wavell to proceed to Benghazi as fast as possible and turn it into a well-defended naval and air base, then to capture the Dodecanese so as to clear the lines of communications to Greece and Turkey. He was informed that a special force of four Glen ships carrying landing craft and 1,500 commandos was being sent out, and that he was to create a four-division strategic reserve in the Delta as soon as possible.[216]

It was said that *four* divisions was the minimum that Metaxas would accept as assistance against invasion.[217] But it seems that at this point a typographical error crept in, which on 22 February Papagos would try to correct, but which would help lead to ultimate disaster A 9 and a 4 are fairly similar when handwritten. Both the record and common sense show that the Greeks meant nine, but that the British could only find four. This conclusion appears logical, especially later when the British were trying to justify to the Australians having sent inadequate forces.

On 23 January Eden telegraphed Palairet an account of the Turkish Foreign Secretary's meeting with the German ambassador, von Papen, in Ankara, at which the latter had said that the Germans were in Rumania defensively to meet the threat posed by British landings after they cleaned up in Libya. However the Germans did not regard the current level of British activity in Greece as dangerous, nor did they have any intention of going into Bulgaria. The Turkish Foreign Minister had not believed von Papen, and his country's partial mobilization was proceeding. At the same time in Moscow the German ambassador had let it be known that his country had not forgotten "the fatal Salonika front."[218] On the twenty-first Athens had heard from Rumanian sources that the Germans would attack Salonika through Bulgaria.[219] On the twenty-second Eden had lunched with the Yugoslav ambassador, who stated categorically that Salonika was absolutely vital to his country and that she would fight to protect it. He and the Turkish and Russian ambassadors also agreed that British forces in the Middle East were too small to get involved in Europe and that the Germans were already in Bulgaria: the British were too late.[220]

London received on 22 January a status report on airfields in Crete which indicated that Heraklion had been ready for use since the end of the year, with 1,000 yards of runway laid and rolled; that work had commenced on Retimo; that Maleme near Suda Bay could now take fighter aircraft; and that a new site had been found at Pediada Kastelli fifteen miles southwest of Heraklion which allowed approximately 1,500 yards for take-off in any direction.[221]

In Cairo two senior doctors, Col. N. Hamilton Fairley and Col. J.S.K. Boyd, gave Wavell a medical appreciation of the dangers of malaria in southeast Europe. Fairley was consulting physician to the Australian Imperial forces in the Middle East and consultant in tropical diseases to the British forces, while his colleague was the deputy director of pathology for the British forces. Both were worried because there had already been trouble in the training areas in Palestine, especially in Arab villages where more than 20 percent of the children had the disease. Antimalarial measures at this time were mostly confined to avoiding known infectious areas and control of mosquito-breeding sites near camp. Quinine was only used clinically, followed by atabrine. Malaria was not a significant problem in the Desert because there was almost no water, but Greece was another matter.[222]

The Fairley-Boyd report, apparently drawn up at Wavell's request, dealt with both Greece and Turkey. It was compiled by men with great authority and was based upon both research and personal experience. The report pointed out that malaria was hyper-endemic in the plains of Macedonia and in the Struma and Vardar river basins. In 1916-1918 the British army in these areas had suffered extremely heavy casualties from the disease. Now the area had many refugees, as a result of the exchange of populations with Anatolia, and there were great dangers in using unseasoned troops there. Moreover, the Germans knew more than the British about the problem, as they had established a major research center in the area. Fairley and Boyd reported that only in October-through-May season would it be medically safe to conduct military operations in northern Greece. Wavell asked about the antimalarial work the Greeks had done and concluded that their analysis was "typical of non-medical and non-military experience." But after a 7 February meeting with Greek officers he agreed to help carry out measures needed to mitigate hazards.[223]

While this discussion was going on, Prime Minister Churchill had been trying to get a commitment from the Turks, his old Gallipoli enemies of the First World War. This simply exacerbated the tensions between London and Cairo over supplies. Already the AOC-in-C had been told that he was to regard Malta's defense as his first priority. Longmore had been forced to signal back that he had not yet received three squadrons of fighters promised and that he could not guarantee to fly them into the island in winter. The response from London was to tell him that he could form as many additional squadrons as possible from what he had. Once those in London had made a decision, they seemed to assume that sufficient material and trained personnel would be found—which was true enough in England but not in the Middle East where there was usually a three to six months' lag between order and delivery.

For instance, 21 Battalion, New Zealand Army in England was ordered to go to Egypt on 26 November 1940. The first vehicles were sent off on 28 November, but the battalion did not march out from its Camberley barracks until 3 January 1941; the *Duchess of Bedford* sailed on the fifth, only to anchor off Newport, Monmouthshire, for several days, finally leaving Belfast for Cape Town on the twelfth. It called at Freetown, Sierra Leone, and reached Table Bay on 8 February. Four days later it sailed again, passed through the Gulf of Aden, arrived at Port Tewfik on 3 March, and began to disembark on the eighth. The battalion was still unloading on 14 March when it was put on forty-eight-hours warning for Greece, arriving finally at the Piraeus on 29 March, four months after it was ordered from Britain.[224] It is scarcely any wonder that Wavell and his fellow commanders viewed London's orders of 21 January as instructions to live on "their leanness" for the next three months.[225]

There were two basic reasons that supply was a constant bone of contention between London and Cairo—time and distance. London forgot that ships could only make two round trips a year, and they tended to think that once items were ordered shipped they could be considered as being on hand in the Middle East. Nor did London appreciate the geometric scale of the increase in supply needs with the distances involved. And decision makers in London underestimated the needs of modern war, especially in maintenance and communications, and the breakdowns of untested equipment in its early battlefield use—a common problem after a long period of peace.

The relationship with Turkey at this point well illustrates the very frustrating position in which Longmore, in particular, found himself because of the actions taken by Churchill and Portal in London.

Alerted by ULTRA and expecting the attack in Greece any day, London was terribly anxious to get Turkey into the war. But the Turks were realists. They were dissatisfied over the slow delivery of the aircraft they had been promised, they needed fighters and antiaircraft guns, and many Turkish squadrons were grounded, and their training delayed for lack of spares. While they for their part had promised to hasten the development of ports and airfields, they had no wish to provoke the Germans while they were themselves unready, as they patiently explained during staff talks. The report of these conversations reached London on 22 January. Churchill then appealed to the president of Turkey, Inönü, and promised him ten squadrons of fighters and bombers as soon as they could be received, and 100 A/A guns from Egypt with more to follow. This, he reasoned, should allow Turkey to make a threat against both the Rumanian and the Russian oilfields. On the twenty-fourth the air attaché in Ankara signaled Longmore that the Turks wanted five hundred first-line aircraft of the latest type with bombs, fuel, training aircraft, lorries, and so on.[226]

This coincided with a signal from London telling Longmore to work up plans to knock the Luftwaffe out of Rhodes and Sicily, to which he had reasonably responded, Had the air staff worked out the maximum number of squadrons the Middle East could maintain, given existing air and sea communications? Nor was Longmore happy when he learned that he was to supply the ten squadrons promised by the Prime Minister, even though London told him that by the end of March he would have a further 100 Hurricanes, 120 Blenheims, 45 Marylands, and 35 Wellingtons.[227]

Additionally on 24 January the Chiefs of Staff ordered the C-in-C's in Cairo to plan and prepare for the invasion of Sicily, an operation to follow shortly after that in the Dodecanese, especially if there was a falling out between the Italians and the Germans. Moreover, the C-in-C's were to provide all the necessary forces from their own resources, though they might retain shipping as it arrived in the Middle East. And even though the feasibility of the whole operation might be in some doubt, the commanders and their forces were to be nominated.[228]

This was followed two days later by a signal from Churchill admitting that the message of the twenty fourth was sent at his urging, but returning to the theme of support for Wavell only if he was not wasteful of resources in his rearward areas. This signal made clear that the reason for invading Sicily was to open the Narrows of the Mediterranean and to shorten the route to the Middle East for troop convoys, a hope which was dashed by the arrival of the German air force in the Mediterranean. The second paragraph was devoted to puzzlement over Wavell's recent refusal of another South African division unless it came fully supplied with its own administrative tail. Churchill pointed out that the offer of the South African division was part of a master plan gradually to get the Afrikaaners committed to the main theater of war: "On no account must General Smuts be discouraged from his bold and sound policy of gradually working South African Forces into the main theatre." He then went on to conclude that the Germans were active in the Balkans: "We must expect a series of very heavy disastrous blows in the Balkans, and possibly a general submission there to German aims. The stronger the strategic reserve which you can build up in the Delta, and the more advanced your preparations to transfer it to the European shores, the better will be the chances of securing a favourable crystallization."[229]

To this Wavell responded on 27 January that he could assure the Prime Minister that "my demands for rearward services are the result of the most careful and prolonged examination and that every one of my principal administrative officers is working on what he (and I) regards as dangerously low margins. At the moment my forward movements in Cyrenaica, in the Sudan and in E. Africa are all in danger of coming to a halt, not from lack of fighting troops, but for want of transport, signals, wokshops and such." And he went on to point out that he had 100,000 prisoners of war to guard, which further strained his manpower. Then he reminded London that his two divisions had defeated eleven enemy divisions by their superior equipment and mobility, only made possible by superior rearward services. As for the South African division, none of the telegrams he had seen had ever suggested that they could be used north of Kenya, as that was Smuts' political pledge. If they could, he would welcome them, provided they came with a full complement of administrative services. As far as the Balkans was concerned, he fully agreed on the danger there and on the need for a strong general reserve in the Nile Delta, "but such reserve will be useless unless it is fully equipped with the necessary proportion of modern weapons . . . and unless administrative services and base units are available to enable it to be transferred and maintained in overseas theatre. This is policy on which I must continue to work so long as you entrust me with responsibility for this theatre. I need hardly point out again that Army operations anywhere are entirely dependent on effective air support and that air reinforcement must continue to keep pace with reinforcement of troops. . . . Possibly most effective deterrent to German advance in Balkans would be knowledge that any infringement of Bulgarian neutrality would at once bring heavy air attack on Rumanian oilfields."[230]

There followed another long signal later in the day from Cairo to London detailing the shipping problems occasioned by the capture of Benghazi, which entailed running a coastal convoy service over a distance equivalent to that from John O'Groats to Lands End, in an area already starved of shipping. This had already required that three ships be taken off the Greek and Turkish services. Certainly OPERATION MANDIBLES needed to be done, but it would be early April before the Glen assault ships arrived. The capture of Rhodes was urgent, but would have to start with the taking of Kasos, and even when all of Cyrenaica was in British hands fighters would have to be retained in Egypt to guard against attacks from Rhodes. And apart from Longmore's problems in forming new fighter squadrons from the material trickling in, he was saddled with the defense of Malta; but owing to distances and weather, even fighters with long-range tanks could not easily get through to the island.[231]

On 29 January Churchill replied, "I quite understand that your rearward services must be specially maintained because of the great distances and the absence of local reserves and repair facilities such as we have here." But then he went on to say that he was preparing another analysis of Middle Eastern ration strength which he was sending out and he expected Wavell to "help in every possible way." He added that Smuts said he could send troops anywhere in Africa—but there was no hurry, as far as Churchill was concerned, in taking the division. He ended by saying that London would be considering the impact of various new events in the Aegean, including the possible collapse of Greece and abstention of Turkey.[232]

While London was trying to push Turkey and Yugoslavia together, Knatchbull-Hugessen telegraphed from Ankara that the German military attaché had told his Greek opposite number that the Germans expected to walk into Salonika on 2 March without opposition; that would give them Mediterranean bases there, at Trieste, and at Gibraltar. The Greek had hotly replied that Turkey would fight on the side of Greece.[233]

Meanwhile on 27 January air intelligence had been able to point out accurately that the Germans now had 80 long-range divebombers at Benina, near Benghazi (but the Middle East was not as yet able to make full use of such intelligence). It was also able to warn Admiral Cunningham three days ahead that the Germans were going to mine the Suez Canal.[234]

But perhaps the most important development was taking place in Athens, where on the eighteenth Metaxas had had to cancel a meeting with Longmore and had ever since been increasingly, but secretly, ill.[235]

## 29 January 1941

Early on Wednesday, 29 January, General Ioannis Metaxas, president of the Council and prime minister of Greece, died. Seventy years old and suffering from a variety of ailments, he passed away lying on the old leather couch at his home in Kifisis, surrounded by his wife and daughters. According to what Metaxas' son-in-law told Laird Archer that morning, the doughty old man died of a combination of diabetes, intestinal troubles (kidney infections), and influenza, as well as a heart attack. The seriousness of his condition had been kept a secret, as people pinned their hopes of ultimate victory on this little man of rugged fortitude and undoubted patriotism. Casson says he died after a tonsil operation.[236]

The prime minister lay in state in the Greek Orthodox cathedral, the Mitropolis on Miropoleos Street, attended only by four Efzones, the elite Greek soldiers, in their traditional white kilts. The British ambassador and the four attachés went, knelt, kissed the icon, and departed in sorrow at the loss of a personal friend.[237]

C.L. Sulzberger of the *New York Times*, then a young correspondent in the Balkans, found that the short, fatherly-looking dictator, known as "the Little Moltke," despite his unpopularity, inspired an immense outpouring from the emotional Greek people on his passing, perhaps because fear of Germany now replaced euphoria. Wavell, writing in *The Army Quarterly* just before his own death in 1950, said that Metaxas was the heart of the Greek defenses, that "he may have been an arbitrary politician, but he was a very stout-hearted and skillful director of his country's defense at a critical hour." Sir David Hunt, who was present in Athens at the time, called his funeral the burial of British military luck in Greece.[238]

Ioannis Metaxas was a significant figure in the early history of the Second World War. To a non-Greek not involved in the emotions of internal Hellenic politics of then and now, the scales of justice seem to tip decisively toward a verdict of patriotism, realism, and strategic soundness, if not genius. He knew his country and he knew the Balkans. Britain was lucky that he was there steadfastly to deflect foolish proposals concocted in London and dutifully relayed by Cairo (where it was hoped he would turn them down). As a contemporary, it was his fate to have to be associated with Churchill's ideas in both World Wars. But as the leader of a lesser power and a man of fewer words, he was the greater realist.

Certain moments are decisive in history because they see the release of historically decisive forces that turn the footsteps of Fate in a certain direction. The death of Metaxas was one of these. Greece was, as he recognized, marching inevitably to tragedy even if she had the power and the luck and the time to push the Italians out of Albania. By the time of his death, and perhaps helping to cause it, the Little Moltke knew that the Germans were going to combine with Greece's traditional enemy, Bulgaria, to invade Hellas. That the British were in Greece was less the excuse than, on the petty level, the settling of old Balkan scores left from 1913; at a higher level the motivation was to stabilize Italian and German spheres of influence on the Balkans before Hitler began the great crusade against the Soviet Union.

Whether they realized it or not, the British were in a race against time in Libya and the Mediterranean. They needed to clear North Africa and save Malta, in order to open the Mediterranean to convoys, protect shipping, and shorten their supply routes; and they needed to clear the Dodecanese, and probably Syria, in order to bolster Turkey. Aside from the proper strategic necessity of securing Crete, aid to Greece was a noble distraction, but an irrational one which the United Kingdom could not at that time afford. Yet, unfortunately, Churchill and Eden insisted on setting Britain on the same path to tragedy that Greece was taking. Self-analysis and rational calculation were not British strong points, and Churchill still tended to fight the Second World War as though it was the Kitchener expedition to avenge General Gordon, an operation in which he himself had fought. Had Metaxas lived, he might have saved the British Empire by keeping Wavell on the path to Tripoli.

# III

## The Garden of Eden
### 29 January 1941 - 4 March 1941

*During the winter of 1940-1941 British armaments production climbed, but so did shipping losses as the U-boats took their toll. Civilian casualties mounted during the Blitz (the nighttime German air raids) and exceeded military losses. Most dangerous of all, the supply of dollars was fast running down as exports were curtailed and armaments sucked bank accounts dry. But once safely reelected, FDR came to the rescue with Lend-Lease, which enabled the British to borrow weapons, and other helpful measures. In fact, Britain found she was better off by late March than she had thought, for a judicial review came to the decision that the Air Ministry had far overestimated the size of the German air force, while evidence from many sources, including ULTRA, began to point toward German activity in the east rather than an invasion of the British Isles.*

*To secure their flank for their move toward Russia, and to smooth the flow of badly needed raw materials, especially Rumanian oil, the Germans were determined to clean up the mess made by Mussolini's ambitions in Greece, and to block his schemes elsewhere in the Balkans. To this end in December they began shifting troops to Rumania, put on pressure to obtain bases in Bulgaria, and sought to coerce Yugoslavia to allow passage to Salonika. The Turks played a waiting game.*

*By early 1941 all the rest of continental Europe, with the exception of the neutral Iberia, Switzerland, and Sweden, was essentially under German hegemony. Neither the United States nor the United Kingdom could destroy that control without Soviet help, and that was unavailable before 22 June.*

The weeks after the death of Metaxas were less significant for Greek than for British history. The story we have now to tell explains a great deal about how history is made by people, not by luck, and how the ignoring of geographical and timely obstacles leads to disaster. The Prime Minister in London kept changing his mind about the objectives like a puppy in a fire-hydrant factory. The presence of senior politicians in unusual places complicated the decision-making process, while the timorousness of those who had doubts again prevented timely warnings. Once the rational Metaxas was removed from the scene, there was no one to say "Ochi," and it was all a tragic march to the final evacuation at the end of April.

The passing of the tough little Greek leader was but an incident, of course, in an ongoing drama. Other themes continued to develop. The C-in-C's in Cairo asked whether in the event of a ceasefire between Italy and Greece the policy was still to hold Crete, to which the COS replied in the affirmative.[1] The question of Turkey remained unsettled. On 23 January AVM Elmhirst had reported that the Turks badly needed 500 planes to re-equip their air force and that, in addition to supplying spares for the British machines they already possessed, they wanted the British to build and stock all-weather airfields, especially in Thrace, so that in the event of war the RAF could move in rapidly. Elmhirst then left on a tour of Turkish positions, not to return to Cairo until 15 February. To meet Turkish demands, Portal proposed that three fighter and two bomber squadrons plus 100 A/A guns be diverted to Turkey (in spite of their virtual nonexistence in the Middle East).

After the news of Metaxas' death reached London, Churchill and the COS settled on a new policy, which was not to give priority to the seizure of Benghazi, but to aim instead at neutralizing Bulgaria. This was coupled with a scheme to bomb the Rumanian oilfields from Turkish airfields. Once again the trouble with London's strategic vision was that Churchill thought that the vast forces in the Middle East were underemployed, and that the capture of Benghazi and of the Dodecanese would not occupy them sufficiently. Not surprisingly, when Longmore heard of the cavalier offer of his forces to Turkey, he was astounded. Eden noted in his dairy that Churchill and Portal were touting the plan as the key to the Balkans, because in their view Wavell did not see the dangers there sufficiently.[2]

On 30 January Portal sent Longmore a personal signal which began, "This is a warning telegram only. It is possible that during the next few days Turkish Government may agree to suggestion His Majesty's Government are making that they should allow us to infiltrate air forces into Turkey forthwith. . . . We suggest three fighter, four Blenheim, three Wellington at first, possibly followed later by two more fighter and three more Blenheim squadrons from Greece. Actual dispatch of any squadrons would be subject to stabilized situation in Libya, but it would take priority over operations against East Africa, Abyssinia, Sicily, and further assistance to Greece." And the signal ended that all of this would be most urgent and might have to be accomplished immediately if the Turks accepted.[3]

Longmore's popularity in London was surely not improved by his reply, which began,

Quite frankly contents astound me, but, as both Wavell and Cunningham will be seriously affected by the removal of squadrons concerned to Turkey, full reply cannot be sent until after consultation with them. In meantime, I cannot believe you fully appreciate present situation Middle East, in which Libyan drive in full career and Sudan offensive into Eritrea progressing satisfactorily. Neither shows signs of immediate stabilization. Arrival of aircraft in Middle East all routes now hardly keeping pace with casualties Libya, Sudan, Greece, Malta, and there is no chance of forming Nos. 250, 251, 89 or 91 Fighter Squadrons in immediate future. Nos. 47 and 223 Squadrons in Sudan are still operating Wellesleys, No. 237 a mixture of Lysanders and Hardys. No. 39 has no aircraft at all until Glen[n] Martin's arrive here. Have not sufficient personnel or stocks of bombs to disperse them in Turkey whilst still meeting our existing commitments. . . . Under these circumstances and however strong the political advantages may be of impressing the Turks, can you really afford to lock up the squadrons you propose in Turkey, where they might well remain for some time inoperative even against the Dodecanese, until the Turks declare their hand? Would it not be forsaking the substance for the shadow?[4]

To this Portal replied that he could understand Longmore's astonishment, but the limit on cipher signals did not make it possible to keep him fully informed. It was the considered opinion in London that they were putting first things first, by deterring Germany from taking Greece, Turkey, and the eastern Mediterranean through fear of having the Rumanian oilfields bombed. Besides, by the end of March Longmore should have an additional 100 Hurricanes, 120 Blenheim IV's, 45 Glen[n] Martins and 35 Wellingtons. As to the shortage of bombs, the CAS could not understand this, as Middle East Command had 4,500 tons on hand, according to London's count, and 7,000 tons en route, while Turkey would need only 350 tons per month.

On the thirty-first Churchill sent a message directly to the president of Turkey formally offering 100 antiaircraft guns and ten RAF squadrons. Unprepared to fight until 1942, the Turks saw this as a declaration of war and refused all but some instructors.[5] So next the government in London decided that the way to force Turkey's hand was to give all aid to Greece.

Longmore had hoped that success in the Desert, if not elsewhere, would allow him to rest and refresh his tired squadrons. In Greece D'Albiac could do not much else, except try to rebuild the RHAF. Some reinforcement of the RAF in Greece took place, but it could not be raised to the anticipated strength of fourteen squadrons by 15 April until all-weather airfields could be built.[6]

Meanwhile in London Cadogan and Eden had been discussing which of them should visit the Middle East; the under-secretary was reluctant because he thought he was too much like the "chaps out there," but on the other hand he thought that if Anthony went he would scare the Balkan governments out of their wits.[7]

In his recent assessment of the state of British intelligence at this time, Hinsley has come to the conclusion that the British knew a good deal about the German plans but not very much about Greek, Turkish, or Yugoslav plans, and that it seems clear that Whitehall's hopes of cooperation with those Balkan countries were largely based upon wishful thinking.[8]

## 29 - 30 January 1941

A secret memo circulating at the top of the War Office identified Field Marshal List as commanding the German 12th Army in southeast Europe, and set the date for his attack on Greece as the first week of March, an estimate based in part on "Most Secret" Luftwaffe sources. We now know this was from ULTRA decrypts.[9]

In Athens the king summoned Alexander Koryzis to be prime minister. He was an honest banker who had been the minister of public assistance from 1936 to 1939 and was highly respected for the reforms he had made in the departments of national health and hygiene. Meeting with Laird Archer for the last time as chairman of the Greek War Relief Committee, he left an impression of a conscientious, upstanding self-made man with a high degree of integrity. Koryzis knew he had been drafted by the king, in spite of His Majesty's own doubts and the advice of his friends, on the strength of his record and reputation. But he was not a politician, though he had been in the government, for he was fiery, impetuous, disdainful of political expediency or party popularity. A towering figure of a man with a handsome broad head and great driving force, he was in many ways the antithesis of little Metaxas, but as Archer sadly concluded his diary entry, he said goodbye to the Greek War Relief Committee as one going to his death, for he was not a well man.[10] And it was true; the events of the next three months would kill him.

D'Albiac, Turle, and Heywood were most unhappy over the appointment of Koryzis, as they did not think that he had what it would take to keep Greece in the war. At the same time the orthodox D'Albiac complained about Papagos, who wished to use the RAF as flying artillery, while D'Albiac himself wished to maintain a wide-ranging, independent role for the RAF.

Papagos and Koryzis now told Heywood that the Greeks had only a two-months' supply of artillery ammunition, and Koryzis also said that he did not think that the Germans would attack Greece. If they did, outside help could not arrive in time, and the premature dispatch of an effective British force to Greece could only mean disaster.[11]

The distances spanned in the Cyrenaica campaign were now beginning to affect wireless traffic. Because of the shortage of sets, transmissions from Athens to Cairo were limited to the 0800-1200 and the 2200-0200 watches, but the latter fell into the dead time when signals would not pass because of atmospheric conditions.[12]

Meanwhile in London on 29 January Eden had a talk with the Soviet ambassador, Maisky, to try and get an assurance that if the Germans went further into the Balkans the Russians would stay neutral to Turkey; but Maisky was noncommittal. In response to a question from Maisky, Eden said that Germany's attitude to the war in Albania "was to disinterest herself in the operations there."

The next day the Foreign Office received a 24 December letter from George Rendel in Sofia, informing them that in late November and early December the British and Turkish air attachés had discussed whether or not the German use of Bulgarian bases for attacks on Greece would create a state of war. The view just before Christmas in Sofia was that this was a hypothetical question as the Germans did not wish to get involved in that part of the world and that it was "extremely dangerous for us to draw them in here as it would mean the destruction of Greece. German policy aims to neutralize the Balkans for fear of the ultimate political complications with Russia. But only 'until the Spring' as the Germans say here."

Enclosed with this letter was a copy of one written by the assistant British air attaché, S/Ldr. Aidan M. Crawley, to Air Commodore R.A. George, who was air attaché to both Ankara and Athens, in which he predicted an air attack on Greece and noted that eight to ten all-weather bases with satellites already existed in Bulgaria. Crawley went on to predict that a German air attack in the face of the very weak Greek and British air forces could devastate every town of importance in Greece, as well as road and rail junctions and RAF airfields, and all in two weeks. Greece would collapse; Yugoslavia would be isolated. In his opinion the best approach for the Turks was to attack Bulgaria as soon as the Germans started to move in, to try to seize the country first, and let winter thus save Greece for a few months.[13]

Lincoln MacVeagh cabled home from Athens that the view common in Athens was that the Turks would not move and that the Yugoslavs probably could not, and that the new prime minister thought that the ultimate German aim was the Ukraine.[14]

Late that night a Luftwaffe raid led by a former Suez Canal pilot flew from Sicily, refueled at Rhodes, and successfully dropped eleven parachute mines into the Canal and nine on the banks. As these proved to be new delayed-action acoustic-magnetic mines, they defied sweeping and wreaked havoc for thirteen days. Between the third and the sixth of

February four vessels were destroyed in the Canal and a fifth damaged, reducing the fairway from 197 feet to 85 and the permissible draught from 34 feet to 26 feet, 3 inches. Most seriously it deprived Admiral Cunningham of his only carrier, since *Illustrious* had been bombed on 10 January. *Formidable* had been ordered round from the South Atlantic via the Cape, but was held for ten days at the south end of the Canal. This meant that Cunningham had to stop worrying about Malta while he got the stopper out of the Canal. On 13 February he had Egyptian sentries placed along the whole length of it to spot falling mines as an aid in sweeping. This whole incident meant that the docks at Alexandria, the only ones equipped to handle large amounts of cargo, worked well below capacity, while a large number of vessels began to back up at Suez awaiting a place to unload; and all of this compounded the shortage of shipping. The Luftwaffe raids were effective enough to close the Canal for sixty-six days in 1941, forty-five of them while the British were aiding Greece.[15]

## 31 January 1941

Sir Stafford Cripps, the British ambassador in Moscow, reported to London that the German news bureau representative in Moscow had told the Yugoslav ambassador that Germany had no territorial ambitions in the Balkans, but that Yugoslavia would be offered Salonika and that "Greece would have to be occupied because of the British front which was being organized there; the Germans knew for a fact that there were 7 to 10,000 British motorized troops in Greece."[16]

It has never been easy to sift the kernels from the chaff in this sort of intelligence. But an understanding of German economic as well as historical interests in the area helps to explain the attitudes of both Germany and the Balkan states. The reason the British did so poorly in the area is that they had devoted little time to the Balkans, a place generally regarded as a comic or sinister backwater through which characters in Graham Greene and Agatha Christie novels passed on the Orient Express.

On this Friday in London a massive intelligence review including Enigma sources indicated that only the renewal of the invasion of the United Kingdom would give Germany the victory she so desperately needed in 1942, but the Chiefs of Staff concluded that the Germans would not make the great gamble until autumn 1941, hoping in the meantime to wear the British down at sea and in the Balkans. When she did strike, Germany would mobilize her full resources against England, which would, air intelligence concluded, mean a Luftwaffe of 14,000 aircraft. This estimate was later proved to be way too high, but, unfortunately, the Chiefs of Staff refused during February to sanction the dispatch overseas of any more armor or divisions because the air intelligence estimate gave only a three-weeks' strategic notice.[17]

The problem had been, starting in October, that the egocentric British were thinking along different lines from the Germans. When in early January intelligence in London made its first reassessment since October of German aims, it failed to envision a German attack upon Russia, making the mistake of assuming that what was logical from the British point of view was also what the Germans would see as desirable.

The Air Staff were not so much concerned with impressing the Turks as with deterring the Germans from using Bulgaria. They, therefore, wished to make the threat to the Rumanian oilfields, and they gave this a higher priority than beating the Italians in Africa. The trouble was that the Air Staff had learned nothing from the campaigns of 1940, when their efforts to bomb the German back areas had been impotent in the face of the blitzkrieg. Prewar RAF doctrine of the grand-strategic use of air power had already been visible in Athens in the arguments between D'Albiac and the Greeks over the tactical employment of his force. It was a fine theory when based on an insular set of airfields, but it was not very helpful in the face of actual battlefield necessities. The arguments about bombing the Rumanian oilfields were really vitiated by more practical considerations—there simply were neither the aircraft nor the airfields for the job, nor would Balkan winter weather permit it. On top of this, grand-strategic air power was not much use if the Germans could overrun its bases, which was exactly what Hitler intended to do.[18]

At the end of January the fate of the Middle Eastern theater hung in the balance. Wavell signaled that the taking of Benghazi was a month away, but on 5/6 February the highly mobile O'Connor was at the gates, while a flanking force had struck across the desert to cut the coastal road, closing the escape route to Tripoli. In Greece, the outnumbered Greek army under Papagos was about to start a winter offensive aimed at capturing Valona before the Germans intervened, and D'Albiac had been persuaded to use his aircraft in close support. In London it had been decided to send Eden back again to Cairo.

## 1 - 5 February 1941

The military attaché in Athens reported to the War Office that his visit to the Albanian front had revealed that Greek morale was high, but their losses of pack animals due to bad weather was from 30 to 70 percent in December and early January, while the bulk of the troop casualties were from frostbite, not the Italians.[19]

In Cairo, Wavell had once again over the weekend to deal with Churchill's incessant complaint that his administrative forces were too large, and Wavell's blunt, soldierly, telegraphic prose, was not really to

Churchill's liking: "Experience in Libya, Eritrea and East Africa continues to confirm necessity for ample rearward services. Tail in each instance is so long that it simply has to wag the dog, but you may rely on me to ask for nothing unnecessary."[20] In this respect it was especially unfortunate that Wavell and Churchill had never gotten to know each other in peacetime, and that Churchill the historian overlooked the fact that an underdog general who was a master of the art of deception and realism, whether on peacetime maneuvers or in war, would be unlikely to have a fatter tail than necessity demanded.

Wavell also got a signal from the COS that the Prime Minister had decided that the C-in-C ME's priorities should be arranged so that "steps to counter German infiltration into Bulgaria must now have the highest priority." He could go on to Benghazi as long as this could be "done without prejudice to European interests. . . . We must repeat that the Graeco-Turkish situation predominates and should have first place in your thoughts."[21]

From his own brilliant Brigadier John Shearer the C-in-C received an appraisal of the situation in southeast Europe which took the view that the Germans wanted an Italian victory in Albania to compensate for Italy's loss of prestige in North Africa, and to quiet the Balkans. "Her first objective, therefore, is likely to be the settlement of this conflict and the resumption of active trading notably in tobacco of which a large part of her requirements normally come from GREECE."[22]

It seems highly likely that Wavell, a soldier who had spent much time studying politicians and one who had been trained by Allenby in the First World War (and had long ago learned the necessity of not hinting to anyone what was in his mind), had by this time worked out his own plan. He indeed had a grand strategy for his vast theater, in which he would try to deal with an "option of difficulties," but because of faulty British intelligence, a paucity of resources, and the normal bad breaks of war, he did not quite succeed. He never revealed his plan, but we can hazard a guess as to what it was.

## 2 - 5 February 1941

In Athens the king told Heywood he thanked God that the new prime minister had no knowledge of military affairs, and he told MacVeagh that the appointment of Koryzis was his own idea, since Metaxas had always refused to discuss a successor.[23] In London L.S. Amery, a distinguished elder statesman and friend of Churchill's, proposed that the British take Tripoli, but his letter never reached high places. (After the war Wavell said that he could never have done it because of the wear and tear on his vehicles, inferior numbers, and the reluctance of the navy.)[24]

On 4 February Heywood had extended discussions with Koryzis

about the Greek arms situation in which it became plain that, since Metaxas had refused British support and the Greeks had no sources of supply for their metric weapons except captured Italian matériel, their war effort would fizzle in about sixty days.[25] At the same time Wavell flew up to Bomba in the Desert and talked with Lieutenant-General Sir Maitland ("Jumbo") Wilson, who was the military governor of Cyrenaica. Wilson was a pedestrian commander. Technically he was the mercurial, birdlike O'Connor's superior, and as long as Wavell kept his hand in things worked well.[26] O'Connor's forces were already beyond their supply line on the way to Benghazi, but Wavell and O'Connor, well supplied with decrypted information from Italian signals, decided on the bold run across the desert to cut the coastal road.[27]

On 5 February the Defence Committee decided to send the largest possible land and air forces from Africa to Greece to oppose a probable German attack through Bulgaria. In order to concert action, Eden and Dill would visit Cairo, Athens, and Ankara.[28]

Unfortunately there were several faults in this whole scheme, starting with the evolution of Churchill's sixth of January mythical four-division reserve in the Middle East into a viable force. First, there was the lack of double-checking that there was shipping available to move a force to Greece rapidly. Second, there was no solution to the Greek ammunition problem. Third, there was a failure to ensure the availability of airfields for the fourteen squadrons Longmore had specified earlier, or of the planes to use them. Palairet cabled the Foreign Office on 5 February that D'Albiac hoped that the airfields would be ready at the end of April—but that date was two months after the Germans were expected to be able to attack! And a month before that the Greeks might well be out of ammunition.

Even if troops were to be shipped out from England to the Middle East, the twelve-week voyage around Africa was so debilitating that the staff in the Middle East reckoned that the troops would need a total of three months more than if they had come through the Mediterranean, to be ready for action.[29] If these questions did not occur to those in London who were making the decisions, they did occur to the C-in-C's and their staffs in the Middle East, who made themselves unpopular by asking Whitehall if they had thought about such things. (Small wonder, then, that by mid-summer 1941 two of the three C-in-C's had been removed from active command in the Middle East, with Longmore on the road to retirement and Wavell moving into exile in India.)

Already other serious problems were developing. The Luftwaffe attacked Tobruk on the fourth and Benghazi on the eighth. The lack of small ships and of A/A defenses ashore caused the C-in-C Med' to refuse to run more than one convoy a fortnight to Benghazi, so it could not be built up as a major base. The first convoy to reach Benghazi was so heavily attacked that it retired (Tedder claimed prematurely) to Tobruk to unload. Long-more was relieved when the advance stopped, because he felt that the long lines of vehicles were far too vulnerable to air attack, and besides, he was worried about the Greek situation.[30] Aircraft arriving over the route from Takoradi were a mere trickle (less than wastage), and almost no Hurricanes had come in by sea.

About this time a change began to emerge in intelligence available in London. Though it had been known since October that the Germans planned a major campaign in the Balkans, its precise nature had not been determinable from the normal intelligence sources. It was only when the Luftwaffe began to move into the Balkans that large amounts of Enigma intelligence suddenly began to flow in. Even so, its significance was nearly lost because of lack of knowledge of the mundane: On 6-7 February, Bletchley had broken by hand methods a variant of Enigma used by the German railway administration, but only by bringing in experts from the British Railway Research Service had they been able to determine that this mass of messages dealt with movements orders and railway needs.[31]

Meanwhile, the German army, which had not fought since the June 1940 blitzkrieg, had been able to assimilate the lessons of combat, expand, and improve. What could be deployed in the Balkans was only limited in quantity or quality by the Balkan road system. On the other hand, Wavell's forces were in the midst of a series of scattered, mostly colonial, campaigns which had exhausted their men and matériel, and Wavell wished to complete the campaigns in East Africa and the Sudan before he undertook any more assignments. The 2nd Armoured Division had just arrived from England, but it had been sent out with tanks whose tracks needed replacement. The Australian-made substitutes would not work, so the division was partly equipped with captured Italian tanks. And its commander, Major-General J. Tilly, died suddenly in January.[32]

By the time Benghazi was taken on 6 February, the 7th Armoured Division had been continuously in action for eight months and it was "mechanically incapable of further action"—it had no tanks! So it had to be withdrawn and its men dispersed to other units.

Battle fatigue of a sort was surfacing elsewhere, too. Even though he was an old Etonian, the gang at the Foreign Office were getting fed up with Sir Michael Palairet by early February 1941 after at least three months of his signals and dispatches urging aid for the Greeks. Now he was sending *secret* messages in general telegrams and these were getting double distribution, as they were repeated to Sofia and Belgrade, where recipients had had to be instructed to *utterly* destroy those parts. It was decided that since many of Palairet's questions could not be given a simple reply, a short telegram should be sent to him to say they were under consideration. The staff were also irritated because Palairet, who after all had been in the Foreign Service since 1905, failed to read the copies of messages that were sent to him and went on asking questions which these repeats were intended to answer.[33]

The fifth of February was significant because the Australian prime minister arrived in the Middle East on his way to London. Menzies stayed in Cairo until 13 February discussing with Wavell the general proposal to offer a force to Greece. In the course of these discussions the six-foot Menzies got the impression that the force to be sent would amount to 200,000 men.

"Chips" Channon, a wealthy member of Parliament who had been sent as an informal emissary to encourage the Yugoslav regent, had by now arrived back in dirty, sunny Cairo from cold Belgrade and was present that evening for the cocktail party on a barge on the Nile given by General and Lady Blamey. Here he again met Lady Eugenia Wavell ("Queenie," as her husband called her), whom he liked enormously, confiding to his diary, "She is a vague, motherly, lazy, humorous creature. . . . Of course, he is altogether more charming, more cultured, more silent—a very rare bird indeed." Menzies was there, too, "jolly, rubicund, witty, only 46 with a rapier-like intelligence and gifts of a raconteur."[34]

## 6 February 1941

In London the government was as usual upset by events and changing its mind. The capture of Benghazi had come a month ahead of prediction, no doubt because Wavell was protecting himself against impatience at No. 10 Downing Street. Churchill had switched the priorities to the Balkans when early March was the date for Benghazi, but now he decided that the Italians could be cleaned out of North Africa completely if priority was returned to that area.[35]

But there were now two schools of thought on this in the Desert because of the state of the troops. When on 6 February the Italians surrendered on the coastal road, the Rifle Brigade was out of antitank ammunition and the 7th Armoured Division was down to the last 10 of its 350 tanks. Only 50 of the whole war establishment were considered salvageable, and these were being returned by sea to Alexandria for repairs. XIII Corps was regarded as exhausted.[36] Standing against these pessimists were those who argued that nothing succeeds like success, that the Italians were on the run and in a hopeless funk, and that all of North Africa was there for the taking. These included the Joint Staff Planners in Cairo, who were just putting the finishing touches to their appreciation, and also O'Connor and his staff in the Desert. In the end, waffling in London allowed the whole thing to fall flat as a pancake.

In Athens Prime Minister Koryzis was just back from a tour to the front, where he was shocked by the starving children along the road begging for food in the cold. As Laird Archer noted, few ships were getting through with any food. Most of the Greek merchant marine was in British service outside the Mediterranean and, with the Suez Canal blocked by the new German mines, there was an acute shortage of shipping within the Mediterranean and the Aegean.[37]

On Thursday, 6 February, Longmore reported from Cairo that he was using everything he had including Gauntlets, the obsolete biplane fighter predecessors of the obsolescent Gladiators, that he was 90, repeat 90, Blenheims short of his program, and that he had 32 Merlin engines in depots awaiting spares before they could be overhauled. The Mohawks were "out of sight with a major engine defect and the Tomahawks an unknown quantity. With hardly straw sufficient for bricks to meet minimum local requirements difficult to export in qty. visualized, but all preliminary preparations now in hand."[38]

At the same time Churchill sent Portal a personal minute noting that some time ago Portal had proposed offering the Turks ten squadrons while also pushing the Greeks for airfields for up to fourteen. Now it looked as if the Turks were likely to accept, and what was the CAS going to do? "I am afraid that you have got to look at this very seriously. I am in it with you up to the neck. But have we not promised to sell the same pig to two customers? . . . Nothing was said about time or priority, so we have that to veer and haul on. W.S.C." Portal replied the same day that he did not think that any pledges had been given to Greece about further squadrons. All Longmore had said to Metaxas was that he could not operate any more aircraft in Greece until more airfields were ready. After the January refusal by the Greeks of additional air and ground units, Portal did not feel that Britain was in any way bound to provide reinforcements in the future. And this was substantiated, Portal thought, by Longmore's account of his talk with Papagos on the seventeenth in which he had refused to promise any further air support at distant dates because we were anxious to avoid promises we might not be able to fulfill. But Churchill wrote across the bottom of this "Superseded by later developments. W.S.C. 11.2.41."[39]

## 7 February 1941

On this Friday the military mission in Athens reported on the likelihood of an Italian collapse in Albania, and on the Greek response if the Germans attacked. General Heywood said that, with 170 battalions in Albania plus many Fascist leaders, an Italian collapse was unlikely unless fine weather allowed the Greeks to make real progress. If the Germans attacked before the Albanian situation was cleared up, the Greeks could offer no effective resistance in Macedonia without Yugoslav participation and British assistance. As the country had not been prepared for a war against Germany, such a war would be a severe strain on morale, and resistance might only be nominal unless the king gave a strong lead. One of Heywood's assistants had talked with General Papagos, just back from the front, who believed that the Germans would go into Bulgaria but that their ability to strike then at Greece, Turkey, or Yugoslavia would be sufficient to quiet the Balkans without war: "If Germany did attack Greece, Greece would resist, but, as neither Jugo Slavia nor Turkey appeared willing to assist and Great Britain was unable to afford the necessary help, Greek resistance would be more of a political than an effective military operation and could only be short lived. He thought the German Army would not increase its glory by overrunning small nations like Greece, and, therefore, would not do so unless provoked by the arrival of British forces intended for operations against Germany."

Papagos still felt that any British reinforcement before the Germans actually crossed the Greek frontier would only provoke Germany into immediate action; he suggested that the British prepare plans based on what forces they could send, but he was not prepared to allow an officer to reconnoiter the Aliakmon position until the British knew what forces they could send to assist in holding it. Heywood concluded that Papagos was gambling that the Germans would not intervene but that, if they did, there was little he could do about it. The British officer believed that Papagos was falling for German propaganda, as had all the other small states.[40]

On the whole Papagos' assessment was right, and Heywood reported it correctly. Unfortunately Heywood's reputation had been tarnished by his failure to see the weakness of the French army in the 1930's, and so it is likely that Wavell discounted what he reported from Athens. If Wavell appears to have leaned the wrong way, assuming that the noble Greeks were stronger than they were, he was an unwitting victim of the "aura of allies" phenomenon.

Wavell's reaction on 7 February to an earlier order to send two battalions of infantry to Malta was simply that he did not have them to spare.[41] Undoubtedly the most significant signal that he received in many a day was the order received on the seventh to secure his flank in Cyrenaica and to swtich his forces to Greece. Succinct but fateful, it was arguably a major grand-strategic blunder. He obeyed it because he was a dutiful soldier.

The trouble in part was that Wavell had been too successful. His forces under O'Connor, never more than two divisions strong, had destroyed ten Italian divisions while taking 130,000 prisoners, 180 medium and 200 light tanks, and 845 guns. The small British air force had captured 91 Italian aircraft intact, and shot down 58.[42] The rest of his few divisions were either actively campaigning in East Africa, garrisoning widely scattered holdings from Iraq to Aden to Palestine, or under training.

In the past the British have blamed the switch of direction on the

Greeks. But Koryzis, as we shall see, sent no urgent plea for help. Nor was Wavell influenced by a plethora of ULTRA material. He had developed his own intelligence organization in the Middle East, including a small codes and ciphers section which worked on tactical intelligence faster than it could be sent to Bletchley Park and back.[43] It must be remembered that not until 14 March was ULTRA teletyped directly to the Middle East, and that was only three weeks before the campaign in Greece began. On that date two special cipher officers reported into BAFG headquarters in Athens to handle the materials sent there, but not until 5 April, the day before the German attack, was the British commanding officer in Greece given ULTRA and told what it was. (He was then kept supplied throughout the campaign, a fact which would seem to explain the very few serious engagements that took place before evacuation.)[44] Wavell got some UL-TRA, of which there is no trace, and of his reaction there is even less. Such messages were hand delivered by the cipher officer, signed for, read in his presence, and then destroyed. We do know that Wavell got one such message on 6 February telling him that Rommel had arrived in Tripoli, but the War Office had no file on "this obscure German officer." If the significance of the arrival of Germans in Tripoli was lost on the British, it was in part because of what Roberta Wohlstetter has called "noise"[45] and in part because the British were expecting the Italians to withdraw. They were further misled (in spite of the fact that the textbooks on blitzkrieg had been written by Wavell's friends J.F.C. Fuller and B.H. Liddell Hart) by the British view that no one could get organized in under three months. Rommel, if they had only known, was one of those unorthodox generals who felt he did not have to be bound by the rulebooks.[46]

## 8 - 9 February 1941

On the eighth intelligence came in from Sofia that the roads leading to the Struma (sometimes written Strymon) Gorge were being widened and strengthened and that it was reckoned that the Germans would need ten days to cross Bulgaria on their way to Greece.[47] In Athens it was clear that the king was interested in knowing just how many British troops could be sent to Greece, in view of the pressure from both the minister and the military mission that he accept some, but it was becoming clear, too, that neither Papagos nor Koryzis was aware that on 18 January Metaxas had refused the aid proferred. When he found out about that action, Koryzis gave the British a declaration that Greece would fight to the end, and yet also sensibly suggested that the document of 18 January should be carefully reexamined (though that is not quite how the British interpreted his request: Palairet forwarded it as a plea for help). A second note from Koryzis essentially left it up to the British to decide whether reinforcements should be sent to Greece and, if so, when.[48]

The fact that the Greek officials in Athens usually went to the British legation for meetings would seem to indicate that they either feared that their own quarters were not secure, or suffered from a built-in deference to Great Britain and its representatives, or both. On the other hand, General Papagos, as the senior officer, usually relied on military protocol and required General Heywood to visit him at his headquarters in the Hotel Grande Bretagne.

That Saturday afternoon, 8 February, Palairet had tea with the king and told him that his government ought to be strengthened by the inclusion of members of the opposition, including Venizelists, as neither Koryzis himself nor any other minister seemed ideal for their jobs. Then he wondered aloud if the army would fight the Germans, and asked bluntly whether His Majesty was satisfied with the military position and with his commanders. Although it was all done tactfully, it is said, the king's responses were mostly negative. But George II did say he trusted his commanders and was satisfied with progress in Albania.[49]

That night General Papagos sent for Heywood and said that, when he had implied that the Greeks would not ask for British help until the Germans crossed the Greek frontier, he had not known that on 18 January Metaxas had said both orally and in writing that he would appeal for British aid when the Germans crossed either the Danube or the Dobruja frontier into northern Bulgaria. Papagos now thought it probable the Germans would cross into Bulgaria at the end of February or the beginning of March, and possible courses of action in the event of German attack should be studied as quickly as possible.

There were really two choices, according to the Greek commander: if Yugoslavia came in, to hold the line along the Struma River or east of it; if they did not, to hold the Aliakmon to cover Thessaly and the rear of the army in Albania. If the British were going to send reinforcements, it was desirable to start building up stocks, supplies, and ammunition at once, but to avoid arousing German suspicions these should be delivered to the Greeks at the Piraeus and Volos, to be held for the incoming British forces.[50]

The next day the British military mission met with King George II at the legation and then reported to Wavell that the increasing German menace and the death of Metaxas had unfavorably affected the Greek nation: "The new president does not possess the personality or the pugnacious optimism of his predecessor. There is a growing feeling of doubt amongst the Greek population as to whether the Army can go on winning without Metaxas. Many people realize the strategic situation is difficult and even critical. . . . We felt it was our duty to point out to you that there was a danger that military and political situation might deteriorate rapidly and in consequence security of existing British forces in Greece might become jeopardized." The king had pointed out that it was difficult to plan without knowing what the British might send, and the military mission went on to say that it thought the information should be given.[51]

From Cairo Longmore signaled Portal that he had now given warning orders for No. 274 Hurricane and No. 45 Blenheim squadrons to withdraw to the Delta to refit and subsequently join Nos. 37 and 38 Wellington Squadrons in what he proposed to call his "Balkan Reserve." In two or three weeks he hoped to be able to withdraw two or three incomplete squadrons from Eritrea, and possibly one from Aden, refit them, and add them to the reserve. With air infiltration into Turkey now accepted, he was concerned to establish a headquarters somewhere in Greece or Turkey to control the operations of that force. He thought that the best plan was to operate the forces in Greece and Turkey as one, not to allocate squadrons to one country or the other. And what did Portal think of his appointing Tedder to the command?

To this Portal replied, with some logic, that a single headquarters below Longmore's own did not make good sense; the RAF in Greece was operating against the Italians in Albania, while the force in Turkey would only be preparing for operations against the Germans. It would be difficult for one headquarters to keep closely in touch with both the Greeks and the Turks. Moreover, if the Germans attacked Greece and the Greeks could not hold the Thracian line, then forces would have to be withdrawn either to Turkey or at least to positions south of the Lepanto-Lamia line, "if you believe that the Greeks can hold that." To have the same headquarters trying to run a retreat on the one hand and offensive operations from another country on the other would be difficult. So Portal favored leaving D'Albiac in Greece and sending Elmhirst to Turkey until the Germans attacked, when Tedder might be sent to command. Meanwhile the Turks had been promised ten squadrons and Longmore was to be prepared to send these at once if the Turks accepted. "On the other hand, Greece has been promised only one more squadron, and you should carefully avoid any further commitment. If deterrent succeeds and Germans do not advance into Macedonia, question of sending units across from Turkey to help Greece against Italy might arise, but this must be dealt with at the time."[52]

In London on the eighth the government changed its mind again and decided that Wavell should not be allowed to go on to Tripoli because he lacked air support and because, although he might be able to take it, Tripoli would be difficult to maintain. Why this was so was not entirely clear, since although convoys to there from the east would have to travel along the inhospitable Cyrenaican and Libyan coast, with protection and air cover from Crete, the shore, and Malta they should have been able to survive. And while it was true that aircraft from Tripoli could not have covered convoys coming from the west in the Narrows between Sicily and

North Africa, Malta could have been used as an advanced landing ground for such operations. This procedure would have immeasurably shortened the route from Britain and shifted the locus of the war from the eastern to the central Mediterranean. It seems fairly illogical for London to have considered mounting attacks on Pantelleria (WORKSHOP) and Sicily (INFLUX) and not to have chosen to clear the coast of North Africa. The ultimate argument against going to Tripoli advanced in London was the fallacious one that to hold it would use up the reserve needed for the Balkans.

Once it was decided that Wavell should halt at Benghazi, the question then was where the British should concentrate their forces in opposition to the Germans in Rumania. It was argued that it was logical now to follow up on Koryzis' request for a study of the size of the force the British could send to Greece. Thanks to Palairet, this request was misinterpreted in London as "a definite invitation to us to send troops," whereas it was intended only to bring about a realistic assessment, with the hope of dissuading the British from acting in their own worst interests. It was with this misapprehension in mind that the War Cabinet decided on Saturday that Eden and Dill should visit Athens to offer assistance.[53]

In London, AVM Charles Medhurst, director of plans at the Air Ministry, sent a note to the private secretary of the secretary of state for air that no promise had been made to the Greeks of fourteen RAF squadrons: Longmore in January had asked Metaxas if airfields for up to fourteen squadrons could be prepared, and it was clear that the Greeks had taken this to mean that fourteen squadrons would be sent. Medhurst concluded by noting that the most that the British had said they would send was nine.[54] At the same time a memorandum was circulating in the Foreign Office pointing out that if these airfields were to be of any use against a German attack they had to be ready long before the end of April, since everything pointed to the Germans making an early move in the Greek direction.[55] (In fact, we now know that the Germans had planned to attack on 7 February but had had to postpone the operation because of bad weather.) And in a more elegant office Cadogan noted on the eighth that the reply from the Turks was not too discouraging; they even seemed to consider a visit by Anthony Eden to Angora.[56]

In the Middle East the first inklings of the German arrival in North Africa were trickling in, and as the deputy AOC-in-C, Tedder, put it later, "Rommel had no 'Balkan mirage' to lead him astray." Because of their poor knowledge of the enemy's communications with North Africa and the fact that Rommel was an unknown, the speed of the German build-up would come as a nasty surprise to the British high command in Cairo.[57]

On 9 February, a balmy Sunday night, Chips Channon dined at Air House, sitting between Tedder and Wavell. The latter was silent and bored at first, but gradually thawed. Chips noticed that with his single eye he suffered occasionally from knocking things over. After the meal they sat in embarrassed silence listening to Churchill's broadcast, during which Wavell hid behind a door while the Prime Minister's fulsome comments upon his leadership rolled from the set. Chips was ill at ease with the forced language. Afterwards Wavell offered to drive him back to the embassy, but he had already arranged to travel with Menzies. The invitation only further put him in Wavell's palm: "I cannot get over Wavell's modesty, his lack of surface brilliance, his intellectual detachment and seeming boredom with military matters. He is on a high scale and as great as he is charming."[58]

## 10 February 1941

By 10 February Wavell had received O'Connor's response to the idea of going on to Tripoli brought back by his chief of staff, Brigadier John Harding, and had begun to feel that the long-range benefits outweighed the risks. He believed that a small force could do the job and would make an immense difference to the French in Tunisia. O'Connor, however, unlike Nelson, refused to put his earphones on the back of his head and present Cairo and London with a *fait accompli*.[59] (Interestingly, Rommel believed that if the British had attacked Tripoli before mid-April they could have succeeded.)[60]

In London on 10 February the Defence Committee agreed that Eden should go to the Middle East and support Greece, which was fighting the Axis, as opposed to Turkey, which was avoiding its obligations. This was decided in defiance of Eden's report that the Greeks would not be able to hold in the face of the Germans, and that the British did not have sufficient forces to help them, unless—and then only possibly—the Turks came in. The Defence Committee, nevertheless, decided to honor the 1939 guarantee treaty, although France was no longer a party to that obligation.[61] In a sense the Joint Planning Staff in London supported this move by recommending that Britain's best response for the moment was to subdue the Italian Dodecanese, to assist Greece, and to strengthen Crete. The next day Churchill told the C-in-C's that, failing a satisfactory agreement with the Greeks, they had to try to salvage as much as possible from the wreck, but that at all costs Crete and those Greek islands which could be used as air bases had to be held. Unfortunately, Crete, which was the linchpin of such a grand strategy, and a vital bastion of British power in the eastern Mediterranean, was never the center of policy or planning. By mid-February it should have been the base for operations against airfields on Rhodes, only seventy miles to the northeast, from which the Germans were mining the Suez Canal. Its far from exalted place in British thinking is exemplified by the fact that in six months it had six different commanders.[62]

The tenth also saw the emergence of the whole Blamey-Menzies problem. Menzies, the Australian prime minister, was told by Wavell that the "aggregation principle," under which the Australian Imperial Force was gradually accumulated and consolidated, was fine, but it should not be so rigidly applied that he could not make use of less than the whole corps when necessary, as there would not always be a front large enough for it. When Menzies told the Australian commander this the next day, Blamey, a blunt soldier who had a low opinion of Menzies anyway, said that "Australian forces must be regarded as national under national command. This does not exclude the use of smaller units in special places, but all must be subject to the consent of the G.O.C., A.I.F. If you give these British generals an inch, they'll take an ell!"[63]

Blamey was a redoubtable character who looked something like Colonel Blimp, the Australian cartoonist Lowe's famous character. In September 1938, at the time of Munich, Blamey was fifty-four and had been out of the army for thirteen years. Left in financial straits, he had taken a job as a broadcaster, and he was largely, according to his official biographer, an outcast. However, he had been chief of staff on the Western Front from May 1918 to the end of the war, when Sir John Monash commanded the Australian Corps, and after the war as a general he had kept active as a militia officer. Thus several men in high places had their eyes on him after Munich, and Sir Frederick Sheddon, the secretary to the War Cabinet in Canberra, got the Cabinet to make him chairman of the Manpower Committee. Blamey had a reputation as a drinker, which probably did not count against him in Australia, and he had a powerful personality and the ability to talk even a hostile prime minister like J.A. Lyons into his camp. In April 1939, when Menzies succeeded to power, he supported Blamey, who on 28 September 1939 was appointed as GOC 6th Division. At 5 feet, 6-1/2 inches, with dark hair turning grey and a clipped mustache, Blamey gave the impression of being taller than he was. When he was appointed to command the Australian forces, he had his charter drawn up by the best legal minds down under, because he had acute memories of Gallipoli and France, where he had had firshand experience of how the British treated colonials. In this distrust he was quite right. One of his first rows with the British in Palestine and Egypt was over the presence of his wife; it was quite silly, considering that the British had their own wives along.[64]

## 11 - 12 February 1941

On Tuesday the planning for OPERATION LUSTRE, as the expedition to Greece was misnamed, began. At ten that morning, when General Dorman Smith, sent back by O'Connor to plead with Wavell for permission to go on, walked into Wavell's office, the walls were hung with maps of

Greece. The C-in-C ME greeted him with his quiet smile, saying, "You'll find me busy with my Spring campaign." While he listened to Smith, Wavell arranged the pencils on his desk in neat drill formations.[65]

Wavell had just signaled the CIGS that aid to Greece or Turkey was limited not so much by reserves as by shipping and escorts. This signal crossed the one from the Chiefs of Staff saying that their review showed he should send the four-division reserve. To this Wavell responded that the following reserves were available at the present: one armored brigade group and the New Zealand Division of two brigades only; by mid-March there would be another brigade group, the New Zealand Division would be complete, and there would be one Australian division of two brigades only. But all of this was dependent upon the arrival of equipment then in passage and on progress in East Africa. The administrative and base units then on their way out in convoys would be sufficient, but all the A/A units would only give a low-scale protection in Greece. Moreover, medium support artillery was in a low scale. The major limiting factor was likely to be shipping, which would also affect the building up of a reserve of supplies and ammunition at the Greek ports. (It was obviously inadvisable to stock large reserves at Salonika if this was unlikely to be held.)[66]

Another puzzle still bothered the Foreign Office in London: did the ten squadrons for Turkey come out of the fourteen squadrons that Longmore had promised Greece? "It certainly would be useful to get this point cleared up," wrote a Foreign Office staffer, to which Eden added a note to the effect that the Greeks obviously thought they were getting the eight additional squadrons. Another hand added, "This is disturbing. I had understood when we offered ten squadrons to Turkey that the Greeks had refused to prepare aerodromes for which we had asked near Salonika. Clearly this is not so. We shall have to find some squadrons for them from somewhere."[67]

Over at the War Office the director of military operations, Kennedy, was joyfully noting that Greece was "still refusing our aid and we at the General Staff think we are well out of it." In the comfortable Old War Office Building, Dill, that unimpressive, charming person, as Cadogan called him, was trying to get Kennedy sent to the Mediterranean in his stead, but Churchill would have none of it. Dill in his nice rational way was also trying to tell the Prime Minister that the troops in the Middle East were fully employed, and that none were available for Greece. Churchill, who had made up the four-division Middle East reserve in his own mind, lost his temper and said that what the Middle East needed was a good court-martial. Dill told Kennedy later that he should have said, "And who do you want to shoot?"[68]

That afternoon the director of military intelligence gave the Defence Committee a timetable, sent by the military attaché in Sofia, for the German invasion of Yugoslavia and Greece. It was to start on 17 February with the move into Bulgaria, arrive at the Greek frontier by 12 March, and reach Salonika on 24 March. Ten divisions would then march down through Greece to Athens between mid-April and mid-May. Given this schedule, there was time to render help; and so this was the basis for the decision to stop the advance to Tripoli and switch the forces to northern Greece.[69] But the shipping problem remained.

The DMI's assessment was made three days after the first Germans left Naples for Sicily, but it was eleven days before the British woke up to the reason why the convoys between Naples and Tripoli were being escorted by the German air force. Nor did they put two and two together when heavy air transport flights were also observed. Because British thinking had been preconditioned to the idea that the Italians would evacuate, it never occurred to them that the Germans might be sending in reinforcements. It was not until HQ ME signaled contact with Germans on the ground on 22 February that the awful truth dawned in London, and even so German broadcasts were dismissed as propaganda until 27 February.[70]

From Athens on 12 February Heywood told Dill and Wavell that Papagos had reported that, in response to Wavell's queries about the Greek reaction to a German attack, he was forming a new division of two infantry regiments and a mountain artillery regiment to be stationed at Edessa-Veria, and erecting supply depots at Florina, Corowits (Amyndeon), Kosani, and Kastoria. He intended to renew the offensive in Albania on the thirteenth, though a serious problem was Italian superiority in the air. He had appealed personally to the AOC-in-C ME, and asked Heywood to appeal also to Dill and Wavell, for all possible air reinforcements. Sent a copy of this the next day, Churchill demanded, "Please report on all possibilities. W.S.C."[71] At the same time Heywood was ordered to arrange passage on RAF transport on the thirteenth so as to be in Cairo on the fifteenth.[72]

In an air-raid shelter in Athens Lincoln MacVeagh had a long talk with the king on the night of the eleventh. His Majesty said that he regarded the German attack against Greece as "overwhelmingly probable," and that to oppose such a stab in the back Greece had now only three divisions. The British had so far only proposed sending one artillery regiment to Salonika. Turkey's attitude was undetermined, and Yugoslavia showed "the lethargy of a rabbit faced by the snake which will devour it." The king's plan was, therefore, to shorten the Albanian line and to move some troops to oppose the Germans. He asked for complete secrecy, as only the C-in-C, himself, and the staff knew of this. He declared that "no less than Finland, this country is fighting in civilization's front line." After three months not to have gotten planes from the United States was heartbreaking. The December 1940 statement of the British Purchasing Commission that the British had 400 planes helping

Greece, when in fact there were now only 32, "is shocking." He went on to tell MacVeagh—with admirable restraint, in the ambassador's phrase—"I realize England's desperate need for supplies, but the 30 or 60 planes that we need quite as desperately won't break the British Empire."[73]

The Prime Minister on 12 February cabled Wavell his congratulations on the Cyrenaican campaign and then went on, "Defence Committee considered whole situation last night, comprising extremely favourable developments in United States supplies. . . . Undoubted serious probability of attempt invasion here. In this general setting we must settle Mediterranean plans. . . . Your major effort must now be to aid Greece and/or Turkey. This rules out any serious effort against Tripoli, although minor demonstrations thitherwards would be a useful feint. You should therefore make yourself secure at Benghazi and concentrate all available forces in the Delta in preparation for movement to Europe."

He went on to say that he was afraid that Greece and Turkey would make the mistake of the Low Countries and fool away their chances of combined resistance. The Greeks were obviously the ally most needing support at the moment and must have some idea of fighting the Germans: "If they have a good plan it would be worth our while to back it with all our strength and fight the Germans in Greece, hoping thereby to draw in both Turks and Yugoslavs. You should begin forthwith plans and timetables as well as any preparatory movements of shipping. . . . It is not intended that you delay Mandibles which we regard as most urgent."

Churchill then announced that he was sending out the Foreign Secretary and the CIGS to undertake discussions in Cairo, Athens, and Ankara. "It is hoped that at least four divisions, including one armoured division, and whatever additional air forces the Greek airfields are ready for, together with all available munitions, may be offered in the best possible way and in the shortest time. . . . We must at all costs keep Crete and take any Greek islands which are of use as air bases. We could also reconsider the advance on Tripoli. But these will only be consolation prizes after the classic race has been lost. There will, of course, always remain the support of Turkey."[74]

In their supplemental signal containing what Churchill called "operative orders," the Chiefs of Staff told the commanders-in-chief that "the only way to make sure that the Turks do fight is to give sufficient support to the Greeks to ensure that they fight." And they went on to suggest that now that the ten RAF squadrons did not have to go to Turkey; they could be sent instead to Greece. They wanted the British forces landed at Salonika, but thought that the Piraeus was going to have to be accepted. In addition they stressed the need to occupy at once the Greek islands of Mytilene, Lemnos, and Levithia in order to keep the passage open to the Straits. The C-in-C's were to collect shipping and have timetables ready for discussion by the time Eden and Dill reached Cairo.

Churchill laid down that Eden should do everything in his power to aid Greece, including if necessary slowing down the campaigns in East Africa and the Mediterranean except for the Dodecanese. According to the Cabinet minutes, "The governing principle stated by the Prime Minister was to secure the highest form of war economy in the armies and air forces of the Middle East for all the above purposes and to make sure the many valuable military units in that theatre fitted into a coherent scheme and pulled their weight."[75]

## 13 - 14 February 1941

Knowing that Heywood was going to Cairo to see Wavell, Papagos called him in and gave him a briefing on the Greek estimates of a German attack. The Greek staff estimated that the Germans had twenty divisions with 400 aircraft in Rumania, and the staff calculated that they could concentrate seven to eight of those on the Greek frontier twelve days after crossing the Danube. To meet this threat the Greeks had 10,000 frontier troops backed by three divisions. Though the Greeks had frontier defenses, these could easily be turned, and Papagos' guess was that the Germans would strike with impunity through Yugoslav territory and be in Salonika within twenty-four to forty-eight hours. The most economical line to hold was that along the Vardar, but it meant giving up Salonika or the line from the mouth of the Aliakmon to Veria, Edessa, and Kajmakalan. His problem was whether to defend the frontier or to withdraw to the Vardar. The latter was more logical, but impossible for reasons of internal policy. He considered, therefore, that he had to defend the frontier while preparing to hold the Aliakmon Line, and that it was essential that that position be held for twenty to twenty-five days to give time to withdraw his forces from Albania. "He reckoned that we could count on having 25-30 days from the time the Germans crossed the Danube before they could arrive in any strength opposite the ALIAKMON position. We have to consider, therefore," Heywood's report continued, "what can be done in one month, remembering that once SALONIKA is gone the two Northern Corps in ALBANIA, which are supplied by the SALONIKA-FLORINA railway, will have to be supplied by M.T. [Motor Transport]."[76]

On this Thursday, 13 February, Wavell cabled that he thought he could do better than he had proposed, as Menzies was agreeable and Wavell expected the Australians to make some more concessions. Menzies had talked with Blamey, but they had not discussed the idea of using the Australians in Greece, and when Churchill's directive arrived on the twelfth, Blamey was in Cyrenaica at I Australian Corps headquarters. And Menzies left for England before they did discuss it. Later Wavell told Eden that Major- General Freyberg, of the New Zealand forces, was prepared to go ahead in Greece, but that Blamey had not been consulted.

Blamey wrote Percy Spender, minister for the army in Canberra, on the twelfth that his views had not been sought; he was simply instructed. When he asked what additional formations would be available, he was told perhaps an armored division at an unknown date. He told Wavell that he considered the enterprise "most hazardous." To Spender he wrote that neither Dill nor Wavell appreciated the German ability to improve communications in Greece rapidly, or the German strength in the air. Blamey concluded that as action was going to take place, adequate forces should be provided as rapidly as possible.[77]

On the eve of Dill's departure from London, he and the DMO, Kennedy, had a long talk and agreed that the government was trying to cram an unsound policy down Wavell's throat, and down those of the Greeks and Turks also. It was playing the German game to get involved on the Continent again. Moreover, Dill and Kennedy did not accept the argument that Britain's prestige would suffer in America if she backed out now, and that Lend-Lease might not pass Congress, for they felt that Britain's prestige would suffer far more if she failed in Greece as they were sure she would. Dill was surprised that Portal and Pound, the First Sea Lord, favored the idea. Churchill considered Portal to be the real strategist among the Chiefs of Staff, and Portal's idea was to use Greece as a platform to bomb Rumania and Italy.[78] (This latter was a revival of the cockeyed prewar strategic thought of basing the RAF in the Low Countries to bomb Germany, regardless of retaliation.)[79]

According to Sir John Colville, Churchill's personal secretary, the two members of the Chiefs of Staff Committee left behind in England were both similar and different. Both were reticent and observant, but they were otherwise dissimilar. Sir Dudley Pound, who would die in harness, had a long, straight nose, a pointed chin, and deep-set eyes. He appeared lethargic, but—courageous, matter-of-fact, and with a fine mind—he was willing to oppose Churchill and take great risks to support Wavell. He had a wry sense of humor. Sir Charles Portal was tall and slim, with streaky, untidy, receding hair. He never volunteered any information or an opinion unless asked. He ate alone daily at the Travellers' Club in Pall Mall except when ordered to have his meal with the secretary of state or the Prime Minister. He understood and sympathized with Churchill, and dominated everyone in the Air Ministry and the RAF except his eventual successor at Bomber Command, Sir Arthur Harris.[80]

February in England is not always the best time for flying, and so it proved in 1941. Eden and Dill, Eden's parliamentary private secretary, Ralph Stevenson, and Pierson Dixon of the Southern Department of the Foreign Office, together with Dill's aide Brigadier Mallaby, traveled down by train to Poole on 12 February, where they found the weather too bad for their Sunderland to take off, and so there they sat, incognito. On the thirteenth it was too bad to land at Gibraltar, and they did not finally get away until just before midnight on the fourteenth, the day Menzies, Colonel Donovan, and Chips Channon left Cairo for London. They then ran into more bad weather, and the pilot is reputed to have said that he doubted if they could make Gibraltar: they would have to make a choice between Tangier or the Spanish coast, either of which might mean internment for the duration. It was decided to try for Gibraltar and hope that if they had to come down at sea they would be rescued by a patrol from the Rock. Five and a half hours later they landed at Gibraltar with what the pilot said was ten minutes' fuel left (though actually it turned out to be more like an hour's supply). At any rate it was a good enough story to repeat to Col. Raymond Lee when they got back in April.[81]

Eden and Dill were then delayed in Gibraltar for several days. They discussed the danger of attack by the Axis, talked among themselves about future actions in the Near East, and dispatched signals to Middle East Headquarters. And they opened and digested Churchill's sealed orders, which, in the best naval tradition, Eden had been forbidden to read until en route. These read, " . . . First, to send speedy succour to Greece against a German attack. Second, to make both Turks and Yugo-Slavs fight or do the best they can. Third, to provide for necessary help to Turkey in case Germany attacks her." While MANDIBLES should be executed at the earliest possible moment, it should not delay assistance to Greece, and it might be necessary to leave the Italians in Ethiopia to rot in order to find the necessary forces.

"Anglo-Greek operations must aim at establishing a defensive front which will have a reasonable chance of withstanding or at least checking a German attack. . . . It may well be necessary to establish the line further south perhaps, covering Athens and the Morea. In any event it will be necessary to hold the Greek Islands. . . . A possible alternative means of helping Greece is by Anglo-Turkish operations in Thrace. . . . Meanwhile, whatever plan is adopted, it will be necessary to send to Greece air reinforcements at the earliest date by which aerodromes are ready for them."[82]

Eden and Dill agreed that aid to Greece would depend on Greek plans and the rate of movement to Greece of British forces. Limitations were the garrisoning of Cyrenaica, the earliest possible inception of OPERATION MANDIBLES, and the urgent need to finish the campaign in Eritrea. On the alternative plan, an Anglo-Turkish operation in Thrace, Wavell should seek the opinion of General Marshall-Cornwall, as the new commander of British troops in Egypt had had extensive experience in Thrace as a boundary commission member in 1924-1925.

On 13 February in London, conversations between the Foreign Office staff and the Greek counselor seemed to show that Prime Minister Koryzis was changing his mind. While on the one hand he was adhering absolutely to Metaxas' January declaration to the effect that the Greek government would appeal to the British for aid as soon as the Germans crossed into Bulgaria, rather than waiting until they reached the Greek frontier, on the other hand Koryzis thought the two general staffs should discuss the matter. It was puzzling that the Greeks wanted to wait until the Germans committed an actual act of aggression, which meant waiting too long. The Greek counselor said he thought Koryzis hoped that the Germans would stop in Bulgaria, but Cadogan said that that was not likely.[83] On the same day Portal told the Prime Minister that Longmore already had the authority to send aid to Greece, and that he had been told that he could go ahead and draw on the ten mythical squadrons allocated to aid Turkey to do this.[84]

On Valentine's Day Admiral Cunningham signaled the Admiralty on the difficulties of operations in the Aegean in the face of German aircraft operating out of Bulgaria, and especially his concern with magnetic and acoustic mines, for which he had inadequate counterforces. And he concluded, "If I can feel sure more anti-mine resources are actually on their way more risks can be taken at Egyptian and Libyan ports so as to provide something for Greek ports. But it would be illusory to embark on this new undertaking without facing facts that mine risks are considerable and that my reserves for combating them are extremely slender."[85]

The commanders-in-chief in Cairo told London on 14 February that they felt they had to go on record, in spite of the later arrival of an additional signal from the COS, that they were overstretched and that London seemed not to understand that they could not undertake operations in all directions until reinforcements and equipment promised actually arrived and were available for operations in the theater. Until MANDIBLES was carried out and the Axis menace in the Dodecanese Islands was eliminated, defensive forces had to be kept in the Delta and especially to safeguard the Suez Canal, at that moment closed by mines, as well as to guard the Benghazi area against increasing German air activities from Tripoli and Sicily. Longmore also told Portal that he was so short of medium bombers that he was probably going to have to convert some squadrons with Tomahawks. He could not supply all ten squadrons promised the Turks or anyone else because he did not have them. Moreover he was in urgent need of more long-distance communications aircraft and wondered if another six Lockheed Lodestars could be acquired from the United States. (To this Portal replied on the fifteenth that there were 79 Blenheim IV's and 6 Glenn Martins at sea, and 19 Blenheim IV's and 23 Glenn Martins at Takoradi, and that Longmore would know the numbers en route between Takoradi and Egypt. They would look into communications aircraft. On the nineteenth Air Chief Marshal Sir Christopher Courtney, the air member for supply and organization, told Longmore that he might be able to send out a few twin-engined transports for BOAC and 16 Bombays; he hoped that these would help.)[86]

On 14 February, ME HQ prepared an order of battle for the GHQ Overseas Reserve. This was eventually to consist of one corps of three infantry divisions and one armored division, but for the present, HQ had to consider what units were available then, what would be available in mid-March, and what would become available after that date. To be included at some time would be the New Zealand and 7th and 9th Australian divisions. The whole order of battle was to be ready by noon on that day, as the C-in-C required it for a conference early on the fifteenth.[87] (Wavell would have presented this to Eden on Saturday, 15 February, if the latter had arrived on time.)

On Valentine's Day in London Cadogan—noted in his diary—it sounds like the best British music-hall tradition that he gave the Bulgarian minister a lecture and told him that his country must fight! Poor Sir Alexander, the Bulgarians had long since been in the German pocket. In Greece the Greek high command moved from their long-time command post at Janina to the area of Grevena-Kozani, in order to be in a better position to face the Germano-Bulgarian threat.

## 15 - 16 February 1941

On the fifteenth Ankara wired that the Axis ambassadors there said that Germany would soon face a settlement of the Graeco-Italian war. The Italian minister said that the Germans would advance in the Balkans, as British help to Greece was beyond allowable bounds. Beneath this someone at the Foreign Office scrawled "tittle-tattle."[88]

The headquarters of the 1st Australian Corps had just moved out into the Desert, and General Blamey went with it. He did not at that time know of the decision to go to Greece. The next day he lunched at Barce with Jumbo Wilson and was told to report to Wavell in Cairo; he rode back after lunch with O'Connor, whom he had just succeeded in the Desert command.[89]

In England Sir John Kennedy went down to spend the weekend with Churchill and was summoned at the unusually early hour, for Winston, of 10:30 on Sunday morning to hear a three-hour discourse on what was wrong with Dill. The CIGS' great failing, Churchill said, was that he allowed his mind to be impressed by the enemy's will. Churchill did not argue with Kennedy when he gave his own views of the Balkans; he merely brushed them aside. So as soon as Kennedy got back to the office on Monday he dictated a long memorandum for the record on this conversation, which is reproduced in full in his memoirs. The gist of it was that Britain could hardly be too strong at home, and that all of her strategy had to be directed to safeguarding her sea communications. "An immediate measure in which the Army can assist is the seizure of Tripoli." And that was the view of the general staff. Otherwise, Britain must not throw away its power of offensive action by an unsound strategy in the Middle East, where the real bastion of its position was Turkey. And, Kennedy concluded, "It is essential to cling to things that matter, and not to waste our strength on things that are not vital to our strategy."[90]

## 17 February 1941

On Monday the Turks, having learned that the Yugoslavs had been talking to the Germans in Vienna, signed a nonaggression agreement with the Bulgarians which allowed the Germans to deploy behind the Bulgarians provided they did not go within fifty kilometers of the Turkish frontier.

Wavell reported to the War Office conversations which General Marshall-Cornwall, who had been sent from Egypt on a special mission to Turkey with Air Vice Marshal Thomas Elmhirst, had held in Turkey. The officers' impression was that the Turks expected eventually to fight on the British side, but thought they would do better by procrastinating to improve their material position. They considered the offer of ten squadrons a drop in the bucket in the face of the 1,500 German aircraft in Rumania and Bulgaria that could be deployed against them; they claimed they needed 1,300 aircraft to assure their frontier and communications across the Straits to Anatolia. An extremely heated argument had developed in Ankara between Marshal Çakmak and the Turkish delegation on the one side, and Marshall-Cornwall and Elmhirst on the other. Both British officers spoke Turkish from long association with the area, and knew many of their verbal opponents well. But they had to report to Wavell that, in spite of lacing their arguments with examples from the Battle of Britain and the Libyan campaign and pointing out that the Germans would be just as much hampered by the lack of airfields as the Turks were, they had made no impression with their contention that five RAF fighter squadrons (sixty aircraft) would be a sufficient addition to the Turkish air force. But at least one beneficial result of the discussion was that the Turks realized the urgent necessity for expanding the number of airfields and letting the RAF establish and improve bases at Ismir and Kilia. At this time London said that if the Turks would not accept complete units, then they should not get equipment, as the British would then lose control over it and it would not be available for Greece.[91]

A proposal had been made in London on 14 February to send out a division in Convoy WS-7 without its 15,000 administrative troops, because with the capture of Benghazi the Middle East did not now need so many people on the lines of communications. Now, on 17 February, Wavell sent a personal message to the secretary of state for war to the effect that the proposal did not make good sense: the fall of Benghazi had only released some transport units, and advanced bases had to be established there and at Tobruk, while the work of supply and ordnance services was spread over a wide area. "Operations in the Balkans will mean establishment of one or more bases and advanced bases, much engineer work, road construction, etc. Balkans is notoriously unhealthy area in summer and it would be folly to weaken medical services or allow scale of reinforcements to be reduced. . . . Operations in the Balkans against German troops will require full artillery support. Arrival of additional division would emphasize lack of supporting corps troops. We are already 3,000 signallers under establishment and recent operations have been hampered by this shortage." Therefore, as much as he wanted another division, he refused it in favor of the administrative personnel already agreed upon. He then indicated what effect cuts would have, pointing out that he could not tolerate "any reduction of artillery in view of present shortage and as the Australians have no Corps artillery." All told he could only see cuts of 5,076 administrative troops and possibly 2,000 infantry.[92] At about the same time Hitler announced the formation of the Deutsch Afrika Korps.[93]

Also on the seventeenth Major-General Bernard Freyberg, V.C., was told that the New Zealand Division would be the advanced guard of the troops going to Greece. Freyberg was upset. He thought Wavell had gone over his head and bypassed his charter, which gave him the right to consult his own government, but actually the fault lay in London, where Eden had suggested the arrangement to Churchill; the latter had gotten the Dominions Office to get the permission of the New Zealand government, which assumed that Freyberg had been consulted.[94]

The respected Australian official historian, Gavin Long, wrote that Wavell's notes showed his unhappiness with the Greek plan. With Greece and Turkey politically hesitant, to say nothing of the Yugoslavs, the British were going to be put in a difficult situation. The military objective in the Balkans was, Wavell noted, purely defensive for the present, and it was likely to be a long time before this could be an offensive front, so that it should get the minimum force. But if it became an offensive area (as eventually it was in the First World War), the British would need Salonika and the Bulgarian passes to be able to hit the Rumanian oilfields. "Unfortunately," the C-in-C wrote, "our forces are very limited and it is doubtful if they can arrive in time." The use of the Aliakmon Line would help. He had told Menzies, when the Australian passed through, that his headquarters suspected that the Greeks would not hold against the Germans. Though regular convoys were arriving from the United Kingdom, they carried mostly depot units, equipment, and reinforcements; except for the ill-equipped 2nd Armoured Division, no fighting units had reached the Middle East since the fall of France. Freyberg was upset enough after his talk with Wavell that he told his New Zealanders going to Greece that everything was still makeshift: "The strategy behind the move to Greece was fundamentally unsound." And though the troops were issued pith helmets and mosquito nets, the Cairo bootblacks and Greek restaurateurs told them they were going to Greece. And indeed they were soon boarding small, overcrowded ships for the voyage north in early March.[95]

To the west Eden and Dill were still delayed in Gibraltar, as it was too rough for the Sunderland to take off. Dill proposed that if they could reach Malta they should then proceed in a Martin Maryland, but the only one there was too badly needed for photographic reconnaisance to be available for courier duties. So they remained at the Rock, where they had been visited the day before by Sir Samual Hoare, the ambassador at Madrid.

Ironically that same day Cadogan repeated his music-hall act and lectured the Yugoslav minister in London on his failure to get together with the Turks, as the only hope for the Balkans lay in creating a bloc.[96] Meanwhile just a short walk up Whitehall on the Thames-side in the Old War Office Building, Sir John Kennedy was noting in his diary that the Germans had twenty to twenty-five divisions in Rumania and would move south through Bulgaria in late March or early April, as soon as the weather permitted. A political front in the Balkans was useless without a military one, but the Greek case was hopeless and in one month their four divisions would suck up all Britain's ammunition reserves in the Middle East. As far as he was concerned, Britain should be prepared to lose anything that was put into Greece for political reasons, and she would lose so much that she would not be able to keep up the Middle East offensives or defend Egypt.[97]

## 18 - 19 February 1941

On the eighteenth Blamey met again with Wavell and was gloomy from the start about the Greek expedition. Three days earlier he had warned Menzies that 1942 was going to be the big year for the war on land, if the army was not forced to fight piecemeal in places like the Balkans.[98] At their meeting Wavell outlined the plan to the Australian commander, who said that the 6th rather than the 7th Australian division ought to go, as it was better trained.

Not far from Cairo the Germans successfully mined the Suez Canal once more on 18 February and again four days later, closing it until 8 March.

For the RAF, the wing commander, Administrative Plans, produced a paper showing the provisional schedule of reinforcements and shipping for the RAF in Greece, which included a rough order of battle. This envisaged three squadrons being sent by 15 March and six by 15 April.

His estimate was that by 15 April there would be six fighter, seven bomber, two heavy bomber, and two army cooperation squadrons available for Greece, a total of seventeen, but airfield space for only fourteen. In Greece D'Albiac was arranging for the gradual remounting of his fighter squadrons on Hurricanes.[99]

Meanwhile in London the Foreign Office had heard in a roundbout way from the Poles that the Greek Foreign Office had on 8 February said that the war in Albania had to be terminated because of the situation in the Balkans, where British help would be too limited: the RAF had already been sent back from Greece to Libya. The Air Ministry pointed out that it was true that one squadron had been withdrawn to Libya, but that had been because of the weather, which made the Greek airfields unusable.[100] Cadogan noted that various telegrams showed that unless the British could make a really good show in the Balkans they would be better off cleaning up in Africa.[101]

Planning for the movement of the LUSTRE forces to Greece was proceeding apace in Cairo. A meeting was held at 3:30 on 19 February in "G" Conference Room to coordinate sailing priorities of force, corps, base, and lines of communication units in proportion to the fighting troops of the first three flights of Phase I and the first three of Phase II. For planning purposes LUSTRE was assumed to consist of one armored and three infantry divisions, with each flight to consist of 8,400 personnel and 1,200 vehicles proceeding at two- to three-day intervals with an additional two days between the third and fourth flights. The total at this stage would amount to 50,400 men and 7,200 vehicles. Units were then placed on twelve-hours notice to move to Greece, with movements prepared to begin as soon as 21 February or as late as 21 March.[102]

Eden and Dill finally got away from Gibraltar and passed through Malta and Crete, landing late in the evening on the Nile at Cairo, where they were met by Longmore and Hutchinson. It had taken them twenty-nine hours from Gibraltar.

In London on that Wednesday the Foreign Office staff was discussing the possible Greek collapse and what it would mean. These effects were divided between the strategic consequences, which were the concern of the Chiefs of Staff, and the political ones, which were in the realm of the Foreign Office. It was concluded that it would be best, to avoid total collapse and the appearance that siding with Britain was fatal, that the Greek government be persuaded to move to Crete and carry on the war from there. Greek troops not needed in the islands could be used to garrison Cyrenaica. Certainly a "Greek Dunkirk" was seen as very likely and needed to be planned for at once.

So Sir Alexander Cadogan dictated and sent to Churchill, then also acting foreign secretary, a memorandum on the pros and cons of a Balkan expedition. He pointed out the need to get General Weygand, the Vichy commander in Tunisia, into the British camp, and noted that the word from Vichy was that Pétain was delaying negotiations with the Germans in the hopes that the British Army of the Nile would take Tripoli and arrive victorious on the borders of Tunisia; such an event might impel Weygand into action. Unless a German advance into the Balkans could be held, Britain would lose there anyway, said Cadogan, while on the other hand victory in Tripolitania would eliminate the Italians in Africa for the most part, possibly stiffen the French in North Africa, and allow the British to undertake counter-infiltration. He realized that a change of policy would be embarrassing for Eden, now on his way to Athens and Ankara, and that it might be thought cynical to abandon Greece, but he feared that nowadays one had to do that. Moreover, he had a nasty feeling that the Germans wanted to entice the British into the Balkans to destroy them there, while there were signs that the Germans were apprehensive about their success in North Africa. "If by any chance we do abandon Greece we should have to explain to America, as you will remember that Colonel Donovan was very insistent on our retaining a foothold in the Balkans (but can we?)"

Churchill replied the same day that it was impossible to advance to Tripoli without taking the forces needed for effective aid to Greece and Turkey. All the points Cadogan had raised had been considered by the COS and by himself and were not to be denied. "It may well be that neither Turkey nor Greece could accept our aid, judging it the offer of a 6-foot plank to bridge a 10-foot stream. If however Greece resolves to resist the German advance, we shall have to help them with whatever troops we can get there in time. They will not I fear be very numerous." The alternative was a separate Greek peace, and that might well happen.[103]

## 20 February 1941

While Eden and Dill were in Cairo, probably on the twentieth, the director of military intelligence there, Brigadier E. J. Shearer, sent up a paper which showed the very great dangers of a campaign in Greece. It was returned with a note, "War is an option of difficulties—Wolfe. A.P.W." De Guingand has said that the staff questioned this judgment. John Connell, in his biography, says that Wavell wrote across Shearer's appreciation that it was better to be active than passive, and to go to Greece, provided there was a good chance of being able to establish a front there against the Germans.[104] The decision was based upon locally available intelligence, as Wavell got little ULTRA from London until after 13 March. Eden and Dill thus brought tremendous confirmatory evidence to an assessment based upon meager intelligence.[105]

On 19 February Marshall-Cornwall had returned sick from Turkey and had a long conversation with Wavell, who told him with a heavy heart that he had decided to go to Greece. Marshall-Cornwall was horrified and said it was a gamble that could only lead to military disaster. Wavell replied, very slowly, that strategy was only the handmaiden of policy, and here political considerations must come first. "The policy of our Government is to build up a Balkan front." The next day, sick as he was, Marshall-Cornwall was called in to see Eden, who insisted that he make greater efforts to get the Turks into the war and was astonished when Wavell and Longmore both supported the Turkish-speaking general's arguments that Turkey would be more of a liability than an asset, with her bow-and-arrow army. The next day Marshall-Cornwall went into the hospital, where he was looked after by the Wavell's oldest daughter, Pamela, who was a nursing sister. [106]

Connell, Wavell's official biographer (who, in spite of recent family denials that such papers existed, worked from Wavell's own manuscript on the Greek affair), says that Wavell had made an early military appreciation which recognized the risks in the Balkans, the wastage of shipping, and the Cyrenaican problem, but which came to the conclusion that to save Salonika would put new heart into Greece, Yugoslavia, and Turkey; the effort might force the Germans to fight, where they hoped to make a peaceful penetration, and so would make it more difficult for the Germans to exploit the corn and oil of southeast Europe. Not to act, Wavell argued, would lose Britain almost as much prestige as defeat, and it would end the chance of gaining Yugoslavia and Turkey as allies, put fresh heart into the Italians, and render the whole Mediterranean more difficult. He believed that the Axis forces could not counterattack in Cyrenaica because they did not have control of the sea and were short of transport for an advance from Tripoli to Cyrenaica. He, therefore, concluded that the British would more likely be playing the enemy's game by being inactive than by taking action in the Balkans: "Providing the conversations with the Greeks show that there is a good chance of establishing a front against the Germans with our assistance, I think we should take it." Wavell now saw the problem as one of finding the means to implement the choice he had already made between two sets of "difficulties." [107]

(Dill appended a note to his official diary about Wavell's appreciation, and Eden mentions that he only saw it after he got back to England in April. [108] I have never been able to locate this analysis. It is in neither the Dill nor the Avon (Eden) papers. It may just be lost, or it could have been deliberately misfiled by being placed in some harmless folder called up from the registry and innocently returned slightly thicker than when received, or pushed out the back of a drawer and ever since stuck in the CIGS' old desk—all possibilities suggested by J.F.C. Fuller's experiences in the War Office.)

Another of the peculiar things about the background of the British decision was that de Guingand wrote to Heywood's GSO-1, Colonel Salisbury-Jones, that he never could find in Cairo the reports that he had sent from Athens on the talks with Papagos and the unhappy factors in the Greek situation.[109] It is not clear if de Guingand meant talks that he, or Salisbury-Jones, or Heywood had with Papagos. It is not clear either whether or not Wavell had those papers at one time. (I know they existed because I have a set.) What *is* clear is that Cairo had sufficient information upon which to base an accurate appreciation.

On 20 February Heywood drew up in Cairo a seven-page memorandum, including a map of the Yugoslav situation, entitled "APPRECIATION OF THE SITUATION IN MACEDONIA WITH REFERENCE TO POSSIBLE GERMAN ATTACK ON GREECE." This pointed out that the combined German-Italian forces available to be brought against Greece from Rumania and Albania totaled more than fifty divisions, plus fourteen Bulgarian divisions then three-fourths mobilized; against this, Greece had perhaps twenty divisions. Within the next two months the British were assumed to have available one armored division and three infantry divisions "with a low scale of Anti-Aircraft, Anti-Tank and Medium Artillery." To these might be added sixteen to twenty-four Yugoslav divisions, not fully mobilized, and forty Turkish divisions. The report then described briefly the primitive state of the ground and the prevalence of malaria: "The mountainous nature of the country and the paucity of communications make the ground on the whole unfavourable to the employment of mechanized forces, . . . [whose] operations must be confined to the plains. The prevalence of malaria, however, makes it advisable for British troops to avoid the plains."

Much of the rest of the report was based on Greek staff estimates of the likely German course of action, and would prove in April to be quite accurate. It was envisaged that less than three British divisions would be called for on the Aliakmon Line, if that was the one which had to be held, because of the unsuitability of the area for forces equipped with mechanical transport. Heywood recommended the formation of pools of pack transport to be used as sector troops until communications could be improved. And he concluded, "In any of the alternatives considered, the early despatch of medium artillery is recommended as BALKAN armies are particularly short of artillery."[110]

It is likely that Heywood's analysis introduced for the first time the possibility that three British divisions would be sufficient. The Greeks had 10,000 frontier and fortress troops in Macedonia, backed by three mountain divisions and another forming in Salonika. The third position that might be held was the Struma line, which was estimated to need only seven divisions all told. British troops would have to be landed at Salonika *en masse* and be in place before the Germans arrived, and that—the Greek staff estimated—would be ten days after motorized troops crossed the Danube.

At 11 a.m. on that Thursday in Cairo the secretary of state for foreign affairs, the chief of the Imperial General Staff, and the three commanders-in-chief sat down for informal talks of which no record was kept. Evidently, when Wavell was asked what he could provide, he replied that he had the new Australian division, the Indian motorized brigade under training, and the one armoured brigade of the 7th Division; he could put these in Cyrenaica. He would keep the 4th and 5th Indian divisions to clean up Eritrea. He would reduce the troops in Kenya, and as soon as shipping was available he would move the South African Division to the Middle East. For OPERATION MANDIBLES against Rhodes he would use the new 6th British Division then being formed out of oddments.

This left for Greece, ready to sail: one armored group and the New Zealand Division (less one brigade still on its way from England), two medium artillery regiments, and some A/A artillery. Later the Polish Brigade Group, one armored brigade, and another Australian division could be moved. The first lot could go thirty days after a decision was made, and the second and third at three-week intervals; the movement would need at least fifty ships and would have many side effects. Very few aircraft could be sent to Greece, now that the Luftwaffe had appeared in the Mediterranean and losses were rising. If all went to Greece, there would be nothing for Turkey, and it would be best, therefore, to tell the Turks that, by helping Greece, the British were helping all their friends.

"Guido" Salisbury-Jones reported from Athens to Cairo that discussions with the Greek general staff on British participation could be summed up as follows at this point: To hold Salonika would take nine divisions on the easternmost Nestos River–Rupel Pass line, eight on the hills west of Kavalla and Drama, and seven for the position along the Struma River up to the Rupel Pass. Only about three divisions would be Greek, unless there were a major change in the Albanian situation. The Greeks considered the "minimum additional force required to hold Salonika would be two Corps [eight divisions], which should be in position on the Struma from the start. Unless these additional forces are available, it will be necessary to concentrate on defence of Thessaly." For the latter there were four possible main lines stretching westward to the sea, all of which utilized the Aliakmon River: (1) Aliakmon–Veria–Edessa–Albanian frontier to the sea. (2) The same except from Mt. Grammos via the Kalamas River to the sea. (3) Aliakmon–Venetikos River–Mt. Vradeton–Kalamas River to the sea. (4) Aliakmon–Venetikos River–E——–Arackthos River to the sea. (The signal was blank for E——.)

It was estimated that the first and second positions needed fifteen divisions, the third fourteen, and the last, which would become the basic

Aliakmon Line, twelve. The last position would entail a morale-straining Greek retreat and re-forming, which might not be feasible. But the first two would expose Greek forces in Albania to being cut off if the Germans broke through at Veria or Edessa. Salisbury-Jones said that from other sources he had gathered that the Greeks were determined to fight and that the Ministry of Security said that there were still another 300,000 men in the country who could be mobilized.[111]

The trouble with the Aliakmon Line was that it was not a line at all in the World War I or even the French sense. It was a series of passes through very sharp and steep mountains, but with weak, relatively narrow, flat flanks which could be turned. Even more important, there were no lateral road or railway systems; the whole was much more like a garden fork with the vital passes at the tips of the tines. All supplies and reinforcements had to pass to and from the shank or handle, which meant that any one pass might be overwhelmed before sufficient forces could be brought up to block it. Moreover, even this concept assumed that the enemy would not have mountain troops who might scale the slopes in between if blocked in the passes.

On the evening of 20 February a second signal from Salisbury-Jones reported that Papagos had just given him a brief appreciation of the German threat in Bulgaria. If Yugoslavia stood firm, the Struma valley would be unattractive to the Germans, but if she were neutral Salonika would have to be abandoned. If the Germans attacked before Papagos could clean up Albania, it would be a disaster, so he had decided to do nothing to precipitate German action before the Greeks could establish themselves on the line Berat-Valona. The Greek C-in-C could then consolidate and shift some troops to northeast Greece. He had arranged for the newly formed 20th Division to move to the Edessa–Florina area, and for the 19th to go to Veria to prevent a German rush through. Greece would not make a separate peace with Germany. Salisbury-Jones concluded, "Capital importance of Jugo Slav position being clarified cannot be over-estimated."[112]

A third signal from Salisbury-Jones that evening indicated that Steers and Major Miles Reid of the special HQ Liaison Regiment might shortly be allowed to make a reconnaissance of the north in plain clothes.[113]

The best news of the day was that the first six Hurricanes sent to support the Greek offensive against Valona arrived at the front. Eight days later they put on a real morale-building performance by teaming up with some Gladiators to shoot down twenty or twenty-six enemy aircraft in full sight of both armies, a performance which, in D'Albiac's words, "caused the greatest jubilation."[114]

At six o'clock all the principals met at the embassy in Cairo again for another conference, then for dinner with Wild Bill Donovan, followed by a further conference over the wording of a telegram to the Prime Minister which, it was eventually decided, had better wait until clearer heads could draft it in the morning.

At dinner the evening after they arrived, Eden, Dill, and Wavell had been briefed by Donovan on his strategic appraisal of the Balkans, with which all three agreed, stressing in particular the necessity of aircraft and mechanized equipment to make any effort effective. After dinner Donovan cabled President Roosevelt that the British were acutely worried about their shortage of shipping and equipment. Whatever developed in southeastern Europe would seriously strain shipping, and convoys from the UK would have to be cannibalized for the Mediterranean, so anything FDR could do to make more shipping available would be an important contribution to Britain's war effort.[115]

In the course of conversations with Eden and Dill, Wavell proposed that Salonika be defended. (Both Longmore and Cunningham were doubtful, however, and on the twenty-first Eden cabled London that an evacuation might have to be undertaken.) Wavell in early February had come to the conclusion that risks were worth taking in the Balkans, if only for two months, in order to put new heart into the Greeks and make the Yugoslavs and the Turks fight. If we assume, as we must, that Wavell drew up his appreciation, within a few days of Metaxas' death (if not earlier), because he was a general much more interested in political nuances than in military affairs, then we can begin to unwrap the enigma about Wavell's decision to go to Greece. It seems logical to assume the following undocumented sequence of actions: aware of the stakes in keeping the Greeks in the war, and at that time unaware of the German threat in Tripoli, Wavell worked on the political possibilities. Then he received confusing messages from London, including the word that Eden *and* Dill were on their way out, due on 12 February. Naturally, militarily and dutifully, as any sound and proper manager would do, he prepared plans for likely eventualities and alerted those who would have to act upon them, for he expected that he would be ordered to send troops in force to Greece shortly after the twelfth, when Eden and Dill were to arrive. This did not happen, simply because of the vagaries of the weather, which delayed their flight out. Moreover, he reasoned, if he were not to be ordered to campaign in Greece, why had London interfered with his highly successful drive to the west? There remains then merely the question as to why Dill did not show Eden Wavell's appreciation until late April. One answer is that it was not required, as it was a military paper. But it did point to eventual evacuation, and Dill sent it over in London when the disaster occurred, saying, in effect, we told you so.

In Cairo the decision to proceed was taken in spite of Salisbury-Jones' warning. Unfortunately General Heywood was killed shortly after Crete fell in May, and so he was not able to speak for himself, but Salisbury-Jones claims that he did send a memorandum to the War Office setting the record straight, after No. 27 Military Mission was criticized for not having properly represented the military situation.[116] The criticism was unjustified, but neither General Wilson nor Brigadier Alexander Galloway, his chief of staff, liked Heywood. The military mission had reported that to hold the Aliakmon Line would require two corps, but before the inevitable post-disaster inquest in Cairo, de Guingand was lobbied to water down the views he was widely known to have held that the whole thing was a mistake from the beginning.[117]

One of the puzzles of the British decision to aid Greece in 1941 is Wavell's change of mind. Was he a loyal soldier following orders to make plans according to directive from London? Had he intended only to make plans, relying on Dill (who was pro-Turk) and Eden to face realities? Was he expecting that the Greeks would again reject what Britain had to offer? Was he planning simply to show by the rational process that the British could not succeed because they did not have the men, materials, or shipping and could not hope even to begin to occupy positions until months after the German attack? Was he hoping that the Germans would, in fact, make their overt moves first and save him from moving? Was he stalling for time to get rid of the Balkan problem and then go on to Tripoli? Wavell was no fool, and he was not a hidebound World-War-I-style general. He may have looked at the map of Greece, realized what the terrain was like and the impossibility of holding there without adequate transport, guns, and air support, and believed that others seeing this would make the rational decision on political-military grounds not to go. Or he may have been misled ultimately by his powerful sense of duty.

But even these questions may not be the right ones. For it may well be that the solution lies in a circle of assumptions. Wavell assumed that Eden, as in October, would be sensible and would clearly see that Middle East Command simply could not undertake the Grecian campaign, and that Dill would support him. But Eden and Dill thought they were there to reconnoiter for Churchill and the Chiefs of Staff, who for their part now thought that the people on the spot should make the decision. And in Athens Koryzis was too deeply embroiled and too much aware of his lack of expertise to interfere; he relied on Papagos, who did try to be rational but, like Wavell, felt that it was a political decision.

Above all, these men were tired. They had been working night and day under arduous circumstances for more than three months. They wanted to do the right thing, but they were too tired to think clearly. And for one reason or another they all deferred to Eden, a dangerously mercurial character holding *carte blanche* from Churchill.

Later in the war, on 1 October 1942, in a speech in the House of Lords, Viscount Cranborne, God's courteous, outspoken gift to Eden, defended the government by saying that Wavell was *always* in favor of "the Greek episode," nor was his advice ever disregarded.[118] This was queried by

Churchill, so on 9 October old Etonian Cranborne wrote to Wavell for confirmation. The loyal Wavell replied then, as he wrote in 1948 to Liddell Hart, that he had always believed the Grecian decision the right one, that militarily it had a chance, but above all that politically and psychologically it was the right choice.[119] (Still burdened with the ULTRA secret, could he have answered otherwise?)

In London the War Cabinet met at noon on 20 February. The Prime Minister told them that Eden and Dill had arrived in Cairo on their way to Athens and Ankara, and that the object of the visit was to see what help could be given to the Greeks and the Turks in the event of a German advance south through Bulgaria, and to ascertain how the diplomatic situation in that part of the world could be made to conform to the military situation. The minutes include Churchill's conclusions:

> If the Greeks decided to oppose a German advance into their country, we should have to help them to the full extent of our power and Mr. Eden would inform them of what help we could give. . . . If the Greeks decided to fight, we should do what we could. It was possible, of course, that before making their advance the Germans would offer the Greeks such attractive terms that they would feel bound to make peace. In that case we could not very well blame them, nor should we take such a decision on the part of the Greeks too tragically. We should have done our duty and should then have to content ourselves by making our position in the Greek Islands as strong as possible. From these Islands we could wage air war against Germany, which might eventually turn in our favour.

Churchill then went on to say that the extremely experienced RAF pilots in the Middle East were being remounted on the best machines available, and that if Greece fell and Turkey remained an honest neutral, "it would remain for consideration what we should do with our strong forces now in the delta. In that event, the question of advancing into Tripoli would again arise. He hoped that we should not have to put any large part of our army into Greece. In fact it was unlikely that it would be possible for a large British force to get there before the Germans."[120]

The Prime Minister also noted that the Germans were politely pressing Yugoslavia and that there were signs of German infiltration into North Africa.[121] Apparently by this time Churchill had begun to come to his senses, but Eden's hopes had now gone the opposite way; and that is the stuff of which tragedies are made.

## 21 February 1941

On 21 February Lincoln MacVeagh cabled Washington that the Greek under-secretary for Foreign Affairs had called the Bulgarian-Turkish non-aggression agreement of 17 February a British diplomatic defeat.[122]

Salisbury-Jones sent a "Most Secret Officers Only" to Wavell and the VCIGS: "Operation has been delayed by bad weather. Country unbelievably difficult for example to go due west from point on road Berat-Klissoura to top of Shendeliru distance 7 miles as crow flies takes two days."[123]

(Much later, in his final report on the campaign in Greece, Jumbo Wilson, the defeated British commander, started with a blistering description of the Greek roads and communications system. In 1941 British wireless sets simply would not work in the mountainous areas of Greece, and the best communications were by liaison officers, who often took twenty four hours to make the round trip from their front-line posts to headquarters and back again. The campaign in Greece encountered many such disadvantages, compared to Western Desert warfare of the same day. By 1945 the quantum jump in the efficiency of wireless sets and the availability of radio/voice communication, liaison aeroplanes, and even helicopters would significantly alter operations in mountainous terrain. But none of these improvements could overcome the failure to have gathered adequate information on the country in the first place.)

The deputy director of military intelligence in Cairo issued on 21 February an appreciation which followed the line taken by Brigadier Shearer at the end of January, but went further and insisted that it was inconceivable that the Germans would commit their forces to invade Turkey and Iraq: dumps of supplies were nonexistent.[124]

At 11:45 Eden, Dill, Mallaby, Dixon, Wavell, Cunningham, and Longmore sat down again to go over the situation; for part of this discussion, AVM Elmhirst was present. It was agreed that "our best course in the whole world" would be to get the Turks to declare war on Germany. "All our information points to the fact that the Germans intend to eliminate the Greeks . . . . Our object is to forestall, not to precipitate, a German attack." And similar sentences dot Pierson Dixon's record of the discussions. In the afternoon Dill went off to see the Free French General Georges Catroux, Churchill's "Frenchman in the Levant." In the evening the group reassembled and read a message received from the Prime Minister, which said in part, "Do not consider yourselves obligated to a Greek enterprise if in your heart of hearts you feel it will be another Norwegian fiasco. If no good plan can be made, please say so. But, of course, you know how valuable success would be."[125]

The group in Cairo then discussed once again the line of approach to the Greeks, and Cairo 358 was finally dispatched to the Foreign Office that evening: Palairet had advised from Athens that Koryzis felt that a meeting in Crete would be impracticable and impossible to keep secret. He therefore suggested that the British party fly into Menidi airfield and meet at the nearby royal palace at Tatoi. Palairet would meet them there.

On the same day London had cabled that Hugh Dalton, the minister for economic warfare, wished the Rumanian oilfields bombed in connection with a program of subversive operations which was expected to start on the twenty-eighth. This would require the use of Greek airfields, which might bring German retaliation against Greece: would this be a difficulty? The Foreign Office had no objection to violating Bulgarian air space. Would Eden discuss this in Athens and let London know?

And the chief of the Air Staff had warned Longmore that he was getting more commitments for Hurricanes in the Middle East than the spares situation would stand in the future, and the same might apply to the Tomahawks.

From Cairo Eden reported the consensus that limited air resources would not allow Britain to help both Greece and Turkey at the same time. There followed a long paragraph in which Eden laid out the air situation, which really had not changed a great deal from what it had been in October 1940 when he was last out there, and noted especially that Longmore had a "much smaller margin of modern aircraft suitable to meet the Germans than we had estimated." And rate of wastage would rise as Germans rather than Italians were encountered. After further technical comments, Eden went on, "Present limited air forces available make it doubtful whether we can hold a line covering Salonica. . . . Commander-in-Chief of Mediterranean considers that he can supply the necessary protection at sea to enable Salonica to be used as base, but emphasizes that to do this he will need air protection, which we fear would prove an insuperable difficulty. Question of line to be held in Greece will be discussed with Greeks whom we hope to meet Sunday."

He then limned out Wavell's dispositions and the forces he could send to Greece, concluding, "Despatch of this force will inevitably strain administrative resources to the utmost and must involve much improvisation." Nevertheless, those in Cairo were agreed that immediate help should go to the Greeks and that the Turks should later get air reinforcements if their volume would allow it. "My present intention is to tell the Greeks of the help we are prepared to give them now and to urge them to accept it as fast as it can be shipped to them. If they will accept this help and brave any risk it may entail of involving them in early hostilities with Germany, there is a fair chance we can hold a line in Greece. If we now split our small resources, especially in the air, we can effectively help neither Greece nor Turkey."[126]

Eden emphasized that Longmore's squadrons were simply not up to the standard of those at home, because they had been chasing Italians all over the place and because "many good troopers are still mounted on wretched ponies." He also reported that Longmore and Cunningham were in agreement that Salonika was not possible, but Eden and Dill would reserve judgment until they had talked to the Greeks.

> As regards general prospects of a Greek campaign, it is, of course, a gamble to send forces to the mainland of Europe to fight Germans at this time. No one can give a guarantee of success, but when we discussed this matter in London we were prepared to run the risk of failure, thinking it better to suffer with the Greeks than to make no attempt to help them. That is the conviction we all hold here. Moreover, though campaign is a daring venture, we are not without hope that it might succeed to the extent of halting the Germans before they overrun all Greece. It has to be remembered that the stakes are big. But if the Greeks do not want us to come, then we shall have to think afresh, but all my efforts will be concentrated on trying to induce the Greeks to accept our help now.

As to the question of command in Greece, they had decided that they needed a first-class tactical man who could command the respect of the Greeks, and they had selected General Wilson, then governor of Cyrenaica. "We have carefully considered the claims of O'Connor, but, although a dashing leader, we do not think he is of the same stature as Wilson. Moreover, Wilson will have to command an Australian corps and a New Zealand division, both of them led by strong personalities who are also senior soldiers." Wilson's "appointment to lead the forces in Greece will be a guarantee to the Greeks that we are giving of our best."

## 22 - 23 February 1941

In the pleasant early morning stillness of Cairo in spring, at eight o'clock on the twenty-second the party drove out to Heliopolis airfield, where they boarded two Lockheed 18's for the flight to Athens. As a security measure, the word was leaked that they were paying a visit to the Western Desert. In addition to Eden, Dill, Wavell, and Longmore, there were Lieutenant-Colonel de Guingand, Major-General Heywood, Major Smith-Dorrien, and others, making in all a total of ten with their baggage, in those days usually consisting of good solid leather suitcases and portmanteaus.

In North Africa Jumbo Wilson got a signal to meet Wavell at the airfield at El Adem. He flew in the four hundred miles from his headquarters at Barce to find that no one knew anything; but at 11:15 two planes landed, and out stepped Eden, Dill, and Wavell. Wavell said, "We are off to Athens to discuss sending a force to Greece. If it is decided to do so, you are to command it, but don't say anything to anyone about it until you hear from me again!" And he got back into his airplane and at 12:15 flew off.[127]

Jumbo Wilson, the nephew of General Sir Henry Maitland Wilson, who had been commander of the XII Corps at Salonika in 1918,[128] had been one of Wavell's brigade commanders in the 2nd Division at Aldershot before the war, and had succeeded him as GOC there in 1937. Described by one colleague as "un bon soldat ordinaire,"[129] Wilson was now sharing a house with Wavell in Cairo. Sulzberger of the *New York Times* later said that Wilson told him shortly after this episode that the meeting took place at Benghazi and that he was promised fourteen divisions but eventually got three.[130] Wilson himself later commented on the whole Balkan policy that it involved "strategical gymnastics." He also claimed that he only learned of the really poor state of the Greek forces after he arrived in Athens. A further problem for Wilson was that, just as in North Africa, the British had not built up an intelligence service in the Balkans prior to the war.[131] And other difficulties included shortages of staff officers to go view the ground, the Greek refusal to allow reconnaissance, and the lack of a dossier system on the Balkans.

And if Rommel was an unknown to the British, this was perhaps scarcely surprising. In February 1940 London had sent out a senior major-general of the Royal Engineers to take command of the 4th Indian Division. Though he was a VC and the author of an appreciation of why Hitler would attack Russia, Philip Neame was unknown to Wavell, who relied on O'Connor's judgment that Neame was all right, and on the VC as evidence that he was a brave soldier, and so gave him the command in Cyrenaica when Wilson was moved to Greece.[132] Neame wrote in his memoirs that he could not imagine that Rommel had been sent to the Desert in a passive role, as GHQ intelligence in Cairo maintained.[133] But the forces left to guard Cyrenaica—one armored regiment mostly in Italian tanks, one brigade group of infantry and all arms, and a motorized brigade of 1,000 Indian cavalry armed with rifles (and the whole supplied from Tobruk 450 miles to the rear)—were too small to do anything to counter Rommel.

In Athens MacVeagh on 22 February penned a long letter to the American secretary of state, Cordell Hull, in which he noted that King George II was carrying on the Metaxas tradition of upholding the honor of Greece by vowing to fight, but that resolution might wither and die if the Germans escalated the pressure slowly.[134]

At 3:15 the two Lockheed Lodestars bearing the British party, now in mufti, settled down on Menidi airfield north of Athens. The visitors were met by Palairet, D'Albiac, Blunt, and a guard of honor, though their arrival was supposed to be a secret. (The German ambassador was still in Athens, where people were no longer saying *if* the Germans attack, but *when*.)[135]

Reconnaissance party in Crete, November 1940. In the background are Royal Navy ships in Suda Bay. Below, Wavell landing in Crete (probably at Suda) 15 November 1940.

Above, "Father and son":
Anthony Eden and Winston
Churchill.

Left, Air Chief Marshal Sir
Charles Portal was regarded by
Churchill as the master strategist
of the Chiefs of Staff.

Air Chief Marshal Sir Arthur Longmore with his son's mother-in-law, Lady Wavell, in Cairo, October 1940.

The chief of
the Imperial
General Staff,
Field Marshal
Sir John Dill,
talking to an
RAF officer
in Cairo.

Above, No. 80 Squadron's "A" Flight (the only one equipped with Hurricanes) in Egypt, October 1940. Below, the Gloster Gladiator, last of the RAF's biplane fighters, was the mainstay of the RAF fighter force sent to Greece. Here pilots return from a Western Desert flight.

Above, a Blenheim aircraft flying over typical Greek countryside. Below, the first contingent of the RAF arrives at the Piraeus. (The sailors are Greek.)

Above, Air Commodore John H. D'Albiac, immediately after his arrival in Athens—probably at the Hotel Grande Bretagne. Below, Major-General Gambier-Parry, Prime Minister Metaxas, King George II of Greece, Air Commodore D'Albiac, and General Papagos meeting in December 1940.

The Hotel Grande Bretagne on Syntagma Square, Athens, as it appeared in 1940. The Grande Bretagne was the headquarters of the Greek general staff and also at times of British groups assigned to Greece. Courtesy of Lefteris Pavlides.

Loading supplies into an Australian Hobart-class cruiser for a fast run to Greece, November 1940.

Designed to stop the traditional Greek enemy, the Bulgarians, the Metaxas Line could not hold a German blitzkrieg attack. Courtesy of Greek Army History Directorate.

Above, Palestinians unload a ship somewhere in Cyrenaica, February 1941. (Unfortunately, the few photographs in the Imperial War Museum from this period have only censored captions.) Below, a meeting of Greek ox-drawn carts and British motor vehicles.

Above, a British liaison officer on a motorcycle in a Greek village. Below, the motorized artillery moving up; corners had to be watched at both ends.

Anthony Eden, Sir Miles Lampson, and Sir Alexander Cadogan.

Dill, Wavell, Eden, Dixon, and Arthur Smith in conference.

Lieutenant-General Sir Richard O'Connor and General Wavell in the
Western Desert.

General "Jumbo" Wilson demonstrating the reason for his nickname.

Admiral Sir Andrew Cunningham with Wavell's chief of staff, Arthur Smith.

Brigadier Galloway with General "Jumbo" Wilson, then commanding British troops in Egypt.

That *éminence barbu*, Field Marshal Smuts of South Africa, second from left, talks with Brigadier Guy Salisbury-Jones.

Blamey, Prime Minister Menzies, Galloway, and Arthur Smith beside a Lockheed Lodestar in early 1941, probably at Barce.

Above, RAF ground crews evacuated from Greece arrive in Alexandria; below, others, less lucky, are rounded up in Greece to be sent to POW camps.

Brigadier Frederick de Guingand studying a map with Wavell's successor, Field Marshal Sir Claude Auchinleck.

General Sir Archibald Wavell lecturing to the British staff in Singapore, November 1941; behind him is the map of his Middle East Command.

The party drove at once up the winding road through the pines for about three miles, then down into the vale in which the secluded Tatoi Palace lay. A Gothic country house, not in 1980 visible even to official visitors, it was something of a miniature Sandringham, a private retreat, yet with adequate facilities for a secret meeting.

Immediately upon his arrival at the palace, Eden had a private audience with the king, at which he told George II that he would not meet with Koryzis alone, as he wanted the discussions to be on a purely military and not on a political basis.[136] Then an English tea was served at a long polished table, at which nine Englishmen (excluding D'Albiac) faced King George II, Koryzis, Papagos (in whom the British lacked confidence), and the under-secretary of state for foreign affairs, who kept the Greek set of minutes. The Greeks felt on the defensive, because they did not have all their experts present, and so would be much more guarded in what they said than were the British.

When the meeting began at 5:30 the Greek prime minister presented a declaration in French. He observed that Greece had received the spontaneous guarantee of Great Britain, had obtained her aid from the moment of the unprovoked Italian attack, and had become her faithful ally. In the course of the struggle against Italy Greece had committed all but three divisions, which were still on the Bulgarian frontier. In consequence, Koryzis was asking the purely military question of what would be the number and composition of the forces that the British could send to reinforce the Greeks against a German invasion. There were then twenty-five German divisions in Rumania, plus Bulgarian forces. In effect the Greeks said they were ignoring the intentions of the Turks and the Yugoslavs, as no one knew whose side they would be on. The question was now extremely urgent, and the arrival of Their Excellencies most opportune. And, the declaration concluded, Greece would fight for Macedonia even with only her own forces, no matter what help came.[137]

With General Heywood acting as interpreter, Eden undiplomatically then launched into his own statement. He failed to pay tribute to the Greeks. Instead he noted that the Germans had twenty three divisions in Rumania, and four hundred to five hundred aircraft. In his view the Germans sought control of the Balkans so they could strike decisively at the British in the Middle East. He then said that the British could send three divisions, an armored brigade group, the Polish Infantry Brigade, possibly another armored brigade group, and two medium regiments of artillery, plus some antiaircraft guns. The whole came to 100,000 men, 240 field guns, 202 antitank guns, 32 medium guns, 192 light and heavy A/A guns, and 142 tanks.[138] The first flight would be landed thirty days after the decision was taken, using fifty three ships. This force would be commanded by General Wilson, "the victor in the Desert." "What," Pierson Dixon's record said, "we were offering was the limit of what we could do at the present. The troops were well equipped and well trained and should acquit themselves well." Koryzis then raised the matter of the attitude of Yugoslavia and Turkey, "and Eden replied, 'Frankly, we did not know what they were likely to do.' "

The military session then took place at 6:20 p.m. Papagos and Col. Stylianos Kitrilakis of the Greek headquarters were on one side of the table, with Dill, Wavell, Longmore, Turle, Heywood, and Mallaby on the other. Papagos noted that the Italians had thirty to thirty-four infantry divisions in Albania with 197 light batteries, 39 medium or heavy batteries, 3 cavalry regiments, and 5 tank battalions with perhaps 250 mostly light tanks. In Eastern Macedonia the Greeks had but 4 mountain batteries, 12 field batteries, 17 modern and 8 old heavy batteries (164 guns plus 25 in fortifications, or a total of 189 guns), while in Thrace there were 13 battalions and 3 field and 2 mountain batteries. There were no anti-aircraft or antitank guns in Eastern Macedonia or Thrace. Under the circumstances, the only viable place upon which to make a stand was the Aliakmon Line. Greek forces had to be left in Thrace if the Turks were going to attack Bulgaria, as there was an agreement to this effect, and these forces would in wartime be maintained by the Turks.

As for the Aliakmon Line itself (Mt. Olympus–Veria–Edessa–Kajmakalan), Papagos said that eight divisions would be needed to hold it, with one in reserve (or fifty four battalions). It had to be held for twenty to twenty-five days in order to allow the withdrawal from Albania. He went on, "There might be some difficulty in finding sectors of the line suitable for the high degree of mechanization of the British forces and in deploying so large a number of motor-drawn guns."

Papagos did all the talking at the conference, according to the British notes. At the end he asked Dill and Wavell if they agreed, and they said that they did. It was an acceptable military proposition.[139] De Guingand, writing later in *Generals at War*, said that Wavell blandly gave his opinion, and de Guingand wondered if he was at the time influenced by Eden's enthusiasm. Otherwise either his *military* judgment was unsound or he was arguing for a bad case out of political loyalty.[140] At any rate, with aid on the scale Wavell was citing, and with the Greeks so desperate, the soldiers had no trouble agreeing, though the vital matter of timing was not properly explored.

During the conference Wavell took notes in pencil on sheets of palace stationery stamped with the Greek crown. According to John Connell, who saw them, it is quite clear that at the time Wavell understood that the possibilities depended upon the attitude of the Yugoslavs.[141] It was Wavell's loyalty and sense of duty to his superiors that led him later into agreeing with Eden that the Greeks had misunderstood, when, as will become evident, it was the British who had been slipshod in failing to pass on the decisive information.

Speaking in the United States in 1949, Wavell said:

Papagos made a very clear exposition of the military situation and said the best line to hold was that on the frontier, the Metaxas, which needed 9 divisions, of which the Greeks had 3—we did not have the other 6. The Struma, which we had held in World War I, needed the same number, but the Aliakmon to the Yugoslav border needed only 5. We thought that even if the Germans got into Yugoslavia, it would be some time before the Serbs would allow them to outflank the Aliakmon Line, naturally itself very strong. So after Papagos agreed to move in the three good divisions from the frontier and one from Albania, it did not look like a risk to try to hold the Germans with 4 Greek and 3.3 British divisions dug in on a line Papagos said could be held by 5. The chief danger was German superiority in the air, which Cunningham and Longmore saw rather more clearly at the time than I did. . . . The political advantage was that it showed we would support our only active ally.

What then happened is that we left the Tatoi thinking that the Greeks would be dug in on a fortified line when we arrived, but Papagos maintains that we were not to move until after the attitudes of Turkey and Yugoslavia were known. I don't know whether it was a misunderstanding or whether politically Papagos could not issue the orders to withdraw the divisions. After the return from Ankara, it became a political argument.[142]

The military session broke up about 7:45, and the British delegation then met to brief Eden. Captain R.M. Dick, RN, was now present as stand-in for the C-in-C Mediterranean. It was held that the military discussions had concluded acceptably and that the British would push for their implementation as soon as possible, under a British commander who would be subordinate to Papagos with the right to appeal to Wavell—in the same way in which Blamey and Freyberg already operated.

Everyone then adjourned for dinner, and the sessions resumed at 10:45 (not, as is commonly said, at eight o'clock.)

Papagos led off the discussion with a summary of the military session and concluded that much depended upon whether the attitude of Yugoslavia was ascertained or ignored, assuming she would not move. If the latter, then the Aliakmon Line had to be used as this was the only one the Germans could not turn by coming down the Rupel Pass and the Strumitsa valley.

Wavell said that the only reasonable course was the one Papagos had indicated. It was a strong natural line upon which the Allies could establish their forces before the Germans attacked. From a military point of view, it was wise to establish themselves there in great strength as soon as possible. Roads and tracks needed to be improved so motorized guns could be moved. General Wilson needed to be brought over as soon as possible and allowed to undertake reconnaissances.

Eden said it was clear the British and Greeks agreed militarily. He added that military requirements dictated an immediate withdrawal of Greek forces from Eastern Macedonia to the Aliakmon Line, but politically there would be three possibilities: (1) withdraw now; (2) withdraw while talking to Yugoslavia; (3) wait until Yugoslavia's attitude had been ascertained. He offered to send a message to Prince Paul, and this was accepted. It was decided that Greek troops should be withdrawn to the Aliakmon Line, and it was further agreed that roads and communications in Greece be improved for use by a mechanized force.

A draft instruction was then drawn up for a staff officer to take to Prince Paul, but Dill and Wavell suggested that this might endanger the British convoys moving to Greece, because Prince Paul would be likely to discuss the British move with his government, and with this Papagos agreed. So instead Eden sent word to the British minister in Belgrade to explain to Prince Paul the dangers to Salonika of German activities.

It is clear that at the end of the meeting the Greeks laid particular stress on the attitude of the Yugoslavs, "on which," in the words of the diary of Eden's journey, "depended the choice of the line to defend Greece. The British representatives made clear it would not be safe to count on Yugoslavia." But no one stated precisely what stand had been taken on the schedule for moving Greek forces.

At three in the morning of 23 February the Greeks agreed to accept the British offer and welcomed the appointment of Wilson as the British commander-in-chief subordinate to Papagos. The British thereafter claimed that it had been agreed that Papagos would move his troops at once. When in 1946 Wavell's statement appeared in the London Gazette,[143] the Greeks at once arranged for Papagos' memoirs, with a different conclusion, to be published in English. A misunderstanding had certainly developed. The question is, Why?

It may be suggested that apart from the fact that the minutes were kept in English and Greek, so it would have been difficult to compare them (if any attempt was ever made to do so), and the communiqué was issued in French, Papagos had every reason to think that he was entitled to find out what the Yugoslav position was. Eden had evidently agreed, since he had during the conference sent the specially coded telegram to the British minister at Belgrade. Moreover, though the British claimed urgency, Wavell simply could not move quickly because of lack of shipping, and he was not expecting to be able to concentrate his small force for some sixty to ninety days; why should Papagos have felt that he should issue orders that night for action taking sixty days? What the Yugoslavs did made a very considerable difference because of the great Cherna and

Monastir gaps that pointed at the hinge of the Greek line. (In fact, the whole situation in Yugoslavia changed radically within five weeks; Papagos, long familiar with the Yugoslavs, was correct.)

At any rate, when the conference was over, de Guingand noted that Eden preened himself before the chimney-piece and sent a fulsome signal to Churchill.[144] In his own diary for this time Eden noted that Longmore was weaker in the air than London thought and much weaker than he should have been. He also jotted down that Papagos said that the Germans would need twenty days to get to the Aliakmon if demolitions were made before they could attack.[145] In fact, in April the Germans advanced the whole length of Greece in twenty days, but then the situation was quite different. The Germans were not held up on the Metaxas Line, there were few demolitions to delay them on the plains north of the Aliakmon, and they swept around through a collapsing Yugoslavia and down through the Monastir Gap before the weak British force ever got into place. In retrospect Papagos appears to have been a realist in everything except his hope that Yugoslavia would decide in time to fight, and his faith in British abilities.

In his telegram to Churchill Eden said he had explained the international situation and German intentions in the Balkans as London saw them.[146] And after giving details he concluded by saying that there was full agreement with the Greek government:

> (a) In view of the importance of the Yugoslav attitude as affecting the deployment of troops in Greece, it was agreed that I should make a further effort to persuade the Yugoslav Government to play their part.
>
> (b) That the Greeks should at once make, and begin the execution of, preparations to withdraw the advance troops to the line which we should have to hold if the Yugoslavs were not willing to come in.
>
> (c) The work should immediately be started on improving communications in Greece to facilitate the occupation of this line.
>
> (d) That the movement of British troops should begin forthwith, time being the essence of the problem. The utmost secrecy to be observed and deceptive stratagem devised.

After covering other details, Eden praised the "frankness and fair dealing of the Greeks," and ended by saying, "I am quite sure that it is their determination to resist to the utmost of their strength and that His Majesty's Government has no alternative but to back them whatever the ultimate consequences. While recognizing the risks, we must accept them." He was convinced that they had done the right thing and that time was insufficient to refer it all back to London. "The risks are great, but there is a chance of success." To this Churchill replied that Eden's proposals had been studied that day by the COS and would be studied on Monday by the War Cabinet. "In the meantime you should proceed on the assumption that full approval will be given."[147]

Longmore came away from the Tatoi conference feeling that whatever happened the British were right in honoring their moral obligations.[148] Unfortunately, lack of thorough study cannot be covered by hope and righteousness, as events would soon prove.

At 10:30 a.m. the visiting British party boarded their two Lockheeds at Menidi and departed, ostensibly for Turkey. Flying via Melos, at the west end of Crete, and Alexandria, they reached Heliopolis at 3:15 Cairo time. That evening Dill drafted a reply to the War Office signal requesting action against the Rumanian oilfields. He pointed out that it was impossible, as bad weather over Bulgaria would require violating Turkish air space, and because it was unwise to call attention to the decisions taken at Athens.

While Eden was in Athens economic discussions were also going on with the Yugoslavs, who were anxious about supplies for war and wanted raw materials and petroleum products. Before any resolution could take place, of course, war came.[149]

Prince Paul of Yugoslavia, who had been an undergraduate at Oxford, was in a very difficult situation. On becoming regent in 1934, he had assumed that his mandate was to weld the tripartitioned country of Serbs, Croats, and Slovenes together for the minor King Peter, who would reach his majority in autumn 1941. Though an Anglophile, Paul had to face the realities of geography, internal politics, and German power, with his capital city on the western bank of the Danube at the easternmost edge of the country. Already he had felt threatened by the British, having been told on 12 January that the British were sending a mechanized force to Greece and that, therefore, his neutrality would not be good enough. He was horrified and dismissed the bureaucratic British ambassador, Campbell, with the words, "This stinks of Anthony!" At that time the British offer of help to Greece had, of course, been refused by Metaxas, so Paul was correct in not having moved. It is scarcely surprising, then, that he refused to see Eden.[150] Unfortunately, Chips Channon, who had been sent to sound him out, had left Cairo for London the day Eden left England for Egypt. The situation was also complicated by the muddled work of the Turkish ambassador in Belgrade, which allowed the Knatchbull-Hugesson view of the Yugoslavs as untrustworthy gradually to gain the upper hand at the Foreign Office.[151]

In London Cadogan recorded in his diary his surprise at Eden's telegram from Athens that he had argued for aiding Greece—it was certainly respectable, but Britain would eventually be beaten there. He also noted a suggestion from Belgrade that King George VI wire Prince Paul. Churchill liked the idea, but the king did not, and refused to send a message, saying it would be too peremptory.[152]

In Belgrade the American minister, Arthur Bliss Lane, had presumed to lecture poor Prince Paul, who patiently explained to him that, with the Germans already in Bulgaria, Yugoslavia would be defeated in two weeks, and that if he shifted troops he faced a civil war. The regent commented bitterly to Lane that the British could offer no help and that he wished he were dead, yet he still had pride in his country and believed that the British would win in the long run. Ever since 1935, however, Yugoslavia had faced the dilemma of neutrality between Britain and France on the one side and the Axis on the other. At this time, then, the Yugoslavs sought, unsuccessfully, Mussolini's aid in working out a compromise with the Germans. Thus when Eden inquired about Salonika from Cairo, the regent, discouraged by what Campbell had told him, was uncommunicative.[153]

General Kennedy at the War Office in London lamented that from 21 February things began to shift in "a very curious fashion." Churchill, who had urged the Greek venture from the outset, had sent Eden the signal to drop it if he sensed it would be another Norway. Then another unexpected thing happened: Dill and Wavell changed their minds. On Sunday the twenty-third, the COS met from 4:45 p.m. until 2:30 a.m. and produced a paper which said that on balance the enterprise should go ahead. (But the Cabinet had never asked for nor received a purely military appreciation from either the Chiefs of Staff or Wavell: all service advice given had been colored by political considerations, a very dangerous procedure.) So again on Monday the Prime Minister told the Cabinet that on the evidence he was in favor, and they approved.[154]

Prime Minister Menzies of Australia recorded that the first matter to come before the War Cabinet after he arrived in London was Greece, an issue which Churchill raised at Chequers on Sunday, 23 February.

## 24 February 1941

The day started with a conference at the Marasleon School headquarters of the British forces in Greece with D'Albiac in the chair joined by Turle, Heywood, and their staff. The discussion centered about the arrangements for the arrival of considerable army forces in the guise of reinforcing units for the RAF in Greece. As this would mean that an army commander would take over, it was agreed that the responsibility for arrangements would be split between HQ BFG and the military mission. General Heywood then asked for a photographic mosaic of the Olympus Line, which D'Albiac said the RAF would provide; he would ask the Greeks to make one for the ten to twelve miles in front of the line. Also discussed were the difficulties in the Larissa area: it was a very good target for German bombers, and the army would have to be careful in siting camps not to use ground that the RAF would need for satellite airfields.[155]

Having heard of Eden's visit, MacVeagh went to see Palairet, who did not deny it, merely saying that Eden was then in Cairo. Palairet asserted that the Germans intended to attack Salonika to keep the British from going there; in case of an attack Britain would certainly send aid to the Greeks. He wished there were not so many question marks connected with Turkey.[156]

Salisbury-Jones called in the elderly Major Reid of the HQ Liaison Regiment and told him to get into civilian clothes and go make a reconnaissance of Macedonia. Prince Peter of Greece obtained the permits and Greek vehicles, instead of the conspicuously British ones, and they set off the next day. Secrecy was blown, of course, by having the unit paraded outside the Hotel Grande Bretagne before departure![157]

This Monday in Cairo Dill visited Freyberg and the New Zealand Division, met all the brigadiers and some of the troops, and then interviewed at GHQ Neame, soon to be governor-general of Cyrenaica, and Everts, the commanding general of the 6th Australian Division. He also visited the defence minister and chief of the Egyptian general staff in the morning and spent the afternoon with Jumbo Wilson and the chief ordnance officer. That evening he attended a meeting at the embassy at which the line to be taken with the Turks was discussed. At ten in the evening there was a further meeting in Eden's room to hear a report on the Rumanian situation from Mr. Berthoud of the Bucharest legation, which resulted in a telegram to the Prime Minister and the Chiefs of Staff to urge that one more heavy night bomber (Wellington) squadron be sent out via Malta for the attack on the Ploesti oil targets between 6 and 20 March, the next moon period before the Danube thawed and the stocks at the refineries could be shipped out.[158] This, of course, countered Dill's message sent off just the day before, but that response had been based on insufficient knowledge of the economics of the situation.

The director of military intelligence at the War Office, unaware as yet of the German plans (known as BARBAROSSA) for an attack on Russia, warned the VCIGS that as Field Marshal von Rundstedt had moved to Rumania, the British would lose all forces sent to Greece. With this knowledge, the Chiefs of Staff were inclined to agree that, unless Yugoslavia and Turkey cooperated, going to Greece would not affect the outcome of the war as a whole. But the Cabinet stuck to its decision to go to Greece and, as will be seen, reconfirmed it on 27 February. In Cairo in the meantime, general staff intelligence had been against the Cabinet decision, because they did not think the Germans would attack Greece; but when Dill arrived he changed their minds. Ironically, as Hinsley has pointed out, in early March when London was about to abandon the Greek campaign, Cairo persuaded London to stick with it.[159]

Though it is not in the minutes of the Monday meeting, the Chiefs of Staff in their paper had noted that in creating a Balkan front the British would be forcing the Germans to fight at the end of a long line of communication (though actually it was a great deal shorter than the British one, and was dominated by railways through friendly countries, not by shipping lanes through hostile seas). But the COS also noted that the Greek commitment would be endless and exhausting, using up Britain's reserves in the Middle East and perhaps leaving none for Turkey and Egypt. "The possible military advantages . . . are considerable though their achievement is doubtful and the risks of failure are serious. The disadvantages of leaving Greece to her fate will be certain and far-reaching. Even a complete failure of an honourable attempt to help Greece need not be disastrous to our future ability to defeat Germany."[160]

At the Foreign Office, Cadogan read the Chiefs of Staff report endorsing proposals for a Balkan expedition to help Greece and noted in his diary that on all moral and sentimental (and consequently American) grounds, he was driven to a grim conclusion that in the end it must be a failure. However, it was perhaps better to have failed in a decent project than never to have tried at all. Anthony had rather jumped into it, but what impressed Cadogan was that *Wavell* and Dill endorsed him. He thought the Cabinet had made the right decision, and, when the Greek ambassador said his country did not want help until invaded, he had let this pass because it was useful camouflage.[161]

At five o'clock on 24 February, just in time for a late cup of tea, the War Cabinet met, with Prime Minister Menzies present. They had before them telegrams from Eden and Dill and a report from the Chiefs of Staff, as well as telegrams of 11 February from Churchill and the COS to Wavell and the other C-in-C's. As usual the Prime Minister opened the meeting. He said that the Cabinet had to reach a most important decision, namely, whether or not to open a new theater of war in Greece. He noted that he had warned Eden that if Greece was likely to be another Norwegian fiasco, he should say so; but Eden, Dill, and Wavell had recommended going ahead. What particularly impressed him was the telegram from Dill in which the CIGS, who had always doubted that Germany could be successfully resisted on the mainland of Europe, and had always taken a restrained view about going into Greece, now thought Britain had a reasonable chance of resisting the Germans by going there. As the Chiefs of Staff also thought on balance that the enterprise should go forward, he had given orders for it to proceed pending Cabinet approval. So now was the time for any dissenter to speak up.

Menzies then said that he needed assurances on two points—that shipping would be adequate to get the forces there and into position in time, and that the 7th Australian Division, which was then in Palestine and only equipped to the training scale, would be fully equipped.

The Prime Minister replied that he did not anticipate that the Germans would advance until about 12-15 March and that Allied troops would arrive at their positions at about the same time. The VCIGS said that the 7th Australian Division was almost fully equipped, and it was practically certain that General Blamey would have been called into consultation on this question; he thought that Menzies could rest assured that no Australian division would be put into the line without a full establishment of the necessary weapons.

Asked about the air situation in Greece, Portal said that there were seven RAF squadrons there now, but that Longmore hoped to raise this to fourteen and possibly sixteen *in March* (Portal's italics, in his defense written in response to Australian charges of 22 November 1941 that the RAF had never reached the number of squadrons promised.) Longmore's estimate included three heavy bomber squadrons which would probably operate from Egypt. (This information was telegraphed to Australia by her prime minister after the War Cabinet adjourned. The next day the Dominions Office cabled the New Zealand government that there would only be fourteen squadrons, a signal which was repeated to the British high commissioner in Australia.)[162]

Portal then went into a detailed discussion of the airfield situation in Greece and ended with the statement that the RAF would have some 250 aircraft with which to face about 450 German aircraft over Greece. London's assumption that five more squadrons might go immediately to Greece was noted later by the official New Zealand historian, but no one in these discussions really raised the question of the time that would be absorbed in the shipping process. (Moreover, Longmore did not have, as Turle and others had been led to suppose, twenty squadrons available for Greece: when he did get Hurricanes, he had immediately to dispatch two squadrons to Benina to defend Tobruk against Fliegerkorps X; the one which he did manage to send to Greece late in the campaign was wiped out almost at once.)[163]

Menzies asked if the price of failure would be confined to the equipment of one armored division. Churchill replied that, if they were pressed back, they should be able to evacuate all but the wounded. Menzies then said that if the justification for the enterprise was only a forlorn hope, it had better not be undertaken. Could he say to his colleagues in Australia that the venture had a substantial chance of success? On this Churchill was naturally evasive, saying that it was up to the Australian cabinet to make their own decision based upon what Menzies told them. In Churchill's opinion, the operation was a risk which had to be taken. At the worst he thought the bulk of the men could be got back to Egypt, where new equipment could then be provided. The war turned, he said, on holding England, holding Egypt, retaining command of the sea, obtaining command of the air, and being able to keep open the American arsenals. The enterprise in Greece was an advanced position which Britain could try to hold without jeopardizing her main position.

In response to another question, the Parliamentary under-secretary for foreign affairs, sitting in for Eden, said that aid to Greece would probably make the Turks ask for more material, though they might come into the war; the Yugoslav position was obscure and he did not think there was much chance of her entering the war against Germany. To which Churchill rejoined that the courage of the Serb race must not be forgotten, and helping the Greeks might stiffen Balkan resistance. It was recalled that Colonel Dovovan in his telegram to President Roosevelt had stressed the need to form a Balkan Front, and forsaking now would have a bad effect in the United States. As to the suggestion that Eden should talk with Stalin on this, Churchill had already telegraphed Eden opposing it unless he received a specific invitation.

The minister for aircraft production, Lord Beaverbrook, said he thought that the whole impact of the Greek idea upon the shipping needed for Britain itself had to be looked at, especially if an evacuation was likely to be involved.

The meeting concluded with all the ministers present being in favor of sending military assistance to Greece. Menzies noted that there was almost no discussion, for Churchill dominated the subordinate ministers, who accepted any of his proposals without question.[164]

At 8:15 that evening Churchill signaled Eden that the War Cabinet, including Menzies, was unanimous in support of the action taken in Athens. "Therefore while being under no illusions, we all send you the order 'Full Steam Ahead.' "[165]

## 25 February 1941

On the twenty-fifth Eden told London just before he left Cairo for Ankara that they were going ahead with the decision as taken at Athens, their chief anxiety being that the closing of the Suez Canal would jeopardize the operation.

Some time after this the Greek campaign and its risks were explained to General Sikorski, who agreed to allow the Polish Brigade to participate, though pointing out that it was Free Poland's only fighting force.[166]

On this day the Greek military attaché in Bucharest learned from the Deuxième Bureau of the Rumanian general staff that the Germans were bridging the Danube along its entire length—indicating a concentration against Bulgaria and Yugoslavia—and so informed Athens.[167]

Meanwhile, after a number of false starts, MANDIBLES began on the night of 25-26 February when a landing was made at last, after three abortive attempts, on Castelorizo Island, the easternmost of the Dodecanese, only two miles off the Turkish Coast. HMS *Ladybird* actually sailed into the harbor, but she was driven out by air attacks when day dawned, and had to retreat to Cyprus. And as it turned out, the British had underestimated this operation, and the force put ashore was eventually forced to surrender a few days later; another case of poor intelligence, wishful thinking, and bad planning, although a simulated attack had been made there on 27 July 1940.[168]

## 26 February 1941

Among many concerns mentioned in a signal to Wavell on 26 February, Churchill included this one: "We have great anxiety about closing of Canal particularly on account of 'Mandibles,' which assumes ever-growing urgency. . . . Surely you want about three thousand trustworthy white men watching Canal, but with your large numbers of personnel not incorporated in tactical formations this should present no difficulty. Canal problem must be mastered at all costs.[169]

Wavell replied on the next day, as part of a long response to many questions, "You are mistaken in supposing I have large numbers of white troops available. My only spare battalions are being incorporated in 6 Div. and training for Mandibles operation." As those needed for guarding the Canal had to be permanent and not transients, Middle East headquarters had arranged for Egyptian units to be used. And to Churchill's concern that there would not be enough British troops in the Grecian campaign, he responded that armoured troops, artillery, and administrative services, amounting in all to about one-third of the LUSTRE forces, would be British. But he concluded with the warning, "We have the last two months had only second-class opponents, but I think you will admit we have played quite impressive cricket against them and scored at good pace, now we shall be up against the real thing and shall have to stonewall for a bit."[170]

In London Menzies received an affirmative cable from his Cabinet supporting the Greek adventure, provided the troops were fully equipped and that plans existed for their evacuation. Menzies then asked for an up-to-date appreciation from Wavell and a clear statement from both Eden and Churchill of the broad objectives of aid to Greece. Above all he wanted assurance that to go north would not weaken the Western Desert position.[171] Two days later General Blamey raised with Menzies the idea that he should command the British and the Greek forces, an idea he mentioned to both Wavell and Sir Frederick Shedden, the Australian minister of defence, who was accompanying Menzies and whose brainchild it was in the first place.[172] Once again Menzies was too late; Wilson had already been appointed.

On 26 February the New Zealand government also gave its assent, though it had yet to receive Eden's cable of the twenty-second.

## 27 February 1941

Very early on this Thursday by European time, the New Zealand government in Wellington was in something of an uproar, for it had just discovered that it had agreed to the dispatch of the New Zealand Expeditionary Force to Greece assuming that its commander, General Freyberg, had been consulted. Now a cable arrived from him which clearly indicated that he was in the dark. Normally if confronted with a request from the United Kingdom without an indication of Freyberg's assent, the New Zealand Cabinet would have asked for it, but they thought he knew. They were also confused by London's cable of the twenty-sixth that the Australian government had agreed to send its forces. A second cable arrived, containing more details of the expedition to Greece, after the New Zealand government had given its consent, thus making even stronger the possibility that it had been tricked. A query to London received a surprisingly confident response from the Dominions secretary on 2 March. (Of course this query reached London when it was bouncing high again, before the mess in Athens had become known).[173]

Though Eden's party had a wonderful social time in Ankara, the Turks were implacable in their refusal to move. The only incident of real importance to the Greek story occurred on this Thursday morning, after a party that broke up at four in the morning. Eden called a meeting for 8:00 a.m. The Yugoslav ambassador arrived at that time to report that Belgrade would be unable to make any move, and he was then treated very rudely by Eden and his colleagues, who berated him because his countrymen had gone to Vienna to see Hitler. The minister was dismissed, but he reappeared just before bedtime with a very unsatisfactory reply from Prince Paul to Eden's message from Athens: essentially the regent would take no stand on what Yugoslavia would do if the Germans moved across Bulgaria to attack Greece. Eden was furious.[174]

Meanwhile in Athens Papagos had repeatedly asked Heywood whether or not the British had had a reply from Belgrade, and was each time told no.[175]

And so the critical misunderstanding in Anglo-Greek relations blossomed on the evening of Thursday, 27 February 1941. The fault lay with Eden and his staff member Pierson Dixon. Prince Paul's reply had been negative. Sound diplomatic staff work demanded that the answer be at once communicated to Athens and repeated to London and Cairo, so that Papagos could be informed and the executive order for the movement to the Aliakmon Line could be given. But nothing was done. If Eden and Pierson Dixon told anyone at the time, the others in the party—Dill and Mallaby particularly—assumed that the political head of the mission had taken care of it. Certainly Dill did nothing to inform Papagos or even Heywood in Athens. All of this would lead to recriminations in a few days. Historically, General Papagos' version of the events between 22 February and 2 March on this point is absolutely correct and the British accounts are not.

Equally serious, as late as the War Cabinet meeting on 6 March, London still had no idea that the Yugoslavs were refusing to take any but a neutral stance.

Eden's party spent Friday, the twenty-eighth, in Ankara and then left that night by train. On Saturday, 1 March, just as the Germans moved into Bulgaria, they arrived at Ismid and proceeded to a siding on the jetty at Derince on the Sea of Marmora, where they sat for twenty-four hours awaiting the flying boat from Athens. They were thus incommunicado for almost two whole days.

In Athens the king told MacVeagh that it was an absolute secret that Eden, Dill, and Wavell had come to Greece last Sunday; Greece was not admitting it. The king said that they had talked over military plans and that Greece was still cautious about the British going to Salonika, for to send them there while Yugoslavia's attitude remained uncertain would be pure folly. The Greek defensive line was only designed to hold against the Bulgarians, not against the Germans, so unless the Yugoslavs protected their interests in Salonika, the line now contemplated was in the mountains west of the Vardar.[176]

Meanwhile back in Cairo the 3d Battalion of the Royal Tank Regiment had been ordered to send its tanks to the shops to be repainted from sand to green. By the second half of the month the battalion was fully assembled, but all its tanks were in the shops. On 27 February it was placed on forty-eight-hour notice to move and knew that it was going to Europe, with Greece the most commonly rumored spot. Then it was issued khaki drill and long woollen underwear, made to turn in its battledress, and refused an issue of jerkins. Its brigadier went to see Jumbo Wilson, who agreed that if they were going north they should keep their battledress and draw jerkins! It was all, as Robert Crisp noted, a not untypical mix-up.[177]

And at Helwan the New Zealand 20 Battalion was for the next week also engaged in the throes of departure, being issued weapons and equipment, mosquito cream, antigas ointment, tommy guns, and rain, which frayed tempers and made the many parades irritating. There was a last session in the gas chamber to test respirators (for the December 1940 War Office general staff *Notes on the German Army* still emphasized the use of gas), a final fling in Cairo, and a farewell party in the "Naafi."[178]

In the interim, in London the War Cabinet reconvened at 5:30 p.m. on 27 February to continue its discussion on military assistance to Greece. Churchill said that he had no doubt that the decision taken at the meeting on the twenty-fourth had been right, even though there would be shipping difficulties. He dismissed these, including the enforced use of the long route round the Cape of Good Hope, by saying that after all they had planned to maintain a larger force in the Middle East anyway, so the slightly longer voyage to Greece was not a formidable addition to Britain's difficulties.

Menzies then said that his colleagues in Canberra had given their assent, but with the two concerns already mentioned. Since Dill felt that the forces initially being dispatched were adequate, Menzies would point this out to his own Cabinet. The Dominions secretary, Viscount Cranborne, reported that New Zealand had also given her consent, on condition that the fully equipped New Zealand Division was accompanied by an armored brigade. Like the Australian Cabinet, New Zealand also had doubts, which had been expressed in a second telegram.

Menzies then summed up by pointing out that the decisions had been made on political grounds, but since they involved half of the Australian divisions and the only New Zealand one, the issues involved were of outstanding importance to those down under.

Churchill responded that he deeply appreciated their magnificent response to what was probably the most severe proposal ever put to the Dominion governments. The political value of the military steps just taken could not be ignored. The course adopted was the policy best calculated to retain the eighteen Greek divisions now in the field and twenty-seven Turkish divisions now in Thrace; and these, together with the British forces, would be more than anything the Germans could put into the field for some months. Nor should the possibility of Yugoslavia joining in on the allied side be ignored. He hoped that the 6th Division could be sent as a reinforcement from the Middle East, and the 50th from the United Kingdom, in about two months. Two South African divisions should be available when fighting stepped in East Africa.

As Wavaell's timetable for the move to Greece had not yet been received, the whole business was being kept most secret. It would be a mistake, Churchill added, to draw any pessimistic inferences from the recent clash of British and German armor in Africa. There were no indications that the Germans were preparing to undertake an advance across the Libyan Desert, nor was it known how many German mechanized formations had been ferried over to Libya.[179]

There were at least two problems with this fallacious reasoning. First, Churchill was equating untrained and ill-equipped Allied divisions with well-rested, battle-hardened Germans under experienced commanders. Second, he was overlooking the fact that, thanks to American ineptness and British chicanery, the United States had not yet managed to ship to Greece any of the desperately needed aircraft which had been requested four months earlier. To put it inelegantly in the words of Pilot Officer Prune, RAF, "The Americans had not yet been able to get their finger out." And even if American supply ships sailed at once, it would still take close to three months for the material to arrive at the Piraeus. It should have been evident to London from the comments coming in from its diplomatic listening posts, not to mention by simple intelligent observation, that Wild Bill Donovan had been talking a mouthful of New York Irish blarney.

Meanwhile Longmore had told the chief of the Air Staff that the Grecian airfield situation was terrible. Lines of communication were clogged. The dry airfields were in out-of-the-way places, and others lacked communications. Priority messages on the local telephone system took five to six hours. At Larissa, through which all messages had to be routed, the local air-raid warning net monopolized the lines. And the distances from Athens to the fronts were too great for effective operations. But at least some Hurricanes had arrived: these belonged to No. 33 Squadron, which had finally reached Greece in early February.[180]

Papagos later claimed that during the period January through March 1941 the Greek air force received 12 fighters and 5 bombers from the British. At the same time the RAF in Greece was reinforced to the tune of 24 fighters and 28 bombers, but in view of the German threat these aircraft were reserved for the Macedonian front and were not available for operations in Albania.[181]

That night Cadogan noted that the Cabinet was very gloomy over the shipping situation in general, discussed the contents of Eden's telegram on his talks in Turkey, and agreed to give him some leeway in suggesting revisions of the Italo-Yugoslav border.[182] The latter entry in particular indicates how far removed the British were from the realities of power and international politics in the Balkans: Eden could not even get an invitation to Belgrade!

That Thursday the War Office asked Wavell for an appreciation of the Germans in North Africa since contact had been made on the twenty-fourth. He cabled back that there was no evidence that more than one armored brigade had landed, and that the distance to Benghazi and the lack of communications and water made it unlikely that they could maintain a large enough force to attack in the near future. A larger offensive was extremely unlikely before the end of summer. Cairo had already pointed out that it suffered from a paucity of intelligence from Italy's North African possessions,[183] but the problem went much deeper than that. The British estimates were based on their assumptions that it took three months for troops to get acclimatized and trained in the Desert, which was nonsense as Rommel proved, and apparently no one yet had any information on Rommel. (By the time he got to North Africa in November 1942 the American General George S. Patton, Jr., faced a much better-known Rommel.)[184]

## 28 February 1941

Nine Hurricanes and 19 Gladiators rose on 28 February to challenge an Italian air raid over Tepelene, Albania; they claimed 20 shot down and 8 probables out of 50 attacking aircraft for a loss of 1 Gladiator.[185] The trouble for D'Albiac was that he had been providing, when the weather permitted operations, tactical support for the front lines; this left the Italian airfields immune, and the enemy were now attacking his bases. He decided to revert to his earlier ports and airfields strategy.

In the evening Longmore, visiting in Athens, told Major Crow, the American army air attaché, that the Libyan advance was temporarily slowed down by the activity of the Luftwaffe, but would be resumed when additional air forces became available after the conclusion of the campaign in East Africa and the Sudan. "The ultimate fall of Tripoli is expected," MacVeagh cabled home next day. He added that Malta was under heavy attack and hard to supply, and the Suez Canal was suffering from attacks from Rhodes, against which land, sea, and air operations were planned. Both Yugoslavia and Turkey had changed their attitudes and were stiffening against the Axis, and Turkey had agreed to allow the British to use her airfields in the event of open German aggression in the Balkans. It would be at least a month before the weather improved enough to allow operations and the German force was not yet nearly strong enough for operations against both Greece and Turkey. The Greek government would not make a separate peace with Italy, would strongly resist the Germans, and would allow British troops to operate in Greece in the event of a German threat. Longmore had told Crow he was pleased with the situation, saying, "We have sunk the Italians now and have got to get on with the Germans, which I am afraid is going to be a more difficult proposition."[186]

Far to the north Major Reid and his party of "American correspondents," in their six big Greek military limousines with uniformed drivers, were surveying the area around Serrai on the Struma, where the next day they found that there were no explosives at all in the prepared demolitions.[187]

The GHQ instructions for LUSTRE were issued in 143 copies "For Officers Only" on 28 February 1941. Greece was referred to as 1285. For the lower part of Greece, since there were no maps left over from the First World War, those issued were all in Greek.

Admiral Cunningham was considered by some to be as great as Nelson and was known as "Uncle Ned" or "ABC." During the First World War he had seen a troopship sunk off Gallipoli with all on board, because of insufficient naval escort, and he was determined that that would never happen again. But he was at sea fighting off Matapan when the movements to Greece had to be planned, and his chief of staff, Rear-Admiral

A.U. Willis, had agreed to use both Alexandria and Port Said. When Cunningham returned to port, however, he said he had not enough escorts and that all troops would embark at Alexandria. The Palestine and Egyptian railways had, therefore, hastily to redo all the schedules.[188]

Greater secrecy than normal was exercised for the move to Greece, a precaution that Wavell, no doubt, insisted upon because he was all too familiar with the leaks that abounded in Cairo and the Middle East in general. Thus in the case of the 2nd New Zealand Expeditionary Force all cables to the New Zealand government were sent from divisional head-quarters at Helwan and not from the expeditionary force headquarters. The result was that the move had started before HQ 2NZEF woke up to its responsibilities, and the campaign ended so quickly that the breakdown in support was not noted. However, the lesson was learned and thereafter, according to its official historian, HQ 2NZEF was alert to its responsibilities. That it should have been bypassed in late February is not surprising, since at this time it consisted of the officer in charge of administration, one other officer, and not even a car.[189]

Around Cairo other activities were taking place to ready troops for the journey to Greece. New Zealand 20 Battalion was issued Tommy guns and rumors at Helwan, while 19 Battalion had all its newly issued battledress called back in, and when it had all been checked in, it was reissued again, much to the irritiation of those whose garments had been carefully tailored to fit. Tents were turned in—and it promptly rained for two nights; and topees were issued, some fifty-seven of which ended up in Greece, while others washed overboard on the way over.[190]

## 1 - 2 March 1941

In the meantime, Lt. Col. Freddie de Guingand from Wavell's staff in Cairo had stayed on in Greece and been sent north disguised as a war correspondent to reconnoiter the Aliakmon position, for it was, after all, only a line on the map. He had already visited the wounded in a Greek hospital and had come away very gloomy about the possibilities of doing much for people who were so poor that they were suffering badly from frostbite. Unfortunately, in his memoirs he skims over the vital expedition to the north, saying merely that the members spent six days, looked at the water obstacles, bridges, and mountain passes, and came to the con-clusion that it was pretty vulnerable to the German air force as well as needing a large number of troops to defend it.[191] On the way back he was caught in the Larissa earthquake of 1 March, but fortunately he was staying in the one earthquake-proof hotel in town and so managed to get down intact with his suitcase from the sixth floor and out to the airfield.

This was a major earthquake, which destroyed or damaged half the stone buildings in the town. The RAF spent several days helping the natives dig out, clearing streets, reestablishing phone lines and the like, as well as repairing gaping fissures in the runways. On top of this the Italians bombed the airfield while No. 11 Squadron was trying to fly on and off around the fissures and the working parties.

An RAF pilot took de Guingand for a reconnaissance of the area around Mount Olympus. After viewing that 9,750-foot peak and its very narrow coastal plain, they flew on to Salonika. A depressing view of the Vardar and Struma plains helped convince him that even the Aliakmon position was not likely to be held, because the front by British standards was so immense and even on the narrow coastal plain below Olympus a turning movement was possible. The next day he drove back to Athens, looking at a couple of possible ports along the way, and reported to Wavell's chief of staff, Arthur Smith, who was in Athens to supervise the arrival of the expeditionary force. Major Reid had also been flown down from Salonika to brief Smith and Dill. Tired, de Guingand turned in about eleven o'clock, only to be called up at 1:00 a.m. on 3 March and ordered downstairs at the Hotel King George II to see General Smith, who then dictated a memorandum on the difficulties which had developed with Papagos and ordered de Guingand to take the next plane back to Cairo to report to Wavell.

As de Guingand saw it, Papagos was a realist who saw four principal difficulties: the improbability of Turkish or Yugoslav assistance, the political and morale consequences of withdrawal from northeast Greece, the lack of time, and the doubtful arrival, in time, of adequate British forces. General Smith ended his memo with the sentence, "From the strictly military point of view this would provide us with the opportunity of withdrawing from what appears now to be an unsound venture."

De Guingand left on the 9:00 a.m. plane and passed Wavell's flight on its way to Athens.

(Getting back to Cairo early on the afternoon of the third, de Guingand, finding that the C-in-C had already left for Athens, reported to his own office, the Joint Planning Staff. After listening to his eye-opening description of the condition of the Greek fighting men and of the country, the staff at once agreed that the best thing they could do was to start planning another evacuation. The planners kept their work dead secret, but they knew that once the Aliakmon position was turned they had to be ready with a plan. After a few days it was decided that de Guingand, since he possessed a Greek press pass as a war correspondent, should go to Greece again, to make a reconnaissance of the ports. It happened, he wrote, that while he was waiting for the plane by the Nile in Cairo Wavell appeared, also on his way over. He asked de Guingand what he was up to, and, when told, put him under pain of death to keep it a secret. The next day in Athens, he called de Guingand into his office and had him discuss the nascent plans with a select group of officers. Why the idea of evacuation should be so secret, except that Wavell loved mystery, is open to skepticism, since D'Albiac's directive of 5 November 1940 had required him to make such plans and be prepared to carry them out without reference to higher headquarters.)[192]

Rear-Admiral Turle, in his dual role as head of the military mission and naval attaché, had been considering what should be done about Salonika, and on 1 March he signaled the C-in-C that the military mission had come to the conclusion that they were faced with a complex international problem involving the Greeks, the Yugoslavs, and the Germans, in which time was of the essence. Their recommendation was that Salonika harbor should be mined before the Germans arrived, and that all sweeping gear should be removed, as well as anything larger than a rowing boat located farther north than Volos; while on land all rolling stock, motor vehicles, and militarily useful materials should be withdrawn, and stocks of all oils together with tanks, pipelines, and piers should be destroyed. What they proposed, without apparently seeing the consequences, was a scorched-earth policy that would have further endangered the Greek population. It is scarcely surprising that in the end the Greeks themselves resisted this suicide.[193]

At about this time Longmore noted that photographic reconnaissance showed a complete German division in Tripoli, being supplied by sea and air. What he needed was not Wellingtons, which were a headache in the Middle East because of their maintenance, bomb-loading and refueling problems, but fighters and a transport squadron. Nor did he want to be forced prematurely to reduce air support in East Africa, because that was an area in which victory would be final.[194] As to the Dodecanese bases from which the Italians were operating, and from which the Germans had begun to be a nuisance, Cunningham was right that there had to be a choice of Greece or the Dodecanese. S.W. Roskilll, the naval historian, later wrote that the true solution would have been to pulverize the bases there with long-range bombers, such as Wellingtons (which Longmore did not have).[195]

When he heard of the Bulgarian adherence to the Axis, Churchill cabled Wavell and Eden to try to get Prince Paul, in Yugoslavia, to strike, but he also gave Eden the option of dropping the bargain with Greece. Again, London was simply being unrealistic. Paul sat across the river in Belgrade from large German forces. Yugoslavia's trade was heavily with Germany. Any Yugoslav action was likely to embroil her in a three-front war against Italy, Germany, and Bulgaria, while at the same time leading to the possibility of a Croatian uprising and mutinies at home. The Churchillian suggestion that an attack on Albania would create a disaster for the enemy naively overlooked the realities of Axis politics; Hitler simply would not allow Mussolini to be demolished, especially if it resulted in the establishment of a British-led bloc based on Greece, as in the First World War. The English are a gambling nation and Churchill was no exception, but he was an ill-informed amateur at guessing the odds in the Balkans. The Yugoslavs had been notified by the Bulgarians of their adherence to the Axis, and warned that German troops would be moving through Bulgaria to the Greek border. And when Prince Paul visited Hitler at Berchtesgaden on 4 March the regent emerged from the five-hour confrontation with a sinking heart, knowing where Yugoslavia really stood.[196]

While in a sense much activity took place elsewhere, the center of gravity was for the next few days in Athens. There, on 1 March, it was a pleasant, sunny 50-degree day with light clouds. General Papagos waited to give the decisive order to move to the Aliakmon Line until he had heard from Belgrade. He was faced with a critical decision (which, my own conversations with Greek army commanders in 1979 indicated, was still primarily limited by the geography of Greece). With sufficient forces the logical position to hold for military and especially political purposes was the Metaxas Line on the Bulgarian frontier, but it left a gap on the Greek left flank, since it did not extend to Lake Prespa. If Yugoslavia were neutral or a friendly ally, then that gap was not significant, but if Yugoslavia became a passageway for an enemy, then the whole northeast was at hazard. The only viable position then was the Aliakmon Line, which had to be extended west of Servia in order to cover the Monastir Gap. Potentially it was a strong position if prepared in depth and held by adequate forces backed by strong artillery and a good communications net. Its weakness lay in its roadless geography and lack of communications, which made lateral reinforcement behind the lines impossible without lengthy journeys back almost to the plains of Thessaly.

For Papagos the German move into Bulgaria posed not only the military problem of being caught in the flat Thracian and Macedonian plains but also the political-psychological one of retreat and abandonment of the population. Although the Germans were then temporarily held up by snow in the Bulgarian passes, there was no telling when they might decide to attack. Nor was air cover available. These were the crucial questions with which the leaders in Athens had to grapple, while in Egypt the expeditionary force was moving toward the docks in Alexandria.

Sunday, 2 March, was also a lovely day in Athens. Mere puffs of clouds gave less than two-tenths cover, the temperature rose to the low fifties, and there was a pleasant northeast wind. Though in Belgrade it was raining, it remained dry in the Greek capital.

That morning some 700 RAF and 3,300 other British troops landed at the Piraeus, and there was a rumor that more had landed farther north. It is said that when they had sailed from Alexandria, Major-General B.O.

Hutchison, the QMG, told Wavell the news, and the C-in-C ME replied, "I suppose it is worth it."[197]

Much further north that Sunday the weather-delayed flying boat finally arrived in the Sea of Marmora at eleven in the morning, and Eden's party embarked. Shortly after two they arrived at Salamina Island, close by the classical battlefield of Salamis, disembarked by launch, crossed over to Attica proper and motored to Athens for tea at the British legation. Some of the party were put up at the home of M. Efgenides, at the corner of Vassilis Sofia Avenue and Ag. S. Pyrri, and the rest at the Hotel Grande Bretagne. They were back in circulation again.

Eden and Dill stayed in the legation (which is now the British ambassador's residence, opposite the Byzantine Museum). A stately Greek Georgian house, it had been built for Eleftherios Venizelos and on his death in 1936 had been bought for the legation. The British party drove up the short curved driveway and stopped under the portico. Sir Michael Palairet conducted them through the twin bronze doors, up the white marble steps, and across the front hall, turning right past the three-person lift through double doors in a cast iron screen into the Grand Hall. After the normal pleasantries and an examination of the famous Thomas Phillips portrait of Byron at Missolonghi, and of one of his letters, the visitors were no doubt shown to the guest suites on the second floor.

During his stay in Athens Eden appeared in public in the sartorial splendor of a gray, impeccably cut, light tropical suit with one of his famous soft felt hats. Instantly recognized, he was widely cheered by the Greeks, and C.L. Sulzberger came down from Belgrade to interview him. Elegant and courageous, in Sulzberger's words, Eden quizzed him about Yugoslavia and was highly pleased when the young American told him that the Yugoslavs would fight.[198] (Eden also talked with Campbell, the British ambassador to Belgrade, who spelled out Prince Paul's difficulties, including the fact that the Serbs were pro-Allies but the Croats pro-German. He added that the Yugoslavs were scared of Germany, but there was a chance that, if they knew of the British plans for aiding Greece, they might help.)[199]

At 5:15 on the afternoon of 2 March, in the diningroom of the legation, thirteen Englishmen, including General Arthur Smith from Cairo and Ronald Campbell from Belgrade, first heard from a reluctant Eden, who tried to avoid the subject, about his visit to Turkey, his impressions of the Turks and of their intentions, and likely British aid to Turkey—which boiled down to nothing much. Eden was obviously, according to the Greek version of the minutes, embarrassed.[200] The Greeks moved the conversation to the subject of Yugoslavia. Eden said that he did not expect the Yugoslavs to do anything, though under cross-examination he and Campbell took the view that in the end Prince Paul was to be trusted to do the right thing. Prime Minister Koryzis then expressed his own views that the Greeks would be forced to surrender, and the king and the government would be evacuated to one of the islands; the people would suffer greatly under an occupation unless Britain could immediately supply substantial aid. To boost Greek morale he asked for the freeing of economic controls from British dominance and the promise of Cyprus for Greece. The group then went on to discuss the implications of the withdrawal to the Macedonian position. The Greek minutes, signed by Papagos, end at a little before 10:00 p.m.

A full meeting then convened, with the military present. A detailed exchange took place between Papagos and Dill as to what the Turks would do if the Germans made a move to the south: Dill seemed to think that the Turks would allow the British to fly over their territory but would not declare war until they felt themselves suitably armed. This ambiguity led, therefore, quite naturally back to the Aliakmon position. According to the Greek minutes, Papagos asked if there was any knowledge yet of the Yugoslav position. The British accounts say that then General Heywood reported that General Papagos had not yet moved any troops to the Aliakmon. (Perhaps because Dill himself had not passed on the Yugoslav reply received in Turkey, the CIGS reprimanded Heywood severely for not reporting earlier that Papagos had not moved.)

Because of the detailed nature of the Greek minutes, they deserve to be taken very seriously as accurate. They show that Papagos had a sound grasp not merely of Balkan strategy but of German capabilities as well, and was prepared to expect the enemy to act in much more unorthodox manners than were the British, including winter attacks. Because he did not wish his eastern Macedonian garrisons to be caught on the plains of Thrace by ground or air attack, at this meeting Papagos held out against moving them, stressing that they were better off in their present fortified positions, especially if the British refused to land any farther forward than the Piraeus and Volos. This had not been resolved when Koryzis and Eden came into the room and Eden immediately asked why Papagos had not yet moved his forces. Papagos replied once more: because the order was not to be given until he was informed of Yugoslavia's attitude. Eden then read off the notes his secretary had made of the discussions on 22 February, and Papagos countered by reminding him of the ensuing discussion on the wording of the letter to Yugoslavia; and he repeated that this was a political matter which had to be settled before he as a military commander could give orders. (Other senior British officers felt that the Greek commander-in-chief would rather be stabbed in the back by the Germans than give an inch to the Italians at that point. Though this was not the case, Papagos was anxious that his generals not tell Heywood that they would fight the Italians to the end and then surrender to the Germans, and he sent Prince Peter to tell them so.)[201]

Papagos having bettered him on that one, Eden withdrew.

Papagos and Dill then got into an argument about whose forces would be most exposed if the Germans attacked while they were still moving into position, the Greeks going to the Aliakmon or the British to the forward fortified line. Just before adjourning at midnight, the Greek minutes testify, Papagos reemphasized that they still had not heard of the Yugoslav position, but that the situation had already been changed from what it was on 22 February by the presence of the Germans in Bulgaria.

According to the British accounts, Eden stated at the afternoon meeting that withdrawal to the Aliakmon Line had been agreed upon on 22 February, but "evidently there had been an unfortunate misunderstanding due to General Papagos's hopes that Yugoslavia would in fact come in." Dill testified that it would be militarily unsound to hold another line but the Aliakmon, or to hold even that line with less than eight divisions with one in reserve. The available British forces alone were insufficient. Longmore claimed that the Germans could not get through the passes for a month yet because of snow, and Eden said that he would tell the king, when he saw him that evening, of the British worries.

The group then passed on to a discussion of the air problem, and Longmore said that he could do little for the Turks until late 1941. Repair facilities were inadequate, and there was no ammunition for the American guns in the Tomahawks at Takoradi.

After dinner at the legation, Colonel Casson, intelligence officer of the military mission, gave an account of a German plan for OPERATION MARITA in the Balkans, dated 4 December, which had fallen into British hands.

A series of meetings was then held with the president of the Council, Koryzis, starting at 10:45 and running on until 12:45 the next morning (the Greek transcript says ten to midnight).[202] Eden opened the first session by saying that they could not count on Yugoslavia. Koryzis said that in that case the military should reexamine the question to see if three divisions would be sufficient. Eden responded that this had already been discussed at the Tatoi meetings, that Papagos and Wavell had decided that there was a good chance, and that their decision had been based on no support from either Yugoslavia or Turkey. The Greeks countered that there was now not enough time to move the Greek and British troops. (In this they were quite right, for by Wavell's own schedule the British needed ten weeks to bring over their proposed forces, and that meant they would not be in place on the Aliakmon until early May.)

The meeting then turned into a military discussion. Dill urged speed (without seeming to realize that the Greek forces were geared to the speed of a footsoldier—3.5 kilometers an hour—and the British to cargo-ship speed—10 knots). Papagos pointed out that the Germans now had five divisions in Bulgaria and that they could launch land and air attacks within ten days. If he knew positively that they would not move for fourteen days he could move his troops, but his information was that the Germans already had dumps in the Struma valley. Dill said he thought the Germans could not attack for twenty-one days, as they had only just crossed the Danube, and Papagos admitted that that was possible. Dill added that he did not want to take the risks of disembarkation in the north, though he admitted moving north by land from the Piraeus and Volos would be slow.

The full group came back together just before midnight for a brief discussion of the Tatoi misunderstanding, but quickly broke up so that Dill and Smith could discuss it alone with Papagos. As General Heywood testified the next day, Papagos had repeatedly asked for news from Belgrade, and no one had asked why, or what difference did it make. Nor had Eden or Dill realized that they had failed to pass on the vital answer received in Turkey. When the full meeting resumed right after midnight, there was a further pointless exchange between Dill, Papagos, and Smith, until Papagos said, "If the Yugoslavs fight, the Greeks should stand on the forward line," and Dill said, "General Papagos will have to fight his battle."

At that the meeting broke up. The British went back to the legation and sent a signal to Wavell urging him to fly to Athens at once. That was the morning that Smith sent de Guingand back to Cairo with a written memorandum for Wavell.

The British report on this meeting is most unflattering to Papagos, calling him "frightened" and implying that he knew he was in the wrong and had been caught making excuses for not having moved his men. This is untrue and unfair. The evidence can certainly be interpreted that the Tatoi decision included agreement to determine the Yugoslav position and to take only preparatory action.

Two lessons, of course, emerge from this misunderstanding. First, that the minutes of the meetings should have been drawn up and agreed on before the participants dispersed from such a conference as that on 22 February. Here Eden was at fault because he was not a detail man, nor was Pierson Dixon, whose notes were not transcribed until several days after the conference, and whose record on a number of occasions was considerably at variance with Dill's more precise diary of the trip. Second, if a conditional situation existed, then both sides had a duty to check on it and report back. Heywood probably was at fault for not telling Cairo that Athens had received no reply from Yugoslavia, and that Papagos had not ordered the moves to the Aliakmon to commence. Eden and Dill were equally to blame for not keeping Athens informed of the reply from Yugoslavia. And Eden and Dill were in error in their interpretation of what had been worked out with Papagos as to *preparatory* moves to the Aliakmon position.

Basically, the trouble in March stemmed from that old problem that tired people left a committee meeting thinking that what they wanted to believe had been agreed on. The more polite the meeting, as in such a well-mannered international group, the better the chance for a misunderstanding.

On 2 March the Chiefs of Staff in London told Wavell they assumed that he had planned demolitions in Greece in case of need, and that he had enough materials and British personnel to deal with all the ports, railways, oil stocks, and installations, and for blocking the Corinth Canal. The Greek authorities were not, *repeat not*, to be consulted at this stage.

## 3 - 4 March 1941

Before he departed for Athens on 3 March Wavell cabled the latest appreciation of the German presence in North Africa, which indicated that while the Italians had landed two infantry divisions and two artillery regiments, the Germans had only put ashore one armored brigade and were still very short of transport, though the latest air reconnaissance showed a considerable increase in motor transport on the Tripoli-Sirte road. From Tripoli to Benghazi was 646 miles, with only one road and inadequate water, and these factors would limit the present enemy threat. Wavell did not think the Germans were strong enough to take Benghazi, and, what with shipping risks, difficulty of communications, and the approach of hot weather, it was "unlikely that such an attack could develop before the end of the summer." Effective air and naval attacks might delay the Axis further, but to face 260 German bombers and 60 fighters Longmore had only one squadron of fighters in the Western Desert, one of bombers, and one army cooperation unit. As a temporary measure a second fighter squadron destined for Greece had been retained in the Desert. And while air attack on Egypt from the west was not likely, raids from the Dodecanese had virtually closed the Suez Canal and necessitated maintaining a strong defensive fighter force in Egypt. Only one fighter squadron was available for the whole area, and Longmore would have to divert his heavy bombers to Dodecanese airfield attacks, in order to try to put down that menace, to the detriment of other targets.[203]

In Athens Heywood reported that the Greek military attaché in Bucharest reckoned that the Germans had thirty divisions in Rumania, including one or two Alpine Army corps, that they were crossing the Danube, and that the German headquarters in Bulgaria would be in the monastery at Chamkoria (an aristocratic resort area in the pine trees), near Sofia.[204]

MacVeagh told Washington that the British party had arrived and seen the king. He himself had met with Eden that morning by invitation, and afterwards talked to the Greek under-secretary for foreign affairs and to the Yugoslav minister. Eden told the American that the immediate

German aim was to gain air bases in Greece, but that this would not affect Britain, now rapidly cleaning up the Middle East and Africa. Greece was holding firm, and Britain, Eden said, would give her all possible support in the month before the state of the Balkan roads would allow any action. All the reinforcements were for the air force. Eden was delighted at his reception in Turkey; the Turks were loyal and realistic, but had neither the forces nor the equipment for offensive action. If the Germans attacked Greece, Eden thought the Turks would declare war and allow the British to use their air bases and other facilities. The Yugoslavs had not made up their minds, and the British were still trying to get the Turks and Yugoslavs together. Eden ended, "I believe that Greece, Turkey, and Yugoslavia will all eventually come into the fight, but there will be a lot of slipping and slipping before that happens." Mavroudis, the Greek under-secretary, did not know that MacVeagh had talked with Eden; he said that all that had come out of the visit to Ankara was that the Turks would not fight if the Greeks were attacked by the Germans. Later, Alexander Vouktchević, the Yugoslav minister, confirmed that, despite Eden's cheerful optimism, his trip had not been a success, and Vouktchević became even more defeatist, saying it was now too late to stop the Germans.[205]

About noon Wavell and Wilson arrived from Cairo. Joined by Eden and various staff members, they went over to the Hotel Grande Bretagne for lunch with Prime Minister Koryzis. Afterwards the whole party proceeded to the Acropolis, being given a most enthusiastic reception by the public along the way. When they got back to the legation, the whole position was discussed informally until 6:30 p.m. (6:00 in the Greek version), when General Papagos and Colonel Kitrilakis arrived.

There was more discussion of the Tatoi decision, and at this point Dill, finally, said that the position had to be looked at as it was today. The British would still help if Papagos would put forces on the Aliakmon Line. Papagos said that unfortunately he had no more forces, not even, when pressed by Dill, three more divisions. Dill then proceeded to play his old role of staff college instructor, reminding the Greek commander-in-chief as though he were a student at Camberley that he had one division then forming, and what about the 12th in Thrace? Papagos said that the people of Macedonia would regard its withdrawal in the face of the German presence in Bulgaria as betrayal. Dill then pointed out that Papagos was proposing to hold the Aliakmon with four dividions where heretofore he had said the minimum was nine; wasn't this courting disaster? Papagos said that he could see no alternative, especially as northern Greece was under constant German air reconnaissance. The dilemma was that to hold the Aliakmon indefinitely needed eight to ten British divisions, but as soon as they started to arrive the Germans would attack.

They then went round again about the Tatoi decision. Dill hoped that

Papagos saw the British problem in shipping, and the Greek C-in-C replied that "the problem was insoluble." He went on that Greece was most grateful for the help that Britain had offered, but it *was* limited. Dill then suggested that the whole undertaking had become unsound, to which Papagos responded that that was why the British should come up to the forward line around Salonika.

Dill: "I do not think that that is a sound plan."

Papagos: "Yes, but it is the only feasible one."

Dill, who had never seen the ground, then said he would have to talk to Eden, "as he could not recommend putting the only British reserves in the Middle East into this plan which he considered unsound. It would not be essential to have the nine originally proposed divisions for the Aliakmon Line; if three Greek divisions could be found we would be prepared to build up a line on this basis and would try to operate forward from it." Papagos declared that the only troops which could be brought over from Albania would need thirty days by sea to come from the left flank, and they would be tired troops.

As they were getting nowhere, the meeting adjourned at seven. The king came to a banquet at the legation, and the problems were covered with good manners and good cheer until the next day.

Meanwhile on this day the COS wired Dill that "time is obviously the dominating factor in the Greek enterprise." They gave a detailed analysis of what forces the Germans could bring to bear on the Graeco-Bulgarian frontier: by 6 March they could have four divisions there, with an infantry division in place by the eleventh, but that would be the maximum number that could be maintained until the weather improved, normally about 15 April. Even so, assuming weak Greek delaying forces and ineffective RAF action, the Germans could have two divisions on the Veria line by 15 March and all five by 22 March. They wanted to know if Wavell agreed with this estimate, and "whether you now consider that Allied forces will arrive Veria line in time to hold on it." After asking detailed questions about shipping, Greek munitions supplies, and ports of disembarkation, the COS concluded, "Grateful also for fullest possible appreciation on all points raised in this telegram to enable us to present a clear picture to the War Cabinet."

The staff in Cairo replied at once that Wavell had left that morning for Athens, but then provided all the information requested and gave the following arrival schedule for debarkation at the Piraeus, Eleusis, and Uepalos (Oropos), the ports for Athens:

1st flight, AA and administrative units . . . . . . . . . . . . . .  4 March
2nd flight, Armoured Brigade and NZ Brigade . . . . . . .  7 March
3rd, NZ Brigade . . . . . . . . . . . . . . . . . . . . . . . . . . . . . . 10 March
4th, Australian Brigade . . . . . . . . . . . . . . . . . . . . . . . . . 18 March

5th, remainder NZ Division ...................... 21 March
6th, Australian Brigade............................ 24 March
7th, remainder Australian Division ................. 1 April
8th, Polish Brigade................................. 4 April
9th, Australian Brigade............................ 7 April
10th, Australian Brigade........................... 15 April
11th, remainder Australian Division ................ 18 April

The divisional, corps, and administrative units would be spread among flights, and the whole schedule depended on the Suez Canal's being open all the time. As to MANDIBLES, the first phases, BLUNT (against Kasos) and ABSTENTION (Castelorizzo), would be carried out shortly, with two more phases to follow, but as the C-in-C Med' could not carry out both LUSTRE and the second phase of MANDIBLES concurrently, it had been decided that LUSTRE should take priority and that ARMATURE should be put back to April.[206]

This communication was followed on the fourth by a long signal from Cunningham to the Admiralty in which he noted all his difficulties, "so that their Lordships can strike a just balance with their knowledge of available resources. It would be useless hiding the fact that mine are taxed to the limit and that by normal security standards my commitments exceed available resources. I have, however, considerable hope that all these difficulties can be overcome. We are, I am convinced, pursuing right policy and risk must be faced up to."[207]

Ronald Iran Campbell left Athens at noon on the fourth with a personal letter from Eden to Prince Paul detailing what the British were doing for the Greeks, and would do in the way of revising the Yugoslav-Italian frontier in Istria. But Eden never did get his wish, expressed in this letter, to go to Belgrade for some personal summitry.

In London the Foreign Office was bored and disappointed with Eden and longed for Halifax again.[208]

On the night of 3 March Menzies asked that the Chiefs of Staff make a further appreciation of events in the Balkans, as he was anxious about the timing of British policy. The First Sea Lord, Pound, speaking for the Chiefs, said that they would have by 7:00 p.m. an estimate of how long it would take the Germans to reach the Aliakmon Line, and they proposed to send this out to the C-in-C's ME for their comments to see whether the British could get there in time to hold up the German advance. They also wanted Cairo to provide London with a whole appreciation.[209]

In other words, Menzies, who was in the awkward position of being the outsider in a crucial decision-making process in which his own troops were the pawns, was trying to raise the very obvious question which no one ever seemed to bring into the open: as the American Civil War general put it, Could the British get there "firstest with the mostest?" He had a nasty feeling that they could not, and that, despite the fact that everyone was circulating figures of what the Germans could do and the schedules for the British lifts, there was an invisible curtain between the two sets of calculations, like the emperor's new clothes. (For the War Cabinet meeting on the 5th the Chiefs did produce an *aide memoire* in which they pointed out that the Germans would have five divisions on the start line by 22 March, while the British would have one armored brigade and one New Zealand brigade to meet the first two German divisions to reach the Veria position.)

At eleven in the morning on Tuesday, 4 March, the meetings resumed at the British legation. Papagos said that he was reinforcing the Greeks in Macedonia with the 12th Division from Thrace and the 19th motorized division from Larissa. He had also assigned three divisions to the Aliakmon Line to help the British. In reply to a question by General Wilson he said that no engineers to improve the roads were available, as they were all working in Albania.

For five minutes at 12:15 Dill, Wavell (incognito in mufti), and Wilson went out and discussed Papagos' proposals among themselves. They then returned to the meeting, and Dill said that the eight battalions proposed instead of the thirty-five agreed on "was too small a force to allow our regarding the plan as a sound military proposition." They added that they had asked the king to step over to the legation. He was expected at 12:30, and, no doubt, Papagos would like a word in private with him first. Papagos reiterated that the problem had been caused by his waiting for the Yugoslavian response, to which Dill agreed that there was no doubt that there had been a misunderstanding, but the concern now was what to do next. After the king arrived and talked to Papagos, they decided not to continue the discussions until later, so the meeting adjourned.

Sometime during the afternoon (or it may have been after they reconvened at ten—the minutes and D'Albiac's own report are not clear whether there were one or two meetings on similar points heard through different ears), King George, Koryzis, Papagos, Eden, Dill, and Wavell met with D'Albiac, who at Eden's request described the British air forces in Greece, which now included some Fleet Air Arm Swordfish. There were one Blenheim IV and two Blenheim I light bomber squadrons, and 10 Wellingtons expected to arrive from Egypt for the moon period starting on 8 March. Possible targets included German concentrations in Bulgaria and the Rumanian oilfields, as well as Durazzo and other targets the AOC-in-C ME might designate. D'Albiac proceeded to discuss each of these in turn and noted the dangers of retaliation from the Germans. Unless continuous attacks were carried out on the oilfields, past experience suggested that "against targets of this description, it was pure chance whether much damage would be caused." Durazzo was a far better target and much less likely to spark a German response. At this point the Greeks said that they could not afford to provoke the Germans, but once the Germans attacked D'Albiac would be free to choose targets as the opportunity arose. It was agreed that the Blenheims should be conserved and used in daylight only against advancing German forces. The problem of fighters was then covered, and the AOC pointed out that he had to withdraw his one and a half Hurricane squadrons from Albanian operations in order to cover the British landings. The king and Papagos were not happy about this, as they were relying on that air power to blunt any Italian attack while forces were being moved to the Aliakmon Line. D'Albiac could only respond "that it was quite impossible with the limited forces at his disposal to be strong everywhere . . . [and]although the Hurricanes would be withdrawn, there would still be one complete Gladiator squadron on the Albanian front."[210]

Either at 5:45 (British minutes) or at 6:30 (Greek minutes), the main meeting reconvened with the king, Papagos, and Colonel Kitrilakis facing Dill, Wavell, Heywood, and Mallaby. Papagos promised his 12th, 19th, and 20th divisions for the Aliakmon Line, saying they would be there in ten days, and that he would send some munitions from Salonika to Florina now. In his opinion, however, the best position was the Nestos–Rupel line. Dill thought this was too far forward and too long, so Papagos asked if he was willing to take the Aliakmon with seven battalions from Thrace and the 12th, 19th, and 20th divisions. Dill said yes. He then left the room to consult with Eden, who accepted the plan. Next, Eden came in and suggested that Wilson should command this new force, under Papagos, and the king agreed. These arrangements were put in writing, and Wilson and Papagos sat down to arrange the disposition of the Greek forces until the British could take over the Line.

Later on in Cairo Eden would say that "the real alternative for Greece was whether she should stand up and fight Germany or allow herself to become a victim of German seduction like Rumania." At least, that was his view.

Meanwhile, at six that evening in London, Prime Minister Churchill had told the War Cabinet that the prospects in the Balkans were not promising. Bulgaria was in German control. Yugoslavia would not move until she was surrounded, though she could wipe out the Italians in Albania if she acted at once. He had not heard from Eden, but the movement of troops to Greece was to start today, though they would not arrive for four days. "If General Dill and General Wavell wished the movement to proceed, he (the Prime Minister) was most disinclined to issue countermanding orders. Nevertheless, he still thought the Cabinet might wish to take a final view of the whole position in the light of the information to be received in the next few days." And as the minutes report, "The War Cabinet took note of this statement."[211]

Eden reported to Churchill on 5 March, and his telegram was followed by a very long signal from Eden and Dill to Churchill covering the changed situation they had found on their return to Athens.[212] The British leaders thought Papagos' attitude was "unaccommodating and defeatist," and therefore they had enlisted the aid of the king. Fortunately George II was "calm, determined and helpful." "By a process, which at times painfully resembled the haggling of an oriental bazaar, we were finally offered three Greek divisions . . . together with battalions from Western Thrace, provided the Turks would agree to release them. . . . We were thus faced with the following alternatives. (a) to accept the plan of Papagos, to which he constantly returned, of attempting to dribble our forces piecemeal up to the Macedonian frontier; (b) to accept 3 Greek divisions offered for the Aliakmon line, the equivalent of about 16-23 battalions instead of 35 we had been led to expect on our previous visit, and to build up our concentration behind this; . . . (c) to withdraw our offer of military support altogether."

After some misgivings they had agreed to solution *b*, provided that General Wilson was given command of the whole of the Aliakmon as soon as he could take it over, and this was accepted. Dill did not think it was a hopeless proposition, and at the worst the country behind the line was suitable for rearguard action. But "the hard fact remains that our forces, including Dominion contingents, will be engaged in an operation more hazardous than it seemed a week ago."[213] The Foreign Office in London noted that the Germans were moving south more rapidly than expected. When the Prime Minister read Eden's telegram to the Cabinet, Cadogan noted, they asked with disdain how he could have sent such a jaunty message in the face of complete failure.[214]

McClymont, the New Zealand historian, concluded that those in Athens felt the abandonment of Greece would be the more costly step, while Wavell himself later claimed political and psychological considerations took precedence over military ones.[215] It is doubtful that leaving things as they were in Greece would have brought a disaster. The fate of the Yugoslavs was already foreordained. The Turks were not going to budge and had said so. Lend-Lease would pass in the United States anyway. And D'Albiac had had clear orders from the beginning to evacuate when necessary (and did so in far worse circumstances in April). Time and again the British had been given the chance to back out gracefully, but they had convinced themselves they could not do that. The real problem was the lack of a grand strategy and a purely military appreciation. If a move was to be made in the eastern Mediterranean, it should have been to Crete and the Dodecanese.

Could it be true that Wavell, an expert at deception and at keeping his own counsel, agreed to go along with Eden's wishes as an honorable political gesture? The military argument for this is that Wavell knew he could not afford the help Greece needed. Did he now calculate that because of shipping difficulties little aid would get to Greece before the Germans attacked and dissolved the war in Greece? Perhaps he thought he could make the grand gesture without appreciable losses. The Germans were expected to attack early in March, and his staff appreciation showed that, even with the Suez Canal open, by 22 March only the New Zealand Division would have disembarked at Athens, and very little of it would have been dug in on the Aliakmon Line. Nor by mid-March would the RAF have been present in full strength, as the airfields simply were not ready.

On a higher level, the assumptions and emotions involved in assaying the Yugoslav and Turkish positions were uninformed and unintelligent; the emotional attachment to the Greeks was not reciprocated by Hellenic realists, while a knowledge of American politics would have shown that foreign policy issues were generally settled in the United States by domestic concerns and not by actions overseas.[216]

Meanwhile in Athens, apparently unknown to the British, the Greeks still had contacts with Berlin through Belgrade, by which they were attempting to arrange peace. But Hitler did not trust them, and the British landings in the Piraeus on 4 March confirmed his suspicions that they were merely trying to buy time.[217]

Brigadier W.D'A. Collins arrived at the LUSTRE headquarters in Athens, but since he was without most of his staff he could make few decisions. The Royal Army Service Corps arrived in the first flight of ships, but it never had enough time to operate efficiently before it was thrown out at the end of April. All during March the RASC suffered from an acute shortage of labor, but nevertheless supply depots were built up, and petrol stocks, at least, were no problem.[218]

For 19 and 20 Battalions of the New Zealanders, preparation for departure had started on 27 February at Helwan, but they did not reach the Piraeus until 15 March, a bare three weeks before the German attack.[219] (In fact, 19 Battalion did not arrive until the nineteenth.) Their drill jackets and topees were withdrawn in Athens, and they were loaded, forty-five men at a time, into the famous wagons marked "Hommes 40, Chevaux 8" and sent off by train up country.[220] Their landing was no secret. The German military attaché in Athens greeted the ships in the Piraeus, and one of his colleagues walked through the New Zealanders's camp on Hymettus chatting with the men in perfect English.[221]

Things had been no better managed on 4 March when General Wilson arrived in Athens disguised as "Mr. Watt," with his baggage bearing the initials "H.M.W." On that day the British army magazine hit the newstands in the Greek capital with a full-page front cover of him in uniform. As part of the disguise he was confined to the legation and not even able to get to his headquarters at the Hotel Acropole opposite the

National Museum; nor was he allowed to visit Greek headquarters or go north to reconnoiter the ground until the end of March.[222] (This really was very sportsmanlike, as it gave him about the saem familiarity with the ground as that enjoyed by the German commanders in the short April campaign.) Wilson as commander of "Force W" was thus deprived of even the advantage of knowing the country, and was only able to officially open his headquarters in the little town of Elasson literally just before the Germans attacked.

Wilson's command was to have included the Greek forces known as the Central Macedonian Army, which was originally to have been composed of the 12th Division from Macedonia (six battalions and some guns), the 20th from Florina (six battalions and some guns), and the 19th Mechanized Division from Larissa, a euphemism for an untrained unit with some vehicles which only held part of the line until the New Zealand Division came forward. The rest of the Central Macedonian Army consisted of seven battalions from western Thrace. In his official account of the campaign, Wavell noted that "this Greek force consisted of second line troops of doubtful fighting value, and was a very poor substitute for the original force of five good divisions promised by General Papagos."[223] But one of the questions which certainly arises is whether or not Papagos had promised five good divisions in the first place. In fact on 3 March Dill had forced Papagos to produce battalions without assessing their fitness.

What Wavell said even as early as 1942 was not what he had said in the fall of 1940, or even in early 1941 while General Metaxas was alive. In fact, much as Wavell is to be admired as the premier British general of the first part of the war for his grand strategy in Africa and his strategy and tactics, he is to be criticized for his loyalty in trying to support Eden and Dill. The more one reads the evidence of the way in which the British decision to aid Greece in March 1941 was made, the more one comes to the conclusion that it was a cliff-hanger, in which either Wavell or Dill could have thwarted Eden, or Eden and Wavell could have stymied Dill, and everyone would have been thankful from Athens to London to Berlin. Or London could have remained in control, as it should have, and said *Stop!*

The conference of 4 March was not a very well-kept secret. Major Crow, the assistant United States military air attaché in Athens, heard almost immediately from the economic director of the Greek Foreign Office that there had been a meeting of Eden, the king, and the prime minister, and that the German southward movement was rapid, with five divisions and four hundred aircraft already in Bulgaria. Crow learned, too, that the Greeks now had an entirely inadequate equivalent of six divisions in Macedonia, but bad weather in Albania was preventing them from shortening the line there so as to allow the transfer of more troops, while because of sea transport difficulties it would take the British two months to build up to the total of three divisions. The RAF in Athens,

Major Crow continued, expected the Germans to attack as soon as they were ready, and that date should coincide with the arrival of good weather in about one month.[224] (this latter estimate proved to be absolutely correct, for the Germans attacked on 6 April.)

In London a number of people were worried about developments. The Chiefs of Staff felt that the hazards had increased considerably, as the Greeks were too heavily involved in Albania to disengage there; the force might not be able to reach the Aliakmon Line in time to halt the advance. The navy was worried about the safety of convoys, ports, and the Suez Canal. The Australians in particular were unhappy (their first troops were due to sail from Alexandria on 6 March) because the British raid on Castelorizzo in the Dodecanese had failed on the fourth, German aircraft had appeared over Cyrenaica, where an unblooded Australian division was in garrison, and German armor was reported to be in Tripoli; moreover, the Australians were not at all sure that the protocol signed in Athens between Wilson and Papagos was binding upon them. In London Menzies asked that the Greek plan be reexamined.[225]

The proposed attack on Rhodes, Operation MANDIBLES, was canceled on 4 March on the advice of Admiral Cunningham, who considered that after the fiasco at Castelorizzo the hazards of getting the expeditionary force to Greece were great enough: the transport of 68,000 troops required the use of fifty ships from 4 March to 24 April, (of which six merchantmen and the light cruiser *Bonaventure* would be lost).[226] With the Suez Canal blocked by German mines all sorts of cargo was delayed, including coal for the Greek railways, fuel oil for the Fleet, and war material for Greece and Turkey. Several projects were proposed to bypass the Canal, create new ports, and construct railway routes, but they all required time, which Wavell did not have.

# IV

# Denouement and Disaster
## 5 March 1941 - 26 April 1941

*The final act of this tragedy was played out in two months in the spring of 1941 against a backdrop varying from blinding snow in the north to balmy sunshine in the south of Greece. Almost everywhere to the north of the country were dictatorships, dominated, of course, by Hitler's German one. To the northwest the Italians still clung successfully to Albania, and Mussolini still ruled across the Adriatic. Far to the west was Generalissimo Franco in Spain, and in between was Marshal Pétain in Vichy France. To the east, hostile French forces controlled Syria and blocked the land route between British Palestine and Turkey. Directly north of Greece were the vacillating Yugoslavs, the oil-rich but occupied Rumanians, and the hated Bulgarians. Distantly in the northeast were the Russians, unreliable and inscrutable. The only free country at all likely to be able to help was still Britain, although there was in the wings, of course, that great land of freedom, to which so many Greeks had gone to seek their fortunes, the United States. The situation there was changing, but not fast enough. Lend-Lease was about to be signed into law, ripping down much of the neutrality legislation, but, in spite of Colonel Donovan's words, America was still powerless. And Britain was in not much better case.*

*The war in the Mediterranean theater was still very much one in which Wavell was an underdog commander forced to use all his wiles, even against the Italians, who were still active in East Africa as well as alive in Tripoli and the Dodecanese. And the Germans were about to emerge both in the air and on the ground in strengths with which he could not cope, especially when the direction from London chopped and changed and divided his forces.*

## 5 March 1941

Early on 5 March Cairo notified Athens and London that, because of the closing of the Suez Canal, ships for carrying lorries were at a premium; since there were available inside the Mediterranean only half the required ships, motor transport would become the big bottleneck as the LUSTRE forces moved to Greece.

And Eden and Dill sent a third communiqué, on that cloudy day in Athens, outlining the military position: the Germans might attack in the next seven days, by which time the three Greek divisions should be on the Aliakmon Line. The implication was that the Germans should be held long enough on the Rupel and by demolitions, which Wilson was arranging, that all the Greek troops should have time to get into position before the Germans got to the line. At the moment British plans simply called for the armored brigade and one New Zealand brigade to be in place by 19 March and a second New Zealand brigade by 26 March, with the whole of the New Zealand Division complete by the end of March. But the subsequent program had not been arranged. It had been decided that there would be no bombing of Bulgarian communications until after the Germans attacked in order to gain time. And this communication was followed by a further telegram giving the text of the agreement signed by Papagos and Dill.[1]

In London the War Cabinet met at 5:30 in the afternoon after Eden's two telegrams arrived. Cabinet members heard that Eden admitted now that "the situation in Greece had deteriorated considerably. Deprived of the guidance of General Metaxas, General Papagos seemed to have lost confidence." The First Sea Lord observed that on 24 February they had gotten a schedule from the Middle East on the time it would take the British to reach the Aliakmon, but none for the Germans. Until they got this the Chiefs of Staff could not make a reasoned revision of their previous conclusions.

Churchill listened dully, suffering from a cold caused by the snuff he was taking to prevent colds! He reminded the Cabinet that before Eden left he had been told not to hesitate to act on his own authority if the urgency was too great to allow interference from home. But with the failure of the Castelorizzo operation and the postponement of MANDIBLES, Middle East resources were now being further strained to guard the Suez Canal. Given the continuing deterioration of the situation, Churchill had cabled Eden suggesting that he manage things so that London would have the final say in the Greek undertaking. Eden said that they had no choice but to see it through, but the prime minister responded that since the Greeks had not moved to the Aliakmon Line as promised, the British were still free to decide their own course of action. Now, if the British liberated the Greeks from their obligations, the Greeks could make their own terms with the Germans. Churchill, however, politician that he was, was concerned about the reaction in Spain and North Africa if Britain abandoned Greece without a fight. He went on to think out loud about the problem to the War Cabinet, which concluded that it should reconsider the position when the Yugoslav decision was known.

And so Churchill telegraphed Eden and sent along also an appraisal by the Chiefs of Staff. He explained that Eden should leave the Greeks free to accept a German ultimatum, because not much of an Imperial force could arrive in time. And he concluded, "Loss of Greece and the Balkans by no means a major catastrophe for us provided Turkey remains honest neutral." The Chiefs of Staff had noted that the hazards had considerably increased; "Nevertheless . . . we are not as yet in a position to question the military advice of those on the spot."[2]

## 6 March 1941

Thursday was an overcast day with patches of sunlight. No. 33 Hurricane Squadron, which had arrived in Greece in February and was split between between Paramythia on the west coast and Larissa on the plains of Thessaly, was ordered to Eleusis. It was to have three aircraft at readiness during daylight hours and three ready to intercept any enemy aircraft approaching Larissa or Volos.[3]

The Athens press carried the official announcement of the Foreign Secretary's visit, and at the same time the papers published editorials which openly admitted the chance of a new aggression against Greece and proclaimed the country's determination to resist attack now that she was supported by the United States and Britain.[4]

Some time during the day Papagos had one of his regular conversations with Heywood, in which he reported on the disposition of the three Greek divisions assigned to the Aliakmon position. These forces, very thin on the ground, were very lightly equipped to stop a German blitzkrieg. A total of 16 Italian 47-mm antitank guns were allotted to the entire ninety-mile line from the sea west to Mt. Kajmakalan, near Florina (or one every 5.6 miles), together with 15 20-mm antitank guns; in addition 26 old 75-mm artillery pieces were being sent from England to be used as antitank guns, but their date of arrival was unknown. Additional mountain artillery would be sent as soon as breech-blocks had been manufactured for these captured guns, and a group of 155-mm howitzers was also being sent.[5] This list was again evidence of how Papagos and the Greeks were scraping the barrel. And it is such items as this that emphasize how much the whole scheme was put together on the theoretical grounds of what fully equipped and trained divisions could handle, and not in terms of the half-trained and badly underequipped forces actually available. Even an unskilled eye has only to look at some parts of the 144-kilometer line to realize how absurdly inadequate were the proposed defending forces.

During the conversations at the military mission, General Wilson agreed to send his chief engineer, Brigadier H.P.W. Hutson, forward as soon as Major Wavish returned from a preliminary reconnaissance, so that measures for demolitions could be discussed with the Greek officer in charge. As soon as they were available two British field companies were to be sent to work in the Vardar plain and on the Aliakmon position. As for the protection of bridges and airfields against airborne attack, General Papagos thought that the twenty-four tanks of the motorized division might be most usefully employed in this task. Wilson agreed and promised some of his own, when they arrived, to cover the Aliakmon position. The problem of liaison officers and interpreters was then considered, and it was agreed to find as many as possible in Egypt, but in the meantime the Greeks would provide as many as they could. The most serious problem, though, was lack of coal, for by 16 March the Greeks would run out of coal and there would be no trains at all. The military mission was to contact Cairo urgently about this, while a mixed railway commission would handle all transportation problems. The possibility of bringing over a proper ambulance train from Egypt was also to be looked into. Lastly, Wilson raised the problem of refugees and security procedures, and these were discussed down to the immobilization of unattended cars and the destruction of local petrol supplies.

In Belgrade the Crown Council felt it had no alternative but to sign the pact with the Axis.[6] By 6 March Prince Paul knew the British intentions and limitations, and the Yugoslav general staff said that a German thrust into the country would soon take Belgrade, Zagreb, and Ljubliana, leaving the Yugoslavs only the mountains of Bosnia and Herzegovina, where they could hold out for about six weeks before they ran out of supplies. Paul was physically and mentally worn out (and not helped by nightly phone calls from his family in Athens, which were no doubt tapped). From Paul's point of view contacts with Athens had been a failure, because neither Papagos nor Wavell's chief of staff, Arthur Smith, would be specific. Neil Balfour avers that Eden wrote Paul off after hearing from Smith, and so did not read the signals being sent from Belgrade.[7]

At the Piraeus that Thursday morning more British troops landed, camped on the outskirts of Athens, and were inspected by the German consul-general, a fact confirmed by the British legation listening service.[8]

Also on Thursday morning Rear-Admiral Pridham-Wippell with the battleships *Barham* and *Valiant*, escorted by six destroyers, sailed from Alexandria for Suda Bay, Crete, where they arrived the next morning to act as a covering force for the LUSTRE convoys. No. 805 FAA Fighter Squadron and the remains of No. 815 Torpedo-Spotter-Reconnaissance Squadron were sent to Maleme airfield on Crete to provide air cover for this force.

Eden, Dill, and Wavell departed by flying boat from Salamis Bay at 8:30 a.m. Each apparently sat silent. Eden may have preened himself mentally and physically, Dill may have sat in a weary daze. We do know that Wavell sat quietly reading Lewis Carroll's *Alice in Wonderland*, a not at all inappropriate diversion for a general with a sense of humor.[9]

At five o'clock the C-in-C's met with Eden at headquarters in Cairo.

Cunningham said at once that if the Canal were closed, moving forces to Greece would take four months, not two. Otherwise he and Longmore thought that the right decision had been made. Wavell said that "provided we could get our forces into Greece, there was a good prospect of a successful encounter with the Germans. The results of success would be incalculable and might alter the whole aspect of the war." And so the group broke up feeling that they had made the right, if a difficult, decision. Asked one final time by Eden if they should go, Wavell responded, "War is an option of difficulties. We go." Outside, Dill said to Elmhirst, "I am afraid that there will be a lot of bloody noses this spring in the Aegean."[10]

After dinner they assembled quietly in the drawing room of the embassy with the vital and humorous South African prime minister, Smuts, and weighed the decision again. The "Old Baas" said, with Biblical flavor, that since the decision had already been taken, they would have to proceed, and that in balance aiding Greece would be more noble than defeat at the hands of the Germans. After some discussion Smuts said that what really worried him was the timetable—it was getting down to days and even hours. And Egypt must not be hazarded.[11]

After he had seen Blamey, Dill cabled the Dominions secretary in London that Wavell had explained the risks to Blamey and Freyberg and that both had expressed their willingness to continue the operations under the new conditions. What he did not say was that neither Blamey nor Freyberg felt, in Gavin Long's words, that they had been *consulted*. Both were in the awkward dual roles of subordinates as well as national commanders and their governments' principal military advisers. Both found themselves in the invidious position ultimately of being criticized for not having challenged their superior officers either swiftly enough or sharply enough.[12] This was harder for Freyberg to do than for Blamey, for Freyberg had been a close associate of Wavell's before the war and was imbued with the C-in-C's concepts of loyalty.

(Actually Blamey had not agreed; he had been short-circuited by Menzies' presence in the Middle East in February, and he himself had failed to apply the lesson of the Dardanelles Commission report that a senior officer who did have doubts was duty-bound to make them known to the government. It was not, in fact, until it was suggested to him by Maj. Norman Carylon on 8 March that Blamey put forward his view of the situation to which by then the Australians were already committed. Moreover, Blamey, when he did send in his appreciation, was under the misimpression that there would be twenty-three RAF squadrons in Greece, when in fact that was the total RAF in the Middle East.)[13]

At the evening gathering Wavell said that he had talked with Blamey and Freyberg that afternoon; neither of them had wanted to back out. Smuts then stressed the need to strengthen the forces in the Balkans as quickly and heavily as possible. He doubted the Germans intended to invade the United Kingdom and felt that London should realize the need for air reinforcements in the Middle East, as well as the need to fight the Germans in the Balkans rather than keeping large forces idle in the United Kingdom. In his view, the Germans in Tripoli were only a feint. And so the discussions ended there. As they left the room after the meeting, Dill said to Cunningham, "Well, we've taken the decision. I am not at all sure that it's the right one."[14]

Perhaps the one really bright ray of light in the meetings at Cairo was that Smuts said that South African troops could be moved to any place in Africa, by units if needs be, and that while he would like them kept in divisions, he did not want a South African Corps.[15]

Cairo was, of course, a leaky sieve. The American military attaché there reported that the British would send seven to eight divisions, including two armored ones, to Greece. Secretary of State Cordell Hull at once flashed this "extremely confidential" news to MacVeagh.[16]

At the end of the day, Wavell completed a note on the defense of Cyrenaica and made the point that there was a need to get mobile forces forward at once.[17]

After the war Wavell said that when the decision was made to go ahead in Greece despite the changed circumstances, ". . . it was probably the political and psychological considerations that tilted the balance over the military dangers." Troops were already beginning to land and any change of plans would have caused confusion. "So, we decided to carry on, although obviously we were on a much worse wicket. In this case London was apprehensive and they were right and we the men on the spot were wrong, as regards the immediate danger, but not in the long run."[18]

Whether or not those in Cairo had made a good decision on military or moral grounds, they were certainly aware that there were risks. When on 7 April Sir John Dill said goodbye to Wavell just before boarding the plane to return to London, Wavell is reported to have said to him half-jokingly and half-sadly, "Jack, I hope that when this action is reviewed, you will be selected to sit on my court-martial."[19]

Earlier in the day the Prime Minister had told Geoffrey Dawson, editor of the influential *Times*, that the situation in the Balkans was "murky".[20]

Later that night of 6 March Churchill told the War Cabinet that he "did not wish to expose ourselves to the charge that we had caused another small nation to be sacrificed without being able to afford effective help." But he was most anxious that the Greeks understood that all the British could send in March was two brigades. As the Greeks were evidently determined to fight the Germans, in spite of the option to withdraw Churchill had given them in his telegram to Eden stressing that they should feel free to accept a German ultimatum, Palairet had cabled that "the question was whether we would help them or abandon them." The Prime Minister then, according to the minutes, remarked that "It was inconceivable that the chief of the Imperial General Staff would have signed the military agreement with General Papagos [a copy of which the War Cabinet now had before them] if he regarded the chances of success in the operation as hopeless." The Australian prime minister then said that the problem had been presented in a way which made it unnecessarily difficult and what had been hazardous had become even more so, while "no reason was offered why the operation should succeed." He asserted that the War Cabinet had not been well informed, and that the action of the Foreign Secretary "was embarrassing." The War Cabinet was annoyed that it had been rushed into the business by Eden, but happy that a clear scapegoat had been established.

Speaking for the Chiefs of Staff at the War Cabinet, the First Sea Lord said that on 16 March the Germans would have three divisions on the Aliakmon Line when the first New Zealand brigade arrived. CAS Portal added that the RAF had three fighter squadrons and five bomber squadrons to oppose 475 German aircraft. The VCIGS said that the main weakness was the unprotected Yugoslav frontier, where the Germans might push through. In response to a question, the COS replied that to lose in Greece "would not affect the ultimate issue of the war or our successful defence of this country." It was not necessary to tell the Greeks that intervention would be a failure, as they had said that they would fight anyway.

The Prime Minister concluded that the War Cabinet was not in a position to make a decision until Eden replied to their previous telegrams, nor would they go back on the Dill-Papagos agreement unless the Greeks themselves released Britain from it.[21]

Not long after the gathering adjourned for dinner, a short interim reply from Eden in Cairo arrived, reporting on the reexamination of the Greek question carried out that afternoon with Dill and the three C-in-C's, in which it was unanimously agreed that the right decision had been made. This was passed to the reconvened War Cabinet at 10:10 that evening, and at 2:15 in the early morning of the seventh an additional sentence on the discussion with Smuts came through, with a concluding promise that a detailed appreciation would follow in the morning.

## 7 - 9 March 1941

At 3:00 a.m. on 7 March, Churchill cabled to Eden: "All preparations and movements should go forward at utmost speed. . . . But we must not take on our shoulders responsibility of urging Greeks against their better judgment to fight a hopeless battle and involve their country in probable speedy ruin. . . . It must not be said, and on your showing it cannot be said, that, having so little to give, we dragged them in by over-persuasion. I take it from your attitude and from Athens telegrams . . . that you are sure on this point."

Equally important, the Prime Minister had to be able to tell the Dominions that the venture had been undertaken not because Eden had entered into a commitment at Athens, "but because Dill, Wavell, and other C-in-C's are convinced that there is reasonable fighting chance." "Please remember in your stresses that so far you have given us few facts or reasons on their authority which can be presented to these Dominions as justifying the operation on any grounds but *noblesse oblige*. A precise military appreciation is indispensible. . . . You know our hearts are with you and your great officers." [22]

During the morning of that day Smuts sent his old World War I War Cabinet colleague a message:

> We have a reasonable chance to build up a stable front in Greece. Such a front would be a most important development and may possibly become decisive. I build no great hopes on Turkey and Yugoslavia in the immediate future but feel that a firm British front in the Balkans would transform the situation in southern Europe and the Mediterranean basin generally. . . . I would thus urge most strongly that this new front be supported with all our strength. Our chief immediate need here is more aeroplanes. . . . I am expediting another bomber squadron from South Africa and Beaverbrook should surely also disgorge from his hoard. Next in order I place tanks and guns for us and our allies. We are already grievously late and should now move with all possible speed. [23]

Then Eden's long signal came in.

This started with the fundamental assumption that Prime Minister Koryzis's Tatoi declaration was valid and the consistent basis of Greek policy. The Greeks understood there was no honorable peace open to them. More to the point, the British already had eight RAF squadrons and supporting forces in Greece. Then the message reverted again to emotional arguments based on the surplus of forces now that a great victory had been won in Libya. (One senses a political speech written by the Foreign Secretary and not a military appreciation.) Longmore's difficulties were again pointed out, however, and his grave doubts as to whether his forces could face their many commitments. Cunningham felt that the naval situation had deteriorated sharply in the last ten days, but Wavell remained stoically optimistic that *if his forces could be transported to Greece and concentrated on the Aliakmon position*, "there is a good chance of holding the enemy advance." Defeating the Germans in Europe was rated very high for propaganda purposes. And the signal ended with another long paragraph once again supporting the decision taken, in spite of the serious RAF shortages: "The struggle in the air in this theatre will be a stern one. Longmore requires all the help that can be given. If he can hold his own, most of the dangers and difficulties of this enterprise will disappear."[24]

At noon on the seventh the War Cabinet met to consider these messages. Here it was not the shadow of Chanak but the aura of the Battle of Britain which subtly colored the discussion. The view was that the RAF had won against odds before. (No one stopped to consider that the reasons included the radar-backed fighter direction system that Dowding had commanded, short supply lines, and modern aircraft and airfields.)

Having now decided to proceed, Churchill justified the shaky venture by saying that it was not such a bad decision, for the British had a fair chance of reaching the Aliakmon Line before the Germans could break through, there was still hope the Yugoslavs would join the Allies, and, if the Anglo-Greek forces did have to retire, they would be retreating down a narrowing peninsula with a number of strong defensive positions. And the British would shortly have a strong air force in Greece, which, although outnumbered by the Germans, would face about the same odds as in the past. To this Menzies, the only person present who seemed willing to contradict the Prime Minister, said that it was funny that a decision was being made based on the assurances of those in the Middle East all of whose points supported the case against going to Greece. Churchill brushed this off by saying that the military conclusions were already known, although the appreciation had not arrived, so now was the time to make the decision.

So it was settled. (Beaverbrook admitted later that no one dared to stand up to Churchill. And that night Cadogan noted that on a nice balance he thought it right.)[25] Then the earlier message from Greece about not bombing the Rumanian oilfields was read, and the CAS said that no bombing could be undertaken anyway until after 9 March, when three squadrons of Wellingtons would be in Greece. Nevertheless, most of the discussion concentrated irrelevantly on the fact that the Greeks had deprived the British of the bombing initiative.[26] In fact, there was little hope of bombing Rumania in March because of the weather, but (judging with the benefit of hindsight) perhaps it would have been better if the RAF had been allowed to do this. The Germans would then have attacked before the British could have landed many forces, forcing cancelation of the expedition. Though perhaps not what the Greeks wanted, this might have saved them additional bloodshed.

And the COS were right: the RAF in the Middle East was ill-suited for its task. To stop panzers in either Cyrenaica, as it would turn out, or in the plains of northern Greece, the RAF needed long-range fighters to maintain local air superiority, and fighter-bombers to destroy tanks in a country whose topography often channeled armor into ideal target areas. It had neither, and it still looked down upon tactical work, called army cooperation.

On the ninth Churchill told Eden that there was still a chance that Yugoslavia might come in, but he rather thought not. Among other matters he asked Eden to look into the use of manpower in Wavell's command: "Do not overlook those parts of your instructions dealing with economy of the Middle East Armies. Am relying on you to clean this up, and to make sure that every man pulls his weight. A few days might well be devoted to this." Though Eden would remain in the Middle East another month, there are no signals home reporting discovery of fat at any level.

The lack of air resources in the Middle East, while such resources accumulated at home, led to bad feeling starting with Portal's signal of 6 March questioning the wisdom of keeping a fighter squadron at Aden. Longmore replied that Gladiators were better against Italian fighters than were Hurricanes, but Portal still thought it would be better if the crews at least were sent north to learn about Hurricanes in Egypt pending the arrival of sufficient aircraft to reequip the squadron. Longmore did not think so.[27]

The growing irritation between the two men, due largely to lack of contact, signals written by underlings, and inadequate time for the writing of long personal letters exchanging views, was exacerbated during Smuts' one-day visit to Cairo. Evidently at some point in the conversations Eden, Wavell, or Longmore, or possibly even Cunningham, unwisely made a comment about the number of aircraft at home compared to what was available in the Middle East. Or Smuts, as the principal founder of the RAF, put it in himself. At any rate, on the seventh, Portal sent the following tart message to his AOC-in-C ME: "I have seen General Smuts telegram in which he refers to "Beaverbrook disgorging from his hoard." In case you may have the impression that the flow of reinforcements to you is in any way restricted by the views or actions of the minister of aircraft production I wish to assure you that the only limit which now operates is our power to pack and ship the aircraft and to fly them across the Takoradi route and from Europe direct."

And he followed that signal with another, sent in three parts, each of which was to be given to a different officer to decipher; Longmore was to read it by taking alternate words from the second and third parts!

I feel bound to tell you that further emphasis on your shortage of aircraft is quite unnecessary. Certain passages in recent telegrams to Prime Minister from General Smuts and/or Eden presumably included as a result of your representations to them have created a bad impression especially in view of repeated suggestions as to desirability of concentration at decisive point at the expense of less important theaters. . . . Inference can be drawn either (a) that you do not believe my repeated assurances as to our efforts to reinforce you or (b) that you are indirectly disassociating yourself from recent decision on Greece. I am sure that you will agree that confidence and determination must now animate whole command. . . . We will do everything humanly possible to meet your needs.

The message given above is the way it was hand-drafted by Portal, the printed text being very slightly more polite. And Longmore responded on the 10th: "I have received your X.940 ⅔ to which I take grave exception." (Portal received this signal just as he finished writing by hand a personal letter to Longmore explaining that he had been forced by the Prime Minister to send the carefully ciphered signal, since Churchill insisted on reading all messages that passed between Cairo and London. He hoped, Portal scrawled, that Longmore understood how great were the efforts London was making on his behalf.)

Meanwhile the air member for supply and organization had also been increasingly disturbed by the tone of the signals he was receiving from the Middle East. He laid the blame on Air Vice Marshal A.C. Maund in Cairo, who was no doubt thoroughly exasperated. To the AMSO's signal Longmore replied that he agreed that the signals from Maund could have been less acidly expressed, and that he had so informed the author. However, he went on that he felt that the problem was much deeper and that the RAF needed liaison officers similar to those of senior rank who constantly traveled between the War Office and the Middle East, and suggested that this be discussed with the CAS. "Like you we are all working at very high pressure and hard put to it to meet our wide commitments." And he went on to suggest that two officers who were on their way home should stop in at the Air Ministry to give them some firsthand impressions of the maintenance problems in the Command.[28]

On 8 March Menzies sent Deputy Prime Minister A.W. Fadden in Canberra an eight-hundred-word cable. He admitted that he had had a most anxious time of it and hoped that he had posed faithfully all the questions that those at home had asked. But, "Our military advisers discount the possibilities of a successful thrust by a German armoured force in North Africa and there is complete confidence that the Benghazi front can be held without interfering with the new project."

What upset the Dominions was that once again an Imperial minister had committed them without asking. Menzies noted that he attached a high value to the judgment of Smuts, but the timetable was such that the first Australian troops would not get into position much before the end of the month "by which time many things may have happened." He concluded "that although the hazards are considerable the proposal is by no means hopeless" and should be governed by the overwhelming importance of impressing the world, especially America, with the idea that the British were not abandoning the Greeks.

The New Zealand government had already pointed out on 26 February that it thought that the force being sent for what Churchill called this "glorious task" was a bit small, but it had been willing to accept the explanation that if linked with Greek and Turkish forces the whole would probably be as strong as anything that the Germans could bring against it. However, when they heard the revised figures after the conferences of early March, the Auckland Cabinet cabled on 9 March a very realistic appreciation: in effect it saw the emperor's new clothes, and that the position was one of extreme gravity. The Germans had unlimited resources, interior lines, and a superior air force, not to mention the Italian fleet, the Dodecanese Islands, and the likelihood that the Suez Canal would be blocked; the Greeks would collapse quickly, "leaving the British force in the air." Nevertheless, having said what Dill should have said, they felt morally bound to support the Greeks. The New Zealand Cabinet's cable ended with three caveats, however: full air and sea escort for the transport was to be provided; full and immediate consideration was to be given to the means of withdrawal on both land and sea; and the operation should not be mounted unless the full force contemplated could clearly be made available at the appropriate time.[29]

If everyone had not been so busy keeping a stiff upper lip, and so concerned with not letting down the side, they might have seen that there was absolutely no hope of sending anywhere near the full 120,000-man force contemplated. No one seems to have made a chart that showed the time lag between decision and reality. Or it may have been part of Wavell's plan not to have Churchill risking security by asking questions.

The Dominions were further upset on 9 March when the Australian Cabinet received a cable from Blamey asking permission to present his position before the Australian Imperial Force was committed to Greece. The ministers were confused, as they had been told that Blamey was "agreeable" and knew that the force was already committed. Nevertheless, Sir Percy Spender, the minister for the army, told the GOC to go ahead and submit his views.[30]

As McClymont has pointed out, Churchill, under Australian pressure, tried to get Eden to get them all off the hook.[31] Unfortunately for Eden's reputation, he apparently insisted upon being obtuse and failing to see that Churchill was asking him to make the excuses that would allow everyone to repudiate the Dill-Papagos agreement. One fly in the ointment was Palairet and the embarrassment that British troops had landed prematurely at the Piraeus. The latter could have been explained away, however, as having been sent only to provide airfield protection for the

RAF tactical air forces helping the Greeks against the Italians. Or they could have been withdrawn to Crete to bolster its defenses. But somehow Crete was never seen in proper perspective as the right flankguard of the British position in the Middle East in either naval or air terms. Nor were the dangers of the Axis-held Dodecanese airfields fully appreciated.

To compound the coming difficulties, even though Wavell had noted that he needed to strengthen his defenses in Cyrenaica, the signals emanating from London late on Thursday 6 March and early on Friday the seventh injected another miscalculation. Churchill suggested to Eden the possibility of going to Tripoli instead of Greece, but he put the onus for making the decision on Dill and Wavell. To this Eden replied that the Dominions would not make difficulties about going to Greece, while Wavell had pointed out that to reverse plans would create practical military difficulties. So the COS cabled Wavell that the Cabinet accepted full responsibility for the decision to aid Greece and authorized him to proceed, promising that it would communicate with the Australian and New Zealand governments.[32]

De Guingand remarked in *Generals at War* that it would have helped if Wavell had said to Eden and Churchill that Greece would end in evacuation (as he must have concluded that it would). Wavell's confidence in the Greek operation was shown by his attitude to evacuation plans: the Joint Planning Staff in Cairo arranged to meet with Dill's aide, Mallaby, but he refused to answer their questions. Foreseeing disaster, this band of junior staff officers started preparing their own plans for evacuation, only to be stopped by Wavell. However, a few days later, given an indirect hint by Wavell himself, they set to work once again (luckily, for it meant that two-thirds of the force sent was recovered, though all equipment was lost).

As the authors of the official history, *Grand Strategy,* have pointed out, motives of honor are often confused with policy. "In this case Cairo never sent London a military appraisal and Whitehall never for its part appreciated the drain on Middle East resources. In fact, no considered estimate was made of how much we were prepared to lose."[33]

Campaigns have neither tidy beginnings nor neat endings: the administrative side inevitably stretches out at either end. It was, moreover, in part the tail that caused Wavell not to want to change plans again and switch from Greece back to Cyrenaica; he feared the truth of the old military proverb, "Order, counter-order, chaos."

Planning for the Grecian campaign had begun at least as early as 12 February, long before even Eden, Dill and the C-in-C's had agreed on the move. By 17 February road and port forces had received orders which raised the question of mobilization orders for an expeditionary force.[34] Now, as the troops were moved to Greece in March, highest priority was given to armored units, to impress the Greeks, and second highest to the New Zealanders, who were to dig defenses. High enough priorities were not given to medical necessities in a land of large, low-lying, malarial plains. And malaria was not the only disease to create concern—there were also typhoid, paratyphoid, and related fevers. Intestinal diseases were a constant campaigners' worry even in Athens, the one city with modern sanitation. Many hospitals had to be sited in malarial areas in order to obtain adequate water, and this meant a high chance of dysentery. Apart from a high rate of VD (which even engaged D'Albiac and his staff in a debate over whether to issue free sheaths, as at least fifty airmen were constantly hospitalized with the side-effects of pleasure-seeking), there was also a 3 percent rate of pulmonary tuberculosis to worry about.[35]

Though the leading element of the 1st Armoured Brigade landed at the Piraeus on 7 March and proceeded north shortly thereafter when its transport arrived, it was not until 2 April that the New Zealand Division was in line on the Aliakmon, backing up its exposed position on the plains forward on the road to Salonika. And on 2 April the first flight of the Australian Division was just landing at the Piraeus. Command difficulties in Athens were never really straightened out. The navy was scattered about the Piraeus, about three miles away from the army in the Hotel Acropole, while the air force commander reported directly to the Greek C-in-C and had western and eastern wings operating independently of each other and of Wilson. For much of this period the military mission (it never accepted the name change to liaison delegation) had to supply the nucleus intelligence section, liaison officers, interpreters, and a number of administrative staff from its own very small resources, for it was the only group that knew the personalities, the language, and the country.

The Greek and British armies were two almost totally different organizations equipped with incompatible arms. The Greek force was a marching army that lived on its feet, supported by a supply train of mules, donkeys, and women. The British army was a mechanized, technological organization. The Greeks could move up and down mountains and across plains at four kilometers an hour; the British could make hardly any better speed in the mountains, but they and the Germans could move considerably faster on the plains, provided it was dry.[36] The Greeks fully understood that one of the main problems was that the only rail route to their main supply base for the Albanian front ran up the east coast almost to Salonika, and then northwest along a highly vulnerable line with all of the section Plati-Florina lying in front of the Aliakmon position. In the discussions of the British presence in Greece, this fact and the paucity of paved roads had hardly been considered. It was in part to remedy this vulnerability that since 1931 the Greeks had been extending the Volos-Pharsala one-meter-gauge line from Kardista westward to Trikkala and thence north up the valleys to rejoin the main line at Amyndeon. The ballast had been spread but the rails had not been laid before Greece was overrun in April 1941. Besides the shortage of coal and the need to transship goods between gauges, there was also a shortage of meter-gauge waggons.

On the other hand the needs of a mechanized army can be seen from the example of the New Zealand artillery alone. Each of its three field regiments of 45 officers and 590 men had 112 cars and trucks, of which 36 were quads towing guns. There were 48 ammunition trailers, 29 motorcycles, and 72 field guns, plus a headquarters unit of 7 cars and trucks and 2 motorcycles.

Use of the Greek railways in early March was limited by the capacity of the single-track main line to two 25-car trains a day, or a total of 240 tons daily to Larissa. After 10 March this increased to three trains daily. From Volos, loads had to be reduced from 137 to 60 tons because the locomotives simply could not develop enough power burning olivewood in place of coal.[37]

Larissa, a sleepy little provincial town with an airfield, offered no real solution to the supply problem. It flooded in winter, and it had no sidings, so when trains arrived their contents were dumped onto the ground along the tracks. It was mid-March before enough motor transport got through from Athens to begin clearing this mess and organizing a proper dumping system. And even so, Larissa was fifty to one hundred tortuous road miles from the positions along the Aliakmon and in the passes behind that line. Originally GHQ ME had intended that the main base should be moved from Athens to Thebes, but the Greeks would not allow the area about that town to be scouted. The British suggested Stylis (Stilida, the port of Lamia), but the Greeks did not like that idea as they wished to keep the railway line free for the storage of waggons evacuated when the Germans took Salonika. Eleusis was not discovered to be inadequate until after the Piraeus was bombed out of action; then it was found that it would have to be dredged. Another choice was Ithea, the bauxite port below Delphi from which the British had built a road to Larissa via Lamia in World War I. But even a supply of mules proved to be difficult to find. The Middle East was not a mule area and the British were not muleteers. Two shiploads were dispatched, but one was sunk en route. Thus there were never enough mules forward on the Aliakmon, where they were badly needed as many of the best defensive positions could not be reached by vehicles.

As the planners in the Hotel Acropole got to work in the middle of March they discovered that there were many problems which had not been discussed in the plenary talks, though Dill was apparently aware of some of them. The question of fighting delaying actions from the Struma River back was governed not so much by the lack of air cover—the scapegoat of the campaign—as by a lack of bridges which could take lorry columns, and of bridging equipment: on the flat plains in March and April, rivers flooded wide; they were not deep, but they could stall motor vehicles during freshets. As the military tactical realities began to sink in at the Acropole, Brigadier Brunskill says, the administrative staff came to the conclusion that the only solution was a hurried withdrawal and evacuation to prevent the British from being annihilated. And the more they considered the hazardous situation of the roads and the railway and the vulnerable bridges, the more pessimistic they became.[38] In other words, partly because the Greeks had not allowed reconnaissance, partly because the British had not done their homework, and partly because Eden was determined to create a Balkan alliance, the British army was sent into an untenable situation. Perhaps that is the trouble with doing military appreciations only from large-scale maps in the staff-college fashion without viewing the ground.

On Friday, 7 March, *Formidable* finally squeezed through the Suez Canal and the Royal Navy once again had an aircraft carrier in the Mediterranean.[39]

In Cairo, where it might have been most sensible to allow matters to lie fallow, on instructions from London Eden and Dill stayed on, trying to do something about Yugoslavia and Turkey. At midnight Eden decided to compose a message to Churchill, a process for which he liked an audience. He summoned Dill and Wavell from their beds, and the two generals sat on the couch in their brown English wool dressing gowns like two teddy bears and fell asleep while Eden declaimed telegraphic phrases.[40]

Early on Saturday morning in London Cadogan had just got into bed when he was routed out by an irritated Prime Minister who had discovered that the Foreign Office was closed. Churchill needed information about a signal that had just come in from Belgrade that Prince Paul was sending an officer to Athens. After Cadogan had gone over and talked with him, the Prime Minister sent off a telegram to Athens urging that all support be given to this new mission. (Cadogan later got a reprimand from Eden for not going through the Foreign Secretary, who was in Cairo.)[41]

The Yugoslavs had decided upon another delaying tactic, and on 6 March had sent Lt. Col. Milisar Perišić, traveling on a British passport in the name of L[ast] R[ay] Hope, to Athens to talk to "Mr. Watt" (General Wilson). He was to explain the Yugoslav dilemma, request evacuation of the northern Yugoslav armies when the Germans attacked, determine how soon a line could be established from Salonika to Lake Doiran, and ask for aircraft, tanks, and antitank guns. Wilson could give only general replies, while urging the Yugoslavs to attack the Italians in Albania in the rear. Part of the mission of "Forlorn Hope," as the British called him, was, of course, to find out as much about British strength as he could, and the puny British force of three and a half divisions hardly encouraged Yugoslav action.

Perišić met twice with General Arthur Smith, Wilson, D'Albiac, Turle, and Papagos. As the Yugoslav laid especial emphasis upon the necessity of holding Salonika if his country were to come in, this, naturally, made it difficult for the Greeks to evacuate it as long as there was that hope. In the end Papagos concluded that this visit was an act of bad faith; Prince Paul had always given the Greek king friendly assurances, but sixteen days after the meetings in Athens the Yugoslavs signed the treaty with Hitler, receiving a promise that they would get Salonika as their reward.[42]

In Washington on that Saturday, 8 March, the Senate passed Lend-Lease by a vote of sixty to thirty-one, the only fear being that it would allow the president to aid Communist Russia. Roosevelt was already making sure that aid went to England, so Churchill's original fears that a British withdrawal from Greece would hurt her in the United States were no longer valid.[43] Perhaps he sensed this: he now appeared to be willing to pull back, but by this time he had lost his grip over Eden.

At just after midnight Papagos told the British military attaché that the movement of his troops from Thrace by train was going smoothly, even though the Germans were constantly conducting air reconnaissance over all of northern Greece. The morale of the troops was high, but the prospects of a German attack were causing misgivings, especially as the Germans knew all about the arrival of British troops.[44]

The weather on Sunday, 9 March, was not on the side of the British. The Brallos Pass was so badly clogged with snow that A/A guns could not get through and so had to be sent up the coastal road by Thermopylae. Some days later when the road was opened, it proved to be in such bad condition that it was less damaging to the towed guns to send them by rail.[45] Even in the best of weather the road, with its switchback curves and steep winding gradients, was a challenge for British drivers. In the Hotel Acropole well-muffled commanding officers heard that Greece was not at war with Germany, so the German military attaché was free to record the comings and goings of all British units.[46]

On the south shore of the Mediterranean the 6th Australian Division was warned to proceed to Greece in three groups, to begin embarking at Alexandria on 19 March.[47] At the port General Freyberg promulgated an embarkation message for the New Zealanders which said that they would be fighting "in defence of Greece, the birthplace of culture and learning." The message, the New Zealand historian Murphy said, put "the mission . . . in the crusading tradition of Anzac and had overwhelming appeal." It was to be a sparkling adventure compared to the dirt of Egypt.[48]

Bernard Freyberg was the rare VC who rose to general rank and continued to act with distinction. He was a New Zealander, but after the First World War he had become a regular in the British army, attended the

Staff College with Marshal-Cornwall, and retired in 1937 as a major general. He was a huge, broadchested man of six feet with a sometimes grim visage but an eager welcoming smile, a rasping voice, and a good memory for names and faces. The troops called him "Tiny," but his staff called him "the General," a name he liked, or "Bernard," which as a New Zealander he tolerated. He spoke authoritatively on a wide variety of subjects, but his biographer, Major-General W.G. Stevens, who was also a member of his staff, believes he lacked a wider perspective. A fighting soldier much respected by the troops, he had arrived back in Cairo in September 1940 after an absence in England of three months.[49]

Just before bedtime that night in Cairo, Pierson Dixon, filled with the news that Prince Paul might at last see Eden, dropped in at the C-in-C's house, only to find Wavell already in his russet pyjamas. Nevertheless, they had a long conference.

## 10 March 1941

In Athens there were arguments in the Cabinet about the relationship of Mussolini's plans to Hitler's. Prime Minister Koryzis said that they were related, but at least four Cabinet members indicated that they saw no evil in Hitler's plans, and they were supported by some lesser lights. Koryzis argued that control of Greece was essential to Germano-Italian plans to drive the British out of the Mediterranean and was part of the general German plan to seize the Suez Canal and the Mosul oilfields. He also revealed to the Cabinet a secret Metaxas memorandum which expressed distrust of the Germans. Metaxas believed that the Italians had torpedoed the Greek warship *Helle* without Hitler's knowledge, but anticipating a German attack upon Greece.[50] The American director of the Near East Foundation, Laird Archer, added in his report of the discussions that he had been told that Koryzis reaffirmed the Greek determination to resist the Germans in the Metaxas spirit.[51] The American ambassador reported to Washington that the consul-general in Salonika had phoned him that morning to say that British troops had arrived in Salonika[52] (which was quite untrue).

On 10 March General Heywood saw General Papagos and then reported to Wilson. Papagos agreed at once to a British air reconnaissance of the Struma valley and added that the British were now free to make reconnaissances wherever they wished, even of Salonika, but he hoped that they would not send too many people there at once. It was agreed that liaison officers should be attached to the three Greek headquarters at Salonika, Serres, and Kozani, that Heywood himself should visit the Macedonian fortifications, and that British troops going forward of the Aliakmon position should have special passes, but that elsewhere in Greece their ID cards would suffice. The question of Wilson's incognito status was again raised, and Papagos said that the prime minister requested that it remain in being until General Wilson was ready to take over command; Papagos would then publish an order of the day to the Greek army explaining who he was and why he was in Greece; the choice of the exact moment should be left to Wilson.

Papagos sent for Heywood that same evening and raised a number of points about the command of British units forward of the Aliakmon Line. He thought that if they went beyond the Vardar they should be under Greek command, but then, as the whole frontier force retreated and passed through the Aliakmon position, it should come under General Wilson's control. Papagos hoped that Wilson would give him a few days' notice before taking over command, and Heywood assured him that he would, but that he could not do so until his headquarters and communications were established. They then discussed why Germany had not already attacked, and Papagos laid it to the firmer attitude of Yugoslavia. As they parted, Papagos asked Heywood to drop in again the next day, and to keep him informed of the arrival and movements of British troops in Greece.[53]

From Egypt Blamey cabled home that neither the 7th Australian Division nor the New Zealand Division had ever trained as divisions, and both the 6th Australian Division and the armored division were unready. That left no other troops in the Middle East not fully engaged. Because of shipping difficulties the arrival of troops would be uncertain and the movements now ordered would take two months. In contrast, he said, the Germans already had available as many divisions as the roads would carry, and would have more by the time the Australians arrived and were in position—and that these troops would be completely trained and conditioned. Blamey felt that to land a small British force was only asking the Germans to attack and knock the British off the Continent. The choice appeared to be between the public-opinion effect, especially on Japan, of not sending aid and that of another evacuation. He concluded, "Military operations are extremely hazardous in view of the disparity between the opposing forces in numbers and training." Blamey's cable much upset the Australian Cabinet, which, however, waited until 18 March to respond.

From Cairo Wavell could report that Papagos was much more cheerful and helpful, that Wilson on his way back from his meeting with "Mr. Hope" had visited the Aliakmon Line and made contact with the Greek commanders, and that the seven battalions from Thrace had begun to move onto the position. Equally good news was that the Suez Canal was open again and that, while the second and third flights had had to sail at half strength, another flight would be fitted in before the fourth one scheduled to carry over the rest of the two first groups.

Eden cabled the Prime Minister that "I still have hopes of a triumph, but we are not home yet." Smuts could only stay in Cairo one night, as his parliament was in session, and so Eden had not extended Churchill's invitation to visit London. And as to the matter of the economy of the British army in the Middle East, Wavell agreed that a general officer should be sent out from Home to make a thorough investigation and report.

There followed a message from Wavell to the War Office pointing out that Portal was being shortsighted in trying to get Longmore to pull in his forces from the Sudan and East Africa just when they were needed to help wrap up those campaigns, whose completion would free both military and naval forces for operations elsewhere. Moreover, the C-in-C ME noted, on 21 February it had been suggested that Italian East Africa could be liquidated if air reinforcements were sent, but they had not been.

The military mission in Athens reported that the three Greek divisions were now in line from the Aegean Sea to Kajmakalan.[54]

At noon in London the War Cabinet met and began a discussion (which in the end dragged on until after the Germans attacked Hellas) as to when to announce that aid was being given Greece. It was pointed out that the Germans and the press would report the arrival of troops immediately, but Menzies argued for waiting until the agreement of the Dominions had been received. As the Prime Minister was not present, it was agreed that the Ministry of Information should hold a session that afternoon to draft a communiqué, but that it should not be released until the Prime Minister gave his approval.[55] No agreement with Wavell was reached on this before the German attack on 6 April made it academic.

## 11 March 1941

In Athens on Tuesday Major Crow reported to MacVeagh that the two RAF Gladiator squadrons had finally got Hurricanes and that the mixed Blenheim squadron had been converted fully to fighters. More RAF squadrons were expected when they could be released from Africa; the RAF anticipated the German attack within a month.[56]

Starting on 11 March there were rumors that various Greeks, from Cabinet members to generals, had approached the Germans for a "peace with honor" (an expression first used by Disraeli upon his return from the Congress of Berlin in 1878).[57] Metaxas had tried to discuss this with the British in 1938-1939 without success, and now Papagos faced the same dilemma. Some of his officers were proposing that the Germans be told that if terms could be arranged they should include Greek assurance that the British would leave the country and give up Crete, which they had seized without Greek assent. The fact that the proposals existed and were apparently emanating from the Central Macedonian Army made the Greek C-in-C's task all the more difficult. Yet again, it may be suggested that if he had broached it to *London*, the Cabinet there would have welcomed a way out of the mess, even if it meant that Eden would have resigned (temporarily?) in a huff at being bypassed and ignored. The point is that the British had built for themselves a house of cards, but no one was willing to knock it down as it deserved.

German air attacks from Rhodes again closed the Suez Canal, this time until 22 March. On the other hand, the Lend-Lease administration in Washington issued two directives declaring the defense of the United Kingdom and of Greece vital to the United States.

The same day Admiral Cunningham signaled the First Sea Lord, Sir Dudley Pound, that there were only sixteen heavy A/A guns between Benghazi and Alexandria, and that these were being concentrated at Tobruk; the rest had gone to Greece. Malta had but eight serviceable Hurricanes, while in the Middle East they had but thirty fighters to face over two hundred Axis machines. He added that London was misinformed about British strength in the air in the Middle East. In fact, Longmore wrote to D'Albiac, "It will help if you are aware of the aircraft position here. It has reached the most acute stage since the war broke out, and for some little time to come, as I have foreseen and warned Air Staff, it will be impossible to keep all our existing squadrons up to establishment. As regards Fighters, the supply for the moment is not keeping pace with wastage. . . . As regards Medium Bombers, 2 squadrons have had to be reduced to cadre already, one having no operational aircraft at all and the other only two. . . ."[58]

By mid-March Air Intelligence in London was becoming, thanks to ULTRA, very accurate. Their estimate of the number of German aircraft in the Balkans was 482 (the actual figure was 490). But Military Intelligence was hopelessly off. On 27 March it reported thirty-five German divisions in the Balkans, when actually only seventeen were present. It was clear from Enigma that an invasion of Britain was unlikely, though in late February, according to Hinsley, London was still not aware of the coming invasion of Russia.[59]

And as if to confirm Cunningham's allegation that London did not fully comprehend the air situation in the Middle East, the COS sent Wavell a telegram suggesting that, since the Germans had not bombed the British landing in Greece, perhaps they could not; it might therefore throw them off balance if the British struck at their lines in Bulgaria. (Yet Eden, who certainly did understand the air situation there, sent a message to Churchill on the thirteenth emphasizing that the suggestion that Longmore get fighters from East Africa hardly made good sense: General Alan Cunningham actually only had *eight*, and even if these were moved to Egypt, it would be some time before they were again fit for action. Of the Hurricanes promised for March, none had yet arrived. Of 44 Wellingtons promised in February and March only eight had reached the Middle East. Malta was a constant drain on the Hurricane supply; would it be possible to fly in some off a carrier from the western Mediterranean? And at the same time fly out 30 Wellingtons to bring the four squadrons in the theater up to strength?)[60]

Far more serious was the fighter defense of Cyrenaica.

## 12 March 1941

As far as the state of his fighters was concerned, Longmore certainly had the backing of Wavell and Cunningham. On 12 March the latter added in a signal to the Admiralty on the problems of Malta: "A.O.C. in C Middle East is doing utmost he can with his meagre force and cannot possibly supply all Malta's needs—which in my opinion are at least two full squadrons of fighters and constant replacement of inevitable wastage in such conditions."[61]

In London Portal was trying to calm Longmore down after the Smuts affair, assuring him that he regularlly got all signals received in London and that cooperation was close. Moreover, "Within military policy laid down by the government I have always recognized your right to make decisions, but this does not relieve me of duty to express opinion when I think this may be of value to you."[62] The air member for supply and organization also wished to be more conciliatory and explained that not only had they been making special efforts since last autumn to fill the Middle East's needs, but also they had established a special section to watch over Longmore's interests in the directorate of equipment and would arrange for a squadron-leader from the equipment branch to travel constantly between the United Kingdom and Egypt. And Portal offered to send either Air Marshal Sir Bertine Sutton, commandant of the RAF Staff College, or Marshal of the RAF Sir John Salmond to help.

Cunningham responded to an Admiralty signal pointing out that aircraft-carriers should not be used except in emergencies for the transport of aircraft: "I am not aware that Longmore has expressed any opinion about the reinforcement of Malta by aircraft from carriers, but I feel that you are not being kept well-informed about fighter situation in the Middle East. Large reinforcements of this type of aircraft are urgently necessary if we are not to find ourselves at all points in serious difficulties. Are you aware that in February only one (*repeat* one) Hurricane was received in the Middle East and that in March none have yet arrived? . . . I agree that by looking ahead it should be quite possible to supply fighter necessity of Malta without use of carriers, but, as you will realize, there has been a definite failure to do this which has placed us in present rather grim situation."[63]

This obviously stung the Air Ministry, which immediately demanded if it was not true that actually in February and early March ME Command had received 27 Hurricanes. To this Longmore replied that Cunningham would have been correct if he had said *Takoradi;* London was correct that 27 Hurricanes had reached the Middle East.[64]

Meanwhile on 12 March Knatchbull-Hugesson, good old "Snatch" in Ankara, informed his listeners that the Turkish Foreign Minister said that the Turks would stand only on the defensive and would neither occupy the bridgeheads the Greeks were abandoning at Demotika and De- deagatch nor destroy the bridges there. He added that he was "sick of Yugoslavia."[65] At the same time the Turkish War Office passed along intelligence from the military attaché in Belgrade which gave details of the estimated seventeen to twenty-one German divisions in Bulgaria. And Wilson signaled a rumor that the Germans would make an airborne assault on Mytilene and Lemnos.[66]

In Cyrenaica Neame and the GOC of the 9th Australian Division, Morshead, had begun to indicate their concern to Cairo about the pres- ence of German units in North Africa. Wavell himself became more anxious, but still gambled that the Germans could not attack until May, by which time the two veteran Indian divisions would be finished in East Africa and moved to the Desert. Group Captain L.O. Borwn, command- ing the Desert air force, was much more anxious, as his small force of PRU planes was bringing in photographic evidence of small ports in use and landing grounds under construction. Though he attacked the main air- fields and Tripoli with the four Wellington squadrons based in the Canal Zone and at Malta, his force was too small to stop enemy activities.[67]

## 13 March 1941

Clues to the presence of ULTRA in Greece are conspicuous by their absence, but in the BFG HQ operations record for this date there is the intriguing entry that Pilot/Officers R.W. Green and A.J. Silver arrived for cipher duties from the Middle East Code and Cypher School.[68] According to Hinsley, these were the first ULTRA officers to reach Athens.

## 14 March 1941

On 14 March the RAF was finally allowed to bomb airfields inside Albania in aid of the Greeks.[69]

Eden's departure from the Middle East was delayed for various rea- sons, so on 14 March Churchill sent him a long message: "I have come to the conclusion that it is better for you to stay in the Middle East until the opening phase of this crisis has matured. Your instructions give you the means of concerting the political and military action of all the factors involved. The attitude of Yugoslavia is still by no means hopeless and situation may at any moment arise which would enable you to go there. Turkey requires stimulus and guidance. No one but you can combine and concert the momentous policy which you have pressed upon us and which we have adopted. The War Cabinet needs a representative on the spot, and I need you there very much indeed."

He then went on to say that General Sikorski had agreed to the use of the Polish Brigade and that he, Churchill, was concerned that not enough Englishmen were in action in the Middle East and so he was sending the 50th Division in W.S.8, leaving on 22 April. He urged that MANDIBLES be undertaken and completed as the 6th Division would be needed shortly; he hoped that MANDIBLES would be over by the end of March. Then he wanted to know why Papagos had not withdrawn three or four divisions from the Albanian front, urged that the Yugoslavs get their new equipment by knocking the Italians out in Albania, and instructed that Lemnos, just reported by the naval attaché in Athens as unmanned, be occupied to prevent the Germans seizing the airfield there. As for Longmore's complaints, they overlooked the fact that 104 Hurricanes and parts for Tomahawks were on the way. In addition every effort was being made to fly out 22 Wellingtons within the next fortnight. And lastly, he wished to point out that it was increasingly difficult to keep the press from mentioning the landings in Greece, especially when the German military attaché had already reported the correct numbers to Berlin. He ended by agreeing with Longmore and Portal that when Eden and Dill did fly home, they should go via Lagos, but it would put them out of action for a critical seven days. "Everything is going quietly here, and we have begun to claw the Huns down in the moonlight to some purpose. God bless you all."[70]

In London Chips Channon had lunch at the Mirabelle with Beaverbrook and Rab Butler, the under-secretary of state for foreign affairs, and agreed that Eden should stay in the Middle East. Elsewhere in town the Prime Minister was being vituperative about everyone, but especially about Wavell (the munching trio suspected jealousy), and referred to Prince Paul as "Palsy."[71]

## 15 - 16 March 1941

Eden sent a long reply to Churchill which really did not say much more than that they were in agreement, except that he wanted Churchill to know that the complaints as to Longmore's needs were not the AOC-in-C's, but his own. And on 16 March Eden and Dill gave Churchill the bad news that MANDIBLES had to be postponed till after 12 April so as not to interfere with LUSTRE, and that even then it would be limited to CORDITE (attacks on Rhodes) because of time and lack of intelligence.[72]

In order to clarify the air situation in the Middle East it is instructive to go through the file prepared in November 1941 for Portal to use in refuting the Australian charges that they had been misled in giving their support to the Greek adventure. We find that on 14 March Churchill had confirmed to the prime minister of Australia that fourteen and possibly sixteen RAF squadrons would be in Greece, though there were airfields for only thirteen south of the Aliakmon Line, and that no more than twenty could be accommodated there before the end of June. The same information was sent to the prime minister of New Zealand, to whom it was also pointed out that the Greeks had on 13 March 21 bomber aircraft, 46 fighters, and 48 old reconnaissance machines, but that their serviceability rarely exceeded 50 percent. British reinforcements in March were to be three Blenheim squadrons, one army cooperation squadron of Hurricanes and Lysanders, and three heavy bomber squadrons, and a further two fighter squadrons if the aircraft became available. In the last four months, Churchill maintained, every aircraft that could be spared from the United Kingdom had been sent out.[73]

Actually none of these aircraft went to Greece, as they could not be spared from the Middle East. Moreover, through bad planning, large quantities of Whitley bombers were being produced in Britain which, according to Postan, Hay, and Scott, the official historians, never went further than packing crates.[74]

On 14 March the Middle East Air Force had (by London's count) 502 aircraft either serviceable or likely to be made so within fourteen days: 9 Bombays, 173 Blenheims, 61 Gladiators, 134 Hurricanes, 38 Wellingtons, 36 Wellesleys, and 51 Lysanders. Three more RAF squadrons were in Aden, and four South African Air force squadrons were in East Africa, which might be made available for operations in Greece when the East African campaign stopped. In addition, there were on their way to Egypt 381 more aircraft, and the flow on the Takoradi route was rising as facilities were expanded.[75]

The trouble with these figures, just as with the ones the RAF quoted about the Greeks, was that for a force constantly on the go, serviceability was often less than 50 percent. Moreover, most of the aircraft listed above had been or were being phased out of operational service in Britain. In other words, though the Middle East air forces were facing first-line German aircraft, they were doing so largely with second-line machines.

By mid-March Wavell in Cairo was increasingly unhappy with the presence of Eden and Dill, whose departure had been delayed since the seventh by bad weather and hopes of a visit to Belgrade. For the commander-in-chief, or for that matter for any commander of an active campaign, to have not only the chief of staff but also the deputy prime minister (as Eden was in effect if not in name) residing in his house, was a strain. This was true for personal relations, especially with someone such as Lady Wavell who could herself be difficult, and in all sorts of other ways, from having to arrange their entertainment and listening to them at meals—especially to Eden who liked to hear himself talk—to ensuring their security and answering their questions about matters which were normally strictly within the purview of the C-in-C. Wavell knew that he needed to get out to the Western Desert to see how Neame was getting on, and to ensure that he had taken the proper tactical and strategic dispositions now that it was becoming increasingly obvious that the Germans were present in Tripoli. Wavell's biographer, John Connell, has rightly noted that the presence of distinguished visitors (coupled with his own lack of a personal aircraft, we should add) meant that he did not get forward in time to view the ground and to convert the salt marshes at El Aghila into a strong defensive position. Wavell was later to admit that, perhaps because he was not free to focus properly on military matters, he underestimated the speed at which the Germans could build up. Connell suggests that Wavell never got time to read the excellent report, taking Rommel's position, prepared by Brigadier John Shearer of his own staff.[76]

At the same time Wavell was still having to be involved in the diplomatic side of the Greek adventure, which he already regarded as hopeless. As Connell noted, by 15 March Wavell had lost his illusions but could only go on.[77] He had too many problems on his mind to be able to give the necessary thought to them all, for he was being forced into roles which should not have been his as the military C-in-C.

On 15 March the Yugoslav Foreign Minister told the British minister, Campbell, that Yugoslavia would sign the Axis pact, and when Campbell urged a positive stand, he replied, "What do you want us to do, attack Germany?"[78] Campbell's long report on this conversation reached London at 2:25 a.m. on the sixteenth. It said that the Yugoslavs would maintain contact with the Germans, would not fight, and that the minister of Foreign Affairs was defeatist. The latter was a term applied to those who did not jump on the British dream wagon.

Further to the south Eden, Dill, and the C-in-C's had met in Cairo to discuss how to get Turkey to bolster Yugoslavia. The result had been a telegram to Belgrade which suggested political rather than strategical discussions. In the course of these talks Wavell had said that it was vital that Yugoslavia not be lost to the Allies and so Turkey should be urged to declare war if need be to keep her in. On the sixteenth, after they heard Campbell's report, they decided to urge the Turks to come more into the open, and for this purpose Eden and Dixon flew to Cyprus on 18 March.[79]

Meanwhile in London on 15 March the deputy director of Military Intelligence circulated an appreciation which pointed out that the Germans had ample transportation facilities to support the twenty-nine divisions they were estimated to have in the Balkans (including those watching Turkey and Russia) as well as to maintain the 480 aircraft in Rumania and Bulgaria. For operations against Greece the Germans would have four armored, five motorized, two mountain and four infantry divisions.[80]

In Athens the British naval attaché prepared to open discussions the next day with the Greek Admiralty on Greek naval arrangements in case the country was overrun.[81]

Wavell and Dill finally managed to get away to visit Neame at Benghazi. They were appalled to find him pessimistic, demanding reinforcements which Wavell did not have, with crazy dispositions, and with half his cruiser tanks in the shops and the other half unreliable. Wavell's confidence in him was shaken, and as soon as he got back to Cairo on 19 March he dictated detailed instructions.[82] (Neame did not get these until 26 March, as the original was lost while being sent up by air. He claims that by the time he did get them they were unnecessary as his own dispositions had already been made. But the situation, as Dill and Wavell had recognized, was serious, especially as Neame had at his disposal only three daily sorties of Hurricanes and six of medium bombers for all tasks including distant reconnaissance of the Germans west of him.)[83]

## 17 March 1941

By 17 March Wavell had already stopped all reinforcements for LUS-TRE,[84] but the AOC-in-C ME, Longmore, indicated that he hoped to be able to let the Greeks have 18 Hurricanes as soon as reinforcements came through from Takoradi and Nos. 80 and 112 Squadrons in Greece were brought up to strength. One thing was sure, the Greeks were not getting any aircraft from the United States, because of American and British maneuvering.[85]

London asked Cairo for a draft dispatch announcing the landing of British troops in Greece. Menzies wanted it, but Wavell refused. Why he did so is unclear in view of the fact that the arrival of British troops had been reported in most newspapers in Europe and abroad.[86] It would have been better to have released the cover story that the troops were to support the RAF, though the arrival of armor hardly made sense in that case. Churchill's view, that the Foreign Secretary was playing his hand with great skill, seems more complimentary to an ostrich than to a diplomat.

Meanwhile in Athens the American ambassador reported that the Germans had as yet made no demands, but this was thought to be because of the impassible state of the passes south from Bulgaria and the uncertain position of the Yugoslavs. Delay was at any rate from the Greek point of view a blessing.[87]

The blocked passes had not stopped the British air attaché in Sofia, Wing-Commander MacDonald, from dropping into Athens on 16 March and two days later discussing with D'Albiac the problems of evacuating Yugoslavia. At the same time that "rank-unconscious" regular soldier, the Scot Brigadier A. "Sandy" Galloway, Wilson's chief of staff, was taking the view that Prince Paul was a weakling and that nothing could be expected from him, and he said as much to Major Reid at lunch at the Athens Club a few days later.[88] And another interesting English character had rolled into town when the Fleet Air Arm sent Lt. Charles Lamb in his Swordfish to Eleusis. Lamb had a discipline problem on his hands, what with the Germans loose in town, and was constantly afraid that he would be forced to charge one of his pugnacious able-bodied seamen with "assaulting the enemy." Being a boxer himself, Lamb, one suspects, was not averse to a scrap. He had come into Athens in fact to be briefed by D'Albiac on operating out of the field in the valley at Paramythia, which he thought was inside Albania (after all, all foreigners are alike to a sailor). Having topped up with fuel, the Swordfish left at dusk, climbing from the field at 3,000 feet to get over the mountains at 6,000; they then swept down to sea level, literally running their wheels on the water into Durazzo harbor, to drop their torpedoes before heading back in the dark to Eleusis.[89]

(Lamb and D'Albiac were themselves involved in an incident at the Hotel Grande Bretagne, where they had gone to lunch one day late in the month with the senior air staff officer. The German ambassador and his party sat down at the next table to eavesdrop. After a while D'Albiac said, "SASO, have you given any thought to the problem of what we might do with Germany after the war?" Group Captain Willets replied offhand he thought it wouldn't be a bad idea to give it to the Poles. The Germans shortly moved to another table.)

## 18 March 1941

On Tuesday, 18 March, General Blamey sailed from Alexandria on the cruiser HMS *Gloucester*, which seemed to spend most of March as a troopship. By this time the lines of communications between Cairo and Athens had become so sluggish that Blamey actually reached the Hotel Acropole to report to Wilson before the signal announcing his movements was received. Shortly after his arrival he made a quick trip north to see the lie of the land, conferred with Freyberg, and came back to start collecting as much information as he could garner on the roads, towns, and beaches of the Peloponnesus. All of this was carefully plotted on an evacuation-plan map, which he gave to Wavell on 20 April, so that his troops could be withdrawn in the next few days.[90]

When he reported Blamey's arrival to Washington, MacVeagh commented that the German G-2 had told Greek headquarters that the dispatch north of British troops would mean a fight. Under the circumstances MacVeagh felt it was silly that General Wilson was still going around in mufti as Mr. Watt.[91]

Up country in Veria, on the road from Salonika to Kozani, the purple Judas trees were just bursting into bloom at the entrance to the pass.

Freyberg and Brigadier Charrington were headquartered at Kozani until the twenty-fourth, when Charrington moved down to Edessa, on the escarpment overlooking the orchards on the road from Veria westward to Florina.[92]

At the Marasleon School AVM D'Albiac issued a five-page memorandum on air policy in Greece in which he pointed out that while the expectation was that he would have fourteen squadrons by 15 April, reinforcement squadrons were arriving below strength; and in any continuous operations, and especially fighting on two fronts, the rate of serviceability would be low. Given the many tasks facing the force, and its limited size and lack of suitable airfields, discretion by the commanders of the eastern and western wings would play a large part, but for many roles the forces employed would be far below "that considered necessary for the efficient conduct of war."[93]

Eden and Dixon flew to Nicosia on this Tuesday and met with the Turkish Foreign Minister, Saraçoglu, and with Knatchbull-Hugesson from Ankara. In long discussions that afternoon and on into the nineteenth, the Englishmen learned that the Turks expected the Germans to attack Greece down through the Monastir Gap; otherwise Turkey would be the target. The English thought they had persuaded the Turks to send a message to Belgrade urging their common interests, Eden's diary says, but when he got back to Ankara Saraçoglu did not send it. (According to the War Cabinet records in London, however, a telegram was sent.)[94] For this there were in fact good reasons, which Eden already knew, as his official diary for the trip reports. Three days earlier Campbell had learned from the president of the Council that Yugoslavia was going to join Germany, so Eden had sent Terence Shone, the British minister in Cairo, on a personal mission to Shone's friend Prince Paul with a message which he had delivered on the eighteenth.[95] On the nineteenth Eden himself offered once again to go to Belgrade. But this was all too late. By the twentieth the Yugoslav cabinet was in a crisis and the Serbian ministers resigned rather than capitulate to the Germans; this, like the appeals that day from King George VI and Churchill, did no good.

One outcome of this internal maneuvering was that the former prime minister Milan Stojadinović was turned over to the British at the Greek border for safekeeping, so that Hitler could not use him. Channon's reaction perfectly reflected sentiment in London of that day, "No Balkan can ever be relied upon."[96]

In Belgrade, the prime minister, Cincar-Marković, took the view that Churchill merely intended to use Yugoslav arms to support his grand gesture to the Greeks, and since like most small neutrals he regarded Churchill's attitude as arrogant, he was not sure that the little powers should suffer for the benefit of the great. When in the evening the sad Prince Paul and his beautiful Greek wife, Princess Olga, dined with the

American minister, Lane, and were lectured again on their duties, they pointed out to him that unless the Germans attacked after the pact was signed, there was nothing that could be done, since the British had plainly indicated that they could provide nothing but verbal support. And Belgrade was not Zagreb, with its glorious memories of Serbian defiance of Austria in 1914 (nor, he might have added, was Hitler's Germany the waltzing Hapsburg Empire of Franz Joseph II). So that evening the Yugoslav cabinet met and voted fourteen to three for the pact with Germany.

## 19 March 1941

The British dream had blown away like dandelion seeds on the winds of Balkan realities and the lack of British resources. On 19 March Longmore estimated that he was 450 aircraft short of commitments.[97] When in London on the same day the Greek ambassador left one of his regular notes complaining about the lack of British air aid to Greece, this was circulated to the Prime Minister, who sent the under-secretary of state for foreign affairs, R.A. Butler, to tell the ambassador in Churchill's words that "we had been filled with pride in being able to help so gallant an ally." The ambassador was impressed neither with the gesture nor with the suggestion that the Greeks apply to the C-in-C ME and to Eden. He knew there were no aircraft to spare in the theater.[98]

That same Wednesday General Heywood reported to Cairo and London on the extensive travels he had at last been allowed to make in northeastern Greece. His basic conclusions were that the area was well fortified and that morale was very high among both the troops and the commanders, who were determined to acquit themselves as well as their brethren had been doing in Albania. The problem was that not only had a certain number of antitank and other weapons been "borrowed" for the campaign in the west, but that there were large gaps between the fortified areas which were only wired in and very lightly held with no reserves at all, so that multiple breakthroughs were a real possibility. The frontier commander felt that, if the attack did not come until after the British reinforcements had arrived in strength, the line could be held almost indefinitely, but he needed, in addition to adequate air support, field, antitank, and antiaircraft artillery, six battalions of infantry, and the 19th Motorized Division as a mobile reserve to deal with any parachutists or mountain troops that would come down over the Beles to the plain. Daily German air reconnaissance was occurring over Salonika and the rest of the area. Heywood noted that the most likely line of attack for the Germans would be to violate Yugoslav territory and strike down the Strumitsa valley and the Kosturino Pass to the Vardar with mechanized forces, which would outflank the whole frontier position. From the

Yugoslav consul in Salonika he learned that his country's forces were 75 percent mobilized and that no German attack was expected before 25 March. The Yugoslavs thought the British had landed fourteen divisions.[99]

Heywood further reported to London that the recent Italian offensive in Albania had cost the Greeks 5,000 casualties, and there remained only one month's supply of ammunition for 105-mm mountain, 85-mm and 155-mm guns. Papagos was scouring the barrel for reservists.[100]

The British military mission also reported to Wavell, repeated to the War Office and the Admiralty in London, that the king and the president of the Council were thinking how to fight on if Greece were overrun. The Greeks were now prepared, the mission reported, to evacuate Thrace and eastern Macedonia, but they also wanted to raise another army corps of 50,000 men, for which they needed additional equipment. Greek bayonets would make the decision, and while all recognized the great importance of the actions of the British government, the rapid equipment of the new army corps was vital.[101]

The nineteenth was a sad day for the RAF meteorologists in Athens, for the Italians changed their cipher system. Until then the RAF had been able to decode Rome's weather broadcasts, which gave them a most helpful idea of what was coming and especially what would be happening over the Adriatic ports. They were also until then able to use the Bulgarian codes, which applied both to Sofia and to Budapest. But for the next week or so they had only the Yugoslav weather from Belgrade, as that continued to be given in the International Meteorological Code.[102]

## 20 March 1941

On Thursday, in the course of a conversation between Papagos and Wilson it was agreed that when the arrival of more Australian troops allowed the second New Zealand brigade to move to Katerini, it would relieve the 19th Motorized Division, which would be released to General Papagos on about 25 or 26 March. There were further detailed discussions about locating the incoming troops along the Aliakmon Line.[103]

Late that night Papagos talked, as usual, with Heywood and told him that the Greek military attaché in Ankara had earlier been instructed to call on Papagos's friend the assistant chief of the Turkish general staff, Assim Gündüz. The attaché was to ask him what action the Turks would take if Greece were attacked from Bulgaria, in view of the 1934 Graeco-Turkish mutual guarantee of their "common frontier," as Papagos called it. He had now received a private letter, dated 12 March, which he asked Prince Peter to read to Heywood, who, Papagos said, would see how defeatist the Turks had become. In his letter Assim said that the Greeks must not expect anything from the Turks. The military attaché reported that he believed that the German ambassador's pressure tactics were having more and more success in Ankara.[104]

On 20 March, the New Zealand 19 Battalion was traveling north from Athens, having departed at 2:00 p.m. the day before. Their train stopped for breakfast at Larissa for two hours, and then they joggled north through the Tempe Pass to Katerini, snuffling and cursing the colds brought on by a rapid change of climate. By teatime they had detrained, and soon the colds were being sweated out as they began the laborious task of digging defensive positions on the Aliakmon Line.[105]

From Cairo Wavell signaled the War Office that the personnel ships were now through the Suez Canal and that LUSTRE was moving on schedule; the equipping of troops, especially with transport, was still the limiting factor. The preparatory work on demolitions along the Aliakmon and on the canal to Edessa were completed and a start was being made on the River Axios. The situation in Cyrenaica was beginning to worry him, as growing enemy strength indicated an early forward movement; if the British advanced troops were driven from their present positions there was no good covering position south of Benghazi, as the country was a dead-level plain. But he thought that administrative problems would preclude anything but a limited German advance; beyond a large increase in transport, the enemy was showing no offensive intention at present.

## 21 - 23 March 1941

On Friday 24 Battalion of the New Zealanders left Athens by train, while their motor transport of 220 vehicles made up a convoy twenty-two miles long as it crawled up the passes out of Athens, covering one hundred miles the first day. When at last it got to Mount Olympus, the convoy took five hours to crawl past one spot in the road.[106]

The difficulties of operating British forces in Greece were not well understood at the time that the decision was made to go there, perhaps in part because Wavell was weak on the "Q" side of his training and experience. Movements in Egypt and Palestine in the First World War had not been limited to a single-line railway; both shipping and lorries could be used. But in Greece shipping was limited by the shortage of escorts, the few ports, and the fear of air attack; and the use of lorries was severely restricted by the scarce and difficult roads. Moreover, even the single-line railway system was complicated by the fact that there were two gauges in use, a situation that necessitated transshipment. A report made on 26 March to the director general of transportation at HQ ME began: "The difficult and extremely vulnerable line of communication has throughout influenced the general "Q" policy and the tendency is for all services to want "something of everything everywhere" so that we are tending towards a chain of maintenance from rear to front."[107]

Often the ground was so low-lying and soft that at places like Larissa it was only good for "summer dumping"; spurs needed to be constructed to higher ground. And an overall difficulty was a shortage of waggons on the railways. Just to make the port of Volos effective would take nine months' work. And in transportation as in so much else at this stage of the war, the British were simply badly understaffed and lacked the manpower to carry out even those plans that could be properly developed.

Another problem that arose because of the haste of the movement of the LUSTRE forces resulted from rapid and careless handling of ammunition being loaded in Egypt, so that about 20 percent of it arrived at the Piraeus in an unsatisfactory condition—shells with damaged driving bands, antitank mines loose in the hold because the boxes had been smashed, and gelignite rolling around with loose shells. Some 20-mm ammunition for the RAF arrived wet in boxes carefully stenciled "W E T," raising the question of why it was shipped in the first place. Other difficulties also arose in the north from storing ammunition under tarpaulins in the wet winter and spring weather, because condensation accumulated and caused corrosion and rust.[108]

In the post-mortems on the campaign held in Cairo in May a disagreement surfaced between the ordnance and the engineer officers on the conditions in Greece. While ordnance wished to be near rail spurs, the engineers correctly pointed out that, in an environment in which the British suffered from "air inferiority" to the point of having no air force at all, it was essential that dumps be as far from rail lines as possible, that movements be made over widely dispersed roads and generally at night, and that dumps be created that would facilitate movement by freeing transport from carrying unwanted materials and tools.[109]

In London the interminable arguments over how to supply the Greeks with ammunition were still being waged back and forth with Washington, but Cadogan thought the news from the Balkans better, especially after Eden's talk with the Turks on Cyprus; though Churchill kept calling that afternoon to know about the distribution of Anthony's telegrams, he seemed to be in a good mood.[110] That evening Churchill told the Cabinet that he was not afraid about air attacks, invasion, or the Balkans, but he was anxious about the Battle of the Atlantic.[111]

Cadogan was far less cheerful the next day when he found out that the Yugoslavs had sold their souls to the Devil, but what could you expect from people who were trash anyway, poor dears with no arms, no money, and no industry.[112] Eden began dabbling in the idea of a coup proposed by Shone and Campbell and on the 24 March gave full authority to do whatever they thought fit to further a change of government or regime, even by a coup, and to get in touch with those in whom they had confidence. Cambpell telegraphed that the best chance lay with the military, who had, however, to be convinced of British support by the offer of equipment.[113]

Meanwhile on 21, March in London the Greek minister had told the Foreign Office that the United States had at last agreed to give the Royal Hellenic Air Force 45 Grumman Wildcats. He asked at once for help in transporting them to the Middle East. Cairo had suggested flying them from the Gold Coast, but the Air Ministry said it would be better to send them by sea all the way, because the facilities at Takoradi were already strained. This meant an additional six weeks' delay at a most critical time. So in view of the pressing operational needs of the Greek air force, the Greeks asked for the immediate delivery of the 30 Mohawks originally promised out of British stocks, or in their place Hurricanes. When Longmore had last visited Athens, the minister continued, his suggestion had been accepted that the British keep the Mohawks and deliver Hurricanes. But the Greeks could not rely on the RAF in Greece and had to have their own aircraft not subject to other calls.[114]

In fact the interesting and disgraceful story of the Anglo-American buck-passing on the matter of aircraft for Greece revealed a total lack of appreciation for the urgency of the situation, a complacent concern for business as usual, and an attitude that what the RAF did not want could be discarded to the Greeks.[115]

On Saturday, 22 March, the American ambassador in Athens learned from the Turkish ambassador, just back from a visit home accompanied by the Swedish *chargé d'affaires*, that the Germans had two motives in their drive on Greece: to get the British out so that they could not attack the Italians in Albania and thus Italy, and to cut Turkey off from the West. Von Papen, the German ambassador in Ankara, had told the Swede that the Germans had 700,000 troops in the Balkans and that the campaign would take two weeks. The Germans hoped to get Yugoslav permission to use the Monastir Gap, but it was not necessary.[116]

Meanwhile all four RAF squadrons in the Western Desert had been warned to be able to move on short notice and to prepare demolitions, and given special tactical instructions.

And at Suez *Cameronia* of the Anchor Line dropped anchor with the missing 5th Brigade of the New Zealand Division, which had been for six weeks on its way from the United Kingdom. It was immediately greeted with Freyberg's special order of the day saying he expected them to be in action against the Germans very shortly. Four days later they landed at the Piraeus.[117]

In the meantime MO.5 at the War Office in London was trying to find out who was in Greeece and what exactly was the order of battle. Quite a file had been building upon this subject in order to answer queries from the VCIGS and the director of military operations and plans. Even in early

April the estimates contained phrases such as "This seems to mean . . ." and the like. But several things are clear. The 7th Australian Division had been held back in North Africa. The Polish Brigade was re-equipping and would not sail until 12 April, and at the end of the first week in April only the 1st Armoured Brigade and the New Zealand Division were concentrated forward, with the 6th Australian Division just arrived. About 12,000 administrative troops and 33,000 fighting men were in Greece when the Germans attacked with five divisions.[118]

## 24 March 1941

In view of the imminent likelihood of the signing of a Yugoslav-German Pact, early this morning all RAF units in Greece were ordered to "a state of preparedness for defence." The Greek under-secretary for foreign affairs thought the news from Yugoslavia gloomy, especially since the Tripartite Pact signed at Vienna did not specify German "wounded" and there might be troops passing either way through Yugoslavia. He also felt that this new development would have a further depressing effect on a Turkey regarded in Athens as cautious and hesitant.[119]

MacVeagh also bemoaned the fact that after all the efforts to get the Greeks 45 Grumman Wildcats (Martlets, to the British), at the last minute Washington had acceded to a British request to swap these for Hurricanes to be delivered to Greece from Middle East supplies, a proposal which the Greek government had properly, he said, refused, as they knew that the British in the Middle East did not have any spare Hurricanes. The Greeks were thus left on the eve of the German attack exactly where they had been four and a half months earlier, because once again Washington was reexamining the question![120]

On this Monday General Wilson and General Papagos had another tactical discussion, concerned at first with antiparachutist measures in the Salonika and Vardar Valley areas; it was ageed that the Greek air force would be dispersed to satellite airfields and that the 19th Division would be added to the forces available, together with the British 1st Armoured Brigade, to assist in antiparachutist activities. They then discussed disaffection and resignations in Yugoslavia in the wake of the approval of the pact with Germany, and action to be taken, both to contact the opposition in Yugoslavia and to keep in touch with the army there and ensure that it stayed intact. Wilson then asked Papagos what his view was with regard to the disclosure of his identity, to which the Greek C-in-C replied that it ought to be made now, as the Germans obviously knew British troops had disembarked in Greece. It was agreed that if the Greek prime minister and Middle East headquarters concurred, Mr. Watt would become General Wilson on 26 March. General Papagos would announce it in an order of the day to the Greek army.[121]

Shortly after this General Blamey was having a meeting with Jumbo Wilson and his chief of staff in the British embassy in Athens. The purpose was to clarify the role of Blamey's forces. It was agreed that defense of the passes on the Aliakmon Line was of paramount importance, and that work on these defenses should be given priority, a matter which Galloway, the chief of staff, would take up with the New Zealand commander, Freyberg; additional defenses were to be prepared at the Katerini Pass and between Mount Olympus and the sea. The advanced Australian corps headquarters was to be established at Gerania just south of the pass leading to Servia as soon as possible, and Blamey would take over the command of the front as soon as it could be arranged (which was not actually until 12 April). There followed a discussion of the shifting of troops forward as they arrived at Larissa, the need for reserve forces, and the development of lateral roads between the passes. The roads into the passes would have to be closed to Greek civilians the minute the Germans began their advance, and the inhabitants warned by the Greek authorities to remain at home. Advanced HQ was to leave Athens the next day to open on the twenty-sixth at Elasson.[122]

Far to the south of Athens Monday, 24 March, was a significant day, for Neame's outposts in Cyrenaica were being driven in by Rommel's fresh German troops, who took posssession of El Agheila.

In Cairo Eden, having sent a cautious telegram to Belgrade saying that he had no authority to offer matériel to the Yugoslav army, now reiterated London's suggestion that if they attacked the Italians in Albania they would get a rich haul. But after he and Dill heard that the Yugoslavs were on their way to Vienna that afternoon to sign the Axis pact, they left for England. They were in Malta on the 27th, when the coup took place in Belgrade.[123]

The Dominion governments were getting very worried about the prospects for the expedition which at best they now regarded in the slang of the day as "dicey," so the Commander-in-Chief, Mediterranean, was told on 24 March that he should prepare plans for the evacuation of the Dominion forces from Greece. He replied that he already had such contingency work well under way and that he guaranteed that everything possible would be done.[124]

In London the Chiefs of Staff met with an adamant, growling, belligerent Churchill, who demanded that more forces be sent overseas. The COS found themselves forced to back down from the Joint Intelligence Committee's appraisal of 31 January and their own position of 3 March. On 27 March they consented to say that the danger of the invasion of Britain had become less likely, but they were unwilling to go further than that. Even on 10 April they maintained that it was still a priority item. At the same time, they wrongly said that a German attack on the Middle East, via the Balkans and Syria in one prong and via Cyrenaica in the other, was unlikely, as was an attack on Russia, in spite of recent evidence to the contrary. Hinsley notes that it was not until 27 April that battles between the War Office and the Foreign Office began to inject more realism into the JIC's assessments, upon which the COS were basing their strategic predictions and guidance.[125]

By late March as things went wrong and the thinness of Longmore's forces became increasingly obvious in London, Churchill's temper (or was it a guilty conscience?) became more evident. On 24 March he sent the AOC-in-C the following:

> I have been concerned to read your continual complaints of the numbers of aircraft which are sent you. Every conceivable effort has been made under my express directions to reinforce you by every route and method for the last five months. In order to do this the Navy have been deprived of *Argus* and *Furious* and are left without a single A.C. except occasionally *Ark Royal* to cope with the German battle-cruisers in the Atlantic. We are as fully informed as you of what you are getting. A weekly report is submitted to me of all movement via Takoradi. Therefore when I read a telegram from General Smuts in which he refers to "Beaverbrook being persuaded to disgorge his hoard" or when I read the C-in-C. Med's telegram to First Sea Lord stating that "only one Hurricane was received during the month of March," and when I also read your A.442, which seeks to justify this absurd statement, I fear there must be some absurd talk emanating from your Headquarters which is neither accurate nor helpful.[126]

To this Longmore responded two days later that he hoped that when Eden got back to London he would give Churchill the air picture as seen from Cairo, and that he would clear up the misconception that the AOC-in-C was responsible for Smuts' remark about Beaverbrook's hoard. And after saying how grateful he was for "Pageant" (the Hurricane resupply of Malta by carrier), he went on to point out that in the last two weeks he had lost thirty aircraft of which sixteen were Hurricanes. The Middle East's air commitments were growing faster than one air supply line could build them up. For instance, at that moment five air convoys were held up by weather on the route from Takoradi. He added that he had suggested to the CAS that a direct route from America across the Pacific to Basra and then by air would help, or to South Africa, where erection facilities had been offered, after which aircraft could be ferried up (the old Imperial Airways route opened in 1932). He realized this was long-term policy "and that in the meanwhile we are facing a difficult period which you may rest assured we will do with confidence and determination but with our eyes open."[127]

And on the same day Portal told the Prime Minister that the Air Ministry's estimates of the Germans' strength in the Balkans were 314 (less 100 cooperation) aircraft in Bulgaria and 175 in Rumania plus transports, with Italian strength in Albania less than half Palairet's estimates and in the Dodecanese about two-thirds. In contrast the AOC-in-C had ten and a half fighter squadrons in the whole of his command, of which three were South African units not yet released from East Africa. Longmore had, then, three squadrons in Greece, two in Egypt, one in Malta, one in Aden, and the remaining three and a half in the Sudan and Kenya. Portal had several times urged Longmore to concentrate his fighters northwards, but Wavell had replied that, although Greece was recognized as the major theater, it would be better to clear up East Africa before moving the air forces north; the COS had responded that this was a decision for the commanders-in-chief on the spot. (The rest of this letter is missing from the PRO file). So on 28 March Churchill sent a memorandum to Butler and Cadogan at the Foreign Office, saying that Britain could not send out more fighters, but that additional bombers were being flown out to bring the squadrons up from twelve to twenty aircraft each.[128]

## 25 - 26 March 1941

Tuesday, 25 March, was Greek Independence Day, and Churchill had already approved on the twenty-first a message to be dispatched to Athens for the newspapers to use. This put the myths about Greece in a nutshell: "On this day of proud memories, I would add one brief tribute to those which the whole civilized world is paying to the valour of the Greek nation. One hundred and twenty years ago, all that was noblest in England strove in the cause of Greek independence and rejoiced in its achievement. Today that epic struggle is being repeated against greater odds but with equal courage and with no less certainty of success. We in England know that the cause for which Byron died is a sacred cause: we are resolved to sustain it."[129]

In Athens Wilson and Papagos met again to discuss the German terms and conditions given Yugoslavia, which they understood included the right to run hospital and ammunition trains through Yugoslav territory. Papagos had heard from the Greek military attaché in Berlin that the German attack would probably start on 27 March.[130] Wilson proposed, and Papagos agreed, that Ross, the British military attaché at Belgrade, who was then in Athens, should go back to Belgrade and make contact with the dissident elements of the army, and should then return via Skoplje, where he should try to get in touch with the commanding officer of the 3rd Yugoslav Army and arrange a meeting on the border with Wilson. It was agreed that the Greek consul should meet Ross at the railway station and give him the latest information as he passed through.

Ross was to have a special colored handkerchief so that the consul would be able to recognize him at once.

They then talked over the problem of Wilson's taking over command of the Central Macedonian Army, which they both agreed he should do at once, in spite of the fact that both the Greek prime minister and Cairo believed that the announcement of his presence would precipitate a German attack. It was agreed that a secret order would be sent to General Ioannis Kotulas that as soon as Mr. Watt visited him he would hand over command to General Wilson.[131]

Brigadier Brunskill wrote from Athens to Arthur Smith that the Greeks were short not only of ammunition but of regular administrative supplies such as motor transport, food, clothing, barley, and coal. Shipments of these items ordered from the United Kingdom were unpredictable, yet British troops arrived well equipped with transport and adequate reserves. The lavish scale with which the British were building up reserve stocks in a country whose troops and civilians were living on a hand-to-mouth basis was causing adverse comment in the highest circles. One offshoot of the disparity was that Brunskill was forced to provide seventy British lorries to help establish the Greeks on the left wing of the Aliakmon position. More than this, the British needed to supply the Greeks with boots and bully beef immediately; Brunskill wondered if these could not be issued against what was on order, because otherwise Greek morale would suffer. "Though we can hardly go so far as to reduce the British ration, which to the Greek appears to be luxurious, we must give them what direct help we can, as one is particularly anxious to avoid criticism, which might affect adversely the whole manner of the Greeks in relation to our troops, which at the moment is excellent."[132]

Also at the Hotel Acropole, General Staff Intelligence issued a memorandum on possible German tactics in Greece, which made considerable use of knowledge of German tactics in Norway. It pointed out that the Germans were especially adept at working through defiles, but that the same positions gave the British considerable options for defense, if the troops could be positioned ahead of time and reserves sited where they could be moved in rapidly. It also stated that a German infantry divison had 16,762 men, 1,200 motor vehicles, and horses and motorcycles, as well as guns. A motorized division had 17,482 men and 260 tanks, and an armored division had 14,000 men, 480 tanks, and 3,300 other vehicles, plus 1,238 motorcycles.[133] In contrast, a British division consisted of about 14,000 men and 1,400 vehicles, and the understrength Greek ones were almost all on foot.

The sexual appetites of airmen and Australians had already been the cause of considerable consternation in Athens. D'Albiac had devoted part of more than one of his command meetings to the problem.[134] In Kozani Major Reid found that it created problems of a different sort at the local brothel. Having ineffectively, he thought, complained to Athens about the lack of military police to deal with the problem and been assured that none could be spared, he was greeted the next day by a beaming MP sergeant and twenty men. Twenty-four hours later the results of the good sergeant's zeal proved very embarrassing when on raiding the brothel he found the Australians engaged in an altercation with a high Greek officer who regarded the place as his own establishment.[135] Alliances can prove to be rather delicate affairs in which discretion may be the better part of valor.

Greek Independence Day was the beginning of another momentous movement as well. Thanks to a seduction in Washington, the British Security Co-ordination in the American capital had obtained the Italian naval code. (At least that was the cover story for the fact that ULTRA could now be read daily.) This had allowed Admiral Cunningham to be alerted that the Italians were planning an attack on the convoys to Greece, and so on this Tuesday he sailed for what would go down in history as the Battle of Cape Matapan, where he caught the Italians by surprise on 28 March, even though they also could read his signals.[136]

Cunningham was one of the early beneficiaries of ULTRA. In this instance, Enigma traffic from the German air force indicating a major operation coming up was passed to the admiral, who kept his ships on alert after they returned to port on 24 March. Then came a move of all German twin-engined fighters to Palermo, followed by an Italian message that there would be an operation from Rhodes in three days and a request for information on British convoys to and from Greece, together with a request to neutralize British air cover. Cunningham had this information from the Admiralty before lunch on 26 March, and in the afternoon it was confirmed that all the messages referred to one major attempt to disrupt the LUSTRE convoys. Cunningham at once canceled the southbound convoy from the Piraeus and ordered the northbound one from Alexandria to reverse course after nightfall. Then he went to play golf, so as to be seen.

After dark on the twenty-seventh the Fleet sailed and surprised the Italians off Cape Matapan, in the first important naval operation in the Mediterranean in which "sigint" played a significant part. Without it the convoys might have been massacred and LUSTRE would have very early lost its shine.[137]

On 25 and 26 March the imperturbable Wavell was flying to and from Platt's headquarters under the teboldi, known as "Platt's Tree," at Kilo 126, where the battle for Keren in Eritrea was being brought to a successful climax. He had gone to ask for the 4th and 5th Indian Divisions with which to meet Rommel, as these could be moved by rail from Keren back into Egypt. Ever taciturn, when on the morning of the twenty-sixth he flew up to the Tree again and was told that Platt was through to Keren, he merely said, "Then let's have some breakfast," ate, and flew back to Cairo.[138]

But as Wavell flew north from Keren, he had to contemplate the realities that Cunningham could not mop up quickly enough to really help against the Germans in the very near future, that Platt was still involved in East Africa, and that the victors of Cyrenaica had been sent to Greece. Now as the news of Rommel's activities began to reach him in alarming clarity, he had almost nothing to throw in his way. The activities which had sufficed to deal with the Italians were not good enough for the Germans, now threatening his command on two widely separated fronts. Wavell had hoped that the Germans would not attack until May, but on the next day, 27 March, the GOC of the 6th Australian Division, then well forward in the Western Desert, warned of impending attack. This was the one seasoned division left, one that Blamey had earmarked for Greece because of its state of readiness.[139]

On 26 March the Joint Planning Staff in London produced Paper No. 43 for the Middle East planning staff, in which they suggested that because of the paucity of railway and road systems in Turkey, the possibility of a German invasion of Egypt or Iraq through Turkey was not very likely. However, in their view it was essential to control Crete and Cyprus and to plan the sabotage of communications in Turkey.[140]

Also on that day Churchill cabled Wavell that London was concerned at the rapid German advance to El Agheila, as it was their habit to push on whenever their attack was not resisted. "I presume that you are only waiting for the tortoise to stick his head out far enough before chopping it off. It seems extremely important to give them an early taste of our quality. What is the state and location of the 7th Armoured Division? Pray give me your appreciation." As Wavell was then on his way back from the Sudan, General Arthur Smith replied, "Every effort is being made to reinforce our troops in Cyrenaica. I attended conference with C-in-C Mediterranean and AOC today to discuss situation, and urgent need of more aircraft was again emphasised." The deputy chief, general staff, Brigadier John Shearer, signaled British dispositions.

When he got back the next morning, Wavell sent the Prime Minister a "Personal and Most Secret" which included:

> I have to admit to having taken considerable risk in Cyrenaica after capture of Benghazi in order to provide maximum support for Greece. My estimate at that time was that Italians in Tripoli could be disregarded and that Germans were unlikely to accept risk of sending large bodies of armoured troops to Africa in view of inefficiency of Italian Navy. I therefore made arrangements to leave only small armoured force and one partly trained Australian division in Cyrenaica.

After we had accepted Greek liability evidence began to accumulate of German reinforcements to Tripoli, which were coupled with attacks on Malta which prevented bombing of Tripoli from there, on which I had counted. German air attacks on Benghazi, which prevented supply ships using harbour, also increased our difficulties.

Result is that I am weak in Cyrenaica at present and no reinforcements of armoured troops, which are chief requirement, are at present available.

He then went on to tell of his difficulties, including aircraft and transport. The good news was that Keren had fallen, and so Platt would push towards Asmara; and Cunningham, who had taken Harrar the day before, could move to Addis Ababa.[141]

In the Western Desert a conference took place from 27 to 29 March at which Neame, whose earlier fears had been considerably mollifed by assurances from headquarters in Cairo, maintained that only German technical experts were in Tripolitania. On the thirtieth Neame, who had been DCGS of the British Expeditionary Force in France in 1940, went so far as to say in his operational orders that no further enemy action was likely. Unfortunately, the next day, as these orders were being distributed, the enemy achieved surprise and attacked. Rommel had intended only a limited advance, but he seized his opportunity; the British were soon on the run that in twelve days took them four hundred miles and landed Neame in a prisoner-of-war camp. Wavell, too, had been caught by surprise. He should not have been. Rommel had forced the surrender of the 51st Highland Division in France in June 1940 and then charged 250 miles in five days to stop the evacuation at Cherbourg.[142]

## 27 - 30 March 1941

From down under, the deputy prime minister of Australia, Fadden, cabled Prime Minister Menzies, still in London, that the government in Canberra was very resentful of the fact that the Allied High Command had not been consulted. It was most embarrassing in both the Cabinet and the War Council to discover that the assumption that Blamey had been asked about the Grecian operation was incorrect.[143]

But the big news was the coup in Yugoslavia. The takeover in Belgrade was well within the patterns of Yugoslav politics. Prince Paul, an Oxford graduate with the Order of the Garter, was a Yugoslav who had alienated the retired Serbian officers. Brigadier General Bora Mirković of the air force had been planning a Yugoslav-Italian Pact since 1937, yet only in early 1941 had he approached Major-General Dusan Simović, a St. Cyr graduate, and found him willing. But it had never occurred to Mirković, since he kept Goering's autographed portrait in his quarters, that the Germans would react hostilely to his work. The coup succeeded because it was supported by the army, the air force, young officers, leftists, and the Church, and because the prime minister's lax internal security and lack of agents left him uninformed. It was almost bloodless (one policeman was shot at the radio station), and was completed between 11:30 p.m. on 26 March and 3:00 a.m. on the twenty-seventh. Yugoslavia was now free to join Britain, but her new rulers did not realize the press of time. That evening Prince Paul abdicated and left for Athens. George II of Greece wished to allow him to stay there, but Eden and the Foreign Office were adamantly hostile and Churchill backed them, and so Paul was sent to another of Churchill's colonial outposts, Kenya.[144] The young Prince Peter succeeded as Peter II; his godfather was King George VI of Great Britain, who looked after him when as a refugee he arrived in Britain on 21 June. (Later he emigrated to the United States and died in California in 1970.)

Hitler's reaction to the coup was rapid: he at once ordered the invasion of Russia—which would likely be delayed anyway by flooding in Poland—postponed for four weeks while the Balkan mess was cleared up. (The Swiss knew this that evening).[145]

In London some members of Parliament thought the coup was Chips Channon's doing, which pleased him; but he was profoundly sad for his friend Prince Paul and much resented Menzies' *bon mot* that it was a case of "robbing Paul to pay Peter." Nor did the Prime Minister smile at him. He was too busy.[146]

Churchill ordered Eden and Dill back from Malta to Athens to form a united front and to get the Yugoslavs to attack the Italians in order to capture their equipment in Albania and thus arm themselves to stand off the Germans.[147] It was a wild dream which had no relation to Balkan realities.

In his memoirs Papagos blames the British for not taking the leadership at this point and, as the outsiders, appointing a supreme commander in order to avoid personal jealousies.[148] But no matter what happened, the Yugoslavs were incapable of acting at the speed necessary to forestall German action.

Interestingly, perhaps the most realistic assessment was that made by the director of military intelligence at the War Office in London, Major-General F.H.N. Davidson, who told the VCIGS on 28 March that while the coup should have upset the German timetable by about one or two weeks, the Nazis could attack from three directions and would possibly move at once to attack Greece and seize Salonika and then separate Yugoslavia from British forces. It was essential, therefore, that the Allied High Command settle the line south of the Nis River. Papagos was now considering moving forces from the Aliakmon forward. But if the Germans delayed to mid-April they would have not five, but eleven divisions available. Davidson regarded the situation in Yugoslavia as at worst a conflict into which the Germans would move to restore order and at best an Allied front to liquidate the Italians in Albania. So he thought that the British should stimulate the Yugoslavs in every possible way, including naval action up the Adriatic as far as Kotor and Zara, help in armaments, a general officer as liaison, air support, and so forth.[149] Unfortunately his ideas of aid were simply not possible within the time to be allowed, even if the Yugoslavs had been, in fact, one nation indivisible.

Churchill, not unnaturally, since Eden and the Special Operations Executive claimed to have had a hand in the successful coup in Belgrade, proclaimed the rightness of his policy and sent the president of Turkey a telegram telling him the time had arrived for a common front.[150]

There was still an argument going on in air circles in Athens and London as to the proper use of air forces.[151] Now Col. Leslie Hollis of the War Cabinet in Great George Street sent a note over to Sir Orme Sargent at the Foreign Office saying that the coup in Yugoslavia helped, as that country had the best air force in the Balkans, but that the British could not yet say how they were going to help the Greek air force.[152]

The news of the Yugoslav coup caught Eden and Dill still weather-bound in Malta, waiting to go on to Gibraltar and England. They got off secretly, just missed the Italian fleet, and arrived at Scaramanga at dawn on the twenty-eighth. D'Albiac met them, and they at once saw General Wilson and his staff. Late in the day there was a conference with Koryzis and a more optimistic Papagos to discuss combined action with the Yugoslavs. Papagos wished to defend Salonika, but the British doubted that there was time enough to organize that. Papagos noted that a Yugoslav division with its 40,000 men was two and a half times the size of a Greek or Turkish division, and that Yugoslavia had twenty-four such infantry divisions and three cavalry divisions. Turkey had twenty-six infantry, one cavalry, and one armored division in eastern Thrace, with five more divisions in the Dardanelles and ten in the Caucasus. This discussion terminated without any conclusions, but with Eden and Dill wishing to meet with the new ruler of Yugoslavia, Air Vice Marshal Simović.

Later in the evening Eden talked with King George II, whom he found in good spirits but not very confident about the situation in Belgrade, "that hive of intrigue." Yet he hoped for time and, Eden claimed, said that "the presence of British troops had already saved Greece from being overrun." And he went on that "the king expressed satisfaction at the appointment of General Wilson who had made an excellent impression on all who had worked with him. He also spoke cordially of the conduct of the troops who had arrived, although there had unfortunately been complaints of the behaviour of the Australians." The king ended by saying that he would see Prince Paul at the railway station, but that it would be awkward.[153]

On the twenty-seventh, the day of the coup in Belgrade, General Heywood was in Albania visiting the front, and General Wilson was on the way north to his new headquarters at Elasson.

On 28 March Churchill signaled Wavell that he realized how much they were piling on him, "but events at Belgrade have made LUSTRE into a great stroke of policy, quite apart from its purely military aspect." In the meantime he hoped that everything was being done to assure that MANDIBLES would take place as scheduled. On Sunday he was going to make a broadcast and, in addition to mentioning the fine work of the 4th Indian Division in both the Desert and East Africa, he wished to say, "Considerable British and Imperial Forces have arrived in Greece." Since the Germans and the Americans knew, it seemed silly not to tell the Australians and the British. Other exchanges of telegrams this day provided at last for a British battalion to be landed to garrison Lemnos, which was under daily air surveillance, presumably German.[154]

On Saturday morning the twenty-ninth, Eden told Lincoln MacVeagh that he felt that the immediate implications of the Yugoslavian coup were being exaggerated in England and America, but that he had returned to explore the possibility of their development. He went on, "I don't care if the Yugoslavs don't actually repudiate their signature of the Tripartite Pact if only we can get together now and formulate some sort of a common policy after which we can take it to the Turks." He added that the British minister in Belgrade was to talk with the Yugoslav prime minister and would fly to Athens immediately afterwards.

MacVeagh reported to Washington that he had also talked to Dill, Wilson, and D'Albiac, who thought that the situation in Yugoslavia was holding up the German attack. The AOC and Eden both were of the opinion that it had been scheduled for 28 March in conjunction with the Italian naval sweep (which had just ended in the British victory at Cape Matapan). MacVeagh then passed on to Eden and D'Albiac the rush telegram from the American consul in Bulgaria containing the information that the initial German attack would be an air blitz of British and Greek aircraft on their airfields in daylight, "THE TIME VERY SOON." The AOC said that he expected this to be combined with parachute landings at Salonika and other places in the immediate rear of the defending lines. Eden was greatly annoyed at this time by British radio broadcasts of the whereabouts of Prince Paul, and in MacVeagh's presence (he always liked an audience) he dictated a telegram to the British minister (of information?) stating that it would be well if the BBC "ceased speculating" as it embarrassed the king of Greece. MacVeagh only then discovered that Prince Paul and his wife were in Athens.[155]

On Sunday, 30 March, Eden was still waiting to see what developed in the Yugoslav situation, suggesting that he might make a secret visit to Simović, "who personally takes the view that the Yugoslavs will fight if the Germans attack Salonika and has told the Germans so." But Eden was not, absolutely confident, because there were other Yugoslav ministers to be taken into account.[156]

Meanwhile, on Saturday, Terence Shone had arrived from Belgrade to say that a meeting would be fine; but later in the day Campbell telephoned from there to say it was off. On Sunday there was another change of mind when Simović said that he would "receive Sir John Dill very secretly in Belgrade." So it was agreed that Dill should go in mufti (he looked something like a middle-aged professor anyway) and that the CIGS should say that, if the Yugoslavs would cooperate, Anglo-Greek forces would try to hold Salonika, where the Yugoslavs had a vital free port, with "all Anglo-Greek forces in Macedonia under a Greek commander."

## 31 March - 1 April 1941

So on the evening of Monday, 31 March, Dill, Brigadier Mallaby, and Dixon flew to Belgrade and had three hours of talks with General Simović, General Ilić, the minister for war, and General Nikolić, the acting chief of the general staff. The British team got the impression that the Yugoslavs were much preoccupied during this conference; they were frequently called out to deal with problems of the internal state of the country and of mobilization. It seems that a Yugoslav journalist had misled them into believing the British had landed fifteen divisions and a hundred aircraft. Having carried out the coup, they now heard the abysmal truth.[157] They wanted to buy time and so would not attack the Italians in Albania or let Eden make a visit. Moreover, they badly needed arms from Britain. Yet Simović was willing, he said, to sign a mutual declaration of support if Greece was attacked. Because he wanted a strong force about Lake Doiran, he agreed to staff talks which would take place at Florina in two days.

On the following day Mallaby and Dixon had a very unsatisfactory conversation with the Yugoslav general staff, who did not wish to draft and see signed the general accord to which Simović had apparently agreed. Moreover, the general staff argued for limiting Yugoslav support to the case only of an attack west of the Struma valley. This unsatisfactory state of affairs led, then, to a second meeting between Dill and Simović at which the latter withdrew altogether his willingness to sign any agreement, saying that he now found that he would have to submit it to the whole government (presumably meaning his Cabinet) and that as to do so would split the delicate alliance of Serbs, Croats, and Slovenes, he would not do so at all. Nevertheless, General Janković, the director of military operations, would be at Florina with full power to discuss hypotheses and arrive at conclusions on strictly military plans. During all these conversations, Dixon's diary-report avers, Simovich and Ilitch were adamant that they would resist the Germans, but could not say so out loud because of a fear that the Croatians would pull out.[158]

The real difficulty with making any arrangements with Yugoslavia was that the country was neither militarily nor psychologically ready for war. Churchill, Eden, and Papagos were hoping to count on forces which existed only on paper and upon which no one appears to have completed thorough intelligence assessments, any more than the British had studied the Czechs or the French before 1938-1939.

Not until Friday evening, 4 April, did Dill report from Athens on his disappointing visit to Belgrade. He concluded that the Yugoslavs seemed determined to fight, but not until Germany attacked them, when a strong British liaison mission would be needed at once. Dill had discussed the leadership of this with Wavell and Wilson and reported that they wanted the one-eyed General Carton de Wiart, VC, who had lived in Poland before the war, to lead it, with Brigadier George Davy, then on the staff in Athens, as the second in command. Dill reported that he and Eden would not be involved in the forthcoming staff talks, which would be handled by Papagos and Wilson, but would be close at hand if needed.[159]

Meanwhile in the cold rain and wind on the northern slopes of the Aliakmon Line, grim New Zealanders on 30 March began the task of digging in, well aware from intelligence summaries that they faced twenty-one German divisions under Field Marshal List. What they thought about the odds was obscured by the sweat and mist on their goggles as they labored in gas-masks, having been convinced by Lieutenant-Colonel Marnham, a British gas expert, that this was necessary![160]

From Athens Lincoln MacVeagh reported that the people were frightened, and that the prime minister was hoping momentarily for a German *démarche* but was determined to hold to the policy of 28 October. At the same time Koryzis was completely disillusioned with the attitude of the Turks, who gave nothing but praise (in spite of the fact that their military attaché estimated that so far 120,000 British had landed; evidently British secrecy was paying off, as at this time probably not many more than 40,000 troops had landed, of the 58,000 total finally sent).

On the thirtieth Churchill had cabled Fadden in Australia to point out that the British moves initiated late in February were paying dividends, gave renewed hope of a Balkan front of seventy divisions from four powers, and put LUSTRE in its proper setting with risks somewhat lessened.[161] And interestingly, while Churchill knew from agents in Yugoslavia by 28 March that three out of the five German panzer divisions were on their way to Cracow from their threatening positions near Belgrade, a fact that indicated an attack upon Russia and so a warning had been sent to Stalin, it was not until 31 May that the C-in-C's in the Middle East were told of this switch in German intentions.[162]

Blamey cabled Canberra from Athens on 31 March. He was now more in tune with Wilson's feelings, after having toured the Greek positions. They were very weak in the north, and Florina would early be lost to the Germans. Both the railway and the road ran through narrow defiles easily subject to disruption by intensive air attack. The air and ground defenses were hopelessly inadequate, and serious dislocation of the lines of communication was, therefore, likely. The Germans, he reported, had twenty-three to twenty-five divisions in Bulgaria and could concentrate eleven to thirteen against the four Greek divisions on the frontier and six to seven against the Vermion Line held by the one armored brigade, the New Zealand Division, and two Greek divisions. Papagos had wanted nine full divisions on the line with strong air support, but he had got instead eight weak ones with little air support.[163]

If this war had lasted long enough the Greeks would have received their 30 Grumman Wildcats as, in another switch of policy, these had been released by President Roosevelt on 28 March. Some had left on 1 April and the rest left 4 April, but their transit time was six weeks plus set-up and training.[164] In London Rab Butler told the Greek ambassador that the British hoped to be able to send more of the RAF to Greece, "if the menace in Tripoli did not grow."[165]

On April Fool's Day the air attaché, in Belgrade signaled that the Yugoslavs would start to mobilize on the third, and that that would bring their strength to 1,800,000 men under arms.[166]

On the same day the New Zealand Division and the 1st Armoured Brigade were in line on the eastern end of the Aliakmon position, the 19th Greek Division had moved up to the Eastern Macedonian frontier, and the 6th Australian Division was just beginning to arrive on the line. The opinion in British circles was that the Aliakmon Line was as strong as any one of its four passes at Veria, Edessa, Katerini or on the coast, but once the enemy penetrated one of those, a speedy withdrawal was a necessity. The basic weakness of the whole position remained the Monastir Gap from Yugoslavia down past Florina, a route that would allow the whole position to be turned from the west. The New Zealand Division's position was too long, not tankproof, and could not be covered by the divisional artillery. The few lateral communications were mostly over one-way muletracks. Both infantry and artillery were unhappy about their positions.[167]

In these early April days the RAF in Greece was divided into three groups. In the western wing were No. 112 Squadron with Gladiators and No. 211 with Blenheims, both by then obsolescent. In the eastern wing, based at Larissa, were No. 11 and No. 113 with Blenheims, No. 33 with Hurricanes, and No. 208 Army Cooperation with a mixture of Hurricanes

and Lysanders. Grouped in the Athens area were No. 30 with a mixture of
Blenheim fighters and bombers, No. 80 with Gladiators and Hurricanes,
and No. 84 with Blenheim bombers, together with detachments of Nos.
37 and 38 in Wellingtons. Hardly a full-strength, modern fighting force,
based on waterlogged airfields, it would shortly face the first-line strength
of the Luftwaffe. Yet at this period Churchill believed that the war would
be won by aircraft.[168]

One of the flyers who arrived in Greece with No. 33 Squadron was
Vernon "Woody" Woodward of Victoria, British Columbia, who, like the
Malta ace "Buzz" Beurling, had been turned down by the RCAF before
the war because he did not have a college degree, so had joined the RAF.
He had finished flying training and been commissioned a pilot-officer
and posted to No. 33 in Egypt in the spring of 1939. The Italians declared
war on 10 June 1940, and by the end of the month Woodward, flying
biplanes, was an "ace" and had earned the sobriquet "imperturbable" for
taking on nine Italian fighters single-handed after his wingman had been
shot down. The squadron was commanded by one of the RAF's top-
scoring fighter-pilots of World War II, the South African Pat Pattle, who by
the time of his death on 20 April 1941 in Greece had between twenty-eight
and forty-one victories. No. 33 Squadron moved to Greece in February
and was in action escorting Blenheims before the Germans attacked.[169]

On 1 April London raised the question of using the RAF in Greece to
support either Yugoslavia or Turkey or both, if they, but not Greece, were
attacked by Germany. "The basis of our plans must be to give full support
to our own forces, but we must be prepared to assist our allies if they are
attacked." London did not want to move aircraft forward into Yugoslavia
and they could not aid Turkey from Greek bases, so both cases presented
dilemmas for which Greek consent to operations from Greek fields was
needed. Eden replied the next day that these matters had been considered
and that the Greeks had no objection in the case of Yugoslavia. But as no
definite answer could be obtained from the Turks, that was more difficult.[170] In a few days it became irrelevant.

## 2 - 3 April 1941

There are times when men refuse to believe news they do not wish to
hear. In Belgrade the new Yugoslav government insisted that it had time
to mobilize before the Germans were likely to attack. Thus when on 2
April it received two telegrams from the military attaché in Berlin, which
slipped through German intelligence censorship (perhaps because Admiral Canaris, its head, had told him), they refused to believe him that the
attack would open on the sixth with an intense bombing of Belgrade.[171]

From Athens MacVeagh told Washington that the Yugoslav minister
had received word from Belgrade that Yugoslavia would honor the Tripar-

tite Pact of 25 March but treat it as a dead letter and remain friendly to all, and had so informed the Greek government.[172]

The British 1st Armoured Brigade was warned on this Wednesday, 2 April, that the Germans would attack at dawn on Saturday. The attack actually came on Sunday, 6 April.[173]

Toward the rear, 1 NZ General Hospital was not happy about the situation. This 490-bed unit had 350 tons of equipment and no transport of its own. It did not think that the red cross symbol would be a protection from either German or Italian airmen, and so the whole unit was dispersed in tents in a narrow valley twenty miles from its supply base in Larissa.[174]

Further to the rear, in Athens the weather was better than the day before, when it had been cloudy, windy and cold. On this Wednesday the temperature had risen to 60 degrees under an almost cloudless sky with a light breeze. Otherwise things were not so pleasant. The king and the president of the Council had asked urgently once again for ammunition for their Schneider mountain guns, of French manufacture. Could London, they asked Eden, get at the stocks known to exist in the United States, as none were being manufactured elsewhere? They also asked for rifles and light machine-guns, with ammunition for a new army corps. London passed the request to Washington both directly and through FDR's special envoy, W. Averill Harriman, who sent it to the president's aide, Harry Hopkins.[175]

On Tuesday, the day before, London had finally called the British Purchasing Commission in New York and at last discovered that there was no 105-mm mountain ammunition available in the United States. It had, in London's opinion, taken the commission a long time to discover this. Even if production started at once there would be at least a six- to eight-week gap when the Greeks would be out of it. Two days later Lord Hankey's special committee at the Cabinet Office decided that the time had come to propose to the Greeks that their forces be rearmed with British weapons and equipment, which was replaceable, and that the ideal time to make this suggestion was while Eden was still in Athens.[176]

And to try and straighten out the business of providing the Greeks with Hurricanes rather than Tomahawks, Longmore signaled Palairet that because many people were interested in this matter, confusion was resulting. But he had arranged with Papagos that, as the RAF had Hurricanes in Greece and they were satisfactory there, it made better sense for the Greeks to use them rather than the American-made Tomahawks: spares and maintenance would be simplified. As soon as Longmore's own squadrons were supplied, the Greeks would get the eighteen aircraft promised.[177]

In fact Longmore was not in an enviable position. While he was expected to give his primary support to the campaign that was about to develop in Greece, on this Wednesday he had to order a flight of No. 45 Blenheim Squadron sent from Greece to reinforce its parent in the Western Desert. The Wellington squadron had had to be withdrawn from Malta under pressure from Fliegerkorps X of the Luftwaffe, now operating from Sicily just sixty miles to the north. But even these efforts were insufficient, as a crisis was rapidly developing in the Desert which prevented the 7th Australian Division's planned embarkation for Greece.[178]

Wavell decided that Neame had lost control by staying at his headquarters at Barce and prepared to go up to take charge, but he could not find a suitable aircraft. He sent O'Connor by car, followed by a signal to him to take over. This did not make the man who had recommended Neame for the post very happy at all, since the battle was already lost. By the time O'Connor arrived on 3 April Wavell had located an aircraft and beaten him to Barce. That evening the situation was so bad that Wavell told O'Connor to go ahead and evacuate the coast in the face of the dashing Rommel (who, as it turned out, was disobeying orders in attacking).[179] The British situation was exacerbated by the poor condition and shortage of their material, only partly a result of the switch of emphasis to Greece. Some of the inadequacy was due to the lack of ports once Benghazi was abandoned, and the consequent excessive demands upon motor transport. Wavell later pointed out that he had been promised, and had made his plans upon the receipt of 3,000 vehicles a month from January 1941, but in fact had received less than half that number (though at the same time he claimed that 8,000 were lost in Greece).[180] Eden, who was as much to blame as anyone for the mess in the Desert, said later in his memoirs that Neame's defeat was entirely due to the command's faulty appreciation of the speed with which Rommel could mount a desert offensive. But in truth it was just as much due to prewar failures to set up intelligence networks and to wartime dissipation of inadequate resources. Even more, this fatal dispersion of effort was due to an unwillingness to analyze the evidence available. People like Eden and Dill did not need ULTRA; they needed reading glasses and perceptive minds coupled to decisiveness.

On Thursday evening Eden telegraphed from Athens that the RAF was making arrangements to transfer squadrons to Turkey if the need arose, and the Turks themselves had already sent ships to Alexandria to collect the necessary supplies and had other preparations in hand.[181] Late that night Wavell reported from Cairo that he was back from Cyrenaica. When he had left at four o'clock the situation was obscure, but he feared that a large part of the armored brigade and its support force had been overrun by a superior German armored force. This defeat uncovered the flank of the 9th Australian Division and would probably force its withdrawal from the Benghazi area. As it was essential to stop an apparent drive on Egypt, he had had to withdraw the 7th Australian Division from LUSTRE and send it forward; a mobile reserve would be created of what armored units could be pulled together, and the incomplete 6th British Division would be the force reserve, compelling the postponement of MANDIBLES yet again. When the 4th Indian Division arrived from the Sudan it might be possible to release the 7th for Greece. He had asked for the CIGS's and Blamey's views from Athens. And lastly, when O'Connor arrived at Benghazi, Wavell found that he had been sick and that he might become ill again; so, since Neame was doing well in a difficult situation, and it was agreeable to both, it was left that O'Connor would act as Neame's adviser.

On 4 April Wavell had to signal that, since the enemy had taken Msus, the 9th Australians had to be pulled back and Benghazi abandoned. In Greece the concentration of the New Zealand Division was complete except for 21 Batallion, still in Athens, and 7th Field Company, which moved up the next day.

Meanwhile on the second the C-in-C's in Cairo had cabled the Chiefs of Staff that the Mobile Naval Base Defence Organization should be established at Suda Bay, because "the movement of large military and RAF forces into Greece has greatly enhanced the importance of Crete." The air threat from Bulgaria precluded its establishment farther north until more A/A guns were available. So Suda Bay would now become a Fleet base rather than just a refueling base.[182] Thus Crete continued as a ghostly base at the bottom of the priorities ladder, because of the paucity of resources, when its strategic importance should have placed it at the top. In ways it is symbolic of the immaturity and lack of focus of British grand strategy at this period.

Churchill sent Simović a telegram in which he told him that Germans were concentrating against Yugoslavia from as far away as France, and that his only hope was to make "one supreme stroke for victory and safety" by winning "a decisive forestalling victory in Albania" and collecting the "masses of equipment" that would fall into his hands—and to do this before the Germans reached Albania, while he could still fall upon the "rear of the demoralized and rotten Italians."[183]

On 4 April Wilson, whose code address was *Braig, Athens*, cabled that he and Papagos had met with General Janković, "D.M.C. Jug.army, and with M.J. Hope" late on the night of the third, but that the talks had been limited to operations in the event of an Axis attack on Salonika only, for which the Yugoslav army would fight. The Allies produced a plan based on a British army that was twice its present strength, with the Greeks holding their fortified areas and the British and Yugoslavs attacking the line Petrich-Djumaya-Kustendil, at the same time that a Graeco-Yugoslav attack was launched in Albania. The Yugoslavs, who had brought only one copy of their plan, which they took home again, reported that their concentrations were completed on the Bulgarian front and would be on the Albanian by the twelfth. The British were asked to concentrate on an

Axis attack in the Doiran—Valandovo area. Papagos stressed the need for a higher proportion of the Yugoslav divisions in southern Serbia. "I indicated our forces available near future, risk of weak Struma front against attack from east and unsuitability of equipment to terrain. Agreed to recco with view to joining up later on line Struma-Doiran with Jugs, and for three staff to visit Athens for further discussions. D.M.C. some-what defeatist, especially on A.F.V.'s. Meeting ended [at two in the morning] on friendly and cheerful terms."[184]

## 4 April 1941

Starting at 10:10 Friday morning, in the train heading back to Athens from Kenali Station, Papagos, Wilson, D'Albiac, Heywood, and Colonel Kitrilakis discussed what they should do next. When and how might any change in the disposition of their forces be carried out, in view of the fact that the Yugoslavs had four of their 40,000-man divisions fully mobilized in southeast Yugoslavia and the Vardar valley?

General Wilson was of the opinion that, if there was to be an immedi-ate German attack, the best place to meet it was on the Aliakmon Line. If moves were started, they could not be completed during the next moon period (5-19 April). On the whole he thought it best to strengthen the strong Aliakmon position first and then to bolster the Struma, and with this General Papagos agreed. After acknowledging that the Australian brigade, which might be sent to the Veria Gap, would not be available for eight days, the officers agreed to make no changes until after that time had passed.

As to the question of eventually sending the 1st Armoured Brigade to the Lake Doiran area, Wilson said that any move would have to await reconnaissance to find out if the ground was suitable. Holding the Struma would require at least three divisions, and it would be at least a month before they were available. Papagos then asked if any reinforcements could be expected as a result of the victory in Abyssinia, and Wilson replied No, because of the German attack in Cyrenaica. What about the third Australian division, which Blamey had told him about, Papagos asked, and Wilson responded that that would only be much later. Events would move quickly as they had in France, and the Anglo-Greek forces could not afford to be caught on the move. Much of the rest of the conversation was an exchange of views on things that did not happen. But in the course of this, Papagos said that one of the good things about last night's meeting with Janković was the Yugoslav decision to intervene in the case of an attack upon Salonika. On the other hand Papagos was not very happy about the concentration plan of the Yugoslav Army: it was too even, with far more allotted to the Albanian front than was needed. He concluded by saying that he would press his Foreign Secretary to ask that

Yugoslav officers visit Athens to give information on their general plans, a point Wilson had earlier reinforced by saying that the British and the Greeks needed to be allowed to scout north of the Greek borders also.[185]

Churchill on 3 April had sent off a warning to Stalin of the impending German attack on the USSR, (although it took him until the nineteenth to persuade the stubborn Sir Stafford Cripps, the British ambassador in Moscow, to deliver it). At the same time, the Prime Minister received a signal from Wavell saying that Neame had lost control in Cyrenaica. The Chiefs of Staff advised that MANDIBLES, the seizure of Rhodes, be dropped, that the 7th Australian Division be held in Egypt, and that all services concentrate on stabilizing the front in Cyrenaica. The Defence Committee met that night at 10:30 and expressed surprise that the Germans could operate better than one armored division at the end of such a long line of communications. At midnight when the meeting broke up, it was agreed to send a telegram to Eden in Athens that the loss of Benghazi and its airfields was serious and would probably deny the use of Tobruk. Most distressing was the idea that the British could not face the Germans. Eden should, as Wavell also urged, proceed to Cairo.[186]

Upon his return to Athens on Friday the 4th, Eden signaled that he and Dill had just got back from the Yugoslav frontier. They had generally been out of touch for several days, but they felt that what had happened in North Africa was what had been anticipated as a risk taken when aid to Greece was agreed upon. The build-up had been faster than anticipated. Then sensibly he suggested that he and Dill leave for home the next day, the last one with a favorable moon period for flying through the Mediterranean at night. If they went to Cairo it not only would increase the burdens upon Wavell, but also might make everyone there and in the Balkans think the situation even more serious than it was.[187]

Early on Friday Tedder sent the CAS a short report on his trip to Cyrenaica in the absence of the AOC-in-C. He felt that the military situation was "somewhat dangerous owing largely to the armoured advance across the desert towards Mechili. Only immediate means of checking is air action." But the RAF was very thin. He had discussed LUSTRE and MANDIBLES with Wavell, and they had agreed that both would have to take second place to Cyrenaica; he was acting on that basis and sending all replacements there.

At the same time Wavell teletyped that the reverses in the Desert were due to shortages of tanks, transport of all kinds, and antitank and A/A guns. "Recent reverse in Cyrenaica has been due to insufficiency of these, and, unless I can receive them faster than Germans, Egypt will soon be seriously threatened. Western Desert war is almost purely mechanical." And he went on to point out that those in London knew his wants and that he had been disappointed in not receiving promised transport and aircraft from the United States.[188]

Portal responded to Tedder on 4 April that he entirely agreed that absolute priority must be given to Cyrenaica. If necessary, Blenheims were to be operated from Greece, but the squadrons were to be retained there. "We are sending you all we can. Best of luck."[189]

Perhaps the only bright spot on the British side of the war in the Middle East and the Balkans at this time was that London had finally decided that the Enigma decrypts should be sent directly from the United Kingdom to battlefield commanders, and this prevented the clash of main forces which might have proved disastrous to the British. For the first time the commanders in the field were told of the source and reliability of this information. But, as Hinsley notes, how the material was received and acted upon is unknown today.[190] It appears that Wilson in Greece did shortly pay attention to it and skillfully pulled his forces back in time. Wavell may have been less willing to rely upon ULTRA, perhaps because his mind was cluttered with far too much information and engaged in making too many decisions. At the higher level in London, we know that Churchill and others read ULTRA, but they were not getting the correct messages because they did not know the Germans well enough. Raw intelligence is not necessarily intelligible.

Later on the fourth the Prime Minister sent Wavell a telegram, repeated to Eden in Athens, which began, "We are making an intense effort to reinforce you with aircraft and tanks at earliest. Chiefs of Staff are now drafting statement of decisions we have taken to-day. Feel sure you will be surprised as well as encouraged by all this. Press and public have taken evacuation of Benghazi admirably. Confidence in High Command is unshakable. I warned the country a week ago that they must not expect continuance of unbroken successes and take the rough with the smooth. Therefore be quite sure that we shall back you up in adversity even better than in good fortune." And he went on to ask again for a draft announcement of the landing of British forces in Greece.[191]

The promised memorandum from the Chiefs of Staff was sent on 5 April. It basically at last accepted a number of suggestions made by the Middle East, including now a second lift of Hurricanes to Malta in a repeat of OPERATION WINCH, this time with two carriers flying off 24 to 30 non-tropical Mark I Hurricanes, which could be used there or in Greece or in Egypt; much more armor was to be shipped out in a special convoy due in mid-June; and various other actions were listed, as well as approval for the cancelation of MANDIBLES.[192]

## 5 April 1941

Just before he left Athens for Cairo on Saturday, Eden told MacVeagh that the Germans in Libya were formidable, but he was buoyed up by a telegram from "Winston" which said that he would be surprised at how much they could now send from the United Kingdom. Eden, however, stressed that time was the critical factor. He was greatly encouraged by FDR's view that with Eritrea cleared the Red Sea could be opened to American shipping; what the United States could send in the next couple of months would be crucial. He thought the Yugoslav talks had gone well: they were very determined, but anxious not to provoke the Germans before they were ready. He and Dill had toured the British positions, which were "very strong," but he felt that Turkey's attitude was little better than "fluctuating," unless Britain could send more mechanized equipment, "but unfortunately we can't." In a further exchange, Mac-Veagh told Eden that the Greek king had heard that Hitler intended to attack the Ukraine, and if this was successful then to overrun Russia as far as the Urals; Eden responded, "Megalomania." Eden's return to Cairo, MacVeagh told Washington, was being kept secret so as not to alarm the public after the loss of Benghazi.[193]

Major-General I.G. Mackay, commander of the 6th Australian Division, who had just arrived in Athens the day before with his senior staff, drove north under orders to report to Blamey at Gerania, close to the blue house from which Prince Constantine had in 1912 launched his successful campaign against the Ottoman Empire to take Salonika. Mackay was at once ordered to take over the Veria Pass from the 12th Greek Division, even though he only had the 16th Brigade Group available. The actual takeover did not begin until the seventh.[194]

On Saturday, 5 April, Blamey officially opened the headquarters of the 1st Australian Corps and assumed command of all Imperial troops from the Aegean near Mount Olympus to the Veria Pass. His command was far from settled. The New Zealand Division was listed as almost concentrated, but only the forward elements of the 6th Australian were arriving in the front lines.

In its daily status report to the Air Ministry, Air Headquarters Middle East reported in some uncertainty on the location of its squadrons: No. 113 was presumed to be in Greece; No. 45 was also presumed to be there, but the chief of the Air Staff crossed out that note and wrote in by hand "still in Cyrenaica"; No. 208 was presumed to be in Greece. The total strength in Greece at 0900 hours that morning was presumed to be 19 Hurricanes, 16 Gladiators, 30 Blenheim I's and 34 Blenheim IV's, as of six days earlier.[195] Or 99, to face the Luftwaffe's 490!

Wilson had now set up his command post at Elasson, a few miles from Gerania, so that he was within easy telephone and dispatch-rider distance of Blamey. But Papagos was back in Athens, and communications from Elasson to the capital were at best tenuous and at worst took eight hours by car. Under these circumstances, GHQ ME had finally ordered that the headquarters be split, with half in Athens and half forward at Elasson, a solution which did nothing to alleviate the already severe shortage of staff officers in the whole Middle East. Though Brigadier Brunskill, at least, claimed that the lack of staff did not affect the campaign, he did admit that with only the GSO 3 in Athens he was overwhelmed by the combined Greek staff and the British military mission and was unable to get decisions on demolitions in the crucial days of the retreat.[196]

At the same time Wilson wrote GHQ ME that he needed a larger organization in Greece, especially since he would have to hive off a liaison section for work with the Yugoslavs if the line advanced to the Struma. He was short of clerks, and his staff officers were badly overworked because of this, so he appealed for a draft of women clerks to be sent from Egypt or South Africa to act as drivers and for clerical duties, so as to relieve ablebodied clerks with some knowledge of the work to get on with their proper jobs.[197]

On 5 April Wilson, heard from London that the direct Enigma warning service gave the time of the German attack on Greece as 0530, 6 April. Very early the next morning, London transmitted a correction that the time would be 0600—first light.[198] (In contrast to the timeliness of this service, official air mail between HQ in Cairo and headquarters at Larissa was taking more than three weeks northbound and ten days the other way.)

At 11:30 a.m. on the fifth General Kotulas and General Wilson met with three of their staff to discuss the relief of the Greek 12th by the 6th Australian Division. Kotulas was most anxious to make the transfer as soon as possible, as he was very thin on the ground and had only minor local reserves. As the Australians came in, he intended to thicken up the 20th. This would give greater depth on the left flank and provide some excellent battery areas. Wilson said that he was not anxious to put the Australians into the Veria Gap until their commander arrived, but he expected them to take over the Greek front within the next eight days. They then discussed the building of a second bridge across the Aliakmon and of making a track passable for motor vehicles north of the Veria-Kozani road. The two left battalions of the 12th could not be relieved by Imperial troops until the latter were equipped with pack animals, as there were no other means of communication in their area. The group dealt with various other problems, and it was agreed that Wilson would assume command of the Allied forces at the Vermion position as of 1400 hours that day.[199]

Wavell asked Wilson to please explain to Blamey why he had to keep 18 Australian Brigade in the Desert, and he apologized to both commanders for having to upset LUSTRE; the CIGS agreed with him and also conveyed his regrets.[200]

Churchill replied to Eden's signal saying that he was glad that Eden could be so reassuring about the Libyan situation, as it looked pretty serious from London. Since he and Dill felt they could do no good in Cairo, they should return home.

By that Saturday evening the two Englishmen were in Cairo, where they had a full discussion with Wavell and Tedder; Longmore was in the Sudan. They came to the conclusion that the Italo-German operation in the Desert was a major diversion well timed to precede the German attack in the Balkans. Unfortunately, the enemy had succeeded better than he had hoped; but the situation appeared to be becoming less critical, since the Germans were not using their air force to the degree that was to be expected in a major attack. The new cruiser tanks sent out recently seemed to be breaking down much more than they should, and the British were weak both in these and in aircraft. Because of bad weather, Eden and Dill did not expect to leave for home until Monday.[201]

In London Cadogan noted in his diary that they had received sure news that Germany would attack Yugoslavia on the morrow; all the right pepole had been informed, but he did not know what Britain could do. This was followed by the opening entry for the 6th: "7:45 am. Rung up with the news that Yugoslavia attacked—that'll stop the dithering."[202]

And so began the beginning of the end. On 7 April Eden and Dill slipped quietly out of Cairo and headed home for London, where they arrived on the tenth, much to the depression of the Foreign Office.[203] At last Wavell would have friends at court and not in his hair.

## 6 - 26 April 1941

The story of the next three weeks is quickly told. The Germans attacked with standard blitzkrieg, professional tactics; the exhausted Greeks reeled back; and the totally inadequate British forces, which had never got dug in, simply were forced to withdraw in good order as their pitifully small air force was decimated, often on the ground at unprotected airfields. And all of this happened in steadily improving weather, though in northern Greece wet roads meant slow, slick driving until after the eighteenth. After the campaign there would be much outcry that there had been insufficient air cover in Greece and that that was the reason for the failure there. That is both the truth and nonsense. Lack of air power on the Anglo-Greek side was a reality, but it was by no means the prime reason for the British defeat. There never had been an honest military appreciation of all the factors, with the result that some boys had been sent to do a professional army's job. But after the campaign was over Jumbo Wilson, for one, and others who favored a tactical air force, argued that the failure to subordinate the RAF to the army had contributed to the disaster, rather than admit the true facts. The argument may also have been a cover for ULTRA.

Dill was at least more honest and more perceptive. On 21 April 1941, before the campaign was over, he wrote a memorandum (which was not added to the diary of Eden's trip until 21 December 1971 when it was inserted by the Public Record Office staff, who copied it from another file). Dill said that a military appreciation of sending forces to Greece had not been made, and when the discussions took place in Cairo on 20 and 21 February there was an opportunity to condemn the project as unsound for military reasons; and he then gave the reasons both pro and con. It was estimated at that time that the Germans could attack the Greek frontier eighteen days after crossing the Danube. If the British did nothing, the Germans would have their way in the Balkans. So it was unanimously agreed in Cairo to make an offer to Greece, provided (a) the Greek government would accept, and (b) a sound military plan could be agreed on with the Greeks as to the line to be held. But by early March the British could not withdraw because of public opinion in the Middle East. Dill concluded that "the military risks were throughout clearly seen and given full weight. Nevertheless opinion was at the outset unanimous that we should aid Greece . . . and the military authorities concerned were all agreed that even in the altered circumstances of the second visit to Athens, the risks must be accepted and the plan still had a reasonable chance of success."[204]

As even Eden predicted, the Germans came through the Bulgarian passes just as soon as the snows permitted, propelled by events in Yugoslavia and the plans for Russia. It is almost amusing to find the British reporting critically on 3 April that General Janković of Yugoslavia seemed to think that he had months in which to prepare for war, when in fact the whole British plan depended upon not being attacked by the Germans until at the earliest late May. As it was, they were pushed off their positions almost before they had got their privies placed.

Even the briefest account of the campaign shows an army unready for the contest:

At 5:45 on Sunday morning, 6 April 1941, the German minister in Athens handed a note to the Greek Foreign Office stating that Germany was going to attack Greece. This was fifteen minutes after the signal BOCHE (German attack) had been received from the British forward unit in the Struma valley and relayed through Reid to Wilson at Elasson.[205] Simultaneously the frontier posts from Beles to Xanthe were attacked by German troops with air support. War was also declared upon Yugoslavia. In all, the Germans employed twenty divisions with ten in reserve.

Sunday was a brilliant day in Athens, with no clouds, a temperature in the low seventies, and light winds.[206] During much of the month of April the sky was cloudy, but only on the sixteenth did Athens report ¹⁰/₁₀ths cloud cover; the daytime temperature never fell below the mid-fifties, and only for three nights was it in the forties. The winds were light and there was almost no rain. In other words, at least in the Athens area it was ideal campaigning weather. Snow, sleet, rain, and fog persisted farther north until the fourteenth. Most of the time it was ideal flying weather, once the airfields were dry enough for the planes to take off.

At nine o-clock that Sunday evening two flights of German aircraft flew in over the Piraeus and dropped magnetic mines, one of which set on fire the freighter *Clan Fraser*. She was loaded with two hundred tons of explosives for the Greek Powder Factory, and in spite of strenuous efforts to tow her to sea she exploded in the entrance to the main port. Firefighting facilities in Athens had earlier been reported as poor.[207] The *Clan Fraser* disaster was said to have caused the closing of the main Greek port for both maintenance and evacuation. Later it was claimed that all that was left to complete the destruction of the port of the Piraeus was to take the drydock gates into the Saronic Gulf and sink them. Only one other ship discharged at the port of Athens, and the Greek Powder Factory closed down.[208] Reexamination of the photographs of the damage, and measurement of the shock wave, do not show all these statements to be true. The *Clan Fraser* explosion was a useful cover for the lack of magnetic minesweeping gear and of ships fitted with degaussing aparatus. These factors added to the reasons for the British pull-out.

As the Piraeus lay reeling under the shock of the explosion, Wavell sent home a draft communiqué, a short announcement that British troops had landed in Athens.[209] He had now milked the mysterious in that to the maximum.

Sir Claude Auchinleck, the man who would take over as Wavell's successor in Egypt in a few months, noted later, "This was a period of supreme challenge, of a complex mingling of triumph and disaster, of bold decisions and nightmare risks, above all of overwhelming responsibility."[210] Even on a personal level it was a time of trial and tribulations for Wavell. On the evening of the sixth Neame and O'Connor and Gambier-Parry were captured by the Germans in Libya. (They escaped but were recaptured the same night.)[211]

In the meantime the infamous German air attack on Belgrade had taken place in which a reputed 17,000 died, just as Simović signed a friendship pact with the Soviet Union. Stalin canceled the agreement a few days later, when Yugoslavia was overrun and Belgrade fell. Across the world in Washington the Yugoslav military attaché asked the American government for 100 bombers, 100 fighters, 500 reconnaissance planes, 100 medium tanks, 2,000 trucks, 1,500,000 gas masks and helmets and a large number of antitank and antiaircraft guns. As the administrator of the new Lend-Lease program put it, it was "utterly impossible to meet these modest demands," but a plan was drawn up the next day to start supplying material out of stocks on hand, and by the end of April a few guns, trucks, and gas masks were actually starting to move. But by then the war in the Balkans was over, and these and the supplies for which the Greeks had been pressing for more than five months were diverted to the British in the Middle East.[212]

On Monday there was an urgent appeal from Athens for magnetic-minesweeping equipment as a result of the German raid the night before, which had accounted for six ships in addition to the *Clan Fraser*, out of the fifty-three available for the LUSTRE shuttle.[213] The Kent Fortress Troops were rushed to Salonika to undertake demolitions of oil, petrol supplies, and all facilities and dock machinery. They found the Greek high command not cooperative, as they rightly believed that the Germans would overrun Greece in short order and that Salonika would be needed for the well-being of the country. So on the eighth the Kent Corps troops evacuated about 270 Britishers and left. Farther south at Volos the demolition teams had their work done for them by German bombers, so they returned to the Athens area to water the roads, which—in contrast to those in the north—were dry and dusty, destroy stores, and ruin the airfield under construction at Araxos and the scarce machinery that had been imported to make it.[214]

Left behind at Salonika for the Germans were about 1,000 tons of chrome owned by the Ministry of Economic Warfare in London, a quantity of lead considered of little value, and some antimony.[215]

In view of the fact that the Greek air force was negligible and the Yugoslav force had already been reduced to half its strength, D'Albiac decided to use all his aircraft in the tactical support role. But bad weather, especially 250 miles north of Athens, hampered operations until the nineteenth.[216]

Meanwhile farther south in Cairo the tensions were building up as the crises "seemed to go beyond the possibility of human solution." HQ ME became pessimistic enough that a plan was mooted to pull back to Northern Rhodesia, but that was quickly dropped when Churchill had a fit. No one in Cairo had any inkling that Hitler's real objective was Russia.[217] Disconcerting, to say the least, was the outbreak of a revolt in unstable Iraq.

India had seen this coming, and the viceroy, Lord Linlithgow, and the commander-in-chief, Auchinleck, had laid plans, as Mesopotamia had traditionally been an Indian responsibility. Wavell, with more than enough on his plate and without good communications with Iraq, had resisted getting involved there, though London had dumped it into his lap. Unfortunately for poor Wavell, the vigor with which India reacted to events in Iraq only confirmed Churchill's impression that Wavell was a good average colonel, and the constant transmission of that impression did not increase Wavell's confidence in his relationship with the Prime Minister. Churchill was anxious to have Iraq settled in a hurry, as the United States had been persuaded to set up a great aircraft assembly plant at Basra to which crated aircraft could be delivered across the Pacific Ocean more safely—at that time—than across the war-torn Atlantic.[218]

When it met at five o'clock on Monday afternoon 7 April, the War Cabinet had not discussed Greece since noon on 20 March. With Churchill and Menzies present, the Prime Minister said that he had not realized that the 7th Armoured Division would be so completely out of action when it was sent back to refit in Cairo. (For all his love of guns and gadgets, Churchill had little understanding of the complexities of modern technology as his constant complaints about the overstuffed Middle East betrayed.) Churchill then read Wavell's 2 March appreciation of the situation, upon which the War Cabinet had based its own decision to aid Greece. Menzies added that Wavell had underestimated the likelihood of a German advance in Cyrenaica, a question his colleagues in Australia had raised earlier. Now the Germans had upset plans to send more troops to Greece and it would perhaps be unwise to try and hold Benghazi with only partly-trained troops. Churchill agreed and admitted that losses in the Mediterranean, coupled with the failure to take the Dodecanese, had all hurt, but "we had no strategic error with which to reproach ourselves, although we had no doubt underestimated the likelihood of a serious enemy attack in Cyrenaica." (Neither had the German and Italian high commands expected one, as it turned out.) On the whole the Cabinet was very gloomy, and Menzies was worried and critical.[219]

On Tuesday the Anzac and Greek commanders were just starting to sort out their front-line arrangements on the Aliakmon position. The 16th Australian Infantry Brigade was preparing to take over the pass at Veria, where the Aliakmon flowed swiftly down through a gap between the Vermion Range to the west and the Olympus to the east. The town of Veria itself was perched on the edge of an escarpment to the west of the river. Leading back from it was a road, hardly more than a track, which climbed sharply up through the cloud-shrouded mountains, switchbacking its way toward the summit near Kastania until it peaked and hairpinned rapidly down past Polimilos and thence across the plain before rising up and over the hill into Kozani. The 16th and its accompanying field artillery battalion had scarcely started to get into position when Blamey arrived at Corps headquarters at Gerania with the news that Yugoslav resistance in the south had collapsed and that, as far as was known, there were no troops between Monastir and Florina. The decision was taken at once to constitute Mackay Force, a scratch infantry group which was to be rushed forward to look over the beautiful rolling country, just coming into spring flower, which stretched all the way to Florina with but one possible blocking position where the road and railway cut through low hills at Vevi. Mackay Force, in good British fashion, was detached from Blamey's command and placed directly under Wilson's HQ British Troops Greece.

Wavell had flown up to Tobruk on 8 April and had then disappeared.

Never allowed the benefit of a properly maintained and equipped air-plane, he had had to take what was available. On the way back they had to make two forced landings, and he was out of touch for several precious hours.[220]

In the morning on 9 April Papagos told Wilson over the telephone that the Yugoslavs in Veles had surrendered to the Germans and that there were no Yugoslav troops between there and the Greek frontier. He asked that the Mackay Force link up with the Greek reserves forming a line Florina-Kozani. At the same time Papagos said that he was stopping the Albanian offensive and would withdraw reserves from there. The min-utes of the telephone call seemed to bear out that Wilson had had to say earlier about his clerks: "This is the first intermission [sic] received by General WILSON of the collapse of the Southern YUGOSLAV front."[221]

At 6:15 that night Wilson learned that at 5:30 the night before the New Zealand Cavalry Regiment had had the first Imperial contact with Ger-man ground forces in Greece. The more than twenty-three-hour delay in passing such vital information was indicative of the operational difficulties in Greece in 1941.[222]

When he wrote his report later, Wilson took the view that by the ninth the Greek generals were becoming defeatist and the front was likely to crumble (or was this a cover for ULTRA?). The retreat began on 11 April and became a full withdrawal on the twelfth. From 8 through 12 April the Anglo-Greek forces benefited from bad weather in northern Greece that severely limited enemy air activity. But after that, especially when the weather cleared on the fourteenth, the Germans were everywhere, and the normal daylight spacing of ten to twelve vehicles per mile had to be reduced to five. It was not realized until afterwards that the Germans did not fly at night, and that lorries could have operated then with their headlights on and made much better time and had fewer accidents. Taking out casualties from the Aliakmon Line positions was a nightmare for the stretcher-bearers, involving as it did in some cases a carry of seven miles for which mules and donkeys, already in short supply, were neces-sary. Many medical difficulties occurred simply because the units were barely set up before casualties arrived and the withdrawal began.[223]

On Wednesday, 9 April, the Germans swept into Salonika, and Cairo asked permission to withdraw the 1st Battalion of the Bedfordshires and Hertfordshires (the "Beds and Herts") from Lemnos, where it had arrived on the fifth, as this force was now but a hostage to fortune and would be much better placed in the Middle East reserve in the Delta.

At Gerania orders went out to the New Zealand Division to move one brigade group to the Servia Pass south of Kozani to act as a pivot for the subsequent withdrawal of the 12th Greek Division and the 16th Aus-tralian Infantry Brigade. The position was a strong one if covered with enough artillery. The road snaked up the mountain pass from a river crossing down in the shallow valley to the pretty little town of Servia itself, then climbed up the pass past a small white-washed Greek Orthodox chapel on its little graveyard bastion. On Thursday further orders were issued to organize the defensive position and to outline the procedure for withdrawal to the Olympus-Aliakmon Line and arrange the preliminary moves of vehicles out of the area in order to clear the roads.

In London Channon noted in his diary that the tendency was "to blame Wavell, who, after all, only obeyed—and reluctantly, I have reason to believe—orders in withdrawing his forces from Libya and sending them to Greece." And the next day he added, "Why not leave the prosecution of the war to the Generals?"[224]

A gloomy Cabinet met to hear that three British generals had been captured. Cadogan then left the meeting to go to Paddington Station to meet Eden and drive him to the Foreign Office. On the way over in the car Eden told him that the Libyan disaster was due to the muddle by the military command. After a few moments at the Foreign Office, and a short chat with the Prime Minister, Eden went over to his flat nearby, where Cadogan joined him. Eden was upset because Churchill had been difficult, saying he had never wanted to help Greece. Cadogan tried to cheer Eden up by saying that that was just Churchill's mood of the moment, as in the past no one could have been more stoutly and consistently his supporter while he was away than the Prime Minister.[225]

Dill in the meantime arrived tired (he had not slept for three nights) and worried about the situation in the Middle East, especially about Rommel's drive, which had swept in twelve days across the desert that Wavell's fast-moving forces had captured in fifty days. Dill's train was early, and the ACIGS, Sir John Kennedy, missed him at Paddington. Gloomily Dill arrived at the War Office at 4:30 p.m., where Kennedy caught up with him and tried to allay his pessimism about Egypt. They had scarcely begun to talk when Dill received a summons from the Prime Minister. He did not return from No. 10 Downing Street until 6:30, when he went at once again to Kennedy's room and repeated that the situation in Egypt was "desperate—I am terriby tired." He then spoke of the difficulties in Greece and told Kennedy that he feared that a bad mistake had been made. They then discussed a telegram that had been drafted that afternoon telling Wavell to hold onto Tobruk, in spite of Wavell's response to the first signal that it was not a good defensive position. Kennedy said that while Dill was away they had had a lot of trouble with signals being sent out before the War Office saw them. Dill was most unhappy. He put in a call to Eden and used Kennedy's words that London should not dictate strategy and tactics to commanders in the field. Eden agreed and got Churchill to add a sentence giving Wavell a free hand. Before this revised message could be sent, a signal came in from Wavell saying he would stand temporarily at Tobruk. Kennedy carried a copy over to the Prime Minister's office at once, whereupon Churchill canceled his unsent telegram and sent a short one endorsing Wavell's decision. Dill then went off to bed and Kennedy to dinner.

Even the next day Dill was so worn out mentally that he could not concentrate on papers for the Cabinet. On the twelfth he was summoned to Chequers to spend the night with the Prime Minister, and Kennedy spent two hours briefing him on matters that might come up to put him "back into the picture."[226]

And London evidently still did not understand its own lack of power. Knatchbull-Hugesson in Ankara was ordered to tell the Turks to break relations at once with Germany and Italy, and to ally themselves with Yugoslavia, Greece, and Britain.[227] On Thursday the tenth he met with President Inönü and General Marshall-Cornwall, who had known the president years earlier as General Ismet Pasha. As instructed, Marshall-Cornwall urged Turkey to join the Allies and in response to Inönü's question said that Churchill promised 100 Hurricanes and 100 A/A guns. The president roared with laughter and ended by saying that his visitors knew that Turkey was more useful to Britain as a benevolent neutral. And that, of course, was quite true.[228]

On 10 April, only four days after the Germans crossed the Bulgarian border, HQ British Forces Greece began to consider how to withdraw the RAF squadrons from Greece. Wilson had driven over the snaking road from Elasson to Perdika and back again to his headquarters between 10:00 a.m. and 9:00 p.m., only to have to get back on the road an hour later to meet Papagos at Pharsala soon after midnight.

For over an hour they discussed the deteriorating situation. Papagos did not fully know the Yugoslav situation, but he did know that German armored forces were east of the Vardar, while Wilson confirmed that the head of the German column coming down the Monastir Gap had reached Sisteria, where patrol action had taken place. At Perdika Wilson had told General Carassos to start withdrawing as soon as night fell, since he would need three or four nights in which to pull back from Lake Vegoritis, pick up transport at Perdika, and ride to Klissoura and on south. Consideration was then given as to how long Wilson could hold on the Servia-Aliakmon position, but he was unwilling to commit himself. Papagos hoped that he could hold for the five or six days that it would take to march the Greek reserves from the Albanian front to strengthen the Greek left along the Aliakmon. The reserves would have to be a division taken out of the line at Koritsa, as reinforcements from Janina would take fifteen days by route march: because of lack of air cover, they could only move at night. Wilson was worried, as he had no reserves to bring up from the Trikkala area, and Papagos was frightened of an Italian attack if he pulled two divisions out of the Albanian front.

Wilson agreed to send as much British motor transport as possible to help with these moves, but Papagos observed that from Janina to Grevena was 218 miles, and it would take the lorries four days for the round trip. It was agreed the division should start marching and the lorries would pick it up when they met. The meeting ended with a warning from Wilson to keep the Yugoslav troops away from the Greeks, as their morale was very bad, and to check up on the Yugoslav refugees as there could be many enemy agents among them.[229]

So a start was made just before 3:00 a.m. to thin out the 12th Greek Division and to start moving it back, while at the same time the 16th Australian Infantry Brigade began to move to the south bank of the Aliakmon. Because of poor communications the 12th Greek Division was unable to get permission to start its flank battalions moving in spite of the fact that they had very large distances to cover.

On 10 April the last convoy bound for Athens loaded in Egypt and sailed, docking on the twelfth at Old Phaleron, as the Piraeus and Eleusis were closed by magnetic mines.[230]

At the unusually early hour of 11:30 on Good Friday the eleventh the War Cabinet met in London to hear Eden's long account of his trip to the Middle East. He said that when he and Dill went back to Athens in early March they were "shocked" to discover that the four Greek divisions had not been moved, although the Germans were then already in Bulgaria. Eden averred that they were told that these Greek divisions would only fight in western Thrace and Macedonia and not elsewhere. The Greeks had then agreed to provide three other divisions; two of these were then on the Aliakmon Line, but the third had been refused by Wilson, who regarded it as insufficiently trained. Eden then mentioned his trip to Turkey and his impression that the Turkish army was "pre-1914." While he was in Ankara he had talked with Sir Stafford Cripps from Moscow, with the result that a Turco-Soviet rapprochement had been worked out relating to a German attack upon Turkey. He concluded by saying that the Greek resistance and the Yugoslav coup had completely thrown off Hitler's timetable for a peaceful penetration of the Balkans. This would not have happened were it not for the help Britain had given Greece. The Germans would now try to act by force and attack Britain's Middle Eastern position through Cyrenaica. Therefore, it was of the utmost importance that the enemy supply line through Tripoli should be attacked, and Wavell's main needs—for modern aircraft and tanks—should be met.

Dill then spoke briefly about his meeting and many phone calls with Simović. He also read an appreciation from Wavell, which called for holding the enemy as far west as possible in order to keep air attacks away from Alexandria and to keep up Egyptian morale. Wavell admitted that the enemy had been underestimated, and he felt the Western Desert was critical without having to be concerned about Greece.[231]

After the meeting Churchill cabled FDR that the situation was manageable and hopeful, and that Eden and Dill concurred in this assessment. But by Sunday he was telling the Defence Committee that it was grim and that the British might easily be driven out of Egypt.[232]

On 12 April Blamey gave orders for the 12th Greek Division and the 16th Australian Infantry Brigade to leave their defensive positions astride the Veria Pass that night, and to withdraw to new ones on the Servia Pass, where sharp steep heights on either side were virtually impassable. During the afternoon Blamey moved his headquarters back to Elasson, on the main road from Larissa to Katerini, to be next to Wilson. At the same time he officially became commander of the newly recreated ANZAC Corps, composed of the New Zealand and the 6th Australian divisions.

On Sunday the thirteenth the New Zealand Cavalry Regiment on the Aliakmon River north of Katerini was attacked by German infantry covered by artillery and mortar fire. The Germans secured several crossings despite heavy casualties, and after the loss of one motorcycle the New Zealanders broke contact and withdrew to Platamon. That night the elements of Mackay Force known as Lee Force, holding part of the hill area covering the Florina-Kozani approach to the Aliakmon Line at Servia, were attacked and forced back. Since the rooads were still reasonably passable in this area in spite of rain, the force was pulled out by lorry, including elements of the 1st Armoured Brigade, shedding mechanically broken tanks along the way down the road from Kozani to Grevena on the road to Kalambaka.[233]

The thirteenth of April was Easter Sunday. By the following morning the Aliakmon position had been turned. The Germans had breached the defenses at both ends and there was no longer any RAF air cover. The next major position was at Thermopylae, an ancient site now to be menaced not merely by enemy infantry but shortly by hostile aircraft based on the airfields about Larissa. Moreover, both British supply ports were useless: Volos would soon be cut off and the Piraeus had been flattened. No landing craft were then available to use the many beaches along the coast.

Churchill signalled Wavell that Eden and Dill were back "and we all send you our assurance of complete confidence and every wish for good fortune. This is one of the crucial fights in the history of the British Army."[234] The Prime Minister also sent a message to Belgrade that, because of air forces which had not existed in the First World War, no naval forces could be sent into the Adriatic to help Yugoslavia evacuate her troops, while D'Albiac had all the air help that it was possible to give at that time. Churchill continued, "You must remember that the Yugoslavs have given us no chance to help them and refused to make a common plan, but there is no use in recriminations, and you must use your own judgment how much of this bad news you impart to them."[235]

The next day, C.L. Sulzberger visited Wilson at his headquarters at

Elasson. He found him resolute, friendly, and intelligent, especially in his quizzing of the young American correspondent about conditions to the north. Sulzberger later wrote that he felt that Jumbo never got fair credit for all his work.[236]

Orders were given to form Savige Force out of the 17th Australian Infantry Brigade Group and attached forces as a reserve to hold the Kalambaka area, while the New Zealand Cavalry Regiment was ordered to move across from Katerini through Elasson, on the main north-south road on the east coast, to cover the headquarters area from the west.

On Tuesday the fifteenth the eastern wing of the RAF asked permission to withdraw, and this was granted. The AOC signaled the AOC-in-C ME that they would retire to Athens, but that "evacuation was imperative and should start forthwith."[237]

Wilson's headquarters had left Elasson and moved into a farmhouse near Pharsala that was hidden in an oak wood carpeted with asphodels in full bloom, which gave off a pungent smell as the traffic crushed them. The commander had just lost his own car to a direct bomb hit while he and his ADC lay in the ditch nearby. And it kept raining. Reid's special signals set was the only one working; all the rest of the standard Royal Corps of Signals sets had "packed it in," as the expression went.[238]

The decision was made on 15 April to withdraw to the Thermopylae position, and control of the battle in the Aliakmon area was passed from Wilson to Blamey. The latter at once ordered the 19th to move more than two hundred kilometers south to Domokos, where the road and railway end a long run across the Plains of Thessaly via Pharsala. Here the road climbs southward up the pass, while the railway line heads west on a more level route to Lamia. The rearguard position was to be reinforced by two battalions that were on their way up from Athens when the fighting started. The 16th Australian Infantry Brigade was ordered back to Zarkos on the Larissa-Kalambaka road to cover forces retreating along that line, and the 6th New Zealand Brigade Group was moved to a covering position between Elasson and Tyrnavos. The 5th New Zealand Brigade Group withdrew from the Katerini Pass, and the 4th moved out from the Servia Pass; both had a long march over mountainous roads that were difficult to negotiate in the dark and wet.

The New Zealand 21 Battalion was in serious trouble at Platamon, where they held a commanding position overlooking the flat shoreline and the road down which the Germans had advanced alongside the railway line. At this point the line swung seaward and moved into a tunnel along the shore. If the Germans came through the tunnel they would pin the New Zealanders against the mountains of the lower Olympus range. Mount Olympus itself, towering 9,500 feet high, rose up very sharply to the left flank ahead of the position. The motorized New Zealanders were also in trouble because the road south only went as far as the mouth of the Pinios (Tempe) Gorge. And though the railway went through the gorge on a series of ledges and through a number of tunnels, it was not envisaged that lorries and other vehicles could be driven along the tracks. The New Zealanders had to get back nine miles from Platamon to the gorge, at a point where Blamey hoped a stand could be made and to which he sent more guns. Before the situation could be resolved, however, the Yugoslavs capitulated on 15 April.

The next day Longmore reported to Portal that D'Albiac's strength in Greece was rapidly diminishing in the face of enemy attacks on forward airfields. Only 18 Blenheims, 16 Hurricanes, and 12 Gladiators were serviceable, apart from the Wellingtons of No. 37 Squadron. "He sees no possibility of providing the Army with adequate air support, even if they establish themselves on a rear line." So Longmore had ordered the Wellingtons back to Egypt, and one Blenheim fighter and one Hurricane squadron to Crete, and he was sending over Sunderlands and Bombays to move their spares and mechanics to the island. The RAF had been ordered to coordinate with the army on evacuation plans. Meanwhile Longmore himself was planning to go to Iraq to try to stabilize the situation there before the collapse of Greece made it critical.[239]

By this time Nos. 33 and 208 Squadrons had moved to the Athens area, and that evening all "E" Wing Squadrons were instructed to withdraw to Athens. Longmore signaled that he was sending a planning party the next day to Crete. Spare pilots and aircrews were to be evacuated at once to Egypt, while operations personnel were to go to Heraklion or Maleme to open operations rooms there.[240]

After a gallant defense of the Platamon position, on Wednesday the New Zealanders had withdrawn to the Pinios Gorge, where they had taken up a strong defensive position with weak Australian and New Zealand artillery to back them up. But German mountain troops climbed around them and came down through the village of Gonnos on the western side. As elsewhere, the forces were ill-matched, with the advantage to the aggressor.

The reaction in London was pessimistic. Cadogan feared that with the general staff's abilities the Germans would roll right across the Mediterranean and turn the British out of Egypt, too.[241] So on this day the Chiefs of Staff asked the C-in-C's in the Middle East for their proposals for the evacuation of British forces from Greece, if that step were forced upon them. This communication was immediately followed by a signal from Wilson to Wavell: Papagos had told Wilson that the Greeks were getting into administrative difficulties in their retreat, and the Greek commander-in-chief had suggested that "as things may become critical in the future, we should re-embark British troops and save Greece from devastation."[242] Wilson considered that this operation should begin as soon as they had withdrawn to the Thermopylae line, a suggestion with which

Papagos had agreed. Wavell reported that he had ordered the evacuation to start, pending both instructions from home and a formal request from the Greek government. He proposed to make all arrangements; he presumed that Crete was to be held. Longmore concurred and had canceled his proposed trip to Iraq.

London at once replied that the evacuation could proceed as soon as the Greek government approved, trying to save as much material as possible. Crete was to be held in force, and for this it was important that strong elements of the Greek army should be established there, together with the king and the government. And the Prime Minister concluded, "We shall aid and maintain the defence of Crete to the utmost."[243]

All through Thursday the seventeenth the British forces were withdrawing, sending back or destroying stores around Larissa; that morning the ANZAC headquarters closed at Elasson and opened again at Soumpasi (now Hara). Heavy enemy air attacks on the road from Larissa to Lamia became troublesome on the eighteenth, and an appeal was made to Athens for air support, but there was precious little available. ANZAC headquarters moved again, from Soumpasi to Levadia. By midday on the nineteenth the flow of vehicles through Lee Force at Domokos had virtually ceased, and the two-hour strafing of the road by German aircraft, which began at 3:00, was, to quote the war diary of the HQ 1st Australian Corps, "mistimed." During the night Lee Force withdrew from Domokos. Other forces had been driving down the road to Volos and to the Thermopylae position on the coast, or grinding up the switchbacks of the Brallos Pass and on toward Athens.

The remainder of No. 30 Squadron, RAF, was ordered to Crete, while the mobile W/T station was sent south to Argos. The western wing pulled back that night to Patras in the Peloponnesus. All airmen were ordered confined to camp because of the deterioration of the internal situation in Greece.[244]

On the seventeenth Cadogan was still upset. Papagos had asked the British to evacuate and they had agreed, but no one knew what was happening, and "How the hell did the Germans get to N. Africa—no one knows!"[245] Churchill told the War Cabinet that there were no grounds for the charge that it had been imprudent not to finish off the winter campaign by an advance to Tripoli. The arguments that had been put forth by the Chiefs of Staff against such a campaign were entirely convincing. And to the charges of defective intelligence services, the reply had to be made that the military authorities in the Middle East had discounted the possibility of a serious German thrust developing before summer.[246]

An even more significant statement was also made at that meeting on 17 April, though it has so far received little of the highlighting it deserves. It was recorded that *between November 1940 and the end of May 1941, 1,785 aircraft had either been sent or were to be sent to the Middle East. Of these, 905 had actually been sent, but only 377 had by 17 April actually arrived.*[247] In other words, one of the principal themes running all through this diary of a disaster was true: London thought that it had sent far more in the way of air support than Cairo had received. Approximately 4.75 times as much had been allocated as had arrived, and not all of that was by any means first-class material. But because of the lack of liaison between Cairo and London exasperation had tended to replace communication.

On 18 April Canberra reported the very great concern in Australia over the fighting in both Greece and North Africa, since Australian units were involved in both places, and especially because the LUSTRE force had never been brought up to strength. The Australian Cabinet suggested that the time had come to look at the British position in the eastern Mediterranean and make a decision on where the vital center lay, namely about the Suez Canal, and warned that the present division of efforts was disastrous. They signaled, "We agree with you that the decision to send our troops to Greece was strategically correct and retract in no way from that decision," but went on to ask for a candid appreciation, even, if necessary, to include a recommendation of withdrawal before the position became irretrievable. This message was followed at teatime by another, which stressed that immediate evacuation should include equipment, as this would be essential both for holding Crete and for the re-formation of the complete Australian Corps in the Middle East. The New Zealand Cabinet made similar comments, and Churchill was moved to reply that early reembarkation was indeed a necessity, and for this plans had been made some time before and had only to be applied. "Safe withdrawal of the men will have precedence over any other consideration except that of honour. . . . Undoubtedly a phase of acute anxiety lies before us in the Greek theatre, but the highly competent officers on the spot seem to feel good confidence in their ability to solve its problems."[248]

Certainly not everyone felt that way. On the morning of the eighteenth in Athens, the president of the Council, Alexander Koryzis, committed suicide, a victim of the Greek tragedy.

On that same clear morning, ideal for air operations, General Wilson drove over the tortuous road from his new headquarters at Thebes to the Tatoi Palace, where at eleven o'clock he met with the king, Papagos, Palairet, Turle, Heywood, D'Albiac, and others. The military situation was analyzed, and it was agreed that withdrawal to the Thermopylae line was the only possible plan. Wilson was confident he could hold there, although "it would be difficult to do so indefinitely" because of the lack of airfields behind his lines to counter German air forces, Palairet reported to London. It was decided that Wavell would be asked to be present on the next day to discuss whether or not evacuation was necessary and, if so, when. The king agreed that to bolster morale, which was in danger of falling apart, he would announce that he and the government were staying at least for a week, as the general impression was that the war was finished for Greece. In the meantime the ambassador had begun to evacuate British subjects and others as transport became available; he hoped that all would have departed before he himself left with the government for Crete.[249]

Evidently after this meeting, Wilson accompanied D'Albiac back to his headquarters in the Marasleon School for a conference which concluded that evacuation was imperative. Wavell was already on his way, apparently, for at 4:00 p.m. he met with the Greek staff at the Tatoi.[250]

Palairet told London that there was not likely to be much Greek resistance after Athens fell, and that the Greek government would get little support in Crete because the island was Venizelist. "So if it is of the utmost importance to us that the island should be held, we must rely chiefly on our own efforts."[251]

Perhaps thanks to ULTRA, RAF aircraft at Eleusis and Menidi were ordered to Araxos and Tanagra in order to escape an anticipated enemy air attack.[252]

In Cairo the commanders-in-chief sent a long telegram setting forth strongly their views on the need for a War Cabinet member in the Middle East who could be decisive in the face of a well-directed German subversive effort in the area. The recent visit by the secretary of state for foreign affairs had shown how efficacious it was to have a responsible minister present who could make decisions above the departmental level and disburse adequate funds for actions required.[253]

In response to an inquiry about the order of priorities among Libya, the evacuation of Greece, and Iraq, the Chiefs of Staff cabled later on the eighteenth that, if there was a clash, victory in Libya had to take priority, then the evacuation of Greece: they were not to worry about Iraq, as it would go smoothly. Crete would be at first only a receptacle for whatever could get there from Greece, its fuller defense being organized later. Forces there should protect themselves from bombing "by dispersion, and use their bayonets against parachutists or air-borne intruders if any."[254]

Very late on that Friday a meeting was held at General Wilson's house in Levadia to consider the question of evacuation. Present were Wilson, Wavell, D'Albiac, and two other officers. Wavell started out by saying that it was evident that the Greek army was not capable of further resistance and that the government was not in a settled state. "The question was [ran the report of the meeting] should the British leave Greece to avoid further devastation of the country by the enemy. So far as our Government was concerned, if it was the wish of the Greek Government that the British people should go, then we should go. Meanwhile it appeared that there was no Greek Government prepared to form in Greece which could face that decision." The British had the choice of fighting it out or of evacuating, but it was essential that there be "a new Government in Greece to back us, and a new Greek C-in-C to restore the morale of the Army and the people." In general it was better to fight and inflict damage on the enemy than evacuate and probably suffer large naval and shipping casualties; and to remain would help divert enemy resources from Libya and Egypt. On the other hand the British could not stay in Greece without heavy reinforcements. In addition the British would have to feed the civilian population of Athens and Attica if they stayed, yet they could hardly maintain themselves. And lastly, Wavell said, to remain in Greece might well so drain British resources as to threaten the security of the vital center in Egypt.

Wilson agreed with what had been said. He was concerned over signs of a weakening of the morale of the British as well as of the Greek forces. D'Albiac asked if there was really any prospect of taking the offensive again in Greece, and if Britain could afford the drain of at least six fighter squadrons in Greece with a replacement rate of thirty to forty aircraft a week. He thought it a pity not to accept the possibility of withdrawal if there was no hope of future recovery.

Brigadier Galloway then said that it was "a question of sentiment versus facts." The instinct might be to fight it out even at a severe loss, but the lack of RAF cover and the problem of feeding civilians were decisive factors: could they really feed 2.5 million Greeks and maintain an expeditionary force under the present circumstances?

After some further discussion, it was agreed to evacuate, and Wavell laid down the priorities: personnel, then small arms, gunsights, and all optical instruments, then mortars, and fourth, if possible, all antitank and light antiaircraft guns, then guns, and finally transport. It was pointed out that in view of the destruction of the Piraeus, there was scant hope of getting off more than the first two categories. The feeling was that they would be lucky to embark 30 percent of the force, and this was accepted.[255]

There was no mention at this time of an earlier precedent, but it certainly could have been applicable. In mid-June 1940 there had been talk of sending General Sir Alan Brooke back to France with a second expeditionary force to hold Fortress Brittany. Brooke had refused. Without absolute control of sea, air communications, or the ability to keep air superiority over the bridgehead, such an operation would have been a septic drain of Britain's resources at the heart of the Empire. A similar effort could not fail to have been a disaster in ravaged Greece, especially given the paucity of British resources in the Middle East.

On Saturday 19 April Churchill sent a very strongly worded signal to Wavell and Wilson about a lack of reports from Greece. Wavell responded that the problem was interrupted communications due to the facts that two out of three liaison officers had been wounded, that all army cooperation aircraft had been shot down by the end of the second day, and that travel over roads crammed with military convoys and refugees was slow, not to mention that the weather was bad and that officers busy fighting often forgot to send in reports. The staff in forward units were not all highly trained, but nevertheless they would try to do better. He then gave a situation report and instructed Wilson to send daily cables to London.[256]

As in the matter of shifting troops before the agreements of 4-6 March, there is disagreement between the Greek and the British versions of the events of 19 and 20 April. On the fourteenth the Greek High Command had urged an armistice. Then, General Papagos in his memoirs claimed, on the nineteenth it was agreed that the British would evacuate and that the Greeks would keep fighting until this had been accomplished. They would then continue to fight in Crete and the islands. He added that the Greeks had thanked the British for their help, though it had been inadequate. On the twentieth, the intentions of the Greek commander-in-chief were disrupted when the GOC of the 3rd Greek Army Corps arrested the GOC of the Army of the Epirus, his superior officer, mutinied, and surrendered by capitulation on the twenty-first to the Germans.[257]

Wavell, who on the eighteenth was still speaking of holding on in Greece as being less costly than evacuation, on Sunday the twentieth asked Palairet to put it to the government in London that they should not accept Papagos's reason for leaving Greece (to prevent its devastation) as this would be a bad precedent that the Egyptians might use; it would be much better to say that it was due to the collapse of the Greek army under overwhelming numbers (chiefly as a result of the Yugoslav debacle) and the British inability to defend Greece alone. In London Kennedy had come to the conclusion that practically all the purely military considerations pointed to an early evacuation, and he had papers drawn up showing the pros and cons so that the CIGS could explain it to Menzies and to Churchill.[258]

On the British side by Sunday the twentieth the end was obviously rapidly approaching. Headquarters 6 Australian Division asked for naval assistance to pick up parties who might reach the sea at various places, and for motorboats to support the movement of the right flank from Khalkis on Euboea to a coastal area just north of Thermopylae. On Monday the New Zealand Cavalry Regiment was ordered to cross into Euboea and give warning of any Germans coming down that way, and also to form a reserve for the Rangers holding the Khalkis crossing. Another battalion was sent to Thebes to watch for parachutists.

The remaining Blenheims of Nos. 11, 84, and 211 Squadrons were ordered to Crete. Menidi and Eleusis were continually being strafed, and operations from them were difficult. By this time the RAF in Greece had

15 Blenheims, 11 Hurricanes, and 3 Gladiators serviceable. On the following day the Blenheims were used to run a ferry service to transfer crews
and personnel to Crete, while at the Marasleon School and on the airfields
"All papers were destroyed by fire."[259]

At ten o'clock on the morning of 21 April the king and the new
president of the Council, Tsouderos, met with Wavell, Wilson, and Palairet. Wavell asked if the Greeks could support the left flank of the British
at Thermopylae, and the king said no; Wavell then said it was his duty to
reembark.[260] The king told the British that the minister for war and the
commander-in-chief thought that the Greek forces could hold their present positions on the Graeco-Albanian frontier for four or five days.
General Pitsicas had been ordered to arrest General Tsolacoglou, who
had initiated negotiations with the Germans at Epirus. No one believed
that Tsolacoglou was in German pay, just that he was infected with
defeatism. Palairet concluded his report: "It would seem that, after the
long ordeal of the struggle in Albania nobody but Metaxas was strong
enough to make the nation and the army face a second and more powerful
aggressor, especially after the collapse of Yugoslavia."[261]

Palairet's telegram was followed later that day by another one:

> The Greek Government, while expressing to the British Gov-
> ernment and to the gallant Imperial troops their gratitude for the
> aid which they have extended to Greece in her defence against
> the unjust agressor, are obliged to make the following statements:
>
> After having conducted for more than six months a victorious
> struggle against strongly superior enemy forces, the Greek army
> has now reached a state exhaustion and, moreover, finds itself
> completely deprived of certain resources indispensable for the
> pursuit of war, such as munitions, motorised vehicles and aero-
> planes—resources with which it was, in any case, inadequately
> supplied from the outbreak of hostilities. This state of things
> makes it impossible for the Greeks to continue the struggle with
> any chance of success and deprives them of all hope of being able
> to lend some assistance to their valiant Allies. At the same time,
> in view of the importance of the British contingents, of the avia-
> tion at their disposal and of the extent of the front heroically
> defended by them, the Imperial forces have an absolute need for
> the assistance of the Greek army, without which they could not
> prolong their own resistance for more than a few days.
>
> In these conditions the continuation of the struggle, while
> incapable of producing any useful effect, would have no other
> result than to bring about the collapse of the Greek army and
> bloodshed useless to the Allied forces. Consequently, the Royal
> Government is obliged to state that further sacrifice of the British

expeditionary force would be in vain, and that its withdrawal in time seems to be rendered necessary by circumstances and by interests common to the struggle.[262]

More telegrams followed during the day. Martial law was declared that night in Athens, and Wilson signaled Wavell that he was putting the evacuation scheme into force immediately. The next day the New Zealand offer of medical officers to serve on evacuation ships was accepted.[263]

The king and his ministers as well as Palairet were to leave for Crete on the twenty-second, but did not in the end get off until the twenty-third.

The War Cabinet met in London at five that afternoon. At the end of the discussion of the evacuation of Greece, Menzies said that he "thought it was most important to make it clear that the sending of our forces to Greece had been based upon overwhelming moral grounds. We should keep it clearly before the public mind that it would have been impossible for us to have deserted Greece." The minutes report that the War Cabinet "took note of these statements."[264]

On Tuesday 22 April, ANZAC Corps Operational Order No. 2 was issued for the evacuation of Greece. The Thermopylae position was to be abandoned over the next three nights. On the twenty-third ANZAC Corps headquarters made one more move, this time from Levadia to Mandra (near Eleusis). The next day ANZAC closed, headquarters and British Troops Greece took over command for the last three days. The RAF had already ceased operations on the sixteenth.

By the twenty-second the tempo of disaster had increased to a daily drumbeat of telegrams. Blamey had signaled home that the situation looked very bad. Both Fadden in Canberra and Menzies in London backed up their commander on the spot and stressed the need for supplying the troops with the necessities of war to enable them to defend themselves in their awkward situation and to ensure a safe and rapid evacuation. Whitehall had discussed what, if anything, should be said to those down under about evacuation. Churchill and Menzies agreed that nothing should be said until the operation was either well under way, or, preferably, concluded. But in the morning the *Times* reported that the Australian government was under heavy fire, and Palairet had made it plain from Athens that the news of the Epirus armistice would no doubt shortly be announced by German radio. If the Australian and New Zealand governments heard of this development first from the press they would have every right to be indignant, so Lord Cranborne, the Dominions secretary, sensibly prepared a short telegram, which Churchill ordered dispatched at once to those governments, though it did not mention evacuation. It did give the conclusions reached at the Tatoi on the 21st.[265]

Next the Prime Minister cabled Wavell:

> Consider time has come to prepare public in official communiqué for impending Greek collapse. Effect on World opinion is of such importance that I consider communiqué should be issued from Home where various implications can be assessed at their full value. Suggested draft as follows:
>
> At the request of the Greek Government forces of the Empire were dispatched to Greece after the German occupation of Bulgaria to assist our heroic ally in the defence of her country against the threatened German invasion. Before our concentration was complete the Germans wantonly invaded Greece and Yugoslavia with powerful land and air forces. The early collapse of organised military resistance in Yugoslavia enabled the Germans to direct their main effort through the passes of Central Macedonia against the open flank of the Greek and Empire Forces defending the Northern Provinces of Greece. A general withdrawal became necessary during which determined action by our covering forces inflicted heavy casualties on the enemy. In spite of heavy attacks by the bulk of the enemy's armoured forces in Greece and large air forces, the Empire front was never broken, and our troops were able, despite all difficulties, successfully to reach new defensive positions south of Lamia. In the centre, however, a grave situation has developed. Taking advantage of better communications available to them, important German forces succeeded in reaching positions astride the main links of communications of that part of the Greek Army which had been so victorious against the Italians in Albania. . . . Cut off from support and from their main supply bases, the Greeks, with their traditional bravery, have violently resisted ever-increasing pressure by enemy forces in great numerical superiority, but any further withdrawal of this Army as an organised body seems improbable.
>
> Do not wish anything yet said about possibility of our re-embarkation.[266]

On the twenty third General Papagos resigned as commander-in-chief of the Greek forces and passed under a temporary cloud.

At 3:00 a.m. on 24 April D'Albiac embarked on a Sunderland and left Greece. He arrived two hours later at Heraklion and set up his new headquarters there. Later in the day 6 Hurricanes arrived at Maleme and reported that they were all that were left of those that had been at Argos; 13 had been destroyed on a ground which was now untenable.[269] Among those lost was Squadron-Leader Pattle, an RAF ace who has been largely ignored because he fought in a minor, unsuccessful campaign.

The withdrawal through the Peloponessus was as remarkable as the retreat in general. There was only the one bridge across the Corinth Canal, at the western end, and the roads from there were twisting and dusty. The meter–gauge railway ran only to Nauplion and Kalamata. Other than these two ports there were only a few places that could be used for embarkation, though there were other rocky inlets into which small ships could with care be brought, and where boats could be used to bring the men off—a risky situation if enemy aircraft were about. With clear weather from the fourteenth and the RAF withdrawn from the sixteenth, there was no air cover.

Between two and four in the morning on 25 April 530 vehicles crossed the Corinth Canal bridge going south. It seemed obvious to Major Reid, camped out on the southern side, that—as in France—the Germans had left the bridge intact for a purpose. At 1:00 a.m. on the twenty-sixth Brigadier Galloway found Reid sleeping by his lorry near the bridge, woke him, agreed with his assessment, gave him his last orders, and drove on south. At seven am the sky filled with Ju-52's and paratroopers rained down. In spite of forebodings, no one had sited the antiaircraft guns for defense against an airborne attack, nor were the troops disposed for one. In no time the disorganized and isolated British units were surrendering. But someone did manage to blow the demolition charges, and the bridge fell into the canal. Later Reid, while a POW, noted with interest the German aircraft packed onto the landing ground at Corinth, an airfield the RAF had said was unusable.[268]

On 25 April, despite an increased flow of new aircraft, Longmore had but 21 serviceable Hurricanes for the defense of the Western Desert, and 14 for the Delta, with 19 expected within seven days and another 30 sometime after that. There were 12 Tomahawks in the Middle East, 17 *en route*, and 145 at Takoradi. He hoped that their gun and engine troubles were cured enough that they could be sent on operations.[269]

By the twenty-sixth the Western Desert had only 14 Hurricanes available; of these, 4 were in No. 73 Squadron, which Tedder had decided had to be rested at once. Nos. 33 and 80 Squadrons had been evacuated to Crete, where they managed to shoot down eighteen enemy aircraft in fourteen more days, but by then they were exhausted, having lost all spares and equipment in Greece while limping away with five aircraft of which only three were serviceable.[270]

On 26 April HQ ME sent a special message to Greece to urge that all two-pounder antitank guns be brought off, as these were in very short supply. This simply was not possible, as the ships could not take them, so they were destroyed on the spot.[271]

On the twenty-eighth at its usual five o'clock meeting the War Cabinet heard the Prime Minister say that they could congratulate themselves on getting out of Greece with total losses of between 5,000 and 10,000 men (though actually it was a bit over 16,000). "The concluding stages of the

Greek campaign had been a glorious episode in the history of British arms. He felt no regret over the decision to send troops to Greece. Had we not done so, Yugo-Slavia would not now be an open enemy of Germany. Further, the Greek war had caused a marked change in the attitude of the United States."[272]

On Tuesday the twenty-ninth Churchill warned Wavell again (for there had been an earlier alert against an airborne attack in a telegram of the eighteenth) that Crete could expect a heavy airborne attack in the near future. He wanted to know the C-in-C's plans, and he added in his usual bloodthirsty manner, "It ought to be a fine opportunity for killing the parachute troops. The island must be stubbornly defended."[273] (British forces had arrived in Crete from Greece by 28 April and were evacuated by 28 May.)

On Wednesday night Portal signaled Longmore, "Having regard to changes in the air situation in the Middle East, the Prime Minister wishes you to return as soon as possible for discussion on all aspects of air operations. Air Marshal Tedder is being appointed acting A.O.C.-in-C. and Air Vice-Marshal Drummond acting deputy A.O.C.-in-C. Please telegraph dates of your departure and expected arrival."[274]

On 28 April Dill had cabled Wavell, "Can you give me a rough estimate of total losses incurred in Greek venture?" To which Wavell responded that it appeared that 43,000 had been evacuated of the 55,000 to 56,000 actually landed. To this the Prime Minister responded on 1 May: "I congratulate you upon successful evacuation. We have paid our debt of honour with far less loss than I feared. Feel sure that you are waiting to strike a blow. Enemy's difficulties must be immense."[275]

According to Wilson's final report on the campaign, the 10,000 left behind might not have been abandoned if bad luck had not intervened. Some 1,500 had been left stranded at Nauplion, and 700 were lost there when a transport was sunk and the men rescued by destroyers, only to have them sunk in their turn by enemy aircraft. But the biggest loss was some 8,000 men left behind because of a muddle at Kalamata: the enemy broke into town and captured the landing officer, who had the code to signal the warships to come alongside the adequate piers, and there was a rumor of mines. As a result a cruiser and accompanying destroyers did not take off the men on the last night, although the Germans had been driven out of the town again.[276]

On the morning of the thirtieth the Greek royal family, accompanied by Heywood and D'Albiac and Blunt, flew to Egypt. On 1 May D'Albiac was rested by being posted to command the RAF in Palestine and Transjordan. Some time shortly after that Heywood was killed in an air accident, so he, at least, never filed a final report. Though badly shaken by it, Churchill and Eden survived the 6-7 May debate in the House of Commons.

General Papagos had conducted himself with sense and dignity under trying circumstances during a particularly difficult campaign in which he as commander-in-chief had had not only to conduct the campaign but also to be at the political center in Athens. To their shame the politicians decided that the reasons given for the armistice and the surrender of Greece should not be simply his sensible one of preventing needless destruction, but the elaborate ones declared in the official statement of 21 April. Palairet, reporting from Heraklion on the twenty-seventh, said the new president of the Council rejected Papagos's reason, and told the British ambassador "in confidence that General Papagos had completely lost his head lately and had come under the influence of suspected elements in the General Staff . . . . I know many of the Greeks feel they have been betrayed by treachery within Greece."[277]

Fortunately, the Greeks came to their senses. General Papagos was recalled and reinstalled as commander-in-chief. He led the struggle against the guerrillas from 1944 to 1949, was promoted to field-marshal, and then was elected prime minister.

The authors of the official history, *The Mediterranean and Middle East*, took a look at what happened to the structure of command in the Middle East in May and June 1941: Longmore was called home for consultations, while Air Vice Marshal G.G. Dawson was sent out to investigate his command and subsequently to become the head of a new maintenance organization there under the new AOC-in-C, Tedder. Then Dill sent General Sir Robert Haining, the vice chief of the Imperial General Staff as "Intendant-General of the Army of the Middle East," an unprecedented position, to look into the monstrous tail of which Churchill was always complaining. And it was his report, combined with the failure of Wavell's premature BATTLEAXE offensive (thrust on him by Churchill), which caused the replacement of Wavell on 5 July with Sir Claude Auchinleck. And finally in 1942 came the appointment of a minister of state, a position Wavell had long suggested.

As Playfair and his colleagues correctly pointed out, the problem was that people in London were used to waging war from their own country, with all the governmental and industrial apparatus at their beck and call, while Longmore and Wavell had been compelled to operate in another sovereign country not at war with Germany, at the end of a very long supply line, in a new kind of technological war, and without the sort of base organization under its own commander which those in Britain enjoyed. Thus Longmore and Wavell were the victims both of Churchill's own concepts of war-making and of a conflict in which they had to do far too much with much too little.

This diary of a disaster records, then, a Greek tragedy marching to its inevitable conclusion to the beat of a score conducted by Fate, Churchill, and "son" Anthony.

# V

# Conclusion
## July 1985

Forty-five years after the events related here, it is possible to stand back and make some dispassionate comments. Of the senior participants, the only one I know to be still alive and active is General Sir James Marshall-Cornwall, whose memoirs were completed in 1981 and published in 1984. But if the people have passed, recent events have made it seem quite likely that the same sorts of decisions will be made, leading down the same tragic path, for much the same reasons as in the past—human frailties and misjudgments. If we work back now from the smaller points to the final question—Why *did* Wavell decide, or agree, to go to Greece in February and March of 1941?—perhaps we can achieve some solid guidance and understanding for the future.

First, there is the matter of British Air Forces Greece, personified for us by D'Albiac, who commanded this small force of regulars in Attica with a few staff officers and efficient clerks, although neither he nor his staff spoke Greek. As long as their involvement was minimal and kept at the level of about five squadrons or less for attacks against the Italians, the Germans could tolerate the situation. But unfortunately the RAF wore a halo after the summer of 1940, and London thought that their air force could beat anyone. London's vision became misty with thoughts of classical Athens that obscured the reality of the view from Cairo. Yet for the vision to work, the restraining fear of invasion at home had to be thrown off, and the forces in the Middle East had to be reinforced with the best equipment available. The realities of European geography meant that Germany could put her best on interior lines to the Balkan front. The British had to do likewise for success, but they did not see it that way, instead shipping out what they did not want at home. D'Albiac was expected to beat the Italians and parry the Germans with a force one-tenth the size of that of the Home Command, and without the support base, in a situation in which weather, terrain, and operational conditions were abysmal.

As long as British Air Forces Greece was merely a stopgap force ready to evacuate at any minute, a long-range plan was not essential. But when, by the end of November 1940, it became obvious that the force was likely to be staying a while, then it needed such a plan to protect itself against Churchillian schemes for a toehold in Europe (for a war the British would in no way be ready to fight until at least 1942). Crete became symbolic of the lack of a grand strategy. Planning was suspended after Metaxas sensibly vetoed aid on 18 January 1941, to Wavell's delight. But a change came, either with the ULTRA intimation in late January of a German thrust into Greece or with the death of the Greek prime minister three days later. At any rate, it seems highly probable that Wavell began planning the move to Greece at that time (if not earlier, around 15-17 January) because he foresaw that Churchill would not be satisfied without it. Meanwhile D'Albiac remained in Athens at the head of a token force, until he became subordinate to Jumbo Wilson early in April. D'Albiac's job was to fight a limited war within an unlimited one.

Longmore was in the unenviable position of many British senior commanders at the beginning of a war: he was expected to do wonders with very, very little. And in the days between handwritten letters and telephones, the terse exchange of signals without commuting liaison officers served him badly. Like Wavell's, his responsibilities covered an enormous area, but his means were paltry. Just as Wavell should have been relieved by a Cabinet-level minister of much of the essentially political and diplomatic work which he had to undertake in governing the whole of the Middle East in wartime, so Longmore, seriously short of administrative staff (he even had no deputy commander until December 1940), lacked a technical staff officer to organize and run his maintenance. Many of these essential positions were filled after Wavell and Longmore had been relieved.

Linking Wavell and Longmore, too, was the matter of air intelligence. The shortage of suitable aircraft to watch Tripoli and the coast, as well as to keep a close eye on the Dodecanese and other spots, was partly responsible for Wavell's being surprised by Rommel in the spring of 1941. The British forces, which remained on an amateur basis until 1942, simply did not have their priorities straight, though Wavell himself was conscious enough of the need for news. He set up an intelligence organization that rivaled that in London in efficiency, even if it lacked the tools and the sources in certain vital areas. But there was nothing like the interservice understanding that existed by 1945: as the RAF commented, the army tended to ignore what the RAF provided.[1] All of this played an important part, as did the fatigue of the fifty-nine-year-old Wavell, in the hesitation over going on to Tripoli in mid-February 1941. There are arguments pro and con, but it can certainly be said that at this time Wavell was at least distracted with the idea of increasing the commitment to Greece. Not going to Greece would have freed fifty-three ships to help maintain the army on the road to Tripoli, while adequate aircraft on the forward airfields could have provided fighter cover for the navy.

Wavell, a dutiful soldier, interpreted his orders as requiring him to send a force to Greece to maintain a toehold in Europe. Was this a matter of the lessons of Munich, Norway, and Dakar all coming home to roost again at the same time? At Munich the Czechoslovakian army had been thrown away at the stroke of a pen because the British and the French were not ready for war. Now, since there might be a good chance that a Balkan bloc could be created of Yugoslavia, Greece, and Turkey, should not that be tried? Certainly that was London's view. This was to be a political decision, but was it a sensible military one?

Wavell had studied the political aspects of military decisions, and he was experienced in the uses of deception: he had been chief of staff to Allenby when the latter had fooled the Turks and broken through their lines. More than this, he was by nature a taciturn man who could keep a secret, and he was adept at putting out what would now be called disinformation. In January 1941 it must have become obvious to him that the pugnacious and energetic Prime Minister was going to keep on demanding action. Churchill had instructed Wavell to offer support that he did not really have and could not afford to give to the Greeks. Fortunately, Metaxas had responded as one commander-in-chief to another and refused it. But now the little general was dead, and the GOC-in-C ME's intelligence sources all told him that a German invasion of Greece was coming in early March. The answer to the puzzle of why Wavell agreed to go to Greece is that he believed that he could make a gallant gesture at almost no risk at all.

The late February estimate—based on the then available intelligence—of a German attack on 6 March and arrival in Athens three weeks later meant that very little of a British expeditionary force would have even landed in Greece before it would have to be evacuated. If all had gone according to the usual German schedule, if the snows had melted on time in the Bulgarian passes, the Germans should have been well past the Aliakmon Line before the British had even begun to get into position. And the Greeks would have been free to surrender to the Germans, as they knew they inevitably must.

Wavell had no doubt read Heywood's reports. He knew that the Greeks were about to exhaust their supplies of ammunition and that the British could not resupply them. He also knew that the country's economy was barren. Metaxas had seen that he knew the truth, and Papagos knew it also. The people who did not understand the realities were in London. They were the ones whom Wavell had to deceive. Thus OPERATION LUSTRE evolved. It was designed to satisfy Churchill with a show of force, to be a gesture to a gallant ally that would not cost the British and Commonwealth forces too much.

It was a gamble, and the weather shifted the odds.

When he died in 1950, Wavell was given the first state funeral on the Thames since Nelson's in 1805. Prime Minister Attlee attended, but Churchill only sent a representative.

# Notes

For documents that are to be found in government archives, identifying code letters are used in the notes. The British Public Record Office in London contains the documents identified by FO, WO, DEFE, Cab., *Cabinet Telegrams*, PREM, AIR, and ADM. Published records of British Parliamentary debates are cited as HL Deb. AWM refers to documents in the Australian War Memorial. Items identified as NARS, USN, or U.S. Dept. of State are in the United States National Archives; published items are in *Foreign Relations of the United States* (cited as *FRUS*). The Greek government in 1981 published Foreign Office materials in a white paper identified below as *Greece, 1940-1941*. See the Bibliographical Comment for a more complete analysis of these documents.

## I. Prologue

1. Major-General Sir Francis de Guingand, *Generals at War* (London: Hodder and Stoughton, 1964), 46.

2. Major-General Sir Francis de Guingand, *Operation Victory*, rev. ed. (London: Hodder and Stoughton, 1960), 48.

3. F.H. Hinsley et al., *British Intelligence in the Second World War: Its Influence upon Strategy and Operations*, (New York: Cambridge University Press, 1979), 1:214-21. DEFE 3/686 indicates that at least as far as naval decrypts were concerned, these only began to be sent to Cairo on 14 March 1941.

4. Hinsley, *British Intelligence*, 1:198-215.

5. AIR 8/514, 3/8/40. Robert Schlaifer and W.D. Heron, *The Development of Aircraft Engines and Fuels* (Boston: Harvard Business School, 1950), 623. The Blenheims evidently were not yet fitted with the new sintered corundum insulated platinum-tipped plugs for use with high-octane leaded fuels.

6. Hinsley, *British Intelligence*, 1:299-302.

7. C.B.A. Behrens, *Merchant Shipping and the Demands of War* (London: HMSO, 1955), 104, 107.

8. Major-General I.S.O. Playfair, et al., *The Mediterranean and Middle East*, vol. 1, *The Early Successes against Italy (to May 1941)* (London: HMSO, 1954), 186-89.

9. Anthony Eden, *The Eden Memoirs: The Reckoning* (London: Cassell, 1965), 129, 131-33. See also Martin Gilbert, *Winston Churchill* (London: Heinemann, 1983), 6:718, 730, 735. Wavell's visit to London is also covered in John Connell [John Henry Robertson], *Wavell: Soldier and Scholar* (New York: Harcourt, Brace, World, 1964), 251-64. His introduction notes the existence of manuscript memoirs (11), but the family claims they do not exist, although a recent doctoral candidate had access to them! Sir George Mallaby came to know Churchill quite well as one of the Cabinet staff. In *From My Level* (New York: Athenaeum, 1965) he notes especially the great man's dislike of strangers and insistence on being served by those whom he knew.

10. Francis K. Mason, *Battle over Britain* (New York: Doubleday, 1969), 240, 250.

11. Lieutenant-General Sir Henry Pownall, *Chief of Staff: The Diaries of Lieutenant-General Sir Henry Pownall, 1933-1940*, ed. by Brian Bond (Hamden, Conn.: Archon Books, 1973), 1:114.

12. Eden, *The Reckoning*, 135; Sir John Slessor, *The Central Blue: Recollections and Reflections* (London: Cassell, 1956), 299-301, confirms this.

13. Sir Llewellyn Woodward, *British Foreign Policy in the Second World War*, 5 vols. (London: HMSO, 1970), 1:509-10.

14. Bernard Fergusson, *Wavell: Portrait of a Soldier* (London: Collins, 1961), 52-53.

15. R. Parkinson, *Blood, Toil, Tears and Sweat: The War History from Dunkirk to Alamein, Based on the War Cabinet Papers of 1940 to 1942* (London: Hart Davis, 1973; New York: David McKay, 1973), 135.

16. AIR 8/544, 7/10/40.

17. Eden, *The Reckoning*, 144-45.

18. AIR 8/544.

19. AIR 8/544, 24/10/40.

20. Parkinson, *Blood, Toil, Tears and Sweat*, 143-44; Woodward, *British Foreign Policy*, 1:510.

21. AIR 8/544, 25/10/40.

## II. The Metaxas Phase

1. C. L. Sulzberger, *A Long Row of Candles: Memoirs and Diaries* (New York: Macmillan, 1969), 70. Several works provide a background and further bibliographical introduction to the area, including John Iatrides, ed., *Ambassador MacVeagh Reports: Greece, 1933-1947* (Princeton: Princeton University Press, 1980); John S. Koliopoulos, *Greece and the British Connection, 1935-1941* (Oxford: Oxford University Press, 1977); Joseph Rothschild, *East Central Europe between the Two World Wars* (Seattle: University of Washington Press, 1977); Elisabeth Barker, *British Policy in South-East Europe in the Second World War* (New York: Barnes and Noble, 1976); and Frank G. Weber, *The Evasive Neutral: Germany, Great Britain and the Quest for a Turkish Alliance in the Second World War* (Columbia, Mo.: University of Missouri Press, 1979). Michael Howard, *The Continental Commitment* (London: Temple Smith, 1972), deals with the wider theme.

2. NARS, E108/USN, 28/10/40.

3. FO 371/24920, 28/10/40.

4. General Alexander Papagos, *The Battle of Greece, 1940-1941*, trans. by Pat. Eliascos (Athens: J.M. Scazikis "Alpha" Editions, 1949), 257ff.

5. *Cabinet Telegrams*, ME I, 4, 28 October 1940.

6. WO 106/2146.

7. Gilbert, *Churchill*, 6:876.

8. Sir Alexander Cadogan, *The Diaries of Sir Alexander Cadogan, OM, 1938-1945*, ed. by David Dilks (New York: Putnam, 1971), 333.

9. Major-General R.J. Collins, *Lord Wavell, 1883-1941: A Military Biography* (London: Hodder and Stoughton, 1947), 279.

10. Playfair, *Mediterranean and Middle East*, 1:230.

11. AIR 8/544.

12. Sir David Hunt, *A Don at War: An Intelligence Staff Officer in the Desert, Greece, Crete, Sicily and Italy in World War II* (London: Kimber, 1966), 33.

13. *Cabinet Telegrams*, 65/15; Parkinson, *Blood, Toil, Tears and Sweat*, 144.

14. AIR 8/544, 2159/28/10/40.

15. Eden, *The Reckoning*, 174.

16. Woodward, *British Foreign Policy*, 1:510.

17. AIR 8/544, 28/10/40.

18. AIR 8/544, 1652/29/10/40.

19. FO 371/24920, 28 and 29/10/40. Pierson John Dixon was a Cantabrigian who had spent 1927-1928 at the British School of Archaeology in Athens before entering the Foreign Office in 1929 and being subsequently stationed in Madrid, Ankara, and Rome. Later in 1941 he accompanied Eden on his trip to the Middle East, but his diaries for this period have not survived. See Dixon, *Double Diploma* (London: Hutchinson, 1968).

20. AIR 8/505, 30/10/40.

21. FO 371/24920.

22. Ibid.

23. AIR 8/544, 30/10/40.

24. FO 371/24920, 30/10/40.

25. NARS, E108/USN; AIR 44/8/544; Gilbert, *Churchill*, 6:878, 921.

26. U.S. Dept. of State, 740.0011 EW 1939.7501, 15 November 1940.

27. WO 201/89. G.J. Adkin, *From the Ground Up* (Shrewsbury, England: Airlife, 1983), 192, notes that the RAF was not equipped for winter weather and suffered badly in France in 1939-1940.

28. WO 106/2146.

29. General Sir James Marshall-Cornwall and Major-General Sir Guy Salisbury-Jones to author, 1980 and 1981.

30. Hinsley, *British Intelligence*, 1:219.

31. Parkinson, *Blood, Toil, Tears and Sweat*, 134.

32. Cadogan, *Diaries*, 333.

33. AIR 8/544, 31/10/40.

34. AIR 8/544. Times of all signals are in Greenwich Mean Time, or Z (i.e., dispatched at 1127Z).

35. Field Marshal A.P. Wavell, "The British in Greece in 1941," lecture at the U.S. National War College, 30 November 1949.

36. D.M. Davin, *Crete: Official History of New Zealand in the Second World War* (Wellington, N.Z.: Whitcomb & Tombs, 1953), 5.

37. J.L.S. Coulter, *Royal Naval Medical Services* (London: HMSO, 1956), vol. 2, *Operations*, 364-65.

38. WO 106/2146.

39. Parkinson, *Blood, Toil, Tears and Sweat*, 146.

40. WO 106/2146. See also Derek Patmore, *Balkan Correspondent* (New York: Harper, 1941), 261, for a similar assessment by a correspondent.

41. U.S. Dept. of State, 740.0011 EW 1939.7501, 15 November 1940.

42. Parkinson, *Blood, Toil, Tears and Sweat*, 148.

43. Eden, *The Reckoning*, 169.

44. John Hall Spencer, *The Battle for Crete* (London: Heinemann, 1962), 9.

45. Ivone Kirkpatrick, *The Inner Circle* (London: Macmillan, 1959).

46. FO 371/24920, 2/11/40.

47. Woodward, *British Foreign Policy*, 1:511.

48. Gilbert, *Churchill*, 6:883.

49. *Cabinet Telegrams*, ME I.

50. Eden, *The Reckoning*, 170.

51. Parkinson, *Blood, Toil, Tears and Sweat*, 148.

52. AIR 8/544.

53. Raymond E. Lee, *The London Journal of General Raymond E. Lee, 1940-1941*, ed. by James Leutze (Boston: Little Brown, 1971), 120.

54. FO 371/24920.

55. Gilbert, *Churchill*, 6:886.

56. FO 371/24920.

57. Davin, *Crete*, 6.

58. Cab. 65/16.10; Parkinson, *Blood, Toil, Tears and Sweat*, 149.

59. *Cabinet Telegrams*, ME I, 8.

60. Ibid., 9.

61. Cab. 65/16.10; John Herington, *Air War against Germany and Italy, 1939-1943* (Canberra: Australian War Memorial, 1954, reprinted 1961), 77.

62. Cadogan, *Diaries*, 334.

63. Cab. 65/16.10.

64. PREM 3/308, 5/11/40.

65. AIR 8/544.

66. WO 106/2146.

67. AIR 8/505.

68. AIR 8/544.

69. AIR 23/6370.9920; Playfair, *Mediterranean and Middle East*, 1:463-65.

70. AIR 8/544; ACM Sir Arthur Longmore, *From Sea to Sky: 1910-1945* (London: Geoffrey Bles, 1946), 239, 243.

71. Playfair, *Mediterranean and Middle East*, 1:232.

72. Parkinson, *Blood, Toil, Tears and Sweat*, 149.

73. FO 321/24920.

74. AIR 23/6370/9920.

75. WO 201/89.

76. *Cabinet Telegrams*, ME I, 9.

77. AIR 8/544; W. G. McClymont, *To Greece* (Wellington, N.Z.: War History Branch, Dept. of Internal Affairs, 1959), 89.

78. T. H. Wisdom, *"Wings over Olympus": The Story of the Royal Air Force in Libya and Greece* (London: George Allen and Unwin, 1942), 61.

79. AIR 8/544.

80. FO 371/24920.

81. Hinsley, *British Intelligence*, 1:291-93.

82. Wisdom, *"Wings over Olympus,"* 63, 65; AIR 8/505; McClymont, *To Greece*, 90. The report of the mission is in PREM 3/288/7.

83. FO 371/24920.

84. Ibid.

85. AIR 8/514, 8/11/40; 11/11/40.

86. WO 106/2146, 11/11/40.

87. FO 371/24920; Davin, *Crete*, 6.

88. FO 371/24920, 9/11/40.

89. AIR 8/514.

90. FO 371/24920.

91. Ibid.

92. *Greece, 1940-41*, docs. 27-29 (Greek government white paper published in 1981).

93. Field Marshal Ioannis Metaxas, *Diaries* (Athens: General State Papers, 1964), vol. 4, *1933-1941*, translated for me by Major-General Konstantinos Kanakaris, 1981.

94. AIR 8/505.

95. See Winston Churchill, *The Second World War*, vol. 2, *Their Finest Hour* (Boston: Houghton Mifflin, 1949); Parkinson, *Blood, Toil, Tears and Sweat*, 151.

96. WO 201/95.

97. FO 371/24920, 9/11/40 and 13/11/40.

98. Laird Archer, *Balkan Journal: An Unofficial Observer in Greece* (New York: Norton, 1944), 137.

99. AIR 8/544, 11/11/40.

100. Gilbert, *Churchill*, 6:904.

101. Eden, *The Reckoning*, 175; Cadogan, *Diaries*, 335; Parkinson, *Blood, Toil, Tears and Sweat*, 155ff.

102. *Cabinet Telegrams*, ME I; Gavin Long, *To Benghazi* (Canberra: Australian War Memorial, 1952), 116n. See also Adkin, *From the Ground Up*, 206.

103. The instructions for Rear-Admiral Turle are in FO 371/24920, 15/11/40, and those for Major-General Heywood are in AIR 8/514, 13/11/40.

104. AIR 8/544.

105. AIR 8/519.2879, 14/11/40 and 14/12/40; and AIR 8/514, 14/11/40.

106. Sir John Wheeler-Bennett, *King George VI: His Life and Reign* (London: Macmillan, 1965), 491-93.

107. AIR 8/544, 16/11/40.

108. *FRUS, 1940* 3:590.

109. Ibid., 591.

110. G. E. Patrick Murray, "Under Urgent Consideration," *Aerospace Historian*, June 1977, 61-69.

111. AIR 8/544, 18/11/40.

112. Cab. 65/16.32, 19/11/40.

113. U.S. Dept. of State, 740.0011 EW 1939.6798.

114. AIR 8/514.

115. Stanley Casson, *Greece against the Axis* (London: Hamilton, 1941), 7-38.

116. AIR 8/514, 23/11/40.

117. Hunt, *A Don at War*, 24-28.

118. WO 201/95, 22/11/40 - 14/12/40; 16 and 18/1/41.

119. *Cabinet Telegrams*, ME I.

120. Stephanos Zotos, *Greece: The Struggle for Freedom* (New York: Crowell, 1967), 21.

121. Parkinson, *Blood, Toil, Tears and Sweat*, 160; Woodward, *British Foreign Policy*, 1:516.

122. AIR 24/1666; Wisdom, *"Wings over Olympus,"* 77.

123. AIR 8/544, 25/11/40.

124. General Marshall-Cornwall to the author, 7 May 1981; 27 MM Report, WO 201/119; Sir James Marshall-Cornwall, *Wars and Memories of Wars*, (London: Leo Cooper, 1984), 43, 58, 95.

125. WO 201/119.

126. AIR 8/544, 26/11/40.

127. AIR 8/544. But see S. C. Rexford-Welch, *RAF Medical Services* (London: HMSO, 1958), 3:201.

128. AIR 8/544.

129. Ibid.

130. Brigadier Dudley Clark, *Seven Assignments* (London: Cape, 1948), 187-91.

131. Sir Robert Gordon Menzies, *Afternoon Light: Some Memories of Men and Events* (New York: Coward-McCann, 1968), 19.

132. Davin, *Crete*, 7. WO 193/551.65077 of 20 November noted that Suda Bay alone needed 74 more guns than the 20 allocated.

133. Lee, *London Journal*, 142.

134. Admiral of the Fleet Viscount Cunningham, *A Sailor's Odyssey: The Autobiography of Admiral of the Fleet Viscount Cunningham of Hyndhope, KG, GCB, OM, DSO* (New York: Dutton, 1951), 291.

135. PREM 3/205.HP 00437, 5/12/40.

136. AIR 8/514. One of the major difficulties in the Middle East was an extreme shortage of staff officers. See Sir Charles Webster and Noble Frankland, *The Strategic Air Offensive against Germany* (London: HMSO, 1961), 1:149.

137. FO 371/24920.

138. Casson, *Greece*, 25, 28.

139. John George Bitzes, *Hellas and the War: Trials, Triumph and Tragedy, 1939-1941* (Ph.D. dissertation, University of Nebraska, Lincoln, 1976), 169.

140. WO 201/119, App. B.

141. AIR 8/544.

142. AIR 8/514, 5/1/41.

143. Spencer, *Crete*, 11.

144. *FRUS, 1940* 3:570; AIR 24/1666.

145. Cunningham, *A Sailor's Odyssey*, 295; J.R.M. Butler, *From September 1939 to June 1941*, Grand Strategy series, vol. 2 (London: HMSO, 1957), 375.

146. Compare Marshal of the RAF Lord Tedder, *With Prejudice: The War Memoirs of Marshal of the Royal Air Force Lord Tedder*, GCB (London: Cassell, 1966), 33, 50, with Denis Richards, *Portal of Hungerford: The Life of Marshal of the Royal Air Force Viscount Portal of Hungerford, KG, GCB, OM, DSO, MC* (New York: Holmes and Meier, 1978; London: Heinemann, 1977), 230.

147. PREM 3/205.HP 00437.

148. *Cabinet Telegrams*, ME I. Gilbert, *Churchill*, 6:953, says that in December 1940 Enigma decrypts made all who saw them believe that the German build-up in the Balkans was aimed at Turkey and then, in domino-style, down to Egypt. To counter this the Middle East C-in-C's had proposed MANDIBLES, which was designed to stop that claw of the pincers while Wavell cut off the other with COMPASS. But once Churchill knew about COMPASS from Eden, he then tried to direct it and eventually to switch it to the Balkans. This was in part the logic behind the increased aid to Greece. See Lord Ismay, *Memoirs of General Lord Ismay* (New York: Viking, 1960), 60. Yet it can be argued that once the British started to go to Crete or Greece or both, strategy demanded that the Dodecanese be cleared of Italians, something the Turks really wanted.

149. PREM 3/205.HP 00437.

150. WO 201/10. See also in general Martin van Creveld, *Supplying War* (New York: Cambridge University Press, 1977).

151. WO 201/100.

152. Woodward, *British Foreign Policy*, 1:518; Lee, *London Journal*, 193; AIR 8/505.

153. AIR 8/544.

154. Parkinson, *Blood, Toil, Tears and Sweat*, 174; Cadogan, *Diaries*, 345.

155. Winston Churchill, *The Second World War*, vol. 2, *The Grand Alliance* (Boston: Houghton Mifflin, 1950), 4; Basil Collier, *The Defence of the United Kingdom* (London: HMSO, 1957), 219-32.

156. Lee, *London Journal*, 199.

157. AIR 8/544, 29/1/41.

158. AIR 8/514, 3/1/41.

159. Dimitri Kitsikis, "La Grèce entre l'Angleterre et l'Allemagne de 1936 à 1941," *Revue historique*, July-September 1967, 85-116.

160. Churchill, *The Grand Alliance*, 5-14.

161. Ibid., 19; AIR 8/544; Parkinson, *Blood, Toil, Tears and Sweat*, 176.

162. Churchill, *The Grand Alliance*, 14-15.

163. Gavin Long, *Greece, Crete and Syria* (Canberra: Australian War Memorial, 1953), 2.

164. Kitsikis, "La Grèce," 19.

165. Cadogan, *Diaries*, 347.

166. Parkinson, *Blood, Toil, Tears and Sweat*, 177.

167. McClymont, *To Greece*, 94; AIR 8/95.

168. de Guingand, *Operation Victory*, 41.

169. James Leasor, *The Clock with Four Hands: Based on the Experiences of General Sir Leslie Hollis* (New York: Reynal, 1959), 149.

170. Longmore, *From Sea to Sky*, 253.

171. NARS E108/USN.

172. Kitsikis, "La Grèce," 11.

173. Hinsley, *British Intelligence,* 1:351.

174. Ibid., 354-56.

175. U.S. Dept. of State, 740.0011 EW 1939.7534.

176. *Greece, 1940-41,* doc. 65.

177. *Cabinet Telegrams,* ME I.

178. Ibid., 23; Parkinson, *Blood, Toil, Tears and Sweat,* 177.

179. Major-General Sir John Kennedy, *The Business of War: The War Narrative of Major-General Sir John Kennedy, GCMG, KCVO, KVE, CB, MC* (London: Hutchinson, 1957), 72.

180. WO 193/551.65077.

181. Cadogan, *Diaries,* 348; Sir John Colville, *Winston Churchill* (New York: Wyndham Books, 1981), 118; Robert S. Sherwood, *Roosevelt and Hopkins,* rev. ed. (New York: Harper, 1950), 292-93.

182. *Cabinet Telegrams,* ME I, 24.

183. *Ibid.,* 25.

184. NARS, E108/USN.

185. AIR 8/514.

186. When Wavell's account of this meeting was published in the *London Gazette* in 1946 it aroused great interest in Greece. A cable was sent to Papagos, who was then on a visit to the United States, and he agreed that his memoirs should at once be translated into English. This was all that we had from the Greek side for many years, as on 27 April 1941, just before the Germans reached Athens, Papagos had all papers connected with the British intervention in Greece transferred to the Foreign Ministry, where they were to remain locked up under the 50-year rule until 1991, even from the Greek general staff. However, in early 1981 (though dated 1980) a selection of these documents was published officially in Greek, with some sections in English and French.

187. WO 201/100, 19/1/41.

188. Papagos, *The Battle of Greece,* 7-11; Metaxas, *Diaries*; AIR 23/6385.68312 for the minutes of 14 and 15 January, and AIR 8/915.70315 for Wavell's cable to London. The Greek white paper of 1981, *Greece, 1940-41,* 55ff., contains the Greek minutes and diplomatic papers. For additional RAF background and consequences see AIR 23/6388.67978 of 11 and 13 January; AIR 23/6390.67978 of 23 January; AIR 23/6391.68829 of 25 January; and AIR 23/6379.68834 of 28 January 1941.

189. *Cabinet Telegrams,* ME I, 28-29; this is also in a slightly different form in FO 371/29813, 15/1/41; and also in AIR 8/544.

190. Longmore, *From Sea to Sky,* 252; AIR 24/1666; FO 371/29813.

191. U.S. Dept. of State, 740.0011 EW 1939.7633, 14 January 1940; AIR 8/514, 15/1/41.

192. Metaxas, *Diaries,* 15-16 January 1941.

193. Papagos, *The Battle of Greece,* 11-13.

194. Wavell, USNWC lecture, 1949. And see Field Marshal A. P. Wavell, "Operations in the Middle East from 7th February 1941 to 15th July 1941," *London Gazette* Supplement, 1946, 3423.

195. Casson, *Greece,* 43.

196. AIR 8/514, 14/1/41.

197. Ibid.

198. Playfair, *Mediterranean and Middle East,* 1:342-43; *Cabinet Telegrams,* ME I, 30-31, 17 January 1941.

199. *Cabinet Telegrams,* ME I, 14 and 15 January 1941; Trumbull Higgins, *Winston Churchill and the Second Front, 1940-1943* (New York: Oxford University Press, 1957), 25; Playfair, *Mediterranean and Middle East,* 1:315; Parkinson, *Blood, Toil, Tears and Sweat,* 180.

200. *Greece, 1940-41,* docs. 79-80.

201. D. A. Farnie, *East and West of Suez: The Suez Canal in History, 1854-1956* (Oxford: Oxford University Press, 1969), 623.

202. FO 371/29777.

203. WO 201/100, 18/1/41; WO 106/2146.

204. *Cabinet Telegrams*, ME I, 32-34; WO 201/100, 19/1/41.

205. WO 201/100.

206. Long, *Greece, Crete and Syria*, 3.

207. Athens telegram No. 85. The Greek version of the declaration of 18 January 1941 is in the documents released in 1981, with a preamble in Greek and the main text in French. *Greece, 1940-41*, doc. 82.

208. *Greece, 1940-41*, doc. 84, 28 January 1941.

209. U.S. Dept. of State, 740.0011 EW 1939.7758; Casson, *Greece*, 47-51; Seymour Chapin, "Funky Junkers Planes . . . in the 1920's and 1930's," *Aerospace Historian*, June 1981, 94-102; William Green, *Warplanes of the Third Reich* (New York: Doubleday, 1970), 423-25; photographs in the National Archives, Washington.

210. *FRUS, 1941* 2:638-40. Bradley F. Smith, *The Shadow Warriors* (New York: Basic Books, 1983), xv, makes the point that the Office of Strategic Services, which originated with Donovan shortly after the United States went to war, concentrated much more on staying in being than on contributing to the war effort, for it was not in tune with modern war.

211. See Saul Friedlander, *Prelude to Downfall: Hitler and the United States, 1939-1941* (New York: Knopf, 1967; French edition 1963), 187; Sulzberger, *A Long Row of Candles*, 112; Kitsikis, "La Grèce," 8.

212. Parkinson, *Blood, Toil, Tears and Sweat*, 218; Gilbert, *Churchill*, 6:1001-1003; Richards, *Portal of Hungerford*, 276; Longmore, *From Sea to Sky*, 257.

213. Owen Thetford, *Aircraft of the Royal Air Force since 1918* (New York: Funk and Wagnalls, 1968), 318; NARS E108/USN; AIR 20/5202, Dowding's dispatch of 2 August 1941. Daily equipment reports are in AIR 16/943-945.

214. Eden, *The Reckoning*, 175.

215. FO 371/29777, 20/1/41; FO 371/29855.06113; Cadogan, *Diaries*.

216. *Cabinet Telegrams*, ME I, 35.

217. Woodward, *British Foreign Policy*, 1:520-21.

218. FO 371/29777, 23/1/41.

219. Kitsikis, "La Grèce," 12.

220. FO 371/29777, 22/1/41.

221. AIR 8/505.

222. Allan S. Walker, *Clinical Problems of War* (Canberra: Australian War Memorial, 1952), 64.

223. Allan S. Walker, *Middle East and Far East* (Canberra: Australian War Memorial, 1953), 230-31.

224. J.F. Cody, *21 Battalion: Official History of New Zealand in the Second World War, 1939-45* (Wellington, N.Z.: War History Branch, Dept. of Internal Affairs, 1953), 25.

225. Playfair, *Mediterranean and Middle East*, 1:343-45.

226. Longmore, *From Sea to Sky*, 255. We now know that Churchill's message of 26 January to Wavell was based on ULTRA. Gilbert, *Churchill*, 6:1007.

227. Longmore, *From Sea to Sky*, 254-55; Playfair, *Mediterranean and Middle East*, 1:345-46.

228. *Cabinet Telegrams*, ME I.

229. Ibid.

230. Ibid.

231. Ibid.

232. Ibid.

233. FO 371/29777, 27/1/41; AIR 8/514.

234. Hinsley, *British Intelligence*, 385.

235. WO 106/2146.

236. Archer, *Balkan Journal*, 155. Casson, *Greece*, 53; Bitzes, *Hellas and the War*, 181, gives a

less sympathetic story of his death and suggests the true cause was covered up to save Dr. Lorando's reputation.

237. Spencer, *Crete*, 18.

238. Sulzberger, *A Long Row of Candles*, 123; A. P. Wavell, "The British Expedition to Greece, 1941," *Army Quarterly* 59, No. 2 (January 1950): 179; Hunt, *A Don at War*, 29.

## III. The Garden of Eden

1. AIR 8/514.

2. Eden, *The Reckoning*, 188.

3. *Cabinet Telegrams*, ME I, 43.

4. Ibid., 44. See also Butler, *From September 1939 to June 1941*, 383-84.

5. *Cabinet Telegrams*, ME I, 45-46; Woodward, *British Foreign Policy*, 1:523-24; FO 371/29777, 6-7/2/41.

6. AIR 23/6370.

7. Cadogan, *Diaries*, 351.

8. Hinsley, *British Intelligence*, 1:359; Butler, *From September 1939 to June 1941*, 459.

9. WO 106/2146.

10. Archer, *Balkan Journal*, 156.

11. Spencer, *Crete*, 18-19; AIR 23/6389.68312; Woodward, *British Foreign Policy*, 1:521, n. 1; Butler, *From September 1939 to June 1941*, 384.

12. WO 201/95, mislabeled Reco 1/494, according to a note on the file.

13. FO 371/29777.

14. NARS, E108/USN.

15. Farnie, *East and West of Suez*, 623. Some of these mines remained until the Canal was cleared in 1975 (*Reader's Digest*, July 1975, 170); Behrens, *Merchant Shipping and the Demands of War*, 241.

16. FO 371/29777.

17. Hinsley, *British Intelligence*, 1:262.

18. Ibid., 260-61. On my use of the term "grand-strategic use of air power," see Robin Higham, *The Military Intellectuals in Britain* (New Brunswick, N.J.: Rutgers University Press, 1966), 119-205, and more concisely Higham, *Air Power* (Manhattan, Ks: Sunflower University Press, 1984), 5-9; also Lee Kennett, *A History of Strategic Bombing* (New York: Scribner, 1982).

19. *Cabinet Telegrams*, ME I.

20. Ibid.

21. Ibid., 47.

22. WO 201/1574.

23. WO 106/2146; *FRUS, 1941* 2:642.

24. Wavell, "The British Expedition to Greece."

25. AIR 8/544.

26. See Ronald Lewin, *The Chief: Field Marshal Lord Wavell, Commander-in-Chief and Viceroy, 1939-47* (New York: Farrar, Strauss and Giroux, 1980), 87.

27. *Cabinet Telegrams*, ME I; Correlli Barnett, *The Desert Generals*, rev. ed. (Bloomington, In.: Indiana University Press, 1982), 66-67.

28. Woodward, *British Foreign Policy*, 1:522. Eden's official diary of this trip is in FO 371/33145.

29. FO 371/29813; Collins, *Wavell*, 241.

30. Longmore, *From Sea to Sky*, 257.

31. Hinsley, *British Intelligence*, 259, 357.

32. Wavell, "Operations in the Middle East," 3424; Barton Maughan, *Tobruk and El Alamein* (Canberra: Australian War Memorial, 1967), 3-4.

33. FO 371/29777.

34. *CHIPS: The Diaries of Sir Henry Channon*, ed. Robert Rhodes James (London: Weidenfeld and Nicolson, 1967), 280ff.

35. Parkinson, *Blood, Toil, Tears and Sweat*, 188.

36. Collins, *Wavell*, 318-321.

37. Archer, *Balkan Journal*, 156.

38. *Cabinet Telegrams*, ME I.

39. PREM 3/205.HP 00437.

40. *Cabinet Telegrams*, ME I; WO 106/2146, 7/2/41.

41. *Cabinet Telegrams*, ME.

42. Playfair, *Mediterranean and Middle East*, 1:362.

43. Ronald Lewin, *ULTRA Goes to War: The First Account of World War II's Greatest Secret Based on Official Documents* (New York: McGraw-Hill, 1978), 107, 155-56, 159.

44. Ibid., 155-56

45. Ibid., 163-64. The development of the intelligence establishment in the Middle East and Wavell's use of it are explored in the first volume of Hinsley's *British Intelligence in the Second World War*, 570-72, and other references. The difficulty with many of the works on ULTRA is that they cover the later periods of the war when the system was functioning well, but up to the summer of 1941 this was rarely so. For the arrival of the cipher officers in Athens, see RAF Form 540 for BAFG HQ in AIR 24/1666.8299, 13/3/41. DEFE 3/686 gives the date of 14 March when ULTRA became regularly available to overseas commands.

46. Lewin, *ULTRA Goes to War*, 163-64. The lack of information, or "gen," on Rommel is all the more interesting considering that he visited Libya in 1937 with von Brauchitsch and stayed several weeks touring Benghazi, Bardia, Tobruk, and other points of interest; he then "vacationed" in Egypt, spent a week in Alexandria and motored along the Suez Canal. He kept a well-thumbed copy of Wavell's pamphlet on generalship in his library and told his son that Wavell was a genius. Howard M. Sachar, *Europe Leaves the Middle East* (New York: Knopf, 1972), 144, 149. In France as a major general Rommel had taken the surrender of the 51st Highland Division at St. Valéry-en-Caux, and then driven his troops two hundred miles to try and trap the British forces leaving at Cherbourg. Marshall-Cornwall, *Wars and Memories of Wars*, 154, 165.

47. *FRUS, 1941* 2:643.

48. WO 201/100 and WO 208/691, 8/2/41; *Greece, 1940-41*, doc. 96; FO 371/29813, 9/2/41; Woodward, *British Foreign Policy*, 1:521.

49. Spencer, *Crete*, 19.

50. *Cabinet Telegrams*, ME I, 58, 9/2/41. The telegram, which seems to have been sent from Athens on the eighth, is in *Cabinet Telegrams* as the ninth.

51. *Cabinet Telegrams*, ME I.

52. Ibid.

53. FO 371/33145 contains the 108-page account by Pierson Dixon of this journey and may be supplemented by WO 106/2146, the more accurate diary kept by Brigadier Mallaby for the CIGS.

54. AIR 8/544.

55. FO 371/29813, 6/2/41.

56. Cadogan, *Diaries*, 353-54.

57. Tedder, *With Prejudice*, 60.

58. Channon, *Diaries*, 291.

59. Kennedy, *The Business of War*, 75; *Cabinet Telegrams*, ME I, 10/2/41.

60. Ronald Lewin, *The Life and Death of the Afrika Korps* (New York: Quadrangle, 1977), 37; Correlli Barnett, *The Desert Generals* (London: Pan, 1962), 65-67; Tedder, *With Prejudice*, 59.

61. Cadogan, *Diaries*, 354; Eden, *The Reckoning*, 189.

62. Davin, *Crete*, 7, 12.

63. Menzies, *Afternoon Light*, 27.

64. John Hetherington, *Blamey: The Biography of Field-Marshal Sir Thomas Blamey* (Melbourne: F. W. Cheshire, 1954), 1, 6, 70, 72-73, 82, 89.

65. R. W. Thompson, *Generalissimo Churchill* (New York: Charles Scribner's Sons, 1973), 106; Lewin, *The Chief,* 88.

66. FO 371/29813; *Cabinet Telegrams,* ME I, 59.

67. FO 371/29813.

68. Kennedy, *The Business of War,* 74-75; Cadogan, *Diaries,* 374.

69. Hinsley, *British Intelligence,* 1:359-60.

70. Ibid., 387.

71. AIR 8/544.

72. WO 201/100.

73. *FRUS, 1941* 2:644-45.

74. *Cabinet Telegrams,* ME I. Churchill has given the text of his telegram to Wavell of 12 February in *The Grand Alliance* (pp. 64-66), and of his instructions to Eden (p. 68). They are quoted here, however, from the originals, which became available to historians with the general release of World War II documents in the British archives in 1972.

75. PREM 3/63.11

76. WO 201/52.

77. Long, *Greece, Crete and Syria,* 7. Long (p. 18) says that the Wavell-Eden meeting took place on the sixth, but this is impossible, as Eden did not reach Cairo until late on the nineteenth.

78. Kennedy, *The Business of War,* 75.

79. Sir Charles Webster and Noble Frankland, *The Strategic Air Offensive against Germany* (London: HMSO, 1961), 1:76, 81-92.

80. Colville, *Winston Churchill,* 177, 186-87.

81. Lee, *London Journal,* 254.

82. *Cabinet Telegrams,* ME I.

83. FO 371/29813.

84. AIR 8/544.

85. *Cabinet Telegrams,* ME I.

86. Ibid.

87. WO 201/105.

88. FO 371/29813.

89. Hetherington, *Blamey,* 91.

90. Kennedy, *The Business of War,* 77, 81-85.

91. *Cabinet Telegrams,* ME I.

92. Ibid.

93. Playfair, *Mediterranean and Middle East,* 1:369.

94. McClymont, *To Greece,* 99.

95. Long, *Greece, Crete and Syria,* 8; W. E. Murphy, *2nd New Zealand Divisional Artillery* (Wellington, N.Z.: War History Branch, Dept. of Internal Affairs, 1966), 20-21.

96. Cadogan, *Diaries,* 355.

97. Kennedy, *The Business of War,* 82.

98. Hetherington, *Blamey,* 92.

99. WO 201/103. This was essentially the scheme drawn up in the meeting in Cairo in early January 1941 by the AOC and the AOC-in-C; it is to be found in AIR 23/6388, 13/1/41. See AIR 23/6333.61323 for BAFG.

100. FO 371/29813.

101. Cadogan, *Diaries,* 355.

102. WO 201/103, 19-20/2/41.

103. FO 371/29828.

104. de Guingand, *Operation Victory,* 48; Connell, *Wavell,* 239.

105. Lewin, *The Chief,* 95; DEFE 3/686.
106. Marshall-Cornwall, *Wars and Memories of Wars,* 179, 185.
107. Connell, *Wavell,* 336.
108. Eden, *The Reckoning.*
109. de Guingand, *Operation Victory,* 41-42.
110. WO 201/1474.
111. *Cabinet Telegrams,* ME I.
112. WO 106/2146 and *Cabinet Telegrams,* ME I.
113. WO 106/2146.
114. AIR 23/6370, 20/2/41 and 28/2/41. The first day that Hurricanes were operational in Greece was 20 February.
115. *FRUS, 1941* 2:647-48.
116. The memorandum was located in mid-1955.
117. de Guingand, *Generals at War,* 42-43.
118. 124 *HL Deb 5s* 493, 1 October 1942.
119. PREM 3/288/7.HMO8674; Lewin, *The Chief,* 95-96. See also his lecture to the U.S. National War College, typescript, 1949.
120. Cab. 65/21.24; Gilbert, *Churchill,* 6:1012-1015.
121. Parkinson, *Blood, Toil, Tears and Sweat,* 193; Cadogan, *Diaries,* 357, mentions that he got a moderate reply to his minute about going not to Greece but to Tripoli.
122. *FRUS, 1941* 2:648.
123. WO 106/2146.
124. WO 201/1574.
125. FO 457. Interestingly, the *Cabinet Telegrams,* the relevant section of which was printed and distributed to the Cabinet on 7 April 1941, the day after the Germans attacked Greece, contains only this one paragraph of the telegram from Churchill to Eden sent through Foreign Office channels on 21 February.
126. No. 358 to Foreign Office in *Cabinet Telegrams,* ME I.
127. Connell, *Wavell,* 331, dates this the twenty-seventh, but it was 22 February. Jumbo Wilson was 6'1" and 245 pounds, according to David Chandler. Wilson did not like Australian soldiers, but both Menzies and Blamey told him they were there to bother the enemy. H. D. Steward, *Recollections of a Regimental Medical Officer* (Melbourne: Melbourne University Press, 1983), 50.
128. Alan Palmer, *The Gardeners of Salonika* (London: André Deutsch, 1965; New York: Simon and Schuster, 1965), 243.
129. Marshall-Cornwall to author, 17 April 1981.
130. Sulzberger, *A Long Row of Candles,* 124.
131. Field Marshal Lord Wilson, *Eight Years Overseas, 1939-1947* (London: Hutchinson, 1950), 69-70, 74.
132. Connell, *Wavell,* 383.
133. Lieutenant-General Sir Philip Neame, *Playing with Strife: The Autobiography of a Soldier* (London: Harrap, 1947), 257-66.
134. U.S. Dept. of State, 740.0011 EW 1939.9427.
135. Betty Wason, *Miracle in Hellas* (New York: Macmillan, 1943), 24.
136. Churchill, *The Grand Alliance,* 73.
137. *Greece, 1940-41,* doc. 123.
138. de Guingand, *Operation Victory,* 50.
139. The Greek transcript of this discussion is in *Greece, 1940-41,* doc. 123, 101-107; it appears to differ only in details from Brigadier Mallaby's version.
140. de Guingand, *Generals at War,* 28.
141. Lewin, *The Chief,* 99, 102; Connell, *Wavell,* 338-42.
142. USNWC lecture, 1949.

143. Wavell, "Operations in the Middle East," 3425.

144. de Guingand, *Generals at War*, 28.

145. Eden, *The Reckoning*, 204, 199-200.

146. In *Cabinet Telegrams* Eden's dispatch to Churchill on the Tatoi Palace meeting is incorrectly dated 21 February, rather than very early on the twenty-third. The full text of Eden's report on his telegram to Ambassador Campbell in Belgrade is in his telegram of 5 March in *Cabinet Telegrams*, ME I.

147. *Cabinet Telegrams*, ME I.

148. Longmore, *From Sea to Sky*, 263.

149. W. N. Medlicott, *The Economic Blockade*, 2 vols. (London: HMSO, 1952, 1959), 1:599.

150. Neil Balfour and Sally Mackay, *Paul of Yugoslavia: Britain's Maligned Friend* (London: Hamish Hamilton, 1980), 215-22.

151. Ibid., 223.

152. Cadogan, *Diaries*, 358.

153. J. B. Hoptner, *Yugoslavia in Crisis, 1934-1944* (New York: Columbia University Press, 1962), 211, 214-15.

154. Kennedy, *The Business of War*, 85.

155. AIR 23/6388.67978.

156. U.S. Dept. of State, 740.0011 EW 1939.8584.

157. Miles Reid, *Last on the List* (London: Leo Cooper, 1974), 127. In addition to the index to Phantom documents (Index 6/175.65077) there are in WO 215/6-8 the Phantom materials for Greece, including an undated draft history of the operations there and also signals that can be decoded using Reid's memoirs, as well as the handwritten dispatches of Reid and his deputy, covering a period from 13 December until their capture at the Isthmus of Corinth in April.

158. *Cabinet Telegrams*, ME I; WO 106/2145.

159. Hinsley, *British Intelligence*, 1:360ff. For the British intelligence view of the German intentions toward Russia and their relationship to the British needs in the Middle East, see the whole section devoted to BARBAROSSA, pp. 429ff.

160. Parkinson, *Blood, Toil, Tears and Sweat*, 195.

161. Cadogan, *Diaries*, 358.

162. The full text of the telegrams exchanged with the Australian and New Zealand governments is in PREM 3/63/11.HP 00437, 25 February and after. In the telegrams to the Dominions it was clearly stated that the maximum number of squadrons going to Greece would be fourteen.

163. AIR 8/544, 28/11/41; Herington, *Air War against Germany and Italy*, 80-86; AIR 8/544 entries for 24 February 1941.

164. Cab. 65/21.26-30; Long, *Greece, Crete and Syria*, 15.

165. *Cabinet Telegrams*, ME I; PREM 3/63/11.HP 00437.

166. Woodward, *British Foreign Policy*, 1:528, n. 1.

167. Kitsikis, "La Grèce," 85-116.

168. *Cabinet Telegrams*, ME I; S. W. Roskill, *The War at Sea, 1939-1945*, vol. 1, *The Defensive* (London: HMSO, 1954), omits the incident; Playfair, *Mediterranean and Middle East*, 1: 159, 326; Lt. Col. S. M. Rose, "Castelorizzo, 24-28 February 1941," *The Army Quarterly and Defence Journal* 114 (July 1984): 307-19.

169. *Cabinet Telegrams*, ME I.

170. Ibid.

171. PREM 63/11.HP 00437; Menzies, *Afternoon Light*, 33-34.

172. Long, *Greece, Crete and Syria*, 21.

173. McClymont, *To Greece*, 103-104.

174. Fergusson, *Wavell*, 85-87.

175. Papagos, *The Battle of Greece*, 19.

176. *FRUS, 1941* 2:650.

177. Robert Crisp, *Brazen Chariots* (London: Transworld, 1960), 18, 20-23.

178. D.J.C. Pringle and W.A. Glue, *20 Battalion and Armoured Regiment* (Wellington, N.Z.: War History Branch, Dept. of Internal Affairs, 1957), 38.

179. Cab. 65/21.32-41 and PREM 3/65/11.HP 00437.

180. Denis Richards, *The Royal Air Force, 1939-1945* (London: HMSO, 1953), 1:285.

181. Papagos, *The Battle of Greece*, 306-307.

182. Cadogan, *Diaries*, 359; Colville, *Winston Churchill*, 223.

183. Parkinson, *Blood, Toil, Tears and Sweat*, 198.

184. Kenneth Macksey, *Rommel: Battles and Campaigns* (New York: Mayflower, 1979), 25, 28-45; Ladislas Farago, *Patton: Ordeal and Triumph* (New York: Dell, 1965), 120-22.

185. Richards, *The RAF*, 1:285, is in error; see BAFG RAF Form 540, AIR 24/1670. Greek sources say they shot down 26 confirmed and 10 probables (Kanakaris comment on author's draft, August 1980).

186. U.S. Dept. of State 740.0011 EW 1939.8691.

187. Reid, *Last on the List*, 128-30.

188. *Royal Engineers Journal*, December 1978, 266.

189. Major-General W. G. Stevens, *Problems of the 2nd NZEF* (Wellington, N.Z.: War History Branch, Dept. of Internal Affairs, 1958), 36.

190. Pringle and Glue, *20 Battalion*, 34; D. W. Sinclair, *19 Battalion and Armoured Regiment* (Wellington, N.Z.: War History Branch, Dept. of Internal Affairs, 1944), 54.

191. de Guingand, *Operation Victory*, 52-53.

192. Ibid., 52-65. His dates are not to be trusted. Nor are Reid's in *Last on the List*, pp. 131-32. I have adjusted the material to what appear to be the correct times.

193. AIR 23/6385.XL/11744; Playfair, *Mediterranean and Middle East*, 1:465.

194. Longmore, *From Sea to Sky*, 267-68.

195. Roskill, *The War at Sea*, 1:424.

196. Connell, *Wavell*, 346; Churchill, *The Grand Alliance*, 98; Hoptner, *Yugoslavia*, 216.

197. *FRUS, 1941* 2:656; Connell, *Wavell*, 330.

198. Sulzberger, *A Long Row of Candles*, 124.

199. Hoptner, *Yugoslavia*, 213.

200. Up to this point the historian's task has been fairly smooth, because the narratives have been in harmony, but this is not so with the very critical talks of 2 through 6 March in Athens. On a number of occasions in recounting the Eden-Dill journey there are minor discrepancies in the versions of what happened. Dill's official diary by its very nature and precise recording of time would appear to have been kept in log form, while Pierson Dixon's official record for Eden was written the day, or days, after events as time allowed. Wavell's later records are not necessarily reliable. I have therefore employed a historian's license to make the best judgment, subject to correction from some other verifiable source. A case in point is that Pierson Dixon says that *on the morning* of 2 March the British met in the legation. Dill's diary, much more accurately—since the party did not arrive at Salamina until two in the afternoon—records that the meeting took place at 5:15. WO 201/17; FO 371/33145. Pierson Dixon in *Double Diploma*, 70-71, gives a version closer to Mallaby's official diary, saying they did not leave Ismid until 12:35, and landed in Greece at 2:45 p.m. But his memory of the Tatoi decisions is faulty.

201. Spencer, *Crete*, 25-27. Robert C. Ovelman, *The British Decision to Send Troops to Greece, January-April 1941* (Ph.D. dissertation, Notre Dame University, 1979), 309.

202. For the Greek version see *Greece, 1940-41*, doc. 145, 125-30. The minutes of the extended meetings, which lasted into 5 March, are given in detail on the next sixteen pages, concluding with the version in French of the agreement signed by Papagos and Dill. These Greek minutes, translated for me in 1981, provide a slightly different point of view and give a different flavor to the discussions and the pauses, as Colonel Kitrilakis saw them. The

original English-language version of the agreement to reach London is to be found in WO 106/3133.79449, sent from Athens at 1:50 a.m. on 5 March and received in London at 7:10 the same morning.

203. *Cabinet Telegrams*, ME I.

204. WO 106/2146.

205. *FRUS, 1941* 2:653.

206. ARMATURE is not in the list in the Public Record Office's *The Second World War* list of code names, pp. 178-247. WO 106/3132.79062.

207. *Cabinet Telegrams*, ME I.

208. Channon, *Diaries*, 293.

209. Cab. 65/22.

210. AIR 23/6388.67978; for the ten o'clock meeting AIR 23/6385.68312 and AIR 23/6375.66091, which contains minutes, memoranda on the talks, and the 18 March statement of air policy.

211. Cab. 65/22, 4/3/41.

212. FO 371/33145; also WO 201/17.

213. *Cabinet Telegrams*, ME I.

214. FO 371/29855.06113; Cadogan, *Diaries*, 360.

215. McClymont, *To Greece*, 107; Wavell, "The British Expedition to Greece," 182-83.

216. See Forrest C. Pogue, *George C. Marshall: Ordeal and Hope, 1939-1942* (New York: Viking, 1966), 70.

217. Martin van Creveld, *Hitler's Strategy, 1940-1941: The Balkan Clue* (Cambridge: Cambridge University Press, 1973), 132-33.

218. Graeme Crew, *The Royal Army Service Corps* (London: Leo Cooper, 1970; New York: Hilary House, 1971), 212.

219. Pringle and Glue, *20 Battalion*, 38.

220. Sinclair, *19 Battalion*, 55.

221. Alan Moorehead, *The March to Tunis* (New York: Dell, 1968), 185-86.

222. Collins, *Wavell*, 339; Wavell, "Operations in the Middle East," 3426.

223. Ibid.

224. *FRUS, 1941* 2:655.

225. McClymont, *To Greece*, 108; Long, *Greece, Crete and Syria*, 16.

226. RADM Raymond de Belot, *The Struggle for the Mediterranean, 1939-1945* (Princeton: Princeton University Press, 1951), 116.

227. Farnie, *East and West of Suez*, 624.

## IV. Denouement and Disaster

1. *Cabinet Telegrams*, ME I.

2. Cab. 65/22. On Churchill's cold, See Gilbert, *Churchill*, 6:1024, n. 1.

3. AIR 24/1666.

4. U.S. Dept. of State, 740.0011 EW 1939.8870.

5. WO 201/52.

6. Hoptner, *Yugoslavia*, 219-21.

7. Balfour and Mackay, *Paul of Yugoslavia*, 228-34.

8. Major-General Sir Howard Kippenberger, *Infantry Brigadier* (London: Oxford University Press, 1949), 16; Sulzberger, *A Long Row of Candles*, 125.

9. Collins, *Wavell*, 340.

10. Lewin, *The Chief*, 103-104.

11. Dixon, *Double Diploma*, 73.

12. Long, *Greece, Crete and Syria*, 18-19; Cab. 65/22, 6/3/41.

13. Hetherington, *Blamey*, 94; McClymont, *To Greece*, 114; Butler, *From September 1939 to June 1941*, 446, n. 2.

14. FO 371/33145; Cunningham, *A Sailor's Odyssey*, 315.

15. *Cabinet Telegrams*, ME I, 7 March 1941.

16. FRUS, 1941 2:656.

17. Connell, *Wavell*, 383.

18. Wavell, USNWC lecture, 1949.

19. Probably retailed by Dixon or Eden to the American ambassador in London; John Gilbert Winant, *Letter from Grosvenor Square: An Account of a Stewardship* (Boston: Houghton Mifflin, 1947), 91.

20. John Evelyn Wrench, *Geoffrey Dawson and Our Times* (London: Hutchinson, 1955), 437.

21. Cab. 65/22.

22. *Cabinet Telegrams*, ME I.

23. Cab. 65/22.

24. *Cabinet Telegrams*, ME I.

25. Channon, *Diaries*, 300; Cadogan, *Diaries*, 362.

26. Cab. 65/22.

27. AIR 8/519.2879, 6-8 March 1941.

28. AIR 8/519.2879, 8-10 March 1941. Portal's letter is to be found in the Longmore Papers at the RAF Museum, Hendon.

29. PREM 3/63/11.HP 00437.

30. Long, *Greece, Crete and Syria*, 17.

31. McClymont, *To Greece*, 108.

32. *Cabinet Telegrams*, ME I; Long, *Greece, Crete and Syria*, 16.

33. Butler, *From September 1939 to June 1941*, 447.

34. WO 201/60.

35. T. Duncan M. Stout, *The New Zealand Medical Services in the Middle East and Italy* (Wellington, N.Z.: War History Branch, Dept. of Internal Affairs, 1958), 99-107; Walker, *Middle East and Far East*, 236-37; AIR 23/6388, 20/1/41.

36. Brigadier G. S. Brunskill, "The Administrative Aspect of the Campaign in Greece in 1941," *The Army Quarterly*, 54, no. 1 (April 1947): 125ff.

37. WO 201/20.

38. Brunskill, "The Administrative Aspect of the Campaign," 129.

39. Farnie, *East and West of Suez*, 624.

40. Connell, *Wavell*, 354.

41. Cadogan, *Diaries*, 362.

42. Papagos, *The Battle of Greece*, 22-23; WO 106/3133.79449, 10/3/41; see also Spencer, *Crete*, 37.

43. Sherwood, *Roosevelt and Hopkins*, 1:322.

44. WO 106/2146, 9/3/41.

45. Murphy, *2nd NZ Divisional Artillery*, 25.

46. Lt.-Col. R. P. Waller, "With the 1st Armoured Brigade in Greece," *Journal of the Royal Artillery*, July 1945, 162.

47. AWM 2663/534/5/24, 21 July 1941, App. B.

48. Murphy, *2nd NZ Divisional Artillery*, 24.

49. Major-General W. G. Stevens, *Freyberg, V.C., The Man, 1939-1945* (Wellington, N.Z.: War History Branch, Dept. of Internal Affairs, 1958), 1-34.

50. The *Helle* is generally referred to as a light cruiser, but actually she was a British-built destroyer fitted as a mine-layer, as the model in the Armed Forces Museum in Athens makes plain.

51. Archer, *Balkan Journal*, 161.

52. *FRUS*, 1941 2:660.

53. WO 201/52.

54. *Cabinet Telegrams*, ME I.

55. Cab. 65/22.

56. *FRUS, 1941* 2:661-62.

57. For detailed discussion of these overtures see H. Cliadakis, *Greece, 1935-41: The Metaxas Regime and the Diplomatic Background* (Ph.D. dissertation, New York University, 1970), 264ff.

58. Cunningham, *A Sailor's Odyssey,* 319; AIR 23/6391.68829.

59. Hinsley, *British Intelligence,* 1:364.

60. *Cabinet Telegrams,* ME I.

61. AIR 8/519.2879.

62. Ibid.

63. *Cabinet Telegrams,* ME I, 17 March 1941.

64. Ibid., 18 March 1941.

65. Cab. 65/22.

66. WO 106/2146; WO 201/100.

67. Richards, *The RAF,* 1:287.

68. AIR 24/1666.

69. Maj. Edgar O'Ballance, *The Greek Civil War, 1944-49* (New York: Praeger, 1966), 39.

70. *Cabinet Telegrams,* ME I.

71. Channon, *Diaries,* 295.

72. *Cabinet Telegrams,* ME I.

73. AIR 8/544.

74. M.M. Postan, D. Hay, and J.D. Scott, *Design and Development of Weapons* (London: HMSO, 1964), 12.

75. AIR 8/544.

76. Connell, *Wavell,* 384.

77. Ibid., 357.

78. Hoptner, *Yugoslavia,* 225.

79. FO 371/33145.

80. WO 201/1574.

81. FO 371/29814, 16/3/41.

82. Connell, *Wavell,* 385.

83. Neame, *Playing with Strife,* 268-71.

84. Butler, *From September 1939 to June 1941,* 453.

85. FO 371/29814.

86. Ibid., 12-24/3/41 and 27/3/41.

87. *FRUS, 1941* 2:664.

88. Reid, *Last on the List,* 139-40.

89. Commander Charles Lamb, *To War in a Stringbag* (New York: Bantam, 1980), 174-214.

90. Hetherington, *Blamey,* 95.

91. U.S. Dept. of State, 740.0011 EW 1939.9207.

92. Reid, *Last on the List,* 138.

93. AIR 23/6370 or AIR 23/6375.66091; AIR 24/1669.12317.

94. Cab. 65/22, 19/3/41.

95. FO 371/33145; Cab. 65/22.

96. Channon, *Diaries,* 295.

97. Longmore, *From Sea to Sky,* 269.

98. FO 371.29814.

99. *Cabinet Telegrams,* ME I.

100. WO 201/100, 19/3/41; 22/3/41.

101. AIR 8/544.

102. AIR 24/1666.

103. WO 201/52.

104. Ibid.

105. Sinclair, *19 Battalion*, 63.

106. R. M. Burden, *24 Battalion* (Wellington, N.Z.: War History Branch, Dept. of Internal Affairs, 1953), 18.

107. WO 201/21.

108. WO 201/65, 5/4/41.

109. WO 201/68.

110. Cadogan, *Diaries*, 364.

111. Parkinson, *Blood, Toil, Tears and Sweat*, 211.

112. Cadogan, *Diaries*, 365.

113. Woodward, *British Foreign Policy*, 1:541; see also the more sympathetic account in Balfour and Mackay, *Paul of Yugoslavia*, 239-57.

114. FO 371/29814, 21/3/41.

115. This story has been told in detail by Murray, "Under Urgent Consideration," 61-69.

116. *FRUS, 1941* 2:666.

117. Angus Ross, *23 Battalion* (Wellington, N.Z.: War History Branch, Dept. of Internal Affairs, 1959), 23.

118. WO 106/3132.79062. On the Polish Brigade see Michael Alfred Peszke, "The Polish Army Forces in Exile, I," *The Polish Review*, 1981, No. 1, 104.

119. AIR 24/1666; U.S. Dept. of State, 740.0011 EW 1939.9292.

120. *FRUS, 1941* 2:705-706.

121. WO 201/52.

122. AWM 2663/534/5/24, 24 March 1941; WO 201/100, 24/3/41.

123. Woodward, *British Foreign Policy*, 1:542; and Wavell, "The British Expedition to Greece," 183; Dixon, *Double Diploma*, 78-79.

124. McClymont, *To Greece*, 116.

125. Hinsley, *British Intelligence*, 1:263-64.

126. AIR 8/519.2879.

127. Ibid.

128. FO 371/29814.

129. Ibid. For an account of the Greek independence movement, the interest of the British in it, and the role of Lord Byron, see, for instance, David Howarth, *The Greek Adventure* (New York: Athenaeum, 1976).

130. See also WO 201/100, 26/3/41, for the same information sent from Belgrade to Cairo by the Greek military attaché.

131. WO 201/52.

132. WO 201/33.

133. WO 201/19. See also War Office, *Notes on the German Army—War* (December 1940), 3.

134. AIR 23/6388, 20/1/41.

135. Reid, *Last on the List*, 142-43.

136. David Kahn, *The Codebreakers: The Story of Secret Writing* (New York: Macmillan, 1967; London: Weidenfeld and Nicolson, 1967), 487; Gilbert, *Churchill*, 6:1053; Hinsley, *British Intelligence*, 1:371-72

137. Hinsley, *British Intelligence*, 1:404-405. Dixon, *Double Diploma*, 79, provides an interesting sidelight. He and Eden were briefed on the battle, but their pilot was not and they almost flew into it.

138. Henry Maule, *Spearhead General: The Epic Story of General Messervy and His Men in Eritrea, North Africa and Burma* (London: Odhams, 1961), 99.

139. AIR 8/544, 26/3/41, of which page 2 is missing out of three pages.

140. WO 201/1574.

141. *Cabinet Telegrams*, ME I.

142. Richards, *The RAF*, 1:288. Marshall-Cornwall, *Wars and Memories of Wars*, 154-64.

143. Long, *Greece, Crete and Syria*, 19.

144. Hoptner, *Yugoslavia*, 250-53; see also the sympathetic Balfour and Mackay, *Paul of Yugoslavia*, 243ff.

145. H. R. Trevor-Roper, ed., *Blitzkrieg to Defeat, Hitler's War Directives, 1939-1945* (New York: Holt, Rinehart and Winston, 1965), 61-62; Alan Bullock, *Hitler: A Study in Tyranny* (New York: Bantam, 1958), 320; Pierre Accoce and Pierre Quet, *A Man Called Lucy, 1939-45*, trans. A.M. Sheridan-Smith (New York: Coward-McCann, 1967), 89.

146. Channon, *Diaries*, 297-98; Mark C. Wheeler, *Britain and the War for Yugoslavia, 1940-43* (New York: Columbia University Press, 1980), 16-62, especially p. 33, is wrong about the Greek view of the Yugoslavs, basing it as he does mainly on the Foreign Office documents. See also Dixon, *Double Diploma*, 79ff.

147. Churchill, *The Grand Alliance*, 168-69.

148. Papagos, *The Battle of Greece*, 24.

149. WO 190/893.

150. McClymont, *To Greece*, 115; Hoptner, *Yugoslavia*, 241.

151. FO 371/29813, 27/3/41.

152. FO 371/29814, 27/3/41.

153. WO 201/100.

154. *Cabinet Telegrams*, ME I; Wilson's later report says he was Mr. Watt, still confined to the legation, until 2 April.

155. *FRUS, 1941* 2:668.

156. U.S. Dept. of State, 740.0011 EW 1939.9472.

157. Hoptner, *Yugoslavia*, 275; FO 371/33145; FO 371/27982.

158. FO 371/33145; Dixon, *Double Diploma*, 79ff.

159. *Cabinet Telegrams*, ME I.

160. Sinclair, *19 Battalion*, 64-67.

161. McClymont, *To Greece*, 116; Paul Hasluck, *The Government and the People, 1939-1941* (Canberra: Australian War Memorial, 1952), 339.

162. Leasor, *The Clock with Four Hands*, 152-53.

163. Long, *Greece, Crete and Syria*, 27.

164. Edward R. Stettinius, Jr., *Lend-Lease: Weapon for Victory* (New York: Macmillan, 1944), 91; U.S. *Foreign Relations (1941)*, 2:712.

165. FO 371/29815.

166. AIR 24/1666.

167. Burden, *24 Battalion*, 21; Murphy, *2nd NZ Divisional Artillery*, 27-28.

168. Long, *Greece, Crete and Syria*, 22; Kennedy, *The Business of War*, 97.

169. Les Allison, *Canadians in the Royal Air Force* (Roland, Manitoba, 1978), 55.

170. *Cabinet Telegrams*, ME I.

171. Hoptner, *Yugoslavia*, 281.

172. U.S. Dept. of State, 740.0011 EW 1939.9590.

173. WO 190/893; Waller, "With the 1st Armoured Brigade," 163.

174. Stout, *New Zealand Medical Services*, 109.

175. FO 371/29815.

176. FO 371/29814, 1/4/41.

177. FO 371/29815, 3/4/41.

178. Richards, *The RAF*, 1:289.

179. Connell, *Wavell*, 392; de Guingand, *Generals at War*, 48; Macksey, *Rommel*, 49.

180. Neame, *Playing with Strife*, 275; Maughan, *Tobruk and El Alamein* 43; Wavell, "Operations in the Middle East," 3427-28.

181. PREM 3/205.HP 00437.

182. *Cabinet Telegrams*, ME I.

183. Ibid.

184. Ibid.; WO 201/53; FO 371/29782. The Greek account of these meetings is in Greece, *1940-41*, doc. 203.

185. WO 201/52.

186. Parkinson, *Blood, Toil, Tears and Sweat*, 216.

187. *Cabinet Telegrams*, ME I.

188. Ibid., 4 April 1941.

189. Ibid.

190. Hinsley, *British Intelligence*, 1:406-407.

191. *Cabinet Telegrams*, ME I.

192. Ibid.

193. U.S. Dept. of State, 740.0011 EW 1939.9657.

194. AWM 2663/534/5/24.

195. AIR 8/505, 5/4/41.

196. Brunskill, "The Administrative Aspect of the Campaign," 130-32.

197. WO 201/29.

198. Hinsley, *British Intelligence*, 1:373.

199. WO 201/51; WO 201/33.

200. *Cabinet Telegrams*, ME I.

201. Ibid.

202. Cadogan, *Diaries*, 369.

203. Ibid., 298.

204. FO 371/33145.

205. Reid, *Last on the List*, 148. For the campaign sketch that follows, consult U.S. Department of the Army Historical Study, *The German Campaigns in the Balkans* (Washington, Dept. of the Army, 1953); Major-General I.S.O. Playfair, et al., *The Mediterranean and Middle East*, vol. 2, *The Germans Come to the Help of Their Ally, 1941* (London: HMSO, 1956); Long, *Greece, Crete and Syria*; McClymont, *To Greece*. The Greek official history relies upon the British volumes for the campaign on the east coast, since the relevant Greek diplomatic materials were unavailable until 1981, and the campaign mostly involved Imperial troops. The RAF's operational story is in the documents in AIR 23/6378.

206. My thanks are due to the National Observatory Weather Bureau in Athens and the Greek Army Directorate of History for supplying the weather data on Athens used throughout this work.

207. WO 201/65, 23/2/41.

208. Brunskill, "The Administrative Aspect of the Campaign," 132; WO 201/119, App. C; WO 178/24.71298; WO 201/661, 16/4/41.

209. *Cabinet Telegrams*, ME I.

210. John Connell [John Henry Robertson], *Auchinleck: A Biography of Field-Marshal Sir Claude Auchinleck, GCB, GCIE, CSI, DSO, OBE, LLD* (London: Cassell, 1959), 199-200.

211. Ibid. has Wavell lost on the 7th; this is incorrect.

212. Sulzberger, *A Long Row of Candles*, 127; Stettinius, *Lend-Lease*, 91.

213. FO 371/29815.

214. Major-General R.P. Pakenham-Walsh, *History of the Royal Engineers, 1938-1948* (Chatham: The Institution of Royal Engineers, 1948), 8:279; WO 201/119, App. C.

215. Medlicott, *The Economic Blockade*, 1:600.

216. AIR 24/1666.

217. Connell, *Wavell*, 415, 421-22.

218. Connell, *Auchinleck*, 200.

219. Cab. 65/22; Cadogan, *Diaries*, 370.

220. *Cabinet Telegrams*, ME I, 9/4/41.

221. WO 201/51.

222. WO 201/53.

223. Ibid.; Stout, *New Zealand Medical Services*, 107.

224. Channon, *Diaries*, 299.

225. Cadogan, *Diaries*, 370.

226. Kennedy, *The Business of War*, 89-91.

227. Kitsikis, "La Grèce," 14-15.

228. Marshall-Cornwall, *Wars and Memories of Wars*, 181.

229. WO 201/52.

230. WO 106/3132.79062; ADM 199/2226.ERD/7778.

231. Cab. 65/22; Parkinson, *Blood, Toil, Tears and Sweat*, 223-24.

232. Parkinson, *Blood, Toil, Tears and Sweat*, 224.

233. Playfair notes in the British official history that this was a fast-moving campaign in which no one ever got set in his position, and it is easy to be misled when reading about it later. Even more misleading and confusing is the fact that everyone uses different names for the same places. Dispatch riders and non-Greek-speaking liaison officers would have had their troubles with Greek maps and signposts. In 1979 my guide and host in Greece, Major-General Kanakaris, argued that the goodness of the Greek people would have prevented the British from getting lost.

234. *Cabinet Telegrams*, Me I.

235. Ibid.

236. Sulzberger, *A Long Row of Candles*, 135.

237. AIR 24/1666.

238. Reid, *Last on the List*, 170.

239. *Cabinet Telegrams*, ME I; Herington, *Air War against Germany and Italy*, 85, gives a slightly different breakdown, but the same total of 46 aircraft.

240. AIR 24/1666.

241. Cadogan, *Diaries*, 372.

242. *Greece, 1940-41*, doc. 233.

243. *Cabinet Telegrams*, ME I.

244. AIR 24/1666.

245. Cadogan, *Diaries*, 372.

246. Cab. 65/22.

247. Ibid. My italics.

248. PREM 3/206/1.HP 00437.

249. Ibid.; *Greece, 1940-41*, doc. 234.

250. AIR 24/1666; *Greece, 1940-41*, doc. 234.

251. *Cabinet Telegrams*, ME I.

252. AIR 24/1666.

253. *Cabinet Telegrams*, ME I.

254. Ibid.

255. WO 201/53.

256. *Cabinet Telegrams*, ME I.

257. Papagos, *The Battle of Greece*, 382-83.

258. *Cabinet Telegrams*, ME I; WO 106/3133.79449.

259. AIR 24/1666; AIR 23/6389. Actually not all papers were destroyed. HQ BFG unintentionally aided historians by evacuating many of its papers. These, however, lay effectively concealed by the filing system in the Public Record Office even from the researchers at the Air Historical Branch, Air Ministry, and later Ministry of Defence. I am grateful to Syd Wise, the noted Canadian aviation historian, for clues given me in Banff in January 1981, with additional comments by W.A.B. Douglas and Ben Greenhous, as to how the records might be found, and to Cdr. W. E. May for finding them. One thing that comes across from the files is the neat and tidy administrative mind.

260. *Cabinet Telegrams*, ME I; Cab. 65/22.

261. *Cabinet Telegrams*, ME I; PREM 3/206/1. There is no record of this meeting in the collection *Greece, 1940-41*.

262. *Cabinet Telegrams*, ME I; *Greece, 1940-41*, doc. 235.

263. *Cabinet Telegrams*, ME I; Stout, *New Zealand Medical Services*, 148.

264. Cab. 65/22.

265. PREM 3/206/1.HP 00437.

266. *Cabinet Telegrams*, ME I.

267. AIR 24/1666.

268. Reid, *Last on the List*, 178ff.

269. *Cabinet Telegrams*, ME I.

270. Ibid.; Edward Howell, *Escape to Live* (London: Longmans, 1947), 2.

271. Waller, "With the 1st Armoured Brigade," 177.

272. Cab. 65/22. McClymont, *To Greece*, 486, quotes the British Cabinet Historical Office as having concluded that in all the British landed 62,612 officers and men, of whom 903 were killed, 1,250 wounded, and 13,958 taken prisoner, for a total casualty list of 16,111. However, the navy evacuated 50,172. The discrepancy is explained in that some of those evacuated were Greeks, and others were refugees who were carried to Crete. The naval side of the evacuation is covered in Roskill's *The War at Sea*, 1:434-37, and in Playfair, but in more detail in the Australian and New Zealand histories.

273. *Cabinet Telegrams*, ME I.

274. AIR 8/519.2879.

275. *Cabinet Telegrams*, ME I.

276. WO 201/53.

277. *Cabinet Telegrams*, ME I.

## V. Conclusion

1. AIR 23/811.9920.

# Bibliographical Comment

Almost all the work published so far on Graeco-British relations in World War II has focused on the period after the original defeat, concentrating on the guerrilla war of the occupation and the liberation of 1944, and using primarily Foreign Office records. Even as late as 1980 the bibliographic guide *Greece in the 1940's: A Bibliographic Companion* (Hanover, N.H.: University Press of New England), 12, stated that only the Cabinet and Foreign Office records in London had been opened to researchers, whereas in fact almost all of the records for World War II have been open since 1972, as will be noted in Gerald S. Jordan's forthcoming supplemental revision of my 1971 *Guide to the Sources of British Military History* (Berkeley: University of California Press). A good deal of additional military information was also already available in another of my publications, *Official Histories* (Manhattan: Kansas State University Library, 1970). And in preparing this book on events in Greece in 1940 and 1941, ferreting through the various bibliographical sources produced enough autobiographies, biographies, scholarly studies, and other works to make up a typescript bibliography just short of one hundred pages, a number beyond modern publishing economics. Hence this essay, rather than a complete bibliographical list.

In addition to consulting the items referred to in the notes, the reader who wishes to pursue the subject might start with John S. Koliopoulos, *Greece and the British Connection, 1935-1941* (Oxford: Clarendon Press, 1977), which is heavily based upon Greek and British Foreign Office sources. Next, it will become clear that most of the available works follow the lines laid out in the volume edited by John O. Iatrides, *Greece in the 1940's: A Nation in Crisis* (Hanover, N.H.: University Press of New England, 1981), which emphasizes the period after British and Greek government withdrawal in the spring of 1941. Among such works are Procopis Papastratis, *British Policy towards Greece during the Second World War, 1941-1944* (Cambridge: Cambridge University Press, 1984); David Stafford's work on the Special Operations Executive, *Britain and European Resistance, 1940-1945* (Toronto: University of Toronto Press, 1980); Elisabeth Barker, *British Policy in South-East Europe in the Second World War* (New York: Barnes and Noble, 1976); Mark C. Wheeler, *Britain and the War for Yugoslavia, 1940-1943* (Boulder, Co.: East European Monographs, 1980); and Frank G. Weber, *The Evasive Neutral: Germany, Britain and the Quest for a Turkish Alliance in the Second World War* (Columbia: University of Missouri Press, 1979).

Much closer to the subject of British aid to Greece are the official histories. Sir

Llewellyn Woodward's five confidential volumes have replaced his original single volume on *British Foreign Policy during the Second World War,* appearing from Her Majesty's Stationery Office in 1970 and containing a considerably expanded (but still erroneous) account of the Eden mission of February-March 1941. The first two volumes of *The Mediterranean and Middle East,* by I.S.O. Playfair et al., 1954 and 1956, provide a tri-service look at events in the theater as seen from the British point of view. The campaign is covered in its active phase in Christopher Buckley's popular history, *Greece and Crete, 1941* (London: HMSO, 1952). Far better are the New Zealand official volume by W.G. McClymont, *To Greece* (Wellington: War History Branch, Dept. of Internal Affairs, 1959), the series of Kiwi unit histories referred to in the notes, and Gavin Long's Australian official history, *Greece, Crete and Syria* (Canberra: Australian War Memorial, 1953). D.M. Horner's *Australia and Allied Strategy, 1939-1945* (Canberra: Australian War Memorial, 1982) provides an overall view similar, though on a more condensed scale, to that found in J.R.M. Butler's volume *From September 1939 to June 1941* (London: HMSO, 1957), which is part of the British government's Grand Strategy series.

Most of the important individuals in the text are referred to in the notes citations, but one source should perhaps be mentioned here, since it provides a pivotal view of affairs in Athens: the words of the American ambassador, who was a personal friend of President Roosevelt, are recorded in *Ambassador MacVeagh Reports: Greece, 1933-1947,* edited by John O. Iatrides (Princeton: Princeton University Press, 1980). The observations of MacVeagh's friend Laird Archer, the director of the Near East Foundation (the powerful agency set up to help establish the Greeks moved from Asia Minor in the 1923 exchange of populations with Turkey), have also become available, both in his diary documented in the notes and in a diary published by MA/AH Publishing (Manhattan, Kans., 1983), entitled *Athens Journal 1940-1941: The Graeco-Italian and Graeco-German Wars and German Operation;* this work includes notes by Marian Nicolopoulis on the individuals mentioned.

The most detailed history of the campaign in Greece is that of the Hellenic army, in Greek, but for the eastern area of the fighting this is largely based on accounts from the British and Commonwealth units, which were the forces mainly engaged. An earlier clear account from a different perspective is the U.S. Department of the Army, *The German Campaigns in the Balkans, Spring 1941* (1953).

Although a lot has been written since 1974 on ULTRA, the British decoding of German signals, there is little evidence that ULTRA was of much influence in the Middle East at this time. A start on the subject of intelligence can be made with the new and enlarged edition of Correlli Barnett's *The Desert Generals* (Bloomington: Indiana University Press, 1982) which contains sections modifying the author's original 1960 text in the light of more recent revelations. The main source of "sigint" history today is, of course, F.H. Hinsley's *British Intelligence in the Second World War,* of which volume 1 (New York: Cambridge University Press, 1979), takes the story through June 1941.

Outside of the usual official and unofficial histories, one recent work which breaks new ground and deserves special mention—because it provides a wider background on the one service which is central to this story—is John Terraine's *A Time for Courage* (in Britain, *The Right of the Line*): *The Royal Air Force in the European War, 1939-1945* (New York: Macmillan, 1985).

Obviously the most important sources for my work have been the papers preserved at the British Public Record Office. When the archives on the 1939-1945 war were opened, the PRO also made available (as a supplement, in effect, to the well-known revised M.S. Giuseppi *Guide to the Contents of the Public Record Office*) *The Second World War: A Guide to the Documents in the Public Record Office* (1972). This contains a dated list of ministers, a description of each department and its records, and a numbered list of classes (e.g., AIR 8) with one-line descriptions, including an indication of the size of the holdings. Even when using the files, however, it is not at all plain whether the surviving records relating to overseas commands actually came from their drawers, or are what was accumulated in Whitehall during the war, or are a mixture of both. Working from the Second World War guide it is possible, however, by using intuition and an acquired sense of direction, to follow many trails through the files. The only document which I tried unsuccessfully to find was Wavell's late January or early February 1941 assessment of the Greek situation, which Dill carried back to the United Kingdom and gave to Anthony Eden after their return. It must be in some file other than where it belongs—or it has been destroyed as too embarrassing.

While the Foreign Office record has been the traditional source of information, it should not in diplomatic history be the only one. Moreover, its files are very tedious to go through, since there are numerous drafts of proposed signals as well as the one that was actually approved and sent. Much the same is true in reverse with incoming messages, which are subject to all sorts of comments from what was then a very small staff of perhaps half a dozen men including the Foreign Secretary. The flavor of these insiders' comments, in connection with the subject of this book, is reinforced by the diaries of Sir Alexander Cadogan, the Permanent Under-Secretary of State (edited by David Dilks, New York: Putnam, 1971).

Also close to the top in Whitehall are the minutes of the Cabinet, which generally record what the Prime Minister told his colleagues, and related papers that are found in the CAB and PREM series. These can be supplemented with the DEFE series for the few signals of the period which contained ULTRA material (not passed on as such to the Middle East until 14 March 1941). Churchill had batches of the signals to and from the Middle East printed from time to time as the months passed, and these were issued as *Cabinet Telegrams, Middle East*. They must be consulted by date, as the page numbers repeat in fairly short order.

A large and useful collection is WO 106, Military Operations and Intelligence, which contains copies of many of the signals to and from the Middle East, plus special assessments of the situation in the Balkans in general. WO 201 contains the papers of HQ ME; these include copies of the many signals sent by the military mission in Greece, giving a very full picture of the situation there.

For the RAF, AIR 8 contains the papers of the chief of the Air Staff, AIR 23 contains those of Middle East Command, and so on. Some records are kept by squadrons, so it is necessary to consult such books as John Rawlings, *Fighter Squadrons of the RAF and Their Aircraft* (London: Macdonald and Jane's, 1969), Philip Moyes, *Bomber Squadrons* . . . (London: Macdonald and Jane's, 1964), and John Rawlings, *Coastal, Support and Special Squadrons* . . . (Jane's, 1982), in order to get the actual dates and locations after picking up the unit numbers from Playfair. Operational records, kept on the RAF Form 540, are bound as Operational Record Books. The same form was used for other records (those of HQ, British Air Forces Greece, for instance) to log the movements of personnel and other events. Little use has been made here of naval papers, since the Fleet was only involved in convoying to and from Greece and almost all the decision making of importance was handled by HQ in Cairo.

As for papers of the principal British actors, Longmore's are at the RAF Museum at Hendon, but they contain little that was useful for this book; and Wavell's have been inaccessible.

General Alexander Papagos' memoir, *The Battle of Greece, 1940-1941* (Athens: Scazikis, 1949), remained the basic Hellenic statement in English until the Greek government broke the fifty-year rule in 1980 and released the documents locked up since April 1941 in the Foreign Office archives. They appeared as a white paper, *Greece, 1940-1941*, in which the texts are in Greek, French, and occasionally English.

Apart from these British, Commonwealth, and Greek publications, which enabled me to see what the British were doing and thinking and what were their assets and liabilities, there is another valuable source of information: the records of the Americans in Athens. The diaries (already noted above) of Lincoln MacVeagh and Laird Archer provide useful commentaries, and in addition most of Mac-Veagh's official reports to the U.S. State Department, with some from his attachés, have appeared in the *Foreign Relations of the United States* series. Military and naval attaché reports and other diplomatic documents are also available in the National Archives in Washington, or in Army or Navy files.

# Index

ABSTENTION, 147
airfields in Greece, 45, 46, 48, 69, 84, 128, 134
Air Ministry, 5, 6, 14-16, 24, 32, 50, 76, 82
Albania, 2, 16, 48, 50, 56, 64, 80, 90
Aliakmon Line, 88, 90, 98, 104, 109, 110-11,
    113, 119-23, 136-38, 146, 153, 155-57, 162,
    167, 171, 184-85, 189, 196, 200, 215, 216,
    220, 236
Alpine Army Corps, 144
American aid to Greece, 133, 187, 188, 203
Anglo-French guarantee, 8, 23
ANZAC, 6, 222, 223, 229
Archer, Laird, 74
ARMATURE, 147
Army of the Nile, 53, 68, 107
Auchinleck, General Sir Claude, 214, 233
Australian government, 50, 69, 94, 195, 224
Australian troops, 34, 95, 102, 110, 126, 133,
    146, 153, 167, 170, 184, 188, 189, 193, 203,
    204, 207, 209, 210, 215-16, 219, 221, 222,
    223, 227
Axios-Evros line, 59

Balkans, 3, 6, 11, 18, 55, 64, 139, 169, 234, 236
BARBARITY, 14, 27, 33, 41, 42
BARBAROSSA, 126
Battle of Britain, 6, 7, 28, 37, 68, 103, 162
Battle of Cape Matapan, 193, 198
Beaverbrook, Lord William, 37, 38, 129
Benghazi, 2, 68, 73, 77, 82-84, 86, 103, 185,
    207, 208
*Berwick*, H.M.S., 19
Beurling, "Buzz," 202
Blamey, Major-General Thomas 94, 99, 102;
    and Greek expedition, 105, 128, 130, 172,
    201, 209; and role of forces, 158, 165, 189,
    220
Bletchley Code and Cypher School, 3, 18, 85,
    89
Blunt, Colonel Jasper, 20, 21, 28
BLUNT, 147

*Bonaventure*, H.M.S., 153
BONIFACE, 10. *See also* ULTRA
Bowker, R.J., 17
British Expeditionary Force, 7, 24, 59, 137,
    139, 153, 236
British government: and aid to Greece, 1, 4,
    12, 35, 37, 39; and German invasion threat,
    52; and evacuation of Greece, 57; and Turks,
    71, 79; and Tripoli, 91-92
British Military Mission, 49
British Purchasing Commission, 27, 30, 45, 96
Brown, Group Captain L.O., 176
Brunskill, Brigadier, 192, 210
Bulgaria, 43, 59, 66, 69, 77, 89
Bulgarian-Turkish non-aggression agreement,
    115

Cadogan, Sir Alexander, 13, 79, 102, 106-07,
    127, 169, 186
Canaris, Admiral, 202
Casson, Stanley, 40-41, 49, 142
Central Macedonian Army, 152, 173, 192
Channon, Chips, 11, 92, 177, 182, 196, 217
Chiefs of Staff, 6, 8, 26, 27, 30, 56, 127, 144,
    146, 174, 189, 235; and orders to Wavell, 68;
    and German threat to U.K., 81-82; and
    increased hazards in Greece, 153, 156, 160,
    166
Churchill, Winston S., 5, 50, 51, 53, 57, 63,
    64, 104, 107, 191, 197, 202, 205, 207, 223,
    224; and Wavell, 7-8, 82-83, 97; messages of
    to Metaxas, 8, 13; and Middle East, 9; and
    aid to Greece, 23, 27, 40; and Turks, 70, 78;
    and Portal, 87; and orders to Eden, 98, 100;
    and Greeks, 114, 127, 128, 132; and
    Bulgarians, 138; and Greek options, 159,
    160, 162, 170; and Australian charges,
    177-78; and British evacuation, 231, 232; and
    Crete, 235, 236
Cincar-Marković (Yugoslav Prime Minister),
    182

*Clan Fraser*, 49

Clark, Brigadier Dudley, 46

Collins, Brigadier W.D., 151

Combined Bureau, Middle East, 18

COMPASS offensive, 36, 42, 43, 47, 50

CORDITE, 177

Courtney, Sir Christopher, 101

Cranborne, Viscount, 133

Crawley, Aidan M., 80

Crete, 106, 166, 205; and British policy, 2, 8, 9,
   12-14, 34, 77, 93; and defense, 222, 223, 225,
   227, 235

Cripps, Sir Stafford, 42, 81, 207

Cunningham, Admiral Sir Andrew, 5, 64, 101,
   136, 147, 158, 175, 193; and Suez Canal, 74,
   81; and limited resources, 174

Cyrenaica, 80, 185, 189, 194, 207, 219


D'Albiac, Air Vice Marshal John, 4, 26, 27; and
   Drummond, 28-29; and reports from
   Athens, 30-31; and potential airfield sites,
   38, 39; promoted, 45; and Papagos, 79, 82;
   and Greek commitment, 91; and British
   evacuation, 138, 150, 226, 230, 232, 234

Dalton, Hugh, 116

Dardanelles Commission Report, 158

Davidson, General F.H.N., 196

Davin, D.M., 26

Dawson, Air Vice Marshal G.G., 233

Defence Committee of the Cabinet, 16, 53, 84,
   93, 95

de Guingand, Major-General Frederick, 1,
   113, 120-23, 136, 137, 166

Deutsch Afrika Korps, 104

Dill, General Sir John, 24, 54, 84, 99, 212, 217;
   and Churchill, 46-47; and Eden, 100,
   119-24, 126; and Yugoslavs, 131; and Turks,
   141; and Greek meetings, 142-45; and
   Papagos agreement, 160, 165

Dixon, Pierson, 115, 131, 171, 179

Dodecanese Islands, 2, 8, 15, 39, 58, 64, 68,
   71, 77-78, 129, 235

Dominion and Allied governments, 35

Donovan, Colonel William, 53, 67, 112, 129,
   134

Dowding, Air Chief Marshal Sir Hugh, 68

Drummond, Air Vice-Marshal, 13-14, 28-29,
   232

*Duchess of Bedford*, 70


Eden, Anthony, 5-6, 13, 15, 20, 25, 31, 36, 51,
   53, 80, 82, 100, 104, 112, 113, 179, 182, 186,
   189, 197, 199; supports Wavell, 7-8; and
   Churchill, 9-10; and Egypt, 23-24; and

British aid, 54; and Turks, 108; and Greek
   campaign, 116-17; and Tatoi meeting,
   119-23; and Yugoslavs, 131, 134; and Greek
   meeting, 140-46; replies to Churchill, 150,
   155, 161, 177; and African problems, 204,
   207, 209; and British government, 217, 219

Elmhirst, Air Vice Marshal Thomas, 77, 91,
   103

Enigma (ULTRA), 55, 81, 85, 174, 193, 208

Epirus armistice, 227, 228, 229


Fairley-Boyd report, 69-70

Falconer, Professor Arthur Wellesley, 35

50th Division, 133

Foreign Office (British), 3, 85, 95, 106, 147

Foreign Requirements Committee, 30

*Formidable*, H.M.S., 81

Freyberg, Major-General Bernard, 98, 104-05,
   158, 170, 189

*Furious*, H.M.S., 27


Galloway, Brigadier A. "Sandy," 180, 189, 226,
   231

Gambier-Parry, Major-General M.D., 18,
   20-21, 33-34, 41, 213

George II, King of Greece, 9, 12, 22, 83, 90,
   96, 118, 132, 197, 224, 228, 232

George VI, King of England, 39, 182, 196

German attack on Greece, 210, 211-16

German Foreign Office, 17

German interests, 2, 52, 54, 55, 64, 69, 76

German-Italian forces, 109

German reconnaissance, 67, 170, 183

German troops, 85, 92, 133, 138, 142, 144, 152,
   179, 192, 222

Gilbert, Martin, 24

Graeco-Albanian frontier, 228

Graeco-Turkish mutual guarantee, 184

Graeco-Turkish situation, 64, 83

Graeco-Yugoslav attack, 205

Graziani, Marshal, 59, 62

Grazzi, Count Emmanuel, 11

Greece: as a neutral, 2, 8; and Italian attack,
   13; and airfields, 15; as underdeveloped
   country, 36, 136; and transportation
   problems, 185-86

Greek Admiralty, 180

Greek air force. *See* Royal Hellenic Air Force

Greek Army Corps, 227

Greek army, 3, 22, 30, 41, 82, 173, 216

Greek campaign, 126, 167-69

Greek peace offer, 173

Greek Powder and Cartridge Factory, 45

Greek Requirements Committee, 32

Greek resistance, 17, 49, 156, 171, 225

Greek War Relief Committee, 79
Grigg, Sir James, 26
Grigson, Group Captain John, 51
Gündüz, Assim, 184

Haining, Sir Robert, 233
Halifax, Lord Edward, 8, 27, 35, 47
Hankey Committee on Supplies for Greece, 57, 203
Hankey, Lord Maurice, 30
Harriman, W. Averill, 203
Hellenic Telephone Company, 36
Heraklion airfield, 16, 18, 32, 58, 69, 222
Heywood, Major-General T.G.G., 33, 44, 83, 87, 88, 109, 112, 183, 232, 236; and reinforcements, 57, 61
Hitler, Adolf, 2, 8, 14, 23, 104, 131, 138-39, 151, 154, 196, 214; and Balkans, 75, 82
Hoare, Sir Samuel, 105
Hollis, Colonel Leslie, 197
Hopkins, Harry, 57, 203
Horthy, Admiral, 64
Hotel Grande Bretagne, 13, 42, 44, 90, 126, 140, 145, 181
Hull, Cordell, 159
Hunt, Sir David, 41, 74
Hutchinson, Major-General B.O., 139
Hutson, Brigadier H.P.W., 156

Illustrious, H.M.S., 57, 81
Imperial Defence College, 29
Indian troops, 110, 193, 198, 205
Inönü, President, 218
Ismay, General Sir Hastings, 53
Italian government, 1, 5, 10-13
Italian troops, 5, 11, 16, 135, 137, 154, 184, 211

Janković, General, 205
Joint Intelligence Committee, 32
Joint Planning Staff, 9, 20, 26, 86, 93, 137, 166, 194

Kanakis, Major, 44
Kennedy, Major General Sir John, 57, 95, 99, 102, 105, 217, 227
Kirkpatrick, Sir Ivone, 23
Knatchbull-Hugessen, Sir Hughe, 17, 73, 176, 182
Koryzis, Alexander, 79, 86, 89, 101, 119, 141, 142, 171, 200, 224
Kotulas, General Ioannis, 192

Lamb, Lieutenant Charles, 181
Lancashire Regiment, 13
Lane, Arthur Bliss, 125

Larissa earthquake, 136
Lee, Colonel Raymond E., 26, 48
Lend-Lease, 40, 76, 99, 150, 154, 170, 174, 213
Libyan campaign, 103
Lindemann, F.A., 37
Linlithgow, Lord, 214
Liverpool, H.M.S., 20
Longmore, Air Chief Marshal Sir Arthur, 4, 5, 9, 19, 45, 48, 52, 56, 84, 91, 128, 135, 138, 174, 190, 203, 231, 233, 235; and air aid to Greece, 27, 30, 37; and meeting with Greek leaders, 43-44; and British-Greek conference, 60-61; and requests for planes, 64, 66, 70; and orders from London, 71; and Churchill's offer to Turkey, 77-78; and Tatoi meeting, 123-24
Ludlow-Hewitt, Air Chief Marshal Sir Edgar, 39
Luftwaffe, 3, 36, 63, 64, 66, 80-81, 110, 135
LUSTRE, 94, 106, 130, 135, 147, 151, 157, 177, 180, 185-86, 193, 198, 200, 204, 207, 210, 236

MacDonald, Wing-Commander, 180
Mackay, Major-General I.G., 209
Mackay Force, 215, 216, 220
MacVeagh, Lincoln, 22, 54, 55, 80, 198
Maisky (Soviet ambassador), 80
Malta Battalion, 13
MANDIBLES, 39, 51, 73, 97, 100, 110, 129-30, 147, 153, 155, 177, 198, 205, 207, 208
MARITA, 142, 155
Marshall-Cornwall, General Sir James, 51, 100, 103, 108, 234
Maund, Air Vice Marshal A.C., 164
Menzies, Robert, Australian prime minister, 47, 86, 94, 125, 127-28, 130, 133, 147, 153, 160, 162, 164, 229
Metaxas, General Ioannis, 2-3, 9, 10, 11-12, 21, 26, 37, 39, 43, 49, 50, 52, 64, 65, 235, 236; and British conference, 58, 60, 62; death, 74-75
Metaxas Line, 66, 123, 139
Metaxas memorandum, 171
Middle East Air Force, 178
Middle East and British policy, 1, 2, 9
Middle East Command, 3, 5, 15, 35, 55, 113
Middle East Intelligence Centre, 3
Mirković, Brigadier General Bora, 195
Mobile Naval Base Defense Organization, 205. See also Crete
Monastir Gap, 22, 31, 139, 182, 187, 201, 218
Mussolini, Benito, 2, 8, 14, 76, 125, 138, 154

Neame, Lieutenant-General Sir Philip, 118, 126, 176, 189, 195, 213

New Zealand government, 131, 133, 165
New Zealand troops, 31, 34, 70, 95, 102, 104,
    110, 126, 132, 136, 146, 151, 152, 155, 167,
    184, 185, 187, 200, 201, 205, 209, 216,
    221-22, 227
Nichols, Philip, 16
North American Supplies Committee, 30
No. 27 Military Mission, 38, 41, 44-45, 49, 57,
    113

O'Connor, Lieutenant-General Sir Richard
    Nugent, 82, 84, 86, 93, 94, 204-5, 213
*Orion*, H.M.S., 33

Palairet, Sir Michael, 8, 16, 38, 52, 89, 90, 92,
    126, 165, 228
Pantellaria, 48, 64, 92
Papagos, General Alexander, 137, 139, 155,
    156-57, 170, 171, 218, 227, 230, 232, 236; and
    Wilson, 172, 184, 188, 191; and Yugoslavs,
    196, 206, 216
Pattle, Squadron Leader Pat, 202
Paul, Prince of Yugoslavia, 16, 36, 39, 58, 61,
    64, 122, 124, 125, 138-39, 157, 169, 183, 195,
    196
Perišić, Lieutenant Colonel, 169-70
Peter, Prince of Greece, 44, 196
Phillips, Sir Tom, 23
Piraeus, 15, 25, 28, 31, 49, 70, 165, 213, 219,
    220, 226
Polish Brigade, 110, 129, 146, 188
Portal, Sir Charles, 9, 17, 50, 51, 56, 77, 191,
    208; and Longmore, 78, 91, 163-64, 175
Pound, Admiral Sir Dudley, 67, 99
Pridham-Wippell, Rear-Admiral, 33, 157
PRU (Photographic Reconnaissance), 3

RAF, 4, 8, 13, 42, 54, 162, 188, 201, 225, 228,
    229, 234, 235
Red Cross, Provisions of the Geneva
    Convention, 29
Reid, Major, 126, 135, 137, 192, 221, 231
Rendel, George, 64, 80
Rifle Brigade, 86
Rommel, General Erwin, 34, 89, 92, 93, 118,
    134, 189, 193, 194, 195, 204, 217, 235
Roosevelt, President Franklin, 11, 57, 76, 112,
    129, 170, 201, 209
Royal Army Service Corps, 151
Royal Hellenic Air Force (RHAF), 25, 30, 37,
    40, 50, 51, 78, 134, 187
Rupel Pass, 56, 110, 121, 155

Salisbury-Jones, Colonel Guy "Guido," 42,
    110-11, 112

Salonika, 31, 37, 43, 47, 51, 52, 56, 57, 60, 61,
    63, 64, 65, 66, 69, 73, 104, 108, 109, 110,
    111, 122, 171, 181, 183, 198
Saracoglu (Turkish Foreign Minister), 182
2nd Armored Division, 85, 104
7th Armored Division, 6, 85, 86, 110
Shearer, Brigadier John, 83, 107, 179, 194
Shedden, Sir Frederick, 130
Shell Oil Company, 63
Shone, Terence, 182, 186
Simopoulos Charlalampos, 35
Simovic, Major-General Dusan, 195, 197, 199,
    213
6th Division, 133
Smith, General Arthur, 17, 137
Smuts, General Jan Christiaan, 35, 47, 54, 72,
    73, 158-59, 161, 163
South African troops, 72, 110, 133, 159
Stojadinovic, Milan, 182
Struma River, 56, 89, 90, 109, 110, 111, 137,
    143, 210
Suez Canal, 1, 2, 28, 64, 154, 172, 185; and
    mines, 74, 80-81, 87, 93, 105, 129; and raids,
    144, 147, 153, 174
Sutton, Sir Bertine, 175

Tatoi meeting, 116, 119-24
Tatoi misunderstanding, 143, 145
Tatoi Palace, 13
Tedder, Air Vice Marshal Arthur, 50, 91, 207,
    232, 233
Thermopylae Line, 220-22, 224, 228, 229
3rd Battalion of the Royal Tank Regiment, 132
Thracian line, 91
Tilly, Major-General J., 85
Tripartite Pact, 203
Tripoli, 93-94
Tsolacoglou, General, 228
Tupanjarin, Dr. M., 36
Turco-Soviet rapprochement, 219
Turkey, 12, 59, 62, 71, 78, 103, 236
Turkish air force, 103
Turle, Rear-Admiral Charles, 18, 38, 48, 138
20th Greek Division, 110

ULTRA, 3, 18, 52, 55, 57, 71, 76, 79, 174, 193,
    204, 208, 211, 214, 225, 235; and use in
    Greece, 89, 107, 114, 176

Vermion Line, 67, 201
Vouktchević, Alexander, 145

War Cabinet, 4, 8, 14, 153, 215; and aid to
    Greece, 21, 23, 92, 153, 173
War Office, 3, 31, 79

Wavell, General Sir Archibald, 1, 3, 4, 5, 6-7,
9, 11, 13, 18, 37, 39, 48, 50, 72, 74, 82, 84,
85, 88, 89, 95, 98, 103-04, 107, 108, 110, 112,
113, 134, 144, 193-94, 204-05, 207, 214, 226,
232, 233, 234, 235, 236, 237; and Greece, 51,
54, 56, 58, 59, 60, 61, 62, 65-66; and Tatoi
meeting, 120-22; and Eden, 150, 152, 154,
158-59, 178-79
Wavish, Major, 156
Western Desert Force, 25
Weygand, General, 23, 106-07
Willetts, Wing-Commander, 25, 28, 45
Willis, Rear-Admiral A.U., 136
Wilson, Lieutenant-General Sir Henry

Maitland "Jumbo," 115, 117-18, 206, 210,
218, 221, 224, 225, 229, 232, 235; as Mr.
Watt, 151, 169; and Papagos, 188, 191
Wisdom, Squadron Leader T.H., 31, 33, 115,
117-18
Woodward, Sir Llewellyn, 14
Woodward, Vernon, 202
WORKSHOP, 48, 64

Yugoslav government, 12, 31, 36, 37, 132, 202,
206, 213, 215-16; and German pact, 170,
182, 183, 188; and coup, 196, 199
Yugoslavia, 59, 62, 64, 66, 69, 140, 157, 236
Yugoslav-Italian Pact, 195